SOUTHERN
AFRICA

The Thornton Cox
Guide

SOUTHERN AFRICA

A concise guide for individual travellers
to South Africa, Botswana, Lesotho,
Namibia, Swaziland, Zambia
and Zimbabwe

RICHARD COX

THORNTON
COX

Distribution:
Distribution in Great Britain and the Commonwealth by
Verulam Publishing, 152a Park Street Lane, Park Street,
St Albans, Herts, AL2 2AU, United Kingdom.
Telephone: 01727 872770, fax 01727 873866

ISBN 0 902726 54 4

Distributed in the United States and Canada by
Hippocrene Books Inc., 171 Madison Avenue, New York, NY 10016
Orders Dept. Tel: 718 454 2366, Fax 718 454 1391.

US ISBN 0 87052 223 X

Published 1995 by Thornton Cox (1986) Ltd.,
Address for all editorial correspondence: PO Box 88, Alderney,
Channel Islands, GY9 3DH, United Kingdom
Registered office 20-22 Bedford Row, London WC1R 4JS

Published in the United States and Canada by
Hippocrene Books Inc., 171 Madison Avenue, New York, NY 10016

Drawings by Philip Bawcombe, Alison Cotton, and Guy Magnus
Maps by Tom Stalker-Miller, MSIA
Cover design by Eric Rose
South African advisers: Carla Crafford, Alison Whitfield

Cover: Elephant in the Addo Elephant Park, Eastern Cape,
South Africa. Photograph Richard Cox.
Spine photographs Zulu warrior by courtesy of SATOUR,
Urquhart House, Graaff-Reinet, photograph Richard Cox.

Colour photographs on page 65 (below), page 66 (below),
page 67 and page 265 are reproduced by kind permission of SATOUR.
All other colour photographs by Richard Cox.

*Great care has been taken throughout this book to be accurate but
the publishers cannot accept responsibility for any errors which appear.*

Set in 9 on 10 pt Univers by Alderney Printers, Alderney, Channel Islands
Printed in Great Britain by The Guernsey Press Company Limited.

© Thornton Cox (1986) Ltd, 1995

Thornton Cox Guides:

Titles in print in this series include:

The Czech Republic
Egypt   Ireland
Kenya and Northern Tanzania

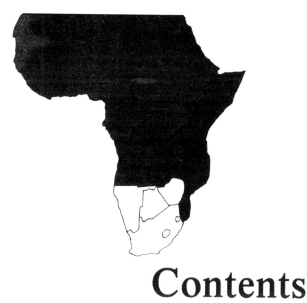

Contents

Acknowledgements

Originally this book was written by a number of local authors and edited by Richard Cox. For this edition the range of sources consulted was hugely expanded, so that advice and comments were received from a much wider spectrum of both local experts and travellers. We have also incorporated readers' comments. Nonetheless, the opinions expressed remain the responsibility of the present author, and not of those of who assisted him.

Special thanks go to Carla Crafford and Alison Whitfield; to Jane Dean; and to Liz Rawlins and Patricia D'Arcy of SATOUR. Emma Cunningham of South African Airways helped organise the very considerable air travel involved. Bill Adams, of Safari Consultants, was a constant source of supplementary detail, as was Haslen Back. Philip and Rosemary James both corrected sections of the book and provided military comment on the Natal battlefields.

In South Africa particularly useful advice was given by Ilse Greyling, Margi Biggs, Solly Blumenfield, Samantha Ford, Jan van Heteren, Elsabeth Muller, Peter Myles, Michael Rattray, Trevor Sandwith, Christa Smit and Vissie Zietsman.

In Botswana we have to thank Cecil Barlett, Claire and Bruce Cantell, Pat Carr-Hartley, Tom Gardner, Jonathan Gibson, Helge Haniger, Patrick Mmalane, Phyllis Palmer, and – not least – the Manager of the Manica travel agency.

In Lesotho the staff of the Lesotho Tourist Board, were very helpful, as were John Dyamdeki and Alec McMath. In Namibia we owe particular thanks to Jenni Schoeman, Wikkie ran Roeyen and Rosalind Rundle. In Swaziland we were helped, among others, by Hazel Hussey and Mark Ward. The Zambian chapter was completely revised by Theo Bull.

The Zimbabwe chapter was greatly assisted by Rob Waters of UTC, Mark Boulle, Anthony de la Rue, Simon Rhodes and the Professional Hunters and Guides Association.

The Author
Richard Cox is a travel writer and novelist, who originated the Thornton Cox guide imprint in 1966 and re-launched it in 1986. He has both lived in Africa and journeyed very extensively there.

Foreword

When you are travelling and deciding your own itinerary what you need are facts and practicalities, not polemics. For years one by-product of the anti-apartheid campaign was a lack of informed travel guidance not merely to South Africa, but to its neighbouring countries as well. Now, happily, the emergence of the 'new' South Africa has lifted the veil from seven countries that offer travel contrasts, experiences and facilities to be found nowhere else in Africa.

Lions and gold, ancient forts and native dancing, the Zambezi plunging down the mile-long arc of the Victoria Falls, the wildlife of the mysterious Okavango delta, gemsbok miraculously surviving in the high dunes of the Namib desert, the wide horizons of the veld and 1,200 miles of beaches from Natal to the Cape are only a few of a host of natural wonders. The vineyards that surround the gracious, cool white Cape Dutch homesteads date back to the 17th century and produce exceptional wines. Historic buildings, imaginative hiking trails, every kind of sporting facility and a distinctive lifestyle all combine to make Southern Africa as many faceted as the celebrated diamonds it produces.

These seven countries are as varied politically as they are physically, from Kingdoms through to multi-party democracies. Yet in practice politics make little difference to the visitor. You can pass freely and easily from any one country into any other, which is more than can be said of other African regions. What you will notice is that the quality of hotels and transport varies, as well as the availability of travel essentials like films and toiletries. But if you are fore-warned you should have no problems.

South Africa is the powerhouse of the region, generating 25 percent of everything the whole African continent produces. In variety of landscape, people wildlife and tourist development she is a giant; as well as, at the time of writing a good holiday 'buy' for your currency. So we make no apology for opening this guide with the Republic.

Readers' comments would be most welcome. Send them to Thornton Cox Ltd, Editorial Office, PO Box 88, Alderney, Channel Islands, GY9 3DH, United Kingdom.

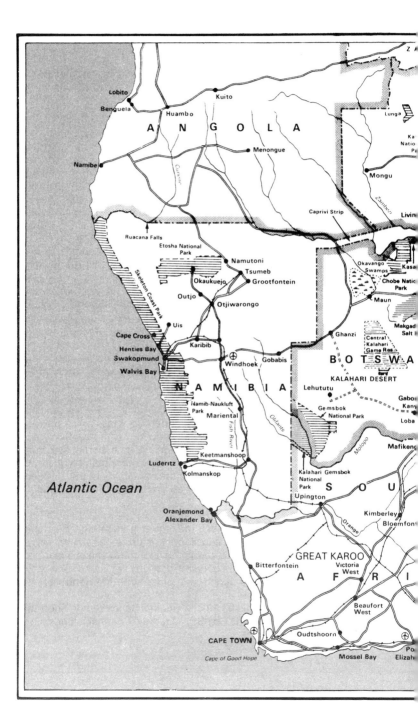

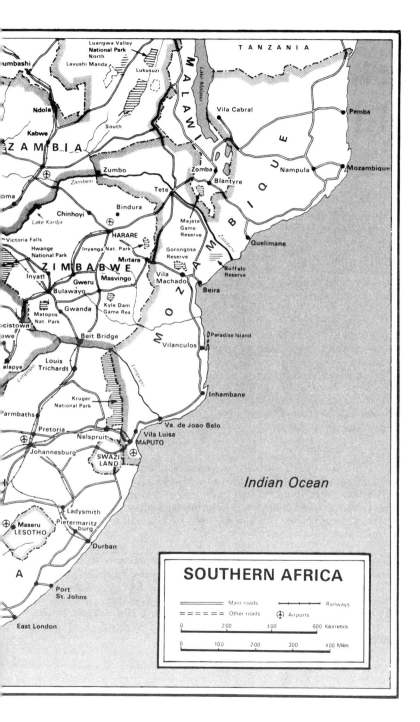

SOUTHERN AFRICA

━━━━━━ Main roads	┝━┿━┥ Railways
═ ═ ═ ═ ═ Other roads	✈ Airports

0   200   400   600 Kilometres

0   100   200   300   400 Miles

General Information

Detailed local advice is given in each country's 'Factfile'.

Getting to Southern Africa

Air from Europe

Johannesburg's international airport is the hub for southern Africa's airline services, although Namibia and Zimbabwe have direct services from Europe on their own airlines. South African Airways operates from London to Johannesburg ten times a week, twice to Cape Town, and twice to Durban. These overnight services use Heathrow's terminal one, where they interline with British Midland flights from Birmingham, East Midlands, Glasgow and Leeds. SAA also flies to Johannesburg from Amsterdam, Brussels, Frankfurt, Lisbon, Paris, Vienna, and Zurich. The airlines of Botswana, Lesotho and Swaziland have onward connections through Johannesburg.

The other international carriers serving the region include British Airways to Gaborone, Harare, Lusaka and Johannesburg; Alitalia, Cathay Pacific, Iberia, KLM, Lufthansa, Olympic, Qantas Sabena, SAS, Swissair, TAP, and UTA to Johannesburg; Air India, Kenya Airways and Quantas to Harare.

Fares

In 1995 South African Airways cheapest return fare London to Johannesburg was £625 – the same as in 1992. Virtually all airlines offer discounted fares through travel agents and consolidators. They are higher at weekends and during the November to mid-February peak season. Fares are usually exclusive of British and other airport taxes.

One British specialist agent dealing with flights to South Africa only is Friends of the Springbok (Friendship House, 49-51 Gresham Road, Staines, Middlesex TW18 2BD; tel 01784 465511). A reliable firm for discount tickets to anywhere in Africa is Trailfinders (46 Earls Court Road, London W8 7RG; tel 0171 938 3366). WEXAS (45 Brompton Road, London SW3 1DE; tel 0171 589 0500) is a reputable travel club for cheap flights.

Air from North America
South African Airways flies four times a week direct from New York to Johannesburg, which with a flight time of 14 hours is easily the fastest service, and twice weekly to Miami. Both have connections to Cape Town. British Airways connects through London, KLM through Amsterdam, and so on. In 1995 the Apex fare to Johannesburg was $1,149.

Services to Botswana, Namibia, Zambia and Zimbabwe all route either through Europe or Johannesburg.

Airport Taxes
Departure taxes are payable in Britain, South Africa, Zambia and Zimbabwe. They are normally payable when you buy the ticket.

Sea
Several cargo companies offer scheduled passenger voyages from Europe to Cape Town, usually continuing to port Elizabeth and Durban In fact they are re-establishing the old traditions of the mailships, though on much larger vessels and with only a handful of well-looked after passengers. They do not carry doctors and may require medical certificates before you sail.

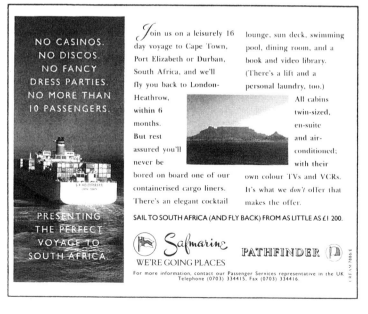
11

General Information

The most frequent and fastest, with 52,000 ton container ships taking 12 passengers in en-suite bedrooms, are Safmarine's ships. They sail 27 times a year from Tilbury, and 27 back, taking 16 days to Cape Town and continuing to Port Elizabeth and Durban. 1995 fares were from US$1,600 per person sharing. Bookings through Pathfinder, PO Box 461, Southampton SO15 2ZE, England; tel 01703 334416. The RM St Helena sails six times a year from Cardiff via the Canaries, Ascension and St Helena, taking a month. A twin-bedded outside cabin costs £2,066 per person. Bookings through Curnow Shipping, Porthlevan, Helston, Cornwell TR13 8TH; tel 03265 63434. Curnow's American agent is Traveltips, 130-07 Depot Road, PO Box 580188, Flushing, New York 11358; tel 718 939 2400.

The Medite Shipping Co goes weekly from Felixstowe taking 17 days to Cape Town at £1,300 per person. Bookings MSC, Cliff House, Chevalier Road, Felixstowe, Suffolk, P11 7ES, tel 01394 676 452. Numerous cruise lines call at South African ports, including Royal Viking, Orient Lines and P&O.

Regional Air Services and Excursions

South Africa has far and away the best network of regional air services on the continent, centred on the hub of Johannesburg International airport 24 km (15 miles) east of the city. Frequent **South African Airways** flights connect Johannesburg to the neighbouring countries of Malawi, Mozambique, Namibia, Zambia and Zimbabwe (Bulawayo, Harare and Victoria Falls), while **SAA** services also extend to the Comores, Ivory Coast, Kenya, Madagascar, Mauritius, Malawi, Mozambique and Zaire. The principal **SAA** reservations office is at Johannesburg, tel 011 333 6504 (24 hours). Overseas offices are given in the South Africa 'Useful Facts' and local offices under the cities concerned.

Within the Republic **SAA** operates a very frequent service between Johannesburg and Durban, up to 15 flights a day each from Johannesburg to Cape Town and several daily flights to Bloemfontein, East London, George, Kimberley, Port Elizabeth and Upington.

Local and Feeder Airlines
The network is re-inforced by feeder airlines, which operate allied routes - usually bookable through **SAA** — to many South African towns and cities.

The principal carriers are **Comair** (reservations through **SAA**) operating from Jan Smuts to Gaborone, Manzini, Nelspruit, Phalaborwa, Richards Bay and Skukuza; **Airlink** (tel 011 973 2941) operates from Johannesburg International to Bloemfontein, East London,

Nelspruit, Pietersburg, Pietermaritzburg and Port Elizabeth and from Durban to Bloemfontein, Maputo, Nelspruit and Umtata. **National Airlines** (tel 011 659 2630) serving the north-western Cape mining towns of Aggeneys, Alexander Bay, Kleinzee, Springbok and Upington from Lanseria airport, Johannesburg, and from Cape Town; and **Theron Airways** (tel 011 659 2738) operating from Lanseria to the northern Transvaal towns of Alldays, Ellisras, Messina, Tshipise, Louis Trichardt and Thohoyandou in Venda. **Transkei Airways** (0471 24636) operates from Johannesburg to Umtata, and Umtata to Bloemfontein, Durban and Port Elizabeth. **Sun Air** (tel 011 394 5555) serves Mmabatho, Sun City and Thaba 'Nchu from Johannesburg International.

Fleets
SAA itself was founded back in 1934, pioneered non-stop flights from Europe and today has a fleet of 50 aircraft, including Boeing 747, 737 and Airbuses, plus an historic 52 for joyriders, with more Airbuses and Boeing 747 400's on order. The airline employs some 10,500 staff and carries out 98 percent of its own aircraft maintenance. The smaller carriers mainly operate twin-engined aircraft from Fokker Friendships down to Cessnas and Pipers.

Special Fares and Excursions
A wide variety of discount and excursion fares are available on **SAA's** scheduled services. These include Apex, Super Apex, late evening 'night flight' specials, standby, weekend excursions, family concessions and senior citizens fares.

A range of tours are sold by **SAA** in Britain, flying out of London, through Jetsave (tel 01342 328231) and marketed by travel agents. They can be booked through SARtravel in Britain (tel 0171 287 1133) and the USA (1100 East Broadway, Glendale, Calif 91205; tel toll-free 800 727 7207).

Air Safaris
Various safari companies offer these (see the Safaris section) and local airline ones are run by **Comair** (as above) and **Progress Air** At Lanseria; details from Safariplan (tel 011 886 1810, fax 011 886 1815), run by the veteran safari organiser Jon Panos. Safariplan's London office is at 62 Tyneham Road, SW11 SX9; tel 0171 924 5557, fax 223 5015. They are also bookable in Britain through Southern African Travel, Pioneer Business Park, York YO3 8TN (tel 01904 692469). The Johannesburg **SAA** reservations number for international tours is 011 333 6504.

Air Charters
Numerous companies operate charter aircraft. Among the largest are

General Information

National Airways Corporation (tel 011 827 9333), which has a fleet from small jets to helicopters at Rand airport, Germiston and **Safair** (as above) with large jets.

The Great Trains

Two of the world's great scheduled train services run through Southern Africa, the famous Blur Train from Capr Town to Johannesburg and Pretoria, and the no less distinguished Rovos Rail, while there are 'ordinary' trains from Johannesburg to the Victoria Falls, via Botswana and Bulawayo. Additionally South Africa and Zimbabwe are among the few countries where steam locomotives are still in constant use; an attraction capitalised on by the organisers of luxury 'steam safaris'. A special 'Great Train Journey' from Cape Town to the Victoria Falls, starting on the Blue Train after a flight from London, is marketed by Southern Africa Travel Pioneer Business Park, York YO3 8TN; tel 01904 692469. They also arrange holidays based on both express and steam train trips.

The Blue Train
From the complimentary half bottle of champagne brought by your steward as the train departs, the Blue Train is in a class by itself. On the 1,000 mile journey from Cape Town to Pretoria, and vice versa, you have excellent meals, compartments with bathrooms, a friendly bar at one end of an observation coach, and air-conditioning throughout. The journey takes just under 26 hours, stopping at Worcester, Beaufort West, de Aar, Kimberley and Johannesburg. Two complete trains enable it to be run in both directions on Mondays, Wednesdays and Fridays. The train manager commands a staff of 25, looking after a maximum of 107 passengers, and everything except alcoholic drink is included in the fare, which varies according to the size of your compartment. Reservations can be made through Spoornet offices in the Republic, Johannesburg number travel agents, or the SARtravel Bureau in London (Rehency House, Warwick Street, London W1R 5WA; tel 0171 287 1133, fax 287 1134). Other expresses are listed in the South Africa 'Useful Facts'.

Johannesburg to Bulawayo and the Victoria Falls
This is actually two sectors on the Spoornet train. The first from Johannesburg to Bulawayo, via Beit Bridge, leaves Johannesburg on Tuesdays and reaches Bulawayo at 1630 the next day. The Bulawayo to Victoria Falls train leaves daily at 1900, arriving at 0730 the next morning. Trains are very frequently late, but the connecting time is adequate. Scenically the trip is an experience, but it is not luxurious, although South African rolling stock is used up to Bulawayo. Check the catering facilities before you embark. Another train, the 'Limpopo', runs from Johannesburg to Harare via Beit Bridge on Fridays. First

class fares are cheaper than flying and passengers over 60 get a 40% discount.

Rovos Rail

This restored Edwardian train is already something of a legend. The brainchild of entrepreneur Rohan Vos, it began taking passengers in vintage luxury steam-hauled coaches to the Kruger Park, with a night stop and game viewing in a private reserve and still does this four day trip. But its main route now is from Pretoria to Cape Town and (connecting) Pretoria to Victoria Falls, doing each every two weeks. Once a year it ventures up to Dares Salaam in Tanzania. The 12 coaches carry only 46 passengers, all with private suites. The train is understandably expensive and heavily booked. Reservations Rovos Rail, PO Box 2837, Pretoria 0001; 012 323 6052, fax 323 0843. It is represented in London by Voyages Jules Verne (tel 0171 723 5066).

Zimbabwe Rail Safaris

Three regular steam services are hauled by huge Garrett locomotives out of Bulawayo, to which trains Rail Safaris (2c Prospect Avenue, Raylton, Bulawayo; tel 75575, fax 42217) attach their own vintage carriages, including a dining car and a lounge. Baths and showers are available on the train and there are gourmet meals. The most interesting run is from Bulawayo up through the big game country of Hwange to the Victoria Falls. This 'Champagne Express' stops at Hwange long enough for a game dive and spends a night at the Victoria Falls before returning, making a four day trip. A variant has sleeping cars stopping for two nights at Dett, while clients game view in Hwange, then going on to the Falls, with a duration of six days. For steam enthusiasts the Railway Museum at Bulawayo is a 'must'. However departures are infrequent, roughly once a month.

Backpacking and Cheap Local Travel

South Africa is no longer so expensive, but there are many new youth hostels (see 'Useful Facts' section) and innumerable campsites, including ones in parks and reserves. It is difficult to find cheap long-distance bus services, as opposed to express coaches. However Translux offers a one week to three month 'all-round South Africa' ticket. The rapidly multiplying 'black taxis' offer very cheap and perfectly safe local and regional transport. It can be dangerous to hitchike. Botswana does not officially say it could do without backpackers, but as one commented 'its tough to get around there, though you can exchange lifts for fuel payments'. Notice boards in the Mall in Gaborone accept notices offering and requesting lifts. Zimbabwe is friendly, with an informal network of information, municipal campsites and cheap, if crowded, buses. Lesotho and Swaziland are friendly too, and it is sim-

ple to locate local African bus stops. You should obtain an International Youth Hostels card before setting out for Africa.

Caravanning

With Southern Africa's climate encouraging an open air life, caravanning has become very popular and caravans can be rented. There are
caravan parks with toilet, washing and cooking facilities all over the
Republic, too many to list. If you want more information write to
SATOUR or to the Automobile Association, (PO Box 596, Johannesburg 2000), or to the Caravan Club of South Africa, (PO Box 50580,
Randburg 2125). Lesotho, Namibia, Swaziland and Zimbabwe also
have well-maintained caravan sites. Botswana has some, but is discouraging do-it-yourself holidays.

Climate

The climate in the countries described varies from sub-tropical in
Botswana, Natal and Zimbabwe, through semi-desert in Namibia to
Mediterranean at the Cape. It is warm and sunny throughout this area,
and rain usually comes in short, sharp downpours.

The biggest single climatic influence is that inland 40 per cent of
South Africa, most of Namibia and all of the other five countries are
part of a plateau, which in fact stretches to the Sahara, and lies 900-
1,220 m (3-4,000 ft) or more above sea level. This means that
though the sun is hot, it is less humid than at the coast, and colder at
night. The further south you go on this plateau, the colder it will be in
winter – in Johannesburg it can snow. Visitors are often caught out by
the tremendous difference between day and night temperatures,
especially in Spring and Autumn. Furthermore hotels may be air conditioned, but central heating is unknown. And do not forget that the
seasons are reversed from European ones, December and January
being the height of summer. The second major influence, which
affects the west coasts of South Africa and Namibia most, is the cool
air brought by winds from the Antarctic, and the cooling effect of the
Benguela sea current. Local variations in climate are detailed in
each chapter.

Complaints

If you have a complaint about a hotel or restaurant, and obtain no satis-
faction from the management, it will be worth contacting the local
Publicity Association in South Africa or Namibia, but less use in the
other countries, although in Lesotho and Swaziland there are efficient
Tourist Offices in the capitals.

Cosmetics

Sun preparations are essential, even in winter when the cooler daytime temperatures can be very deceptive. Moisturisers are vital because the air is so dry, except at the coast, and you should take lip salve on safari. Local South African products are manufactured with these conditions in mind, although many internationally known beauty preparations are sold in South African cities and a good range is available in Lesotho, Namibia and Swaziland. But ensure you take your own sun cream, soap, make-up and toiletries to Zambia and Zimbabwe, also if you are going direct to Botswana's wildlife areas.

Credit Cards

Access/Visa, American Express and Diners Club cards are widely accepted; indeed are essential for car hire. However some well-known safari companies do not accept them.

Currencies

See under each country's Useful Facts sections for denominations and rates of exchange. In early 1995 the South African Rand – the key currency - stood at R5.85 to £1, or to R3.60 to US$1.00. Its previous decline had slowed up.

Customs Duties and Game Trophies

Basic allowances are given in the 'Useful Facts' sections. The three things to be most careful about are the proper documentation for firearms, for which you must obtain permits on entry; the declaration of foreign currency in Zambia and Zimbabwe; and thirdly – when you are leaving – that you can prove the legal ownership of game trophies, skins and other wildlife 'products'. All these countries belong to CITES (the Convention on International Trade in Endangered Wild Fauna and Flora Species). So the export of ivory and cheetah or 'spotted cat' pelts is very strictly controlled. In South Africa permits to export other 'articles manufactured' from endangered wildlife must be obtained from the Department of Nature Conservation. Similar regulations apply elsewhere. Furthermore, you could have problems with your own Customs authorities when you get back home.

Dress – What to Wear

On Safari

The important thing is to be comfortable. Synthetic fabrics can become very sticky in sub-tropical climates. There is no substitute for cotton if you want to stay cool. Laundry is usually done within 24 hours, so it is easy to travel light and keep clothes clean. In lodges there is nothing wrong with jeans and a light shirt, though muted colours are best. In all these countries men wear shorts a lot. Male or female, you will need short-sleeved shirts and at least one long sleeved cotton shirt, and long trousers or a track suit, to keep off mosquitoes in the evenings, plus a lightwear sweater. You also need strong shoes for walking; trainers or desert boots will do.

If you are going to South Africa, then buy on arrival. Style has improved, prices are low (in foreign exchange terms) and there is a wide choice. But in Zimbabwe clothes are expensive and they may be unobtainable in Zambia. In Britain 'Travelling Light', (Morland House, Morland, Penrith, Cumbria; tel 019314 488) is a mail order firm specialising in safari clothes. In the United States the firm which outfitted Ernest Hemingway, Humphrey Bogart and Clark Gable, and still makes exactly the right gear, is Willis and Geiger, now an associate company of Land's Ends at 100 State Street, Madison, Wisconsin 53703; tel 608 823 6515, fax 283 6510. They will mail you a catalog. Or go, less expensively, to Banana Republic on 3rd Avenue and 59th Street in New York.

In Cities and Resorts
Everything is less formal than it used to be. In South Africa the buzzword is 'smart-casual' which means no jeans, shorts or jogging gear, but equally no tie. Unless you are on a business visit a suit is not necessary. The other countries always were less formal, though the more expensive hotels may want a jacket worn. For women light cottons and linens are the thing, preferably washable. Sandals can be bought locally. Swimsuits and beachwear are essential, since so many inland hotels have pools. You will need one pair of flattish shoes, and a raincoat, preferably a lightweight one. Sunglasses and a sunhat (obtainable locally) are vital. Take some lightweight clothes hangers.

Driving and Roads

A vast programme of road building has made most of South Africa's highways as good as you find in many European countries, and with far less traffic, though quite a few minor roads are gravelled. Elsewhere most main roads are tarmaced, though there are still gravel main roads in Botswana. This said, American readers of this book comment that 'South African roads seldom match the standard of American roads' and the 'driving skills' of many people in Southern Africa demand 'concentration and vigilance' from strangers! This is a thousand percent more so on a gravel surface.

There are things you must know about driving on gravel. First, deflate your tyres by ten to fifteen percent. Second, check the road's condition beforehand. If it has rained you may get stuck, or skid. If you go fast on loose stones you will certainly skid. In sand you must have 4WD. Everywhere expect your view to be suddenly blotted out by dust from other vehicles. Third, insure your windscreen and headlights' glass against breakage. Car hire details are given in country chapters. Most rental cars have manual transmissions, not automatic.

Licences and Speed Limits

Throughout Southern Africa you drive on the left. Your home licence is valid, though an international Driving Licence is preferable, and is mandatory in South Africa if your own licence does not bear a photograph. The speed limits in South Africa are 120 kph (75 mph) on main roads and 60 kph (37 mph) in urban areas. Other countries' limits vary only slightly from these, see 'Useful Facts' sections. It is well worth joining the South African Automobile Association, or a similar body, like Rondalia. You get help, free maps, and many other facilities.

Etiquette

In general the welcome you get in Africa is refreshing. Both whites and Africans like to talk to foreign visitors, while normal manners are informally polite. You must be tactful on two points. First there is religion. If you visit an African or Asian Moslem mosque, you must remove your shoes before going inside. It is also best to ask the guardian of the mosque for permission to enter. Second, people may object to being photographed without permission and you should never photograph military installations, or – in countries other than South Africa – any policeman, soldier, airport, or government building.

Gratuities

These are not usually added to hotel and restaurant bills, so give ten percent. Hotel porters, train attendants and others should be happy with R2.00 in South Africa and the equivalent in other countries. In Zambia gratuities are officially discouraged, and so tend to be smaller.

Food and Drink

The great English colonial cooking tradition lies heavy on Southern Africa, except in South Africa and Namibia, where it is alleviated by other influences. So you can expect standard English dishes, though both the splendid cold buffets of South African hotels and the traditional family outdoor barbecue, the braai, have been widely adopted. There are occasional reminders of the Portuguese in the shape of prawns or chicken piri-piri, and of course there are Chinese restaurants and Indian curries. In Namibia the predominant *cuisine* is German, with *apfelstrudel, wiener schnitzels* and the rest making a very welcome change. Zimbabwe produces very good cheeses, including blue, cheddar and brie and camembert types.

In South Africa the braai – short for *braaivleis* – is a nation-wide tradition. Every camp site has its braai place. The Indian communities have brought spicy oriental foods on to the menu, while the Malays at the Cape have had a profound effect on traditional Cape fare. Their *denningvleis* is a fricasse of lamb with spices, *bobotie* is a dish of minced meat with almonds and lemon leaves, while chicken pie is another favourite. South African meat is excellent, Karoo lamb with rosemary being legendarily tender. Fresh trout and seafood, especially crayfish, appear on may menus. Overall, South African cuisine and restaurants are unmatched anywhere else in Africa. Incidentally, a cafe is not a place to eat a snack, it is a small late-night provision shop.

Wines, Spirits, Beers and Water
South African wines are of the world class and widely obtainable in the region, though not in Zambia or Zimbabwe. Much more is said about them in the Western Cape section. Production is strictly controlled and there are six South African 'Wine of Origin' labels. A simple blue band guarantees that the wines come from a particular district, like the French *Appelation Controlee.* The labels of the most distinguished wines bear blue, red, green and black bands on a gold background, denoting exceptional quality as assessed by a panel of experts. A completely gold label denotes exceptional quality. Labels should show the type of grape, the year and the district. Although limited editions of estate wines are the finest, there are widely marketed wines of reliable quality, which you will find everywhere. Such are Simonsig wines, Fleur du Cap Pinotage and Nederburg Cabernet Sauvignon. Furthermore, the South African practice of bottling good wines in 250ml bottles, as well as full-size 750ml ones, is a real bonus if you are eating by yourself. KWV wines are widely available overseas.

Internationally known branded spirits are widely available, though expensive in Zambia and Zimbabwe. But Zimbabwe produces very acceptable wines, locally distilled gin and a range of Jacaranda brand cane-based liqueurs. For instance 'Triple Sec' is a Cointreau equivalent. The best-known South African liqueur is the tangerine-based Van der Hum. Locally brewed beers are available everywhere. Castle is one of many South African brands. Bottled sparkling water has come into fashion, too. In the towns tap water is normally safe, but on safari outside South Africa you should try to drink bottled or purified water.

Health

Immunisation requirements are given in each country's Factfile. Subscribing to the emergency service described below costs from US$9.00 per week - so worthwhile that wes subsidised the ad.

Malaria

Botswana, Zambia, the Zambezi valley, the lowveld of the Transvaal and northern Natal are all malarial. Some malarial parasites are now resistant to single drugs. Two prophylactics recommended by the World Health Organisation are ICI's Paludrine, two tablets once a day after a meal, plus two tablets once a week (on the same day), of Chloroquin. You must start taking these tablets a week before arrival

and continue for four weeks after your return. Prophylactics are sold, without prescription, at the chemist's shop in the domestic terminal at Johannesburg airport, as well as in town chemists.

Inoculations
Basic jabs are yellow fever, typhoid and cholera. Dr Richard Petty of The International Medical Centre (32 Weymouth Street, London W1N 3FA; tel 0171 486 3063) advises 'Top up on polio and tetanus. Rabies is an option, particularly desirable for long overland trips'. But some of the worst dangers come from unhygenic medical equipment. 'Never accept a blood transfusion. Ring your Embassy and ask for access to their disease free blood donor group.'

AIDS and Personal Medical Packs
The dangers of infection with AIDS and hepatitis have led to personal sterile medical packs, which include dressings, sutures, syringes and hypodermic needles. These weigh only three ounces and the idea is that you give one to the doctor or nurse treating you; making sure they actually use it. The International Medical Centre's pack costs £15 by mail order, including a medical advice booklet. British Airways Travel Clinics sell a similar package. These are not necessary in South Africa, Lesotho, Namibia or Swaziland but are elsewhere.

Bilharzia
Finally you should avoid swimming in inland lakes or rivers unless you are told it is safe, since they are often infested with bilharzia, a disease carried by water snails, which causes eventual blindness.

Hiking Trails

The popularity of cross-country hiking in South Africa has spread to neighbouring countries, though not to any extent in Botswana, Zambia and Zimbabwe because of the predators. In South Africa the signed trails laid out by the National Hiking Way Board stretch in a near-complete system from the northern Transvaal to the Cedarberg mountains in the Cape, with many separate trails elsewhere. They range from a one km walk at Bourke's Luck potholes on the Blyde river to the eight-day Outeniqua Trail on the Garden Route. A full list can be had from SATOUR offices or the Hiking Way Board (Private Bag X 447, Pretoria 0001; tel 012 310 3911), which sells maps of individual trails. A Johannesburg company that organises hiking expeditions, as well as canoeing and riding trails, is Drifters, PO Box 48434, Roosevelt Park 2129; tel 011 888 1160, fax 888 1020.

There are hikes in the reserves of Lesotho and Swaziland, while Namibia's five-day Fish River Canyon Trail is renowned, both for its challenge and the spectacular scenery.

General Information

Commonsense rules apply to equipment. Take warm clothing, strong shoes, adequate food and water, check the weather beforehand and stick with your fellow hikers. The right sort of rucksack, with a waist support, is made by Karrimor or Lowe.

Hotels

Nearly all hotels in South Africa are classified from five-star to one-star in a system detailed in the 'useful Facts' section. Hotels in Namibia, Zambia and Zimbabwe have a grading up to five stars. In Botswana, Lesotho and Swaziland there is no grading system, though lists of Tourist Board approved hotels are published. We recommend only those hotels that keep a reasonably high standard, plus some reliable cheaper ones. All the positive recommendations – as opposed to simple mentions – are based on contributors' advice. In 1995 South African hotels prices ranged from R215 (£43) for bed and breakfast per person in a five-star hotel to R60.95 (£12.19) in a two-star one, or around R70 (£14) in a one-star. Some country hotels charge more then their rating would indicate, usually because they have individual character. In Lesotho and Swaziland prices were similar. The other countries were liable to be more expensive and in Zambia and Zimbabwe you had to pay in foreign exchange. Good hotels everywhere accept major credit cards.

Information Overseas

South Africa

The South African Tourism Board (SATOUR) keeps a wealth of brochures at its overseas offices. The London office is at 5-6 Alt Grove, Wimbledon, London SW19 4BZ; tel 0181 944 8080. The United States offices are in New York (500 Fifth Avenue, 20th floor, New York, NY 10110; tel 212 730 2929 or 800 822 5368) and in California (Suite 1524 Airport Boulevard. Los Angles, Calif 90045; tel 310641 8444 or toll-free 800 782 9772). There are also offices in Amsterdam, Frankfurt, Harare, hong Kong, Milan, paris, Sydney, Tel Aviv, Tokyo and Vienna.

Lesotho, Swaziland and Zimbabwe

The Tourist Offices in London are in these countries diplomatic missions at, respectively, the High Commission of the Kingdom of Lesotho (Chesham Place, London SW1 8AN; tel 0171 235 5686), and the Kingdom .of Swaziland High Commission (20 Buckingham Gate, London SW1E 6LB; tel 0171 630 6611). In the United States they are at the Embassy of the Kingdom of Lesotho (2511 Massachusetts Avenue, Washington DC 20008; tel 202 797 5533), and the Embassy of the Kingdom of Swaziland (400 International Drive, Washington DC 20008; tel 202 362 6683). They have only limited information.

The Zimbabwe offices are at the High Commission in London (429 Strand, London WC2R 0QE; tel 0171 240 6169), in New York at the Rockefeller Centre Room 412, 1270 Avenue of the Americans, New York 10020; 212 332 1090) and in South africa at the Carlton Centre, Upper Shopping Level, Johannesburg (PO Box 9398, Johannesburg 2000; tel 011 331 3137).

Namibia Tourism overseas offices are in Cape Town (4 Shell House, Waterkant Street; tel 419 3190), Johannesburg (209 Redroute, Carlton Centre; tel 331 7055), Germany alongside the Air Namibia offices (Im Atzelnest 3, 61352 Bad Hamburg; tel 06172 406650), the United Kingdom at 6 Chandos Street, London W1M 0LQ; tel 0171 636 6244, fax 637 5694. In the USA information is available from the Namibian Embassy (1413 K Street NW, Washington DC 20005; tel 202 234 6047).

Zambia
The Zambia National Tourist Board offices in London are at 2 Palace Gate, London W8 5NF; tel 0171 589 6343. In the United States they are at 237 East 52nd Street, New York, NY 10022; tel 212 308 2155/2162.

Language

English is spoken throughout Southern Africa.

Lavatories

There are very few public toilets in these countries, except at officially recognised campsites and caravan sites. Hotel and restaurant washrooms are usually kept clean.

Photography

The African sunlight can be intense and you should allow a slightly faster exposure than you would in Europe. The DIN, ASA and Weston meter settings recommended by film manufacturers are now for the minimum exposure, not the average, and so are just about right. However, where there is a lot of refracted light, as on the dazzling white sands of the coast or the open veld, you will need a still shorter exposure. A lens hood is invaluable, while an ultra violet filter cuts down the effect of glare.

Photographing Animals and People
Photographing game you are obviously unlikely to get a meter reading

off the animal itself. A good way to check is by taking one off a dull-coloured piece of clothing, remembering to take a reading in shade if your subject is lying in the shade. When using a telephoto lens, it is wise to open the aperture an extra half stop. Taking pictures of Africans, whose dark skins reflect very little light, you need to open the aperture by at least one stop (eg from 1/250th to 1/125th sec).

Developing Film

In South Africa colour prints can be developed in an hour, slides may take three to five days, and black and white film can rarely be coped with. Developing facilities are adequate in Lesotho, Namibia and Swaziland, but should be avoided elsewhere. If taking film around with you be on the look out for old security X-ray equipment at some airports, which will fog your film. Film itself is more expensive throughout Southern Africa than in Europe, and unobtainable in some places. Bring plenty with you.

Regional Tour Operators and Travel Agents

A host of firms sell holidays in the region and advice in the region is given in the next section. An increasing number of travel firms in Britain and America advertise safaris taking in several countries. Few are actually experts. Some even schedule itineraries that are next door to impossible. So it is worth being selective and the following brief listing is of companies that are thoroughly reliable and wide ranging.

Tours

In South Africa Connex has experience since 1922 of luxury tours that now extend to Malawi, Namibia and Zimbabwe. In London they are known as SARtravel (Regency House, Warwick Street, London W1R SWA; tel 0171 287 1133, fax 0171 287 1134). United Touring International (UTI, Travel House, Springvilla Park, Springvilla Road, Edgeware, London HA8 7EB; tel 0181 905 6525) is hughly experienced in Zimbabwe as UTC and is moving into South Africa. Its tours are marketed by the Thomas Cook travel agency. Southern Africa Travel (see next paragraph) has a range of tours throughout the region. So does Wild Africa Safaris, Castlebank House, Oak Road, Leatherhead KT 22 7PG; tel 01372 362288, fax 360147. A small agency that is good on private lodges is Union Castle Travel, 185 Brompton Road, London SW3 1NE; tel 0171 584 0001.

Security

The 1990s have seen a marked increase in car theft and street crime in cities and towns throughout southern Africa. Beggars and street traders - politely called 'informal traders' in south africa - don't help the situation. Nor does unemployment. But the social ills behind the crime don't make it any nicer to be mugged. Keep your eyes open for loitering youths and leave nothing valuable in an unattended car.

Sporting Activities

Sporting facilities are excellent and extensive throughout South Africa, golf courses particularly so. Tennis and bowls are played almost everywhere. Watersports are organised all round the coasts, while inland resorts have been created in the Transvaal, Orange Free State and Northern Cape, as in Lesotho, Namibia, Swaziland, Zambia and Zimbabwe. Ballooning, canoeing, hang-gliding, parascending and white-water rafting on the Breeds, Cunene, Orange, Tugela and Zambezi rivers are among newer activities. There are details in the text, while SATOUR has brochures on what is available in South Africa.

Tailored Itineraries

For wider travel, with personally tailored itineraries taking in Botswana, Namibia and Zimbabwe in particular, we recommend Safari Consultants (Orchard House, Upper Road, Litle Cornard, Suffolk CO10 0NZ; tel 01787 228494, fax 228096). Southern Africa Travel (Pioneer Business Park, York YO3 8TN; tel 01904 692469) arranges both standard tours and special itineraries, as do Abercrombie & Kent (Sloane Square House, Holbein Place, London SW1W 8NS; tel 0171 730 9600) A & K are particularly known for luxury lodge tours. Their United States office is at 1520 Kensington Road, Oakbrook, Illinois 60521; tel 708 954 2944. Safari Drive Ltd (104 Warriner Gardens, London SW11 4DU; tel 0171 622 3891, fax 498 0914) organise self drive expeditions, with camping gear in Botswanna, Namibia and Zimbabwe.

Time

Time throughout the region is two hours ahead of GMT and seven hours ahead of Eastern Standard Time in the USA (six hours during daylight saving). Even in summer the sunsets around 1900, except in the southern Cape, where it remains light until 2100.

Weights and Measures

All seven countries have converted to the metric system.

Safaris and Private Reserves

'Journey' is what the Swahili word safari means and the classic East African luxury safaris move from camp to camp in the wild, using natural sites by rivers or in glades. These do not exist in southern Africa, although countless tours are called 'safaris'. One reason is agricultural development, which has resulted in wildlife being confined to the parks and reserves, or private farms. Another is that it is easy to organise low cost expeditions to well-equipped campsites in reserves and parks, but it is impossible to camp away from those prepared facilities, except on the largest ranches.

Obviously hunting and close-up photography are mutually incompatible, as the game becomes extremely shy in areas that are hunted. So although some of the best hunting firms will take photographic clients – for example, Ker & Downey in Botswana and Greater Kuduland Safaris in the northern Transvaal – many will not. The most enjoyable alternative is to go to camps or lodges in private reserves.

Private Lodges, Reserves and Game Farms

Staying at one of the private game reserves alongside the Kruger National Park, at Mala Mala or Londolozi for example, used to be expensive. But now quite a number of such lodges have opened, all sharing great advantages over conventional ones inside the National Parks, including very reasonably priced ones. Clients are allowed to game view from open vehicles, go on night game drives and make escorted walks. Better still the rangers who guide you at these places mostly have a degree in Natural Sciences before even starting their bush training. They only ever look after four or five clients at a time and impart an understanding of what you are seeing that is a world apart from the average tour leader's commentary.

The best of these reserves are in South Africa, mainly in the Transvaal and northern Natal, and are described in the relevant chapters. A few feature in the brochures of up-market safari organisers. Several South African publications give details. Two are The Hotelogue Collection of Hotels, Country Houses and Game Lodges (PO Box 14160, Greenpoint 8051; tel 021 434 3890, fax 434 0489) and Secluded Country Lodges (PO Box 2473, Parklands 2121; tel 011 442 5640, fax 442 5675). Both can make reservations for you.

In Zimbabwe there are private lodges in several National Parks, while large game farms are opening up in the lowveld near Chiredzi. Game farms are something of a speciality in Namibia, where the Tourism Ministry lists and grades them. Botswanna has, of course, the many camps in the Okavango. See pages 26-27 for agents with specialised knowledge of them.

Lodge Tours
Package tours around the Kruger Park's lodges and to Etosha in Namibia have been going for a long time. Since the late-1980s a more wide-ranging lodge tour circuit has developed from Harare to Lake Kariba, the Zambezi valley, the Victoria Falls and the Hwange National Park in Zimbabwe, continuing to Chobe and the Okavango in Botswana. Tours will often include northern Namibia. British, American and South African firms with specialist knowledge and well-designed lodges itineraries are listed under 'Travel Agents and Tour Operators' in the General Information. But beware of tight schedules based on connecting flights. As someone once wrote in the Harare airport visitors' book 'Everybody will stay here a little longer, if Air Zimbabwe has anything to do with it'. Afro-Ventures (PO Box 2339, Randburg 2125, South Africia; tel 011 789 1078) is one firm with a reasonably priced safari organisation all round Southern Africa.

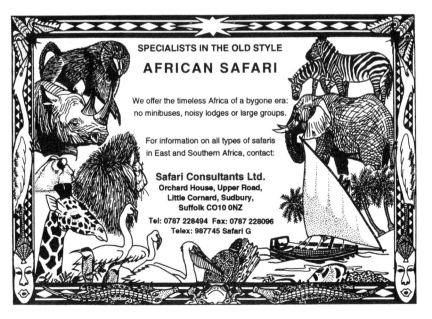

Hunting

What follows is basic information. The opportunities for hunting both big game and plains game, as well as birdshooting, are extremely varied in southern Africa. Serious hunters should contact the professional associations named below for more detailed information. Hunting firms taking you after big game will not usually quote for less than ten days. If you want first-class specimens you should allow yourself two to three weeks. During this time you are excellently looked after, probably shifting between camps in different concession areas, with trackers, gunbearers, cooks, and field and camp staff, as well cold drinks, hot showers, and two-way radio links.

Professionalism

The standards of professional hunters and guides are kept high by their professional organisations. Most professional hunters from Africa attend the Game Conservation International annual conferences in San Antonio, Texas, in early March, or the Safari Club International conference in January.

Game conservation regulations are always strict. In southern Africa cheetah and black rhino are protected everywhere, elephant and white rhino can only be shot very occasionally in South Africa, while elephant are also available in Zimbabwe. But the licences for plains game cover a wide variety of species. Governmental licences and trophy fees can be expensive. Hunting firms quotations are normally exclusive of weapons and ammunition, taxidermy, licences, air fares and hard liquor. Booking deposits of around 40 percent are required.

South Africa

Most hunting is on private farms in the eastern and northern Transvaal, in Zululand, to a very limited extent in the eastern Cape and at Tussen-die-Riviere in the Orange Free State. White rhino are sometimes allocated for culling by the Natal Parks Board. Buffalo can be shot in the eastern Transvaal, where there is a very limited permit allocation for elephant. Trophy fees are only charged for animals either bagged or 'wounded and lost'. A wide variety of plains game is available, from kudu down to duiker. The Professional Hunters Association of South Africa (277 Main Road, Bryanston 2060; tel 011 706 7724, fax 706 1389) can give advice and hunting firms' names.

Botswana

Hunting is expensive. The hunting concessions are in the north, mainly adjacent to Chobe and the Okavango, with firms being based in Kasane or Maun. Cheetah, elephant, giraffe, puku, roan antelope, rhino, and waterbuck are protected. Among species for which licences are available are buffalo, impala, lechwe, leopard, lion, reedbuck, sable antelope, sessebe, sitatunga, wildebeest and zebra. The hunting season is April to mid-September. Safaris are normally sold in a combination package of species/days. Two active companies are Hunters Africa (PO Box 11, Kasane) and Safari South (PO Box 40, Maun; tel 267 660 211, fax 660 379). The American offices are at 13201 Northwest Freeway (Suite 850), Houston, TX 77040; tel toll-free 800 423 4236, fax 713 744 5277. The british ofice is at 18 Albemarle Street, London W1X 3HA; tel 0171 629 2044, fax 491 9177.

Namibia
Hunting is on private game farms in the north, between Windhoek and Etosha. The best opportunities are for eland, gemsbok and greater kudu. The seasons are June-July and August-September. For further details see under 'Safaris' in the Namibia chapter.

Zambia
The hunting areas are in Benguela, Kafue, and bordering the Luangwa valley. Altogether there are 34 game management areas, acting as buffers between the National Parks and farmland, where specialised hunting is allowed. Both the Luangwa and Kafue blocks have numerous buffalo, eland, impala, leopard, lion, puku, warthog, waterbuck and zebra. Cookson's wildebeest is found only in the Luangwa and blue wildebeest in northern Kafue, where hartebeest, roan antelope and sable abound. Lechwe are found only around Lochinvar and Lake Bangweulu. The hunting season is June to October and only members of the Professional Hunters Association of Zambia (tel 260 1 211644) are allowed to take out hunting safaris. Licences are often not actually issued until the season has begun.

Zimbabwe
Hunting is conducted on three categories of land: state safari land, communal land, and private ranches. Big game areas are in the Zambezi valley, western Matabeland, and Manicaland. Hunting on communal land benefits the local population through the 'Campfire' programme, which gives locals monies earned from hunting and meat from the animals shot. Charges comprise a daily rate per hunter and trophy fees according to the species, plus concession fees which vary widely, being high for big game on state and communal land and lower for plains game, mainly on private land. The average hunt is ten days for big game and seven for plains game. The main hunt season is April to November. Only 0.05 percent of the elephant population is allocated for culling by hunting. Birdshooting is available. Hunters must be accompanied by a licenced professional hunter and names can be had from the Zimbabwe Association of Tour and Safari Operators, PO Box 7240, Harare; tel 263 4 733211, fax 794015.

Table Mountain from Bloubergstrand

The Republic of South Africa

The Country

South Africa is a country of breathtaking diversity. Watching the game in the vast Kruger park, you are in the wild Africa that fascinated John Buchan and has provided the locale for some of Wilbur Smith's most exciting scenes. Behind the Indian Ocean shores the sub-tropical valleys of Natal once sheltered the kraals of those bloodthirsty Zulu kings, Chaka and Dingaan. Largely unspoilt beaches run 1,760 km (1,100 miles) from Durban to the Mediterranean climate of the Cape resorts, with magnificent surfing and big game fishing; and that leaves another 1,300 km (812 miles) of sometimes harsh and rocky, sometimes inviting, western coastline from the white sands of the Bloubergstrand to the Orange river. Not that anyone in their right mind would go for a seaside holiday to the barren shores of the Richtersveld, though the adventurous would want to explore its new National Park, just as the Kalahari Gemsbok National Park attracts naturalists to its unique semi-desert environment and wildlife.

Inland you can find stimulating contrasts, from the quiet vineyards and wine presses of Paarl and Stellenbosch to sheep ranching and ostriches in the Great Karoo, or the roaring development of the Witwatersrand. What it all adds up to is a big country, with a long tradition of outdoor living, and energy to match.

Surprisingly few people in Europe and the United States appreciate that although South Africa's 472,675 sq miles make it half the size of Europe, it still only occupies four percent of the African landmass and has six and a half percent of the total African population; yet it produces 40 percent of the continent's industrial output, 45 percent of mining production and is far and away Africa's largest agricultural producer and exporter. While tourist facilities in many other African countries have declined, South Africa's communications, hotel, resorts, art galleries and attractions of every kind for visitors have been transformed in recent years.

Today the country's leaders, black and white, are dealing with the politcal and racial problems left by apartheid. Racial discrimination is a thing of the past and the rest of the world is recognnising South Africa's many qualities, instead of its defects.

Climate

The climate characterising each province is described in the relevant chapters. Overall it is agreeably moderate, with warm summers, while winters are only cold high up on the inland plateau of the Free State, the northern Cape and the southern and western Transvaal. This said, there are considerable variations. The Cape coastal climate is Mediterranean, the Natal coast's humid and sub-tropical, the northern

Transvaal's lowveld and the northern Cape decidedly hot in summer. But it can snow in Johannesburg in winter. Around the Cape coastal belt rain falls mainly in winter (May to September). Over most of the inland plateau and Natal the rain comes in summer. For advice on what to wear see the General Information.

History

The first European settlement in South Africa was established in 1652 when Jan van Riebeeck landed near the Cape of Good Hope. As is recounted in the Cape Province chapter, his mission was to secure this halfway house on the trade route between Europe and the Far East for the Dutch East India Company and to establish gardens that could provision the Company's ships. From this tiny start grew a Dutch colony, which fell into British hands in 1806.

The Bantu Peoples Move Down

When the Cape Colony was founded, the only indigenous inhabitants in this southern tip of Africa were descendants of the hunter - gatherers known as Khoisan, which included the Khoi-Khoin (Hottentots) and San, or Bushmen. Much of the interior was unpeopled, except by the San. By 1660 the Khoi-Khoin had lost their independence and were integrated into the Dutch settlement. Meanwhile the Bantu tribes of Central Africa had been inexorably spreading south since the late 16th century, among them the Nguni tribes (Zulus, Swazis and Xhosas), the Sothos and others. By the time white settlers founded Natal in 1824 the Zulus had already driven the Matabele up beyond the Limpopo river and the Swazis into the mountains (unintentionally ensuring the ultimate survival of the Basuto and Swazi mountain kingdoms, under British protection). The Zulus inevitable confrontation with the whites led to frequent fighting and their eventual defeat in the Zulu War of 1879.

Independent Boer Republics

Meanwhile, during the mid-19th century, the Transvaal and the Orange Free State had been created as independent Boer republics. 'Boer' is the Dutch for farmer, and the republics were founded by Boers – also known today as Afrikaners – who trekked away to the interior from British restrictions at the Cape. The Voortrekkers, as those were called, first moved off at much the same time as American settlers began their historic opening up of the West. The climax was the Great Trek of 1835, which is the most potent symbol of Afrikaner folklore.

Gold, the Anglo-Boer War, and Union

The end of the nineteeth century brought the discovery of gold on the Rand and the Boer War between Britain and the Boer republics. During the struggle the Boer farmer-soldiers added camouflage and trenches to military tactics, and the word 'commando' to military language. In the end it took 200,000 British troops to subdue 180,-000 Boers – men, women and children. That was in 1902. Happily a reconciliation followed and eight years later, on 31st May 1910, the Union was formed as a sovereign State from the four provinces of the Cape, Natal, the Orange Free State and the Transvaal. Pretoria was made the capital and Cape Town the seat of Parliament. Every year officials and diplomats moved down to the Cape for six months Parliamentary session. On May 31, 1961, South Africa became a Republic and left the British Commonwealth.

The international campaign against the policies of apartheid - separate racial development - during the 1960 to 1980s is too well known to need detailing here. Leaders of the African National Congress party, which had been founded in 1912, were forced into exile or into hiding. Nelson Mandela was arrested in 1962. Unrest grew throughout the period and was not allayed by minor constitutional changes. Then in 1990 President F.W. de Klerk released Mandela from jail on Robben Island and lifted the ban on all unlawful organisations. The ANC's President, Oliver Tambo, returned to South Africa after 30 years of exile.

In spite of violence escalating - in 1992 some 20,135 murders were reported to the police - the Republic rejoined the community of nations, economic sanctions were lifted, and national teams took part in the 1992 Olympics. In April, 1994 a fully multiracial election brought a new government to power, with Mandela as President and F.W de Klerk as Deputy President. This government was elected for a five year period to establish a new constitution. The number of provinces was increased to nine, each with a provincial assembly, and existing town councils were replaced by multi-racial provisional authorities. The disparate self-governing tribal states created under apartheid, like the Transkei and Bophuthatswana, were re-integrated into the Republic, which rejoined the British Commonwealth on June 1, 1994.

The People

How the Dutch and British settlers arrived and the Zulus and Xhosa descended from central Africa has just been described. From the end of the 17th century onwards the white settlers at the Cape were joined by Huguenots, Germans and other Europeans, while Malays were brought in as slaves. Inter-marriage of Malays and Hottentots with whites produced the 'coloured' population. Slavery was abolished in 1838. The 1860s saw the racial composition of the country further complicated by the immigration of Indians to work in the sugar fields of Natal.

Today South Africa's 42,700,000 people can be broadly divided into four groups: blacks 33,000,000, whites 5,000,000, coloureds 3,000,000 and Indians 1,000,000.

National Parks

South Africa's National Parks and Reserves are justifiably world-famous. It was this country that initiated the conservation of wildlife and flora in Africa. Sanctuaries were first proposed by President Kruger in 1884 and 13 years later the first reserves on the entire continent were proclaimed at Hluhluwe, Umfolozi and Lake St Lucia in Natal. Since then there has been continual, but extremely selective, growth in the National Parks Board's activity. Confusingly, the important Natal parks and reserves run by the Natal Parks Board, not the National Parks. Separately from the National Parks there are also a substantial number of provincial, municipal and private reserves.

New parks have usually been promulgated to protect specific endangered species or environments of outstanding interest. Thus Cape elephant were near extinction when the Addo Elephant National Park was gazetted in 1931. The Tsitsikamma Coastal and Forest National Park (1964) protects an ecologically unique area if cliffs and shoreline on the Garden Route, while the nearby at Wilderness and Knysna safeguard lake habitats. One of the largest and most exciting conservation projects anywhere in Africa is the Greater St Lucia Wetland Park in northern KwaZulu-Natal, which encompasses 289,-376 ha and is likely to be South Africa's first World Heritage site.

Conservation Policies
Most parks have accommodation in hutted camps or on campsites and how to book them is explained where the parks are described. Conservation is considered compatible with tourism. As one Parks Board publication remarks: 'Sanctuaries must pay their way if they are to have any future.' This does not alter the National Parks mission, which is 'to conserve and manage (parks) for all time in their natural state for the benefit of this country and all its people.' Literature on the parks can be obtained through SATOUR and the Board publishes a very well illustrated monthly magazine called 'Custos.' This often devotes an issue to a particular park. The subscription is small - write to Custos, PO Box 787, Pretoria 0001.

The Union Building, Pretoria

Gauteng (the PWV)

The Province

Most visitors' first sight of south Africa is flying in to Johannesburg airport: and what you see outside the aircraft windows is somewhat different to the travel brochures. In fact for people who imagine Africa as either jungle or oppressed townships this panorama can be a severe culture shock. Below you is a nation's technological heartland: a rapidly expanding and spacious conurbation that might as easily be in California and is known colloguially as the PWV - Pretoria, Witwatersrand, Vereeniging. Within it are the Republic's administrative capital Pretoria, the golden city of Johannesburg, huge African townships like Soweto and the industries of Vereeniging. Pretoria and Johannesburg are quite different in character from each other. In 1994 the PWV was detached from the Transvaal to be a province in its own right and in 1995 was renamed Gauteng (pronounced "Howteng").

The Pretoria-Witwatersrand-Vereeniging Area

Trying to sum up the technological, peri-urban and leisure complexes that have exploded into life around the Rand is like attempting to encapsulate Los Angeles in a single page: not least because there is a parallel in the breadth of activity involved. But the attempt has to be made, because although the PWV comprises far and away the greatest concentration of enterprise and wealth in the African continent, it is not an area in which visitors on vacation – as opposed to business – are likely to spend long. Very often, South Africa's air services being as good as they are, people simply change planes at Johannesburg airport and go straight on to Cape Town, Durban or wherever.

The Diamond Shape of the Gauteng
The Gauteng can be pretty confusing, once you are off the freeways that snake across its 130 km (81 mile) long area: it is appropriately more or less diamond shaped, with Pretoria at the north end and the industrial city of Vereeniging at the southern tip. Johannesburg is slap in the centre, astride the ridge of the gold-bearing Witwatersrand. Johannesburg International airport is to the east of the city, close to the R21 main road up to Pretoria. Broadly, Johannesburg's richer and more fashionable suburbs stretch out towards the capital, where there is very rapid housing development. By contrast, south of Johannesburg is rougher and tougher with suburbs like Turffontein and the huge Soweto township, once so beloved of foreign news reporters both for its riots and as the home of Mrs Winnie Mandela, now a destination for escorted 'township tours'. Beyond, 50 km (31 miles) south of the city, is Vereeniging.

An Economic Dynamo
This emmense complex - the size of two English counties - is the financial dynamo that powers the South African economy: an economy that is responsible for some 25 percent of the entire African continent's gross product. Its needs are commensurately huge. Soon it will be drawing water from the far away Lesotho highlands, part of the largest civil engineering scheme in Africa. The PWV is big in a more American than European way, let alone African way. Within its borders lie the gold mines that made this all possible, airports, resorts based on dams and lakes, numerous shopping hyper-markets, stadiums, theatres, monuments and large nature reserves. We mention some, but any SATOUR office can provide a comprehensive list, as can the cities' Publicity Associations.

Everything Works!
What is more everything here functions. If you want a theatre ticket

Gauteng (the PWV)

then the Computicket service will sell you one by 'phone. If you want a safari to Botswana's Okavango or the Etosha Pan in Namibia, a Johannesburg based safari firm will fix you up. Time and time again in this book you will find that central reservations agencies for safaris or lodges in other countries are here, as is SARTOC, the southern Africa joint tourist promotion organisation. This is the focal point for the whole southern Africa region.

Climate
Summers are warm with an average temperature of 22°C (70°F) and frequent afternoon thunderstorms that last for half an hour or so. Autumn and spring are pronounced seasons, as in Europe, and emphatically unlike most of Africa. In winter it can be cold. Johannesburg occasionally has snow, and the average temperature is 10°C (50°F). But the sunshine averages nine hours a day.

Communications

Johannesburg being the Republic's commercial capital, and Pretoria the official capital, communications from them to the rest of the country and the outside world are excellent. However, local public transport facilities are little short of appalling, from a visitor's viewpoint.

Air
Johannesburg airport, almost equidistant from the two cities, has been rebuilt to make it one of the world's most modern airports, though locals are still rude about it. For airport information call 011 921 6911. Subsidiary airports are Grand Central, Lanseria and Rand. And extraordinarily, although the PWV is criss-crossed with freeways it remains a very slow business travelling around by public transport. You can fly to the remotest parts of the Transvaal faster than you can go between Pretoria and Johannesburg by train. International connections are dealt with in the General Information and provincial ones in the special pages on Regional Air Services. Buses from the International airport run to central Johannesburg and to Pretoria.

Trains and Coaches
Slow trains link Johannesburg, Pretoria, Germiston and Witwatersand towns. For train information call Spoornet on 011 773 2944. There are regular long distance express coach services, notably Greyhound (tel 011 403 6463) and Translux (011 774 3333). Numerous 'black taxis' operate in the cities. If you intend spending any time around the area it is worth hiring a car, since roads and freeways - and road maps - are excellent. Hitch hikers are an endangered species.

Security

Personal security in the cities is a hazard. The centre of Pretoria is all right to walk around by day, the centre of Johannesburg is not, while areas of Johannesburg that used to be fashionable, like Hillbrow and Berea, are beset by beggars and have a menacing feel about them. The elderly white residents, who cannot afford to move, look beleaguered on their doorsteps, while the more affluent in better suburbs like Sandton live behind high walls, with security gates, and 'armed response' security patrol cars wait on corners for radio calls.

Nature Reserves and Recreation

You might imagine that there was not much room left for the wild in Gauteng. In fact there are numerous small reserves, like the Marievale Bird Sanctuary, the Suikerbosrand Nature Reserve near Heidelburg, and the Van Riebeeck Nature Reserve just south of Pretoria. See 'What to do over a weekend' below.

The Witwatersrand

'The ridge of white waters', on which Johannesburg stands, has seen some of the fastest developments of the 20th century anywhere. The place names along it emphasise what it was like before the 1880s. Elandsfontein, and Olifantsfontein, the farms on which were the springs at which eland and elephant used to drink, are now suburbs. The thing that changed the landscape, and made 'The Rand' an international symbol of wealth was, of course, gold.

Gold

Although pockets of gold had been found in the deep forests of the Drakensberg escarpment in the 1870s, causing a minor gold rush, the discovery that really made world news came in 1886. An Australian digger, George Harrison, chanced on a rocky outcrop of a gold-bearing reef on a farm between Potchefstroom and Pretoria. The site of his find is now the George Harrison Park on Main Reef Road in the city and this main reef is now thought to go down eight km (five miles) at an angle of 45 degrees, though three miles is the deepest mine so far planned. In places it is three m (10 ft) thick and the gold mines of the Rand stretch in an unbroken line for 96 km (60 miles) along it. The 55 mines produce nearly 70 percent of the free world's gold and even if four tons of rock have to be mined to extract a single ounce of the precious metal these are still among the world's richest deposits, additionally yielding carbon, green diamonds, platinum, silver and uranium.

Mine Visits; Gold Reef City

The public used to be able to visit certain mines, and if you have specialist or professional reasons it may still be possible through the Chamber of Mines (tel 011 838 8211). However for ordinary visitors the next best thing is the glitzy Gold Reef City, built over the old Crown mine, six km (four miles) from Johannesburg's centre.

You should not be put off going to this entertaining reconstruction of gold rush era Johannesburg by the advertised events there like the 'Just Jungle Juice Rock Show'. The Victorian buildings may be only replicas but they are remarkably authentic ones. The pubs and bars are fun, the jewellers shops well-stocked, and if the atmosphere is of a theme park, the descent of the Crown mine itself is completely real. You go down in a miners' cage wearing a hard hat and escorted by a knowledgeable former miner. True, the jackhammers are not thumping away and there is little dust and sweat. But the visit tells you a lot about mining and you can also watch gold being poured. There are regular African mine dances.

Bus tours depart from the main hotels to Gold Reef City, or it's a 20 minute taxi ride from the city centre. The four-star Gold Reef City Hotel is an agreeable period fake, with Victorian panelling and wrought iron balconies. Nice for a drink, though you might not want to be in this film set location overnight. The Gold Reef City information number is 011 496 1600.

Mine Dances
The Chamber of Mines can also advise on where to see the celebrated African mine dances on Sunday mornings. These are inter-tribal competitions by the mineworkers - who include immigrants from all over Southern Africa - and are extraordinarily robust and energetic. Some dances are war dances, or variants of them, like the Gumboot Dance.

Johannesburg

Postal code 2000. Telephone code 011. Tourist Info. 294961.
Nobody is sure after which Johannes the city was named. What is certain is that whoever he was, he started an amazing transformation. What began as a mining camp of shacks and tents dotted indiscrimately about the veld around the Witwatersrand in 1886 grew with explosive speed. The gold rush was responsible. Within a year the population was 10,000, within eight years 100,000. The town became like the film set for a Western. Single storey, corrugated roof stores had their fronts made fancy by cast iron Victorian verandahs – now faithfully reproduced in Gold Reef City – while horse drawn trams clattered down wide and dusty streets. The city has never stopped growing. Its architects have New York's compulsive desire to tear down and build even bigger all the time. Today the population is at

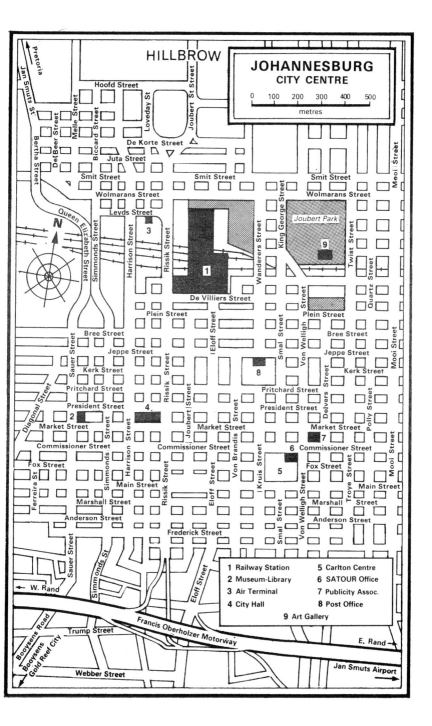

Gauteng (the PWV)

least 1,000,000, with that number again in the township of Soweto, making overall about 3,400,000. Black Africans call the city 'Egoli', which could become its name.

Not that there is anything very African about Johannesburg. This is a European city in the clear sunlight and cold winters of the high veld. Many blacks work there, the shops serve the better - off people of Soweto, and in the evenings the city centre is theirs. But the bustle and chaos of cities like Lagos is missing, although the street vendors and beggars multiply. Right now, what dominates the city centre are budding skyscrapers, like the Anglo-American headquarters, and the Carlton Centre complex, with its associated shopping malls.

The nerve centre of the Republic's telecommunications, the Post Office tower rears up 269 m (880 ft) above the city, all but casting its shadow on the mine dumps and winding gear that remain close to the centre. The mines have dictated the city's growth in an unexpected way too: no high-rise buildings can be constructed south of Commissioner Street because of the risk of subsidence.

Layout of the City
The streets slope upwards sharply north of the railway to Hillbrow, once the Chelsea of the city, and Berea. A couple of kilometres further out are the expensive suburbs like Morningside, Parktown – where Mr Harry Oppenheimer, the mining magnate, lives – and Houghton. Elegant mansions in these suburbs, leafy parks, the Melrose Bird Sanctuary and the Emmerantia Botanic Gardens, are all in high contrast to the mini-Manhattan of the centre.

During the late 1970s and 1980s a pronounced shift of business away from the centre to the outer suburbs took place. Although the Stock Exchange and the financiers remained in the centre, more and more businesses moved out to Rosebank, Sandton and other suburbs close to the freeway encircling the city, where hypermarkets and shopping malls on the American pattern sprang up. For business people this meant that instead of easily accomplishing six or seven appointments in a day, it is now hard to achieve three, and a car is vital. For holiday visitors it resulted in the centre becoming a lot less lively in the evenings, while in the 1990s' Hillbrow, with its bookshops and cafes, has become a pretty rough district at night, as has Berea.

This warning given, we can assure you that, although people work hard, starting at 0830 and finishing at 1700 during the week, Johannesburg as a whole is an extremely lively place, not least culturally. It also has its own moments of beauty, like the sunset on the incredible golden sand mountains of mine tailings outside the city.

Information

The Johannesburg Publicity Association is on the ground floor of Markwell House on the corner of Market and Von Wiellígh Streets (see map) tel 294961, fax 336 4965. The SATOUR offices are on the corner of Kruis and Market Streets, postal address PO Box 1094, Johannesburg 2000; tel 338 8082. There is also a SATOUR office at 181 Jan Smuts Avenue, Parktown North (tel 447 6030) and a most useful one in the Arrivals Hall Johannesburg International Airport (tel 970 1669).

City Centre and Shopping

The central area has a gridiron plan of streets, most of them one way only for traffic and cursed with a formidable array of parking meters. There are, however, several pedestrian malls in the area around the main downtown shopping complex, the Carlton Centre. This is a vast underground shopping area with curio and photographic shops, hairdressing salons and restaurants. Another mall is in Smal Street near the Station, to which pavement hawkers give an atmosphere of bustle. Eloff Street, the main shopping street, has wide pavements and a busway snakes down the middle. This golden street is known for its jewellers and a variety of shops and department stores. The Air Terminal is on Leyds Street (see map).

Markets

The largest and most notable market is the sprawling Oriental Plaza, between Bree Street and Main road in Fordsburg, to the west of the city centre. Something like 270 shops sell all manner of Indian and Western goods. For baskets, fabrics, flowers, fruit and spices try Diagonal Street – famous as a relic of older days – between Market and Kerk Streets. There is a daily flea market centred on second-hand and bric-a-brac shops on Pretoria Street in Hillbrow. Another is set up on Saturday mornings with stalls in Mary Fitzgerald Square, by the Market Theatre. The Artists' Market sells arts and crafts on the first weekend of each month. It's in the open air by the Zoo Lake in the Hermann Eckstein Park on Jan Smuts Avenue, roughly four km (three miles) from the centre to the north.

Accommodation; Restaurants; Entertainment

Among their 100 or more graded hotels Johannesburg and its suburbs have something for most people, including some fine establishments built in recent years. In the Carlton Centre is the city's only five-star hotel, the Carlton with its luxurious extension, the Carlton Court (PO Box 7709; tel 331 8911). The massive three-star Holiday Inn Garden Court is at 84 Smal Street (tel 29 7011), while the small Springbok at 73 Joubert Street (tel 337 8336) is family-run.

Gauteng (the PWV)

Berea, Braamfontein
Slightly away from the central business district are the four-star Parktonian on de Korte Street (PO Box 32278, Braamfontein; tel 403 5740) and the three-star Protea Gardens Hotel at 35 O'Reilly Road, Berea (tel 643 6610).

Parktown, Rosebank, Sandton City
However, it can be a lot more pleasant to stay right out in Sandton, Rosebank, or one of the other fashionable suburbs. One unforgettably delightful place is the four-star Sunnyside Park Hotel at 2 York Road in Parktown (tel 643 7226). This was once Lord Milner's home and remains an elegant mansion in its own gardens, though you must have a room overlooking the garden, not the kitchen backyard.

Sandton has become a self-styled city, with many hotels and exclusive speciality shops. The five-star Sandton Sun (PO Box 484902, Sandton 2146; tel 780 5000, fax 780 5002) and the adjoining Sandton Sun Tower (five-star silver) dominate the district, where the luxurious new Michelangalo (Stocks Hotel; tel 011 806 4192) opens in May 1996 and there are Holiday Inns, Karos and City Lodge hotels. From a visitors viewpoint Sandton is an excellent place to overnight on arrival, since it is easily accessible from the airport and the freeways.

Budget Accommodation, Bed and Breakfast, Youth Hostels
If you are on a budget and want good facilities without trimmings, the City Lodge chain have hotels near the airport at Edenvale (tel 392 1750) and Randburg (tel 706 7800) as well as Sandton (tel 884 9500). The Town Lodge near the airport (tel 974 5204) is also good value. The Publicity Association has lists of one-star hotels and there are numerous bed and breakfast establishments; for listings see the FactFile at the end of the South Africa chapters. The YMCA/YWCA is at 104 Rissik Street near the city centre (tel 724 4541) and the principal Youth Hostel a short way out at 32 Main Street, Townsview (tel 436 2728), near Gold Reef City on the number 47 bus route.

Restaurants
Virtually all two-to five-star hotels have restaurants, except the City Lodges. Exceptionally good ones include the Three Ships in the Carlton and the Prospect Room at the Sunnyside Park. In the city centre try Dentons at 125 Fox Street (tel 331 3806) for lunch. There are some very good restaurants out in Rosebank and Sandton, notably Les Marquis at 12 Fredman Drive, Sandton (tel 783 8947), for classic French cooking; and Lupo's at 281 Jan Smuts Avenue, Dunkeld (tel 880 4850) for delicately delicious Italian fare. Lupo's is not licenced, so you can take your own wine.

There are many, many others. Consult the American Express restaurant guide 'Style'.

If you want to eat for less there are many steak house, such as the Mike's Kitchen chain. The fixed price menus at smaller hotels are often good value, and there are many small restaurants in Hillbrow. But do not go on foot; book a table and phone for a taxi.

Nightclubs
Nightclubs change all the time so consult the local papers. Among the best established is Tiffanys on Henri Street in Braamfontein. A few discos are open all night in Hillbrow. Like any big city, Johannesburg has its clip joints.

Theatres
Johannesburg has a very lively cultural life of concerts and plays. Among many theatres the most active is the Market Theatre complex which incorporates several auditoriums, experimental theatre, exhibitions, a restaurant and bar and pedestrian areas. There are often jazz performances on Sundays. Other notable theatres are the Windybrow, the Civic on the Civic Centre, the Alexander and the Arena. The newspapers carry details of current attractions or you can check with the Publicity Associations. Bookings can be 'phoned for at Computicket (tel 283040). A surprising number of both playwrights and players have emerged from South Africa to hit London and New York, from veteran stars like Glynis Johns to Athol Fugard and Janet Suzman. Fugard's play 'The Road to Mecca' was first performed at the Market and is based on the lady who created the Owl House in the Karoo: see our special article.

Art and Craft
On the last Sunday of each month a number of artists and craftspeople open their workshops on the 'Studio Route'. Ask SATOUR or the Publicity Association for details. And one Joburg artist, Nicky Blumenfield, has made her name encouraging young Africans to paint exterior murals around the city.

Newspapers
The newspapers here maintain high standards. The best known English language papers are the Citizen – effectively South Africa's only English national paper – and the Star. The old Rand Daily Mail has been revived as the Weekly Mail. For a tour of a newspaper being produced tel 633 2341.

Zoo, Bird Sanctuary, Flowers
Even when people live close to wildlife, zoos remain popular. Johannesburg has one out in Parkview. At the Zoo Lake you can go picnick-

ing or boating and there is a good restaurant. Not far from the Zoo is the bird sanctuary Birdhaven in Melrose Road, reached by the bus to Rosebank, plus a pleasant walk of a mile. To see typical South African flora, including proteas, the national flower, go to the 45-acre Wilds on Houghton Drive. September to December is the best time.

Rand Show
Once a year, around Easter, the Rand Show is held at Nasrec, the National Exhibition Centre some ten km (six miles) south of the city, off the N1 or N3 highways. It is a parade of industrial, commercial and agricultural achievement.

Other Places of Interest
Other places worth a visit are the Art Gallery in Joubert Park, near the city centre, which has paintings by Renoir, Cezanne, Picasso and others as well as South African artists; the two Africana Museums, one in the Public Library, the other in the old Market building, Bree Street; and the Planetarium in Braamfontein. For a panoramic view of the city go to the 50th floor of the Carlton Centre on Commissioner Street. Sunset is a good time, because the mine dumps glow like gold. Finally you can watch trading on the Stock Exchange on working days from 0930 to 1530. The Hall of South African Achievement is next to the Visitors Gallery. For children the miniature buildings at the Santarama Miniland in Pioneer Park are a must.

Local Tours
Travel agents or the Publicity Association can arrange various local tours, including ones to the diamond cutting factories, and a hot air balloon over the veld. There are numerous travel agents and tour operators including an American Express office.

Soweto
The sprawling black township of Soweto - standing for South West Township - is barely 15 km from the central business district. Known to TV viewers world-wide for scenes of violence and as the home of Mrs Winnie Mandela, Soweto is now the target of conduct tours. These half day excursions start from the Sandton and downtown hotles and usually include visiting a community centre.

Sport

South Africans are great sporting enthusiasts. Rugby football, the Republic's natural game, is played every Saturday afternoon during the winter at the Ellis Park Stadium. The national team, the Springboks, has an international reputation. In 1995 South Africa hosted the Rugby World Cup.

For a list of all the other sporting clubs and facilities ask the Publicity

Association or consult the newspapers. The Golf Union telephone is 640 3714 and the Squash Racquets Association 883 4390.

Around Johannesburg

Frankly, the neighbourhood of Johannesburg and the Rand is not exciting. It is after all primarily an industrial complex. One of the best excursions is down to the Vaal Dam, near Vereeniging, a drive of 96 km (60 miles) or so. On the way to Krugersdorp, 32 km (20 miles) north-west of the city, there is a Lion Park, while near the town itself is a small game reserve and the Heia Safari Ranch (see Possible Destinations below). From Krugersdorp you can conveniently drive another 11 km (seven miles) to the Sterkfontein caves, known for archaeological finds – including a million-year-old female skull nicknamed 'Mrs Ples'. Beyond Sterkfontein are the scenic spots of the Magaliesburg mountains. The waters of the Hartbeespoort Dam are in this range, 54 km (34 miles) from Pretoria, and pleasant for camping, fishing and boating. Finally there is Africa's largest snake park, the Transvaal Snake Park, at Halfway House, 24 km (15 miles) along the R101 road to Pretoria. You can see snakes being milked for their venom, used in making snake bite serum. It is open on Sundays but closed Tuesdays. Close by is The Train restaurant where a famously varied buffet is served in vintage railway dining cars.

What to do over a Weekend

Johannesburg is not a place to spend the weekend without friends. At weekends people stay in the suburbs or the country, play games of all kinds, cook traditional *braaivleis* (barbecues) and entertain in their homes. Or they leave for weekend resorts. This is fine if you have introductions, or if you belong to a European or American club that reciprocates with a South African country club. If not, then you risk a dull Saturday and Sunday. It is best to fix yourself a weekend tour through a travel agent. But be selective. The snag about many local South African publications and tour firms is that they enthuse wildly about places that overseas visitors are unlikely to find exciting and tribal 'villages' that are thoroughly fake. This said, the 'Transvaal Weekender' magazine is particularly good on how to get to places.

Car Hire and Long Distance Tours

The General Information section has comprehensive details. Avis, Budget, Europcar, and Imperial (linked with Hertz) are all in the city and at the airport. The most comprehensive country-wide coach tours are run by Connex, including a weekend in the Kruger Park. Their Joburg Travel Centre is in Sandton (tel 011 884 8110) and they have branch travel bureaux throughout the country. The immediate rival is Springbok-Atlas, which also has many branches and operates the

Gauteng (the PWV)

Greyhound long distance coaches. Local Johannesburg operators are numerous. Try Welcome (tel 011 442 8905).

Possible Destinations

Some of the best places to go are the Kruger Park, the private game reserves near the Kruger (see Eastern Transvaal section), the relatively nearby Sun City and Lost City casino resort and the adjacent Pilanesberg Game Reserve with its Kwa Maritane lodge (see the North-West Province chapter), or the luxurious Sun International hotel/casino/resort complexes in Lesotho and Swaziland – with the benefit of glimpsing other countries. The Emaweni Game Lodge, near the Vaal river combines a health hydro on a lake island with game viewing drives. All these can be reached by scheduled air services, although it is quicker to drive to Sun City. See the regional air service section of this book or consult a travel agent. The closest game farm to Johannesburg is the 120 ha Heia Safari Ranch (PO Box 1387, Honeydew 2040; tel 011 659 0605), only 45 km (28 miles) from the city near Honeydew. This has luxurious thatched cottages around a pool, Zulu dances and game drives. Its owners have crossed zebras with donkeys, producing a 'zonkey'.

Safaris

One completely reliable company that arranges safaris both in the Republic and in Botswana, Namibia and Zimbabwe is Gametrackers (reservations through Mount Nelson Hotel, Cape Town; tel 021 231050, fax 021 231060). They have their own fleet of light aircraft and camps in Botswana's Okavango Delta, which you can reach inside a morning from Johannesburg. For others see the 'Safaris and Private Reserves' section.

Pretoria

Postal code 0001. Telephone code 012. Tourist Info. 323 1222

Pretoria's life revolves around politicians, diplomats, and the 11 faculties of Pretoria University, one of the largest in South Africa, while UNISA is the largest correspondence university in the world. Where Johannesburg hustles, Pretoria walks at a dignified pace, consonant with being the Republic's administrative capital. It has several really notable buildings –most prominently the Union Buildings looking over the city – and 480 km (300 miles) of its streets are planted with mauve flowering jacaranda trees, which bloom in October.

Founded in 1855 by M.W. Pretorius, first president of the Transvaal Republic, and named after his father, who was the victor of Blood River, the city started at the Fountains Valley. This is now a favourite picnic spot, while the city has spread out to cover 629 sq km (243 sq

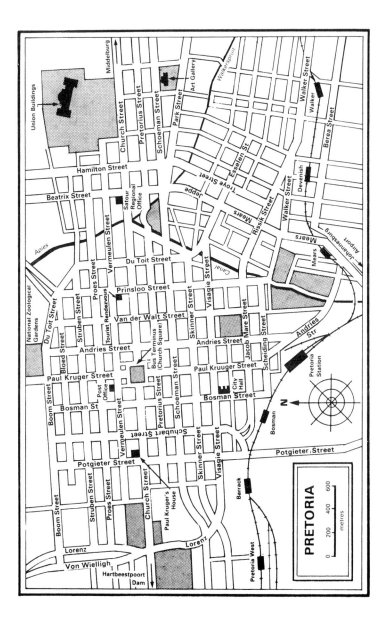

PRETORIA

| 0 | 200 | 400 | 600 |
metres

Union Buildings

Middelburg

Church Street
Pretorius Street
Schoeman Street
Park Street
Art Gallery

Walker Street
Walker
Walker Street
Berea Street

Walkerspruit

Hamilton Street

Isselen St
Troye Street

Beatrix Street

Jeppe

Devenish
Walker Street

Satour
Regional
Office

Vermeulen Street

Mears
Rissik Street
Mears

Apies

Du Toit Street

Mears
Mears

National Zoological
Gardens

Proes Street

Prinsloo Street

Visagie Street
Canal

Johannesburg
Airport

Du Toit Street

Struben Street

Van der Walt Street

Skinner Street

Andries
Str

Tourist Rendezvous

Andries Street

Andries Street

Jacob Mare Street
Scheiding Street

Bloed Street

Bus Terminus
(Church Square)

Paul Kruger Street

Paul Kruuger Street

Pretoria
Station

Boom Street

Post
Office

Pretorius Street

Schoeman Street

City
Hall

Bosman St

Bosman Street

Bosman

Vermeulen Street
Schubart Street

Skinner Street

Visagie Street

N

Potgieter Street

Boom Street

Struben Street

Proes Street

Church Street

Potgieter Street

Paul Kruger's House

Barrack

Lorenz

Lorenz

Von Wielligh

Pretoria West

Hartbeestpoort
Dam

51

miles), including suburbs with their own shopping centres in what was until recently hilly veld. The population is now around 800,000. Some of these suburbs, like Waterkloof, are most attractive.

City Centre
The focal point of the city is Church Square, with its statue of President Kruger, the Raadsaal and the main Post Office. From Church Square Paul Kruger Street runs up to the railway station, while there are shopping streets and malls close to the square. Pretoria's streets are famously long: Church Street stretches 26 km (16 miles).

Information
Pretoria houses the headquarters of SATOUR (tel 347 0600), but it's better to call the regional office in town in the Tourist Rendevous Travel Centre on the corner of Prinsloo and Vermeulen Streets (tel 323 1430). The Pretoria Information Bureau (tel 323 1222) is there too and can make reservations for hotels and tours.

Hotels
Pretoria has plenty of hotels. About the best is the four-star Centurion Lake (tel 663 18256), eight minutes drive south of the city on Lenchen Avenue by a lake. There are two Holiday Inns, on Van der Walt Street and Beatrix Street. The Victoria (tel 323 6052) by the Station has been restored to Edwardian style by Rovos Rail. An attractive hotel on the outskirts is the three-star Farm Inn in 'The Willows' (tel 807 0081). For cheaper hotels and guest houses consult the Tourist Rendezvous' lists.

Restaurants
Pretoria is a young peoples' place at night and most first class restaurants are away from the centre, though you can get a pleasant meal at the Victoria hotel. The Tourist Rendezvous publishes a restaurant guide, categorised by Chinese, French, Greek, Mexican etc and including fast food eateries. Outside the city there are many places: Die Werf (tel 991 1809) on the eastern outskirts serves traditional South African cuisine at a delightful old homestead. Chagall's at Toulouse (tel 341 7511) in Fountains Valley, gets high marks for French food. The chef was trained at the Tour d'Argent in Paris. La Maison at 235 Hilda Street, Hatfield (tel 434341) is much esteemed by locals. The best steaks are reckoned to be at the Hillside Tavern in Lynnwood (tel 473734). Esselen Street in Sunnyside has several well-known restaurants, including La Madeleine (tel 446076). At all these it is advisable to book ahead.

Local Travel
The two places most visitors want to reach from the city are the airport

and Johannesburg. Airport buses leave from the Tourist Rendezvous on the corner of Vermeulen and Prinsloo Streets (enquiries tel 323 1429). Buses for Johannesburg leave from Pretorius Street, between Bosman Street and Volkstem Avenue, arriving at Kruis Street in Johannesburg. The Pretoria Bus Terminal is a short distance away on Church Square. For bus information 'phone 313 0389. Frequent but slow train services also connect the two cities. Travel agents include American Express, Rennies and Connex. The latter deals with both coach tours and rail travel.

There are several car hire firms including Avis, at 70 Schoeman Street (tel 3251490), Budget, 72 Andries Street (tel 323 3658) Europcar on the corner of Hamilton and Vermeulen Streets (tel 326 3715) and Imperial on Potgeiter and Pretorius Streets (tel 323 3259).

Places to See

Historic Buildings
Among Pretoria's historic buildings are Paul Kruger's small unpretentious house, and the beautifully furnished Melrose House, which Lord Kitchener used as his headquarters in the Boer War. Also open are the State Model Schools, where Winston Churchill was kept prisoner and from which he made his celebrated escape the day before he was due

Replica of farm house at the Voortrekker Monument, Pretoria

to be handed back to the British anyway. But the only truly magnificent edifice is the Union Buildings, the seat of the Government on the Meintjieskip Ridge overlooking the city. They were completed in 1913 by Sir Herbert Baker who was sent to Europe to study as a young architect by Cecil Rhodes, designed many splendid South African buildings and became justifiably famous.

State Theatre Complex
An arena, opera auditorium and theatre are part of the State Theatre complex on the corner of Pretorius and Van der Walt streets.

Museum and Reserves
Other places to visit are the Transvaal Museum with its adjoining Geological Museum in Paul Kruger Street; the Zoo with its reptile park, aquarium, and a remarkably complete collection of 'cats' which includes a Bengal tiger; and the Wonderboom Nature Reserve on Boom Street, 13 km (eight miles) from the city. The wonderboom is a fantastic species of fig tree, whose branches sprout when they touch the ground. Over the ages this specimen has formed five concentric circles of growth that can literally shelter a thousand people. The Zoo and the Reserve are open daily. The Natural Cultural History Museum next to the Zoo has an unusual exhibition of Bushmen art. The Sammy Marks Museum is the 1884 mansion of a Victorian magnate in east Pretoria. A real period piece, with fine collections, it has a restaurant in the grounds.

Parks
Among numerous parks, the most pleasant are the Burgerspark and the Austin Roberts Bird Sanctuary in Muckleneuk. Protea Park in Groenkloof is dedicated to 130 species of the Republic's national flower. The National Botanical Garden of 77 ha grows plants and shrubs from all over South Africa. Tours last two and a half hours. The Garden is ten km (six miles) out on Cussonia Avenue.

Voortrekker Monument
About three km (two miles) outside the city to the south rears up the somewhat stern Voortrekker Monument, effectively a shrine of the Afrikaner people. A marble frieze depicts the Great Trek story, and on 16th December, the anniversary of the battle of Blood River, a shaft of sunlight falls on the monument's altar. Nearby is the restored Fort Skenskop, built in 1897/8.

Outside Pretoria

Many sporting facilities and recreation areas are shared with Johannesburg's although the Hartbeespoort dam is nearer Pretoria and the 'What to do over a Weekend' section a few pages back applies to the capital too. Specifically local places of interest are:

Premier Diamond Mine
The Premier Diamond Mine, 40 km (25 miles) east of Pretoria at Cullinan, was once the world's biggest. Barely three years after it was opened in 1902 it yielded a 3,024-carat white diamond measuring five inches across, the largest diamond yet found anywhere. They named it the Cullinan. It was bought by the Transvaal Government for a nominal £150,000 and presented to King Edward VII, who had it cut into more than 100 stones, all of which are now in the British Crown Jewels. The mine itself is now 884 m (2,900 ft) across in one direction and 426 m (1,400 ft) in another, with an average depth of 152 m (500 ft), and has produced seven tons of diamonds so far. It was closed from 1932 until 1950 as uneconomical. Since reopening it has produced a million carats a year, mainly of industrial diamonds. Visits may be arranged through the PRO, Premier Diamond Mine, Cullinan (tel 01213 30050). You cannot descend the mine shafts, but unlike at Gold reef City, you are seeing the real thing. The displays are excellent.

Tswaing (ECO Museum)
A meteorite crater, containing a brine lake, Tswaing is being turned into South Africa's first 'eco museum', focussed on cultural and natural resources. It is 40 km (25 miles) north west of Pretoria.

Game lodge in the Kruger Park

The Northern and Eastern Transvaal

The Provinces

The Transvaal - a name which simply means the country across the Vaal River - was opened up by the Voortrekkers in the 1850s. Subsequently the discovery of gold on the Rand changed the course of its history. But it was already blessed with three great assets. These are the colour and variety of its wide and inspiring landscape; big game living in vast tracts of unchanged Africa; and an excellent climate. No travel agent could ask more for his clients.

Topography
In 1994 the original province was split administratively into two, Northern and Eastern, and lost territory to the new provinces of Gauteng (the PWV) and the North-West. Even so the Transvaal is twice the size of England. The two provinces extend from the Vaal River north to the Limpopo, a distance by road of 643 km (400 miles). In the south and west, on the highveld plateau, the altitude is 1,660 to 2,000 m (5,000 to 6,000 ft). The transition from this highveld to the lowveld cotton farms along the Limpopo and the game ranches of the north east, close to Mozambique, is made by an extension of the Drakensberg Mountains, the same range that is such a feature of Natal. In places this is a most dramatic transition with breathtaking passes and a mile-deep canyon at Blyde River.

Climate
On the lowveld, especially at the north end of the Kruger Park, the daytime temperature can be over 38°C (100°F) in the shade in January and February, though it cools off in the evening. As you get higher, the heat and humidity lessen. Up on the highveld you find a healthy, invigorating climate. Summers are warm with an average temperature of 22°C (70°F). Autumn and spring are pronounced seasons. In winter it can be cold.

History

Historically there is still much to discover in the Transvaal. The Boer trekkers who found this land largely empty, except for teeming herds of game which they unfortunately shot to the point of extinction in places, thought of themselves as pioneers in an uninhabited territory. Research has now revealed that in fact hominids, those creatures of mankind's dawn who evolved between apes and the first men, long ago hunted the golden savannah and tested their prehistoric weapons in the highveld depression that drains into the Vaal River. Ironically the uranium used in the first atomic bombs came from this same area.

Tribal Clashes
There has been more recent unrecorded African history too. Before

The Transvaal

the European came, the movement of Bantu tribes down from Central Africa had led to bloody battles. There were pastoral Bantu clans living here, with whom the renegade Zulu, Mzilikazi, clashed after his hordes crossed the Vaal from Zululand, now part of Natal. Battered and leaderless Africans roamed the veld as the Zulus rounded up their cattle. Finally the whites clashed with the Zulus, chased Mzilikazi into what became Matabeleland in Zimbabwe, and established peace. Today there are still a few Zulus in the province. But the largest groups are of Vendas in the north, Shangaans in the east, Tswanas and Sothos.

Kruger and the Transvaal Republic
In 1857 the Boer farmers declared the Transvaal an independent republic. Its indomitable President, Paul Kruger, led his people in the Boer War that flared up as a result of the discovery in 1896 of the fantastic goldfields of the Witwatersrand, which we shall describe in a moment. You can hardly be in South Africa five minutes without realising that Kruger is a legend. Every town has a street named after him, his statue dominates Church Square in Pretoria and many other lesser places. He stands there in top hat and frock coat, a portly, stumpy man, with a strong bewhiskered face. He was not always like this. In his youth he was an athlete, hunter and soldier. But the overriding image is of 'Oom Paul' (Uncle Paul), puritanical, knowing the Old Testament by heart, leading his people against the British and finally carrying the insignia of state with him in an ox-wagon so that wherever he stopped became the Transvaal's capital. He died in exile in Switzerland in 1904, sadly before the Union and independence of 1910.

National Parks and Reserves

The Transvaal boasts only one National Park, but it is among Africa's most prestigious: the 20,000 sq km (7,800 sq mile) Kruger. Reserves include the Loskop Dam Nature Reserve near Middleburg, the Hans Merensky Game Reserve on the Great Letaba river east of Tzaneen, and the Rust de Winter Nature Reserve north of Pretoria. Altogether there are around 500 proclaimed reserves, many very small like the Cycad Reserve in Letaba. Unlike some Natal reserves and those in Free State, the Transvaal's have lion and other predators and therefore few hiking trails.

Birds and Flora
As well as animals, the Transvaal has magnificent birds and butterflies, while new varieties of plants are often discovered. It has been known for 1,600 species to be identified in one area in one day - as many as are known in the entire British Isles.

Northern Transvaal

The rewarding parts of the Transvaal to explore are the north east and the east, with the Kruger Park often the ultimate destination. The N 1 road leads directly north across the highveld via Pietersburg and Louis Trichardt to the game farms, cotton estates and maize plantations around Messina and the Limpopo river. It's a long way: but corn-on-the-cob harvested here reaches Frankfurt in Germany a day and a night later! By contrast the N 4 road goes straight east to the Nelspruit end of the Kruger Park, with possible diversions to scenic mountain drives and resorts, and some internationally famous private game reserves. The two directions are linked by several roads, which make a good triangular circuit along the magnificent Drakensberg escarpment, stopping off frequently if you have the time. But although it is spectacular the distances are considerable and it is simpler to fly one leg – for example to Nelspruit in the east or to Venda in the north – and then hire a car, returning it at Johannesburg. Wherever you are going, remember that in the summer months of November to February it can be very hot.

Bus Route

If you want to get to the north – and the Zimbabwe border – cheaply Translux runs a service from Johannesburg and Pretoria via Pietersburg and Louis Trichardt to Messina, which goes on to Beit Bridge (tel 011 774 3333 for details) Lebowa Transport also serves Messina.

Through the High Veld to Pietersburg

Apart from providing the Great North Road up to Zimbabwe, the Northern Transvaal is mainly noted for its mineral baths (a complete list of which can be had from SATOUR offices), for mountain scenery, bushman rock paintings, fishing and game. Agriculturally, its citrus fruits, avocados, tea estates and – in the extreme north – cotton plantations are of great economic importance. So are its huge natural resources of copper, phosphates, vermiculite, asbestos and coal. Being mostly upland country it has an invigorating climate and it is increasingly attracting tourist development. Though less well known than the eastern Transvaal it nonetheless offers interesting side trips with an increasing number of lodges and country hotels. Some of the minor roads are not tarred. For exact routes consult the 'AA Guide'.

Warmbaths *Postal code 0480. Telephone code 01533. Tourist Info 62111.*
Taking the road north from Pretoria you come to Warmbaths 112 km (70 miles) on. This is a major local holiday resort, where the mineral

water baths are the centre of an Overvaal tourist complex, with golf, tennis, bowling and a caravan park.

The three-star Mabula Game Lodge (Private Bag X1665; tel 01533 616) in a private 8,000 ha reserves, is some 40 km (25 miles) out.

Nylstroom *Postal code 0510. Telephone code 01470. Info 2211*
This town, so named because the early Voortrekkers thought they had found the source of the Nile here, is the centre for the Waterberg mountains and their lodges. It has a number of historic buildings and was the home of Eugene Marais, a noted poet and writer. The Shangri-La Country Lodge (three-stars, PO Box 262; tel 2381) is a few miles outside town.

The Waterberg
Theses mountains have steep cliffs to their south and stretch a full 100 km west from the Palal river. They include the Tafelberg Nature Reserve and are quite unspoilt, as well as little known to outsiders. The Emaweni Game Lodge (reservations tel 011 442 5640) and the Touchstone Game Ranch (same reservations) are both there. Touchstone offers riding safaris in its 22,000 ha, where there are rhino, elephant and other game.

Potgietersrus
Driving on through to Potgietersrus, an agricultural centre, you should visit the huge caves to the north of the town. In one of these, men blasting for lime exposed a rock face upon which could be 'read' the history of the human race. Fossilised in the strata and in the 800 tons of rock that were excavated there proved to be remains of the earliest hominids, our human ancestors, similar to those found by Lake Turkana in Kenya. The site is being investigated by the University of the Witwatersrand and can be visited by special permit. In the 19th century Chief Makapan and his tribe were cornered in one cave by a Boer commando after they had murdered a party of Voortrekkers at *Moorddrif* (Murder Drift). Potgietersrus also has a small wildlife reserve, where exotic species are bred for the Pretoria Zoo.

Both north and south of the N 1 road between Potgietersrus and Pietersburg – a distance of 59 km (37 miles) – are extensive citrus estates.

Pietersburg

Postal code 0700. Telephone code 01521. SATOUR Info 295 3025
With 35,000 people, this is the largest town and the commercial hub of the northern Transvaal. Situated on the edge of the 1,220 m (4,000

ft) high Pietersburg plateau, it has a refreshing climate with cold nights and is noted for its jacaranda trees, whose dark magenta flowers blossom in October. The local wildlife reserve on a hill above the town has eland, springbok and rhino among its game. South of the town is a traditional North Sotho Bakone Kraal, run as an open air museum.

Pietersburg has a three-star Holiday Inn Garden Court (Box 784; tel 2912030). But the best place is the three-star Ranch (Box 77, tel 293 7180) some 25 km (16 miles) south on the road to Potgieter-srus. The Ranch has first class food and its own airstrip.

Information and Transport
The SATOUR regional office is on the corner of Vorster and Landdros Mare Streets (tel 295 3025). There is a passenger train service from Pretoria, while the Lebowa Transport bus to Messina from Pretoria stops here, though in the middle of the night. By road Pretoria to Pietersburg takes four hours. The airport is three km from the town centre (information tel 295 2011) and is served from Johannesburg by Airlink. Avis, Budget and Imperial have car hire desks.

East from Pietersburg
From Pietersburg many people's destination is what looks like a side-trip to the Magoebaskloof, a huge cleft in the Drakensburg mountains, Tzaneen and the scenic and sporting attractions of the area called Letaba. From Letaba you can drive all the way down the side of the Transvaal Drakensberg to the famous Blyde River Canyon and the Summit Route of the eastern Transvaal. We will deal with this after continuing with the rest of the northern Transvaal.

Pietersburg to Louis Trichardt

Continuing up the Great North Road after Pietersburg you are coming into the dry bushveld and cattle ranching land that stretches up past the Soutspansberg mountains to the Limpopo and has a character we'll enlarge on in a moment. Halfway between Pietersburg and Louis Trichardt a stainless steel monument like a needle marks the Tropic of Capricorn: or rather, since the Tropic shifts, where it will be in the year 2,000.

Ben Lavin Nature Reserve
Then, 32 km after the R 36 turn-off, is the sign to the Wildlife Society's Ben Lavin Nature Reserve. Game includes giraffe, sable antelope and nyala. Hides overlook waterfalls and there are fully equipped huts (bookings tel 01551 3834).

Accommodation

If you need to stop for a meal or the night on this long, straight run there are a couple of small, well-kept roadside hotels on the way. Both are fully licensed. At Bandelierkop, shortly after the turn-off for the gravel R 36 provides another route to the Rain Queen and Tzaneen (see below), there is the one-star Lalapanzi (Box 5, Bandelierkop; tel 0020 and ask for 13). This is 80 km (50 miles) from Pietersburg. Further on is the even more quirkily named Adams Apple (PO Box 338, Louis Trichardt; tel 01551 4117), about 23 km (15 miles) short of the town.

Louis Trichardt and the Soutspansberg

Postal code 0920. Telephone code 01551. Tourist Info 2212

These mountains rising out of the flat bushveld and the town in their forested foothills both come as a surprise. Louis Trichardt benefits from the rain they attract and climatically from being 945 m (3,100 ft) above sea level, though it can be drizzly and cold in summer. After 400 km (250 miles) of driving, even on fast road, many people feel like taking a breather, so this is a good stopping off place on the way to the northern end of the Kruger Park, fog or no fog.

The town is named after a Voortrekker leader and a memorial commemorates his first encounter with the Shangaan and with the Portuguese from Mozambique. Up here there are many monuments, both of stone and in ancestral memory, to the bloody conflicts the trekkers suffered as they laboured their ox-wagons north. Today Louis Trichardt is a centre for forestry and unexpectedly exotic agriculture: the Levubu banana plantations yield 30 percent of the Republic's production, double that of the more obviously sub-tropical plantations in Natal. Citrus fruit, avocados and tea add to prosperity.

Among hotels are the three-star Clouds End (Private Bag X 2409; tel 9621) a couple of kilometres further along the Great North Road, and the Mountain Inn (two-star. PO Box 146; tel 9631) eight km on in glorious mountain scenery with riding, swimming and other sports. The Publicity Association is in the Civic Centre.

The Soutspansberg

The Soutspansberg – the salt-pan mountains – run west to east, jutting into Venda. Quite dramatic, they harbour various species of game, many birds and rare kinds of aloes, while indigenous trees include cycads, yellowwood and the pink flowering Cape chestnut. There is a 91 km (57 mile) hiking trail with designated overnight stops (bookings Northern Transvaal Forest Region in Louis Trichardt, tel 2201).

The Great North Road used to wind among perpendicular cliffs at Wyllie's Poort: now two long tunnels carry the highway through the mountains towards Messina.

Louis Trichardt to the Limpopo

The End of the Road
Beyond the Soutspanberg lies the arid bush that was the furthest destination of the Voortrekkers in the 1850s and is an extension of the Kalahari sand veld. Here in a landscape of acacia thorn bushes and grotesque baobab trees, grey barked and as wrinkled as the hide of the elephants that feed on their fibrous wood, the trekkers established farmsteads and did what they could with the wild and dusty land around the Limpopo valley. Their descendants have ranched cattle, harvested maize and planted cotton. They are tough, shrewd and conservatively cautious people. In the 1970s and 1980s they fought off spasmodic terrorist attacks mounted by the ANC from Zimbabwe. For the whole of the 1980s they had to combat the worse enemy of a drought. Some farmers abandoned raising cattle and the wildlife multiplied, providing an alternative income from hunting and visitors.

Game Farms
There are numerous game farms and lodges in the vicinity of Louis Trichardt and Messina. Notable among them are the three small lodges and camps of Greater Kuduland Safaris (PO Box 1385, Louis Trichardt 0920; tel 015539 720, fax 808) set on two 30,000 acre game reserves near Tshipise.

Gold, Iron and Ancient Sites
The northern veld's other indigenous wealth is under the soil. The ancient African inhabitants exploited copper deposits and possibly gold, since gold beads were among the artefacts found on Mapungubwe Hill 75 km (47 miles) west of Messina. The relics from this natural fortress, inhabited from 950 to 1200 AD, are in the Pretoria Museum. Other sites are at Machemma and Verdun, west of the N 1 road. The iron age smelters, the Bushmen who left rock paintings and the tribes who constructed stone forts similar to Great Zimbabwe all became part of the Venda tribe, briefly established in a self-governing Venda Republic, about whom more in a moment. But there were underground assets they did not exploit: asbestos, coal, tin and vermiculite. The coal is currently a source of dispute because deposits lie inside the northern tip of the Kruger Park. Copper is mined near Messina. In 1989 de Beers started a R2,400 million investment in diamond mining on a farm called Venetia, between the tiny town of Alldays and Messina. So the scene is changing.

The Northern Transvaal

Messina *Postal code 0900. Telephone code 01553. Tourist Info 40211.*
Meantime Messina remains a copper-mining town, hardly ten miles short of the Beit Bridge frontier post with Zimbabwe and within easy reach of the historic sites already mentioned. The town is known for giant baobab trees, some of which are protected in a Nature Reserve along with wild game. There is a one-star hotel, the Impala Lelie (PO Box 392; tel 2197), while the three-star Kate's Hope River Lodge (PO Box 2720, Cresta 2118; bookings 011 476 6217) is 35 km (22 miles) east, with reasonably priced chalets on the Njelele river.

Tshipese Spa
The sulphurous spring here brings forth 675,000 litres a day and people go for cures among the parks and trees of the resort. The snag is that the clean and well-run hotel is liable to be booked up a year in advance. It is managed by Overvaal and its local telephone is 015539 624. From Tshipese a tarmac road leads to the Kruger Park's northern-most gate at Pafuri and you can also reach the Nwanedi National Park in Venda (see below).

The Limpopo and Beit Bridge
Finally at Beit Bridge the road and railway cross the Limpopo river, which Kipling in his 'Just So Stories' called 'the great, green, greasy Limpopo river, all set about with fever trees'. Actually it is muddier down in Mozambique, where it reaches the sea. Like all African rivers its banks are a great watering place for game. The Beitbridge Inn rates two-stars (PO Box 82; tel 214).

Venda

From 1979 to 1994 the people of Venda enjoyed self-rule, but then were re-united with the Republic. Their 'capital' was Thoyandou on the main road between Louis Trichardt and the Kruger's Punda Maria gate. Their ancestral territory centres on the Soutspanberg mountains, a series of ridges, which eventually decline into the lowveld of the arid Malonga Flats in the north – geophysically an extension of the Kalahari sand veldt. The mountain country is very picturesque, but little developed and becoming overgrazed and eroded where the rainfall is sparse: nonetheless it deserves a detour, especially to see the Nwanedi National Park and resort.

The Venda People
An intrinsically interesting people, the Vendas' ancestors moved

Opposite:	Giant baobab, Venda (top left). God's window (top right)
	Johannesburg from the gold mine dumps (below)
Overleaf:	Sibasa market (top)
	Glen Reenen in the Golden Gate National Park (below)

down from what is now Zimbabwe in the early 18th century. The stone forts they built on terraced conical hills – for example at Dzata in the west near the Nshelele river – suggest they were involved in the civilisation of Great Zimbabwe in the 14th and 15th centuries. Equally the very rough barked tree they call *Mutuvhatsindi* is not indigenous, but comes from the Zimbabwe-Mozambique borders. The leader who brought them here was Chief Dimbanyika, whose family lost the succession to the Mphephus in the late 1890s.

Legends and Gods
The Venda are addicted to stories and legends, regard many places, rocks, streams and old ruins as sacred and believe in 'water spirits' that are only half-people, with a single leg, arm and eye. When the mist descends on the mountain forests it is easy to understand these superstitions. Of their traditional dances the most notable is the Domba, best watched between June and August and part of young girls' puberty rites. This is also known as the Python dance, addressed to the python god of fertility who lives in Lake Fundudzi.

Crafts and Rain-making
More practically, the Venda are gifted craftsmen, especially in pottery, weaving and woodcarving. The Lemba people, apparently wandering Judaic-Arab traders in origin, who have become assimilated, are skilled artisans and metal workers. Another sub-group are the Mbedzi, the rain-makers, who have female chiefs, though the present Rain Queen lives further south in Lebowa.

Thoyandou and Sibasa

Telephone code 01581. Tourist Info 21131.

Thohoyandou is a short way off the main R 524 road from Louis Trichardt, set among hills, while the old administrative centre of Sibasa is a little higher up. Sibasa, planted with jacarandas and tulip trees, is alive with market stalls, African music, goats and dust. Thohoyandou is anodyne, with a craft centre, a hospital, and the hotel that has made serious tourism feasible.

Information and Tours
The Tourist Board is very helpful and organises tours and guided hiking trails. It is located in the Ditike Craft House. (PO Box 9 Sibasa; tel 015581 21131.).

Previous page: Zulu Induna or warrior in
traditional dress (top left)
Zulu woman (top right)
Durban's Golden Mile (below)

The Northern Transvaal

Accommodation
The Venda Sun (Sun International. PO Box 766, Sibasa, tel 21011)
keeps a high standard, serves good food, organises local tours for
guests and has a casino, cinema, tennis courts, pool and boutique.
There really is nowhere else with a restaurant to stay in Venda, except
the Nwanedi resort, though there are self-catering chalets at Acacia
Park in the capital, the Mphephu hot springs resort and Sagole Spa in
the north.

Places to See
Roads are mostly untarred and the mountain ridges make for slow
driving. There are a number of attractions reachable within a half-day
tour from the Venda Sun Hotel (see above). These include the
Mahovhohovho waterfalls where you can picnic and swim: the Thathe
Vondo forest to the west, with streams and waterfalls, though part of it
is the Holy Forest where you may not walk; the sacred lake of Fundudzi – no walking the shoreline either; the Dzata ruined fort roughly
38 km (24 miles) west; and further still the Nzhelele dam, with good
fishing and a nature reserve. There is fishing for black bass in the
Vondo dam too. The Mphephu hot springs resort is built around one of
many thermal springs: another is the Sagole Spa, which has chalet
accommodation, but is at the limit of a day's expedition whereas
Mphephu is nearer.

If you have time and 4WD there is a fair amount in the north and east
of Venda: hill villages with their thatched huts; a cycad forest; a mon-
strous baobab, calculated to be 3,000 years old with a trunk 43 m
(141 ft) in circumference, up in the sandveld; bushman paintings;
ruined forts; spectacular waterfalls on the Mutale river where buffalo
lurk in the long grass under the trees; the new Makuya Park; and of
course the Kruger. Quite a few visitors use the Venda Sun as a base for
seeing this remote end of the Kruger.

Makuya National Park and the Kruger
Bordering the Kruger along the spectacular gorge of the Luvuvhu
river, the Park is most easily reached off the main road to Punda Maria
gate. Makuya has elephant, lion, buffalo: everything the Kruger has. A
camp at Gunda (not on any maps) is planned in this landscape of
rugged, dry mountain and riverine forest.

Nwanedi National Park
Here the predators are kept in enclosures. However there are impala,
nyala, kudu and wildebeest among the game in the 12,600 ha. The
park incorporates two dam lakes, between which is a nicely situated
resort complex (tel 015539 723), with thatched bungalows. Charges
are very reasonable. Canoes can be hired by the lake. It is an uphill and

down valley 70 km (45 miles), twisting dirt road drive from Thohoyandou. Access from the Transvaal via Tshepedi is easier, with only 17
km (11 miles) of gravel.

North Eastern Transvaal

Land of the Silver Mists

If, instead of carrying on towards Louis Trichardt from Pietersburg,
you drive east on the R 71 you come into a magical mountain world of
lakes, forests and small resorts. The novelist John Buchan called it the
'land of the silver mists'. Yet it is little known outside South Africa in
spite of its natural beauty, good climate, the dramatic valley of the
Magoebaskloof and a profusion of azaleas and cherry trees that flower
in September and October.

Tzaneen is the main town of this Letaba district, with one of the
Republic's best country hotels. From there you can either turn north
again and visit the land of the Rain Queen, or go south along the edge
of the low veld below the long escarpment of the Drakensberg and
join the much more renowned Summit Route round the Blyde River
Canyon and Graskop.

What opened the area up originally was – hardly a surprise – gold. The
1860s saw the discovery of gold in the mountains and a feverish rush
for riches followed, of which some memorials remain: including a
hollow baobab tree near the now-abandoned mining settlement of
Leydsdorp which the diggers used as a bar counter.

Stage Coach Routes

The gold rush initiated a stage coach route from Pietersburg to
Leydsdorp, beyond Tzaneen. There was only one nation able to build
coaches that could survive the appalling mountain roads: the United
States. The stage coaches that opened up South Africa between
1860 and 1910 were made by the Abbott Downing Coach Company
of Concord, New Hampshire. Several thousand were shipped out.
They were hauled by mule teams that had to be changed every 20 km
(12 miles) or so: which was why a series of staging posts came into
existence along the route.

Haenertsburg *Postal code 0730. Telephone code 0152222*

This tiny town on the winding R 71 road from Pietersburg to the
Letaba river valley was established during the gold rush. Today, there
is yachting on the man-made lake of the Ebenezer dam, and trout and

black bass fishing there and on the Broederstroom river, running down from the Woodbush Forest Reserve. From the town you can either drive along to Tzaneen via the valley of the Great Letaba river or follow the R 71 through the Magoebaskloof, a deep and steep cleft in the hills, clad with forests, that is renowned for its beauty.

The Magoebaskloof
The road up this pass climbs 540 m (1,768 ft) in a mere five km, winding up above a river past a discreet little holiday resort to the splendid views near the three-star Magoebaskloof Hotel (tel 015 276 4276). This is very much a family hotel, with a delightful panelled bar. There is fishing for black bass and trout, lovely walks and two hiking trails. The local Sapekoe tea estates can be visited.

Tzaneen

Postal code 0850. Telephone code 0152. Tourist Info 307 1411
Tzaneen dates from only 1926 and is larger than it looks, with access to several nature reserves and to the well-known attractions of the village of the Modjadji Rain Queen and the Cycad Forest further north. A plaque commemorates John Buchan's stay here. In the town's centre is one excellent restaurant among several eating places, the Steps (tel 21308). Recreations include golf at the Letaba Country Club, hiking trails, sports at various small holiday resorts and nature reserves. The Tourist Information office (PO Box 1808; tel 307 1411) is in the Civic Centre on Agatha Street. There is an airport with flights from Johannesburg on Letaba Airways.

The Siegfried Annecke Research Institute, where research is done on malaria, is the Tourist Office's number one place of interest (open to the public by arrangement). However, from a visitor's viewpoint, the town's current claim to fame is the Coach House at Agatha, 15 km (nine miles) to the south via a gravel road, although there is a three-star Karos Hotel on Joubert Street (tel 307 3140).

The Coach House
Rated the best country hotel in South Africa by American Express this former staging post on the Zeederberg Company's route was built because Agatha – a settlement so small you would otherwise fail to notice it at all –was not plagued by the mosquitoes that delayed the founding of Tzaneen (this area is no longer malarial, though the lowveld is). Restored and re-opened as a hotel in 1983 by Guy Mathews, the Coach House its own 1,500 acres of grounds looking towards the rugged Drakensberg escarpment. The food is excellent, the atmosphere is that of an English country house: in summer you breakfast on the terrace while in winter there are log fires in all the 34

rooms. It fully deserves its five-star rating. (PO Box 554, Tzaneen; tel 307 3641, fax 307 1466).

The hotel also offers a four-night fly-drive joint package with the Motswari Game Lodge in the private Timbavati Game Reserve adjoining the Kruger Park.

Lebowa

A short way north of Tzaneen up the R 36 road, you skirt the district of Lebowa. The immediate interest here is two fold: the Cycad Reserve and the residence of the Modadji Rain Queen. The road climbs up to Duiwelskloof, called 'Devil's Valley' in the old days because of the atrocious road. Today it is a pleasant village in lush, sub-tropical countryside where avocados, mangoes and other exotic fruit are always on sale, and there are hundreds of flowering trees and shrubs. There is a one-star hotel, the Imp Inn (PO Box 17 Duiwelskloof; tel 015236 3253). But finding the Rain Queen is less easy.

The Modadji Rain Queen
We already mentioned that some of the Venda tribe have an hereditary Queen. She actually lives up here in Lebowa and one of her predecessors was the character around whom Rider Haggard devised his novel 'She'. The Rain Queen used to be consulted by Africans from all over the Transvaal, but has become somewhat commercialised. The present-day old lady can be interviewed for a fee. To find her turn off the R 36 at Witkrans six km (four miles) from Duiwelskloof on to a dirt road, then after another ten km (six miles) turn right at Medingen. An unpromising road – misrepresented on most maps though it is signposted – climbs a further 11 km (seven miles) to the Rain Queen's village. After that it is up to you! You may also see some of the Lemba, the Semitic sub-tribe who guard the Venda's holy drums. We were not much attracted by the Rain Queen's attendants – and there's no problem persuading the heavens to open in these hills – so we drove straight on to the cycad forest, also not at all where the maps indicate.

Modadji Nature Reserve
Cycads grow over 30 feet high here in a profusion not often seen. They are the most primitive seed bearing plants on earth, relics of 60 million years ago and we have devoted a special article to them. This tiny, steep-sloped reserve is well kept, with an information centre that contains the Rain Queen's throne and ceremonial leopard skin and a refreshment bar. The sale and transport of cycads is strictly controlled. However, you can buy plants from a cycad nursery near the reserve, which is one of ten Nature Reserves in Lebowa.

Cycads in the Lebowa Cycad Reserve

Cycads

Dinosaurs were familiar with the strange shapes of the cycads 50,000,000 years ago, when fossils show that they grew in other parts of the world. The cycads in the northern Transvaal are a living relic of prehistoric times, the most primitive seed-bearing plants on our planet. They are also among the oddest; and have only survived because they are of no practical use. The cycad's trunk may grow to 13 m (42 ft) high, but it consists of fibre, not wood, and cannot be burnt for fuel. Even the female plant's huge pineapple-like seed cones provide no sustenance if eaten. Nor do the male plant's smaller, pine-cone-shaped ones. In fact the plant's very growth is both capricious and slow. If it is watered too much it becomes soggy and dies. If one of its leaves is cut off another may not grow for ten years. It does not produce leaves every year, incidentally making its age impossible to judge by ring-dating; just as the fibre precludes carbon dating. All you can be sure of is that if you do plant a seedling it is likely to outlive you, your children, and your children's children.

There are some 29 species of cycads. Those illustrated are *encephalatos transvenosus*, growing in the Lebowa Cycad Reserve, near Tzaneen. Being so rare cycads have inevitably become collectors' items for rocky gardens, where they thrive. In consequence their transport around South Africa is controlled by law. But they can be legally bought from nurseries.

Tzaneen to Phalaborwa

Hans Merensky Nature Reserve

East of Tzaneen, via the R 71 and then the R 529 gravel road, is the 5,300 ha Hans Merensky Nature Reserve, a stretch of lowveld with a variety of game. There is a Tshonga kraal, where day to day tribal activities can be watched, and nature trails. Adjoining the reserve is the Overvaal Eiland resort, with self-catering chalets.

Merensky himself was a noted geologist, whose discoveries included diamonds near the Orange river mouth and the enormous copper deposits of Phalaborwa, on the edge of the Kruger Park.

Phalaborwa *Postal code 1390. Telephone code 01524.*

The original hill here containing an estimated 315 million tons of copper ore is now a pit far larger than the Big Hole at Kimberley. But, unless you are on business, the only reason for coming is to enter the central section of the Kruger Park by the Phalaborwa gate. There is a three-star hotel, the Impala Inn (PO Box 139, Phalaborwa 1390; tel 5681). The climate is pretty hot, but who cares in a boom town? From here the thornbush runs right up the African continent through Zimbabwe, Malawi, Tanzania and Kenya until it finally dies out in Somalia not far short of the Red Sea. As Ernest Hemingway succinctly put it 'Just miles and miles of bloody Africa'.

Unless you are going into the Kruger it is better to turn back down the R 530 to the main R 40 road and explore the Summit Route, described below. On the way you pass the access roads to a chain of private game reserves adjoining the Kruger. Technically several are in the Northern Transvaal.

Hoedspruit Cheetah Project

South of this small town on the R 40, near the Klaserie Nature Reserve, is a cheetah research and breeding station; actually closer to the town of Klaserie. More than 40 cheetah can be seen every day, except Sundays. The project is associated with the nearby 11,000 ha Kapama game reserve. The phone for both is 01528 31633.

Thornybush and Tshukudu Game Lodges

These two private lodges are within striking distance of Hoedspruit. Tshukudu, to the north, has both a lodge and a rustic camp and walking trails, as well as plenty of game (reservations tel 01528 32476). Thornybush is to the east near the Timbavati Reserve and the Orpen Gate to the Kruger Park, again with quite luxurious accommodation in a private game reserve (reservations tel 011 883 7918).

The Northern Transvaal

Timbavati Game Reserve
Timbavati became famous a good few years ago for its white lions. Most were transferred to zoos or died, so there was only one left at the time of writing. Overall the reserve covers 740 sq km (289 sq miles) adjoining the Kruger, although - as in the Sabi Sand - the individual lodges do not necessarily have access to all of it. Within this considerable area there are at least 138 species of mammals and 900 of birds.

One of the best lodges is Motswari Game Lodge (reservations tel 011 442 5640). Tanda Tula, in the northern part is equally well-known (bookable through Safariplan PO Box 4245, Randburg 2125; tel 011 886 18100). Both these have air-conditioned chalets. M'bali is a luxury tented camp in a lovely situation by a river, owned by the same people as Motswari. The tents have thatched roofs over them and are on raised wooden platforms, complete with bathrooms. Finally Ngala (reservations 011 803 7400) is slightly larger and works in conjunction with South African Airways.

At all these personal attention and qualifications of the rangers are as high as is described in the private game reserves section of the Eastern Transvaal chapter.

From the Northern Transvaal to the 'Summit Route'
From Tzaneen, two roads wend their way south. The R 40 runs more or less direct to Skuzuza, via Hazyview, with turn-offs to the Phalarborwa and Orpen gates of the park. The R 36 road takes you rather closer to the escarpment through the thorn scrub of the lowveld and past the intriguingly named settlement of Ofalco and a 2000 ha private game farm near Trichardtsdal. 'Ofalco' stands for 'Officers Colonial Land Company', formed by British officers after World War I. A good way beyond Ofalco is a nature reserve always known as 'The Downs' because it is like England. Continuing down the R 36 it is worth stopping at the Olifants river to look along the remarkable cliffs of the escarpment, forming huge natural ramparts and towers where the hard dolerite rock on the top has prevented erosion. The road then climbs up the precipitous Abel Erasmus Pass – now made easier by a tunnel – and out on to the amazingly different uplands of the Summit Route described under 'Eastern Transvaal'.

The Eastern Transvaal

This part of South Africa is best known for the game down on the low-veld, east of the Drakensberg mountain escarpment. But there is much more to it than that, even if the part of the province nearest the PWV is uninspring. Going east from Johannesburg you pass through wide landscapes of middleveld farming country, until gradually it becomes hillier and the plateau ends with the cool, forested highlands around Lydenburg with many mementos of the Anglo-Boer War.

Beyond is the lowveld and the Kruger National Park, to the north east the acclaimed scenery of the Summit Route, pioneer gold mining towns, selected lodges, trout streams, breathtaking views from the escarpment across the Kruger to Mozambique. There is a great deal to explore up here and it's worth having a car, though there are coach tours.

Nelspruit, the capital of the province, is some 325 km (202) miles from both Pretoria and Johannesburg. South of it there is also very pleasant hill country and historic sites around Barberton, from where you can drive easily into Swaziland, or discover recently established game reserves. These are dealt under 'Southern Transvaal'.

Climate
The lowveld east of the Drakensberg escarpment is decidedly hotter and more humid than on the highveld, though the nights can be cold. Unhappily, malarial mosquitoes are around and you must take prophylactics.

Gauteng to Nelspruit

Driving east from the PWV on the fast N 4 towards Nelspruit and the Kruger Park you pass first through the farming lands of the highveld. After Witbank, where Sir Winston Churchill hid during his Boer War escape, is the turn off north to the 12,762 ha Loskop Dam Nature Reserve, with wildlife, many birds and good fishing. You can hire boats to fish, there are rondavels, a restaurant and swimming pool. For reservations write to Loskop Dam Public Resort, Private Bag X1525, Middleburg.

Continuing from Middleburg, with convenient roadside eating places, you come to Belfast, with the Sterkspruit Falls six km (four miles) away, and a first class trout fishing hotel, near Dullstroom, 37 km (23 miles) north on the R 540. This is the Critchley Hackle Lodge (PO Box 141, Dullstroom 1110; tel 01325 40415). Back on the N4 near

The Eastern Transvaal

Machadodorp there are radioactive sulphur baths and trout fishing. A little further the R 36 branches left for Lydenburg and the 'Summit Route'. From here the N4 goes through the Elandsburg Pass - now partly tunnelled. Near Waterval-Boven there is a high waterfall and a nature reserve. However, this section of road is dominated by a paper-works and, if you have time, an attractive deviation would be up the R36 to Schoemanskloof, then taking the lesser road to the Montrose Pass and so to Nelspruit.

The roads south from Tzaneen to the Summit Route and Nelspruit are described later.

Coaches, Flights and Trains
Greyhound runs daily luxury buses from Johannesburg and Pretoria to Middleburg, Belfast and Nelspruit. Airlink and Metavia operate flights from Johannesburg to Nelspruit and Comair from Johannesburg to Skukuza in the Kruger National Park. The 'Komati' express train runs daily from Johannesburg to Nelspruit and on to Komatipoort on the Mozambique border. For booking details see pages 12 - 13 and Factfile at the end of the chapter.

Steam Safari
Rovos Rail's splendid vintage train operates a four day tour from Pretoria, taking in a private game reserve in the eastern Transvaal. See page 15.

Nelspruit

Postal code 1200. Telephone code 01311. Tourist Info 55 1988.
Nelspruit, the junction for the Sabie and the White River railway lines, is the commercial centre of this lowveld citrus fruit area and a stopping place for most coach tours. One of the best hotels is the Promenade (three-star, PO Box 4355; tel 53000). There is a one-star Town Lodge (tel 41444) with family rooms. The Country Club is open to overseas visitors and has good amenities. The airport is 12 km from the centre (information tel 44 996) and has Avis, Budget and Imperial car hire desks. SATOUR'S Eastern Transvaal offices are at Shop No 5, Promenade Centre, Louis Trichardt Street (PO Box 5018; tel 55 1988).

Parks and Botanical Gardens
The town is known for its gardens and parks, its streets are lined with bougainvilleas and jacaranda trees, while just to the north (off the R 40 road to White River) are the Lowveld Botanical Gardens. These are a branch of the Kirstenbosch Botanical Gardens and well worth seeing if you are interested in the flora of the lowveld. They are a cool retreat in summer, when it can be very hot, with a view of the Nel's river falls.

Craft Stalls
A great many craft and produce stalls are active around the town, selling all kinds of curios, while you can buy handwoven rugs and gemstone jewellery in the shops.

Nelspruit to the Kruger

From here the N 4 goes on past the southern edge of the Kruger Park, where there are entrances at Malelane and Crocodile Bridge, to Komatipoort and so to Maputo, the capital of Mozambique. There are various places to stay just outside the National Park which make good bases for day trips into it.

Bongani Lodge
There used to be a self-governing homeland around Nelspruit called Kangwane. Its Parks Board created the Mthethomusha Game Reserve on tribal land in the steep, rocky, Lebombo mountains north of the N4 road close to the Kruger. This 8,000 ha reserve, re-stocked with big game, has a most individually designed luxury lodges, set around a rock kopje, which is now the Bongani Sun Lodge (bookings Southern Sun. Local tel 01315 41114). The turn off to it is 36 km (23 miles) from Nelspruit on the way to Komatipoort. The access road is precipitous and guests are fetched from a guarded car park. Rates include game drives and are moderate to high.

Malelane Lodge
On the southern edge of the park, easily reached from the N 4 is the 102-roomed three-star Malelane Lodge in a 350 ha private reserve close to the Malelane gate (Southern Sun. Local address PO Box 392 Malelane 1320; tel 01313 30331). There is plenty of game in fairly dense bush surrounding it and a day's tour could be to drive through the park to Crocodile Bridge, north to Lower Sabie and back via Skukuza and Jock of the Bushveld (see the full description of the park below). The vegetation around the Crocodile river is lush and there are many elephant.

White River *Postal code 1240. Telephone code 01311.*
Going from Nelspruit to the Numbi and Paul Kruger gates you pass through White River, a pleasant village surrounded by citrus farms and forests. Because of its proximity to the Kruger and the rolling hills between it and the Summit Route, the area around White River has seen the creation of quite a number of country lodges, often in their own small estates, as well as more ordinary holiday resorts. The four-star Winkler (PO Box 12, tel 32317) is an unusual, conical roofed motel in a striking setting and with excellent cuisine 6 km out on the R 538.

The Eastern Transvaal

From here it is a fast run through beautiful country to the Numbi Gate, past the Bushman's Rock, 11 km (7 miles) from the White River, upon which you get wide views over the lowveld. There is a good three-star motel 16 km (10 miles) from Numbi, called the Numbi (PO Box 6, Hazyview; tel 01317 67301). This is by the Numbi turn-off to the Park. Finally, just off the R 536, is the luxurious four-star Kruger Park Lodge (tel 01317 67021, fax 673860), idyllically set by a river and convenient for the park. Lodges between Hazyview and Sabie are described further on.

The Kruger National Park

Proclaimed as a park in 1926, the Kruger's origins go much further back to the ideas about sanctuaries that President Kruger himself began expounding in 1884, following the slaughter of wildlife by hunters in almost every part of South Africa. As such, this park – though much younger than Etosha and the Namib Desert Parks in Namibia – was actually the model for reserves all over the continent: it currently protects a greater variety of wildlife than any other with 137 species of mammals and 493 of birds. It is worth appreciating before you go there that this is emphatically not some kind of super-large European safari park. The priority here is to conserve the area's natural ecological system, to which human access comes very definitely second. So although there are nearly 1,500 miles of roads, plus air-strips and rest camps, there are restrictions on visitors' activities. For instance open safari vehicles are not allowed, through there are conducted wilderness trails. Greater freedom is available in many private reserves that have been established alongside the Kruger's narrowest centre section, between Phalaborwa and Skukuza (see below).

Almost the Largest Park in Africa

Physically the Kruger is huge, albeit slightly smaller than Kenya's Tsavo. Roughly 350 km (218 miles) long, it runs the length of the Mozambique frontier from the N 4 road up to Zimbabwe and is seldom less than 60 km (38 miles) wide. Furthermore, far from being eroded by population pressures as happens in East Africa, the Kruger's 20,000 sq km (7,800 sq miles) is constantly being increased by donations of land. In 1989 another 30,000 ha near Orpen gate was given by businessman Hans Hoheisin, who became one of three South Africans honoured that year by Prince Philip at Buckingham Palace for their contributions to the World Wide Fund for Nature (the WWF).

Basically the Kruger is an enormous tract of flat veld, broken by rivers in which hippo and crocodile laze. The part most visited is the bush and grassland south, mainly as communications are better in the areas around Pretoriuskop, Olifants Camp and Skukuza. The north of the

Park, which used to be closed from October to March because of the rains, is now open all year round. Even on a short visit you can expect to see elephant, giraffe, buffalo, zebra, wildebeest, sable, kudu, water-buck, impala, hippo, crocodile, hyena and possibly lion. In a longer trip, especially one that takes you to the north, you ought to see rhino, leopard and cheetah. The best elephant country is around Shingwedzi in the less dense mopane bush of the north, where the landscape is wilder and more beautiful.

Getting There
By road the park is five hours from Johannesburg, with countless coach firms offering tours (Connex among them). The main airfield at Skukuza has scheduled flights from Johannesburg and from Durban, while fly-drive safaris can be arranged through travel agents. The air-field information tel is 01311 65611 and Avis car hire is available. There are eight road entrances. Along the southern perimeter off the N 4 are Malelane and Crocodile Bridge; in the south west Numbi and Paul Kruger (for Skukuza); in the centre Orpen and Phalaborwa; in the north Punda Maria and – way up – Pafruri. On a day trip it makes sense to enter by one gate and leave by another, though you must allow plenty of time. In the north you may be required to have an accom-modation voucher. The park's administrative nerve-centre is Skukuza, practically a town in its own right, with an information centre, doctor, police station, car hire, post office, shops and a huge rest camp.

Roads
Roughly a third of the park's roads are tarmaced, and even gravel ones are usually suitable for ordinary cars, though you can hire a guide and 4WD through the Parks Board; but do so well in advance. The speed limit is 50 kph (31 mph), on tarmac and 40 kph on gravel. It is strictly enforced, although you should anyway go as slowly as possible if you want to spot game. You are not allowed to get out of your car except in a camp area. The animals are quite used to cars, indeed lions have even learnt to use exhaust fumes to mask their scent when ambush-ing prey, but to leave your car is dangerous. You must be in a camp by sundown and may not leave again before dawn.

Park Information
Useful leaflets are obtainable about the Park both from the Parks Board and SATOUR offices. At Skukuza the Information Centre shows films and videos.

Rest Camps
Due to the popularity of the Kruger, bookings can be made up to 12 months in advance. During Easter and July/August (winter) holiday periods, it is almost impossible to obtain reservations if not made weeks or months ahead.

The Eastern Transvaal

There is now a wide variety of accommodation in the park, from very reasonably priced chalets and huts using communal ablution facilities, all furnished with bedding but without cooking or eating utensils, up to more expensive "donor houses" and private camps. Most huts are air conditioned, and supplied with a small fridge and barbecue area. A limited number of the camps serve groups of tourists and must be booked as a unit. Camp shops are stocked with provisions, curios, books and liquor and the larger camps have restaurants. All rest camps offer cooking and barbecue facilities and most have camping and caravan sites and petrol stations. Pretoriuskop, Berg-on-Dal and Shingwedzi camps have swimming pools. Tap water is drinkable. Book through the National Parks Board offices in Pretoria (PO Box 787, Pretoria 0001; tel 012 343 1991) or Cape Town (tel 021 343 0905).

If accommodation is booked in more than one rest camp, it is essential to check distances and consider the speed limit to allow sufficient time (including game viewing) to get from one to the other. It is by no means possible to travel by road from south to north or vice versa in a single day. Good maps of the Park are available at the National Parks Board, Kruger entrance gates, SATOUR offices, or at shops in the rest camps.

Wilderness Trails

Four trails have been established in the Park. These are three-day walking safaris under the guidance and protection of experienced game rangers, only for people between the ages of 12 and 60. A maximum of eight per group is allowed. Backpacks are not needed. Equipment, tent accommodation, meals and refreshments are provided by trail personnel. Reservations well in advance are essential at the Parks Board.

Private Game Reserves

A number of private game reserves are adjacent to the Kruger – and with similar wildlife, since the fences between them and the park have been removed. They all have advantages seldom obtainable in national parks: exclusivity with small numbers of guests, early morning and sunset game drives in open safari vehicles, walking trails conducted by rangers, their own skilled game trackers and evening meals around a camp fire. Accommodation and food is usually excellent and prices – often payable in US dollars by non-residents – are all inclusive. One of the few restrictions is that you are not allowed to do game drives in your own car. The conservation principles on which they are run are described in the 'Safaris' section at the start of the book.

These reserves are grouped in two main areas. The 140,000 acres of the Sabie Sand Reserve to the west of Skukuza and the Timbavati Reserve north of Orpen, with Manyeleti between them.

Sabi Sand Reserve

Sabie Sand straddles the only perennially flowing river in the district and covers a spectrum of environment from riverine forest to acacia thorn bushveld and glades of open grassland. The wildlife is excellent. You are very likely to see all the 'Big Five' animals and a multitude of others. The various lodges are about six hours drive from the Rand and either have airstrips or collect clients from Skukuza airfield's scheduled services. A small contribution is levied for the overall conservation of Sabi Sand. The road access is either via Newington or from the Hazyview to Skukuza road 36 km (23 miles) from Hazyview, where the lodges are signed.

Mala Mala/Rattray Reserves

The Rattray reserves are the largest privately owned block of game land in the Republic, where originally lions made cattle farming impossible. Princess Alice stayed at Mala Mala in 1930, when it was a hunting box. There has been no shooting since 1960. Mala Mala was the first lodge and has always been exceptional. We flew in unannounced early one morning and were immediately wecomed with a huge breakfast and a game drive. These days you need to book, as the lodge has become internationally famous. The Rattrays own 45,000 acres of land around it and have expanded to two lodges and a camp, yet still taking a total of only 92 clients. They have also opened up their Mt Anderson ranch near Lydenburg for fishing and mountain trails, with comfortable cottages. This is on the Summit Route, described in a moment.

Mala Mala itself, by the Sand river, has a country house atmosphere and is about the most luxurious lodge in the country. Rooms in cottages are air-conditioned, have telephones and have two bathrooms. Kirkman's Kamp is less expensive and takes 20 clients in colonial style cottages, around a carefully restored farmhouse. Harry's is more rustic and less expensive still, with meals either on the river bank or round a camp fire in a reed 'boma' (enclosure). All have swimming pools. There is also a Trekker Trails tented camp. Bookings through PO Box 2575, Randburg 2125, tel 011 789 2677, fax 886 4382; in London at 185-187 Beauchamp Place, SW3 1NE, tel 0171 584 0004; in the USA through Steinberger Reservation Service.

Sabi Sabi Game Reserve

Adjoining Mala Mala, though not quite so up-market, Sabi Sabi (spelt with no 'e') has two lodges in 4,800 ha (11,800 acres), plus the more intimate Selati Camp of thatched cottages. The River Lodge and the Bush Lodge are nine km (six miles) apart. Both have air-conditioned thatched cottage rooms, a great spread of buffet foods at meals and swimming-pools. The River Lodges is especially good for birdwatches. Game viewing hides overlook a waterhole and the management are proud of the training courses they put their rangers through. Bookings PO Box 52665, Saxonwold 2132; tel 011 483 3939. The British representative is African Ethos, 13 Bowman Mews, London SW18 5TN; tel 0181 875 1404.

Londolozi Game Reserve
A few kilometres west of Mala Mala is Londolozi, most easily reached via Newington. It is run on what the owners call a dynamic approach to creative conservation and 'the sensitive management of human impact' (the National Parks' policy of not attempting to change nature is arguably a static approach). Three 'camps' are in the bush along the Sand river with chalets or rondavels. Tree Camp is built around a giant ebony tree, Bush Camp has luxurious chalets in a riverine habitat, the original Main Camp –the largest – still takes only 24 clients. Guided game viewing trails and drives are among facilities. Londolozi is a member of the Relais and Chateaux and is managed by the Conservation Corporation (PO Box 1211, Sunninghill Park 2157; tel 011 803 8421, fax 803 1810).

Singita Game Reserve
This small, recently built, personally run lodge overlooking the Sand river is in a 15,000 ha (37,000 acre) part of the overall Sabi Sand. Friends who have stayed there recommend it highly. It is also run by the Conscorp (Bookings as for Londolozi).

Inyati Game Lodge
Again set by the Sand river, this rather larger lodge is not quite so luxurious as some others and rates are lower. It is at the western edge of the Sabi Sand and is reached via Newington. Bookings PO Box 38838, Booysens 2016; tel 011 493 0755, fax 493 0837.

Manyeleti Game Reserve
Between the Sabi Sand reserve and the Kruger's Orpen gate is the 23,000 ha (57,000 acre) Manyeleti Game Reserve. All the big five game animals are here and among various camps is the Honey Guide tented camp, which takes only 12 clients, provides game rangers for escorted walking trails and night game drives in landrovers equipped with spotlight. Bookings through Safariplan, PO Box 4245, Randburg 2125; tel 011 886 1810, fax 011 886 1815. Khoka Moyo is a Trails Lodge of wooden cabins, where armed rangers conduct game viewing trails, which are the speciality of the reserve overall, more 'back to nature' than the Sabi Sand operations.

To the west of these lowveld big game areas, up in the hills, is the Summit Route.

The 'Summit Route'

This is not so much a route as an area that you can drive – or indeed hike – around in a variety of ways and which is justifiably renowned for its unrivalled landscapes, forests, waterfalls and old settlements from the gold rush days. It lies roughly between the Abel Erasmus Pass in the north and Sabie in the south, entirely on the top of the Drakensberg escarpment. The AA publishes an accurate map and the privately published 'Portfolio of Country Places' gives details of the best hotels. A well-produced book about the area, its history and its happenings, is 'The Golden Escarpment' by Pat Evans, published by C. Struik of Cape Town. One rewarding road to follow is the R 532: either up from Sabie or down from where it turns off near the Abel Erasmus Pass. This description begins at that northern end with the Blyde River Canyon.

Blyde River Canyon
This 600 m (1,960 ft) deep ravine, guarded by natural rock towers – the most impressive being the 'three rondavels' – was formed by the river cutting its way over millions of years into the black granite wall of the escarpment. The road skirts the canyon for 26 km (16 miles), passing the Overvaal Blydepoort resort's self-catering bungalows, both well-built and superbly located (Private Bag 368, Ohrigstad 1122; tel 013231 901), then near the Bourke's Luck potholes, with viewing spots on the way. Many sub-tropical birds haunt the forests in the ravine, and there are both leopard and the leopard's favourite food – baboons – around, while the canyon rock faces are stained red and yellow by lichens. Everyone says 'you must see the canyon': and they are right. It is part of a 26,000 ha (64,000 acre) nature reserve. There is 65 km (40 mile) hiking trail, with overnight huts, one starting point for which is God's Window.

God's Window
Approaching Graskop a deviation is signed to God's Window – a worthwhile one. From a picnic place you can see right across the Kruger to Mozambique, if the weather is clear enough.

Graskop
Graskop is a forestry village with a two-star hotel, the Kowyn (PO Box 64, Graskop 1270) and a steakhouse. There are also guest farms and camps nearby. Despite a patch of indigenous forest called 'Fairyland' and fine views from Kowyn's pass leading to the lowveld, what you want to do here is head out again for the R 533 turn-off to Pilgrim's

The main street of Pilgrim's Rest

Rest and Mount Sheba, two entirely different and memorable places.

Pilgrim's Rest *Postal code 1290. Telephone code 01315. Info 81211.*
You ascend a mountain valley to reach this old mining village, preserved as if in amber from the 1870s with its stoeps and corrugated roofs, a genuine frontier town. People either like this kind of period piece kept alive for tourists or they do not. We did, because of its unhurried and uncommercialised atmosphere. The single street is lined with old one-storey buildings, including operative shops and non-operative museum pieces like the Pilgrim & Sabie News office. A former store has been transformed into a well-organised small museum and Information Office (tel 81211). Above the village, towards the original diggings, is Alanglade. Originally the Mine Manager's house, this is now a museum of Edwardian furnishings.

Gold was found in the stream that runs down the village's valley in 1873 by a lone digger called 'Wheelbarrow' Patterson, who carted his worldly belongings in a barrow. Geologically the gold nuggets in the streambed are an unique mineralisation from ore deposits 2,000 million years old. The second prospector reckoned they signalled the end of his pilgrimage for riches: hence Pilgrim's Rest. In no time there were 1,400 prospectors. The river gold was worked out by 1881, although local mining continued until 1970. In 1974 the Transvaal Administration bought the entire village to preserve it. The one listed hotel is the Royal. It is ungraded and pretty basic, albeit restored to gold rush standards: and a few yards further up is the unlisted European hotel, fractionally more sophisticated with a chintz furnished sitting-room looking exceedingly upright and proper and a dining room where the menu boards are shaped like diggers' spades. Prices are very reasonable.

Mount Sheba
Continuing up the R 533 you pass one of the region's innumerable 'Jock of the Bushveld' monuments to 19th Century transport riders (see under Barberton below) and emerge on to a little partly forested plateau, where there used to be gold diggings. Set on it, among the indigenous yellowwoods, is the four-star Mount Sheba Hotel (PO Box 100, Pilgrims Rest, tel 01315 81241). The estate is a reserve in its own right, harbouring antelope, and at least 100 species of birds. One of the best walks is to Sheba's Lookout, 700 m (1,485 ft) up with panoramic views over the Summit Route and the lowveld.

Sabie River
Between Pilgrim's Rest and Sabie, a forestry town, are several gorges and waterfalls; one is on the Mac-Mac river, an early source of gold and so named because many of the prospectors names began with 'Mac'. We can hardly say too often that this whole area of the Eastern Transvaal is scenically superb and offers great scope for fishing, walking and riding. The Sabie Falls Hotel is comfortable (one-star; PO Box 58, Sabie; tel 0131512 758).

The town lies below Mt Anderson and a splendid drive across the 2,133 m (7,000 ft) Long Tom Pass, named after a long-range Boer War gun positioned on the pass, leads you to Lydenburg, known for its trout streams and an Anglo-Boer war siege. The name means 'town of suffering', a reference to early settlers' hardships. The Long Tom Pass is reckoned to be the southern entry point to the Summit Route. Going through it takes you near the Bridal Veils falls and the Lone Creek falls, both in forest settings.

Mount Anderson Ranch
The mountain is the source of four rivers. In 1990 Michael Rattray, the owner of the Mala Mala Game Reserve, bought 17,300 acres of upland there. He has ended the overgrazing, re-introduced high altitude animals like eland and zebra, created trout lakes and opened a very small lodge. For enquiries contact the addresses under Mala Mala further back.

Where to stay near Sabie

Rather than staying in Sabie itself you should try places nearby; and there are a few outstanding ones, as well as many ordinary 'holiday resorts'. All offer hiking, fishing, bird watching and often riding. The Cybele Forest Lodge (PO Box 346, White River 1240; tel 01311 50511) belongs to the French 'Relais et Chateaux'. It is beautifully situated in the forests off the R 537 Sabie to White River road and in a class of its own. The Casa do Sol is a private resort with many sports, off the R 536 to Hazyview (tel 01317 68111). Or, if you continue straight on past Hazyview you come to the more populist Sabi River Sun (PO Box 13, Hazyview; tel 01317 67311). Now four-star the hotel is air-conditioned, has tennis, a swimming pool and a golf course. It is delightfully situated at the end of the Sabie River Valley, where at the turn of the century the transport riders bringing mining equipment from Delagoa Bay (now Maputo) to the Rand used to water their horses. You can still ride, as mounts are available on the 120-acre estate. Finally there is the Hulala Lakeside Lodge, (PO Box 1382, White River 1240, tel 01311 51710), built by a pine-fringed lake south west of Hazyview.

Hazyview itself has basic shops, but is only on itineraries as a reference point. From it the R 538 goes down to White River and this itinerary joins the main route from the PWV to the Eastern Transvaal.

Southern Transvaal

South of Nelspruit lies the whole of the southern Transvaal bordering Swaziland; or very little, depending how you look at it. In fact the most attractive place is also the nearest.

Barberton

Postal code 1300. Telephone code 01314. Tourist Info 22121.

Born of an 1884 gold discovery and still a mining town with local names like 'Revolver Creek', Barberton nestles at the foot of Swaziland's green Makhonjwa mountains. Its wide streets, lined with flowering trees and old buildings give it a definite aura of its own. The Belhaven House is now a local museum. Sports include golf, tennis and – unusually – hang-gliding. The Information Bureau (PO Box 23; tel 22121) is in the Market Square and there are several hotles. The best, the two-star Impala on de Villiers Street (PO Box 83; tel 22108), was an officers' mess during the Boer War and has some Jock of the Bushveld scene friezes on the lounge wall from that period. These murals were executed by a German travelling painter, Conrad Genal, who became something of a lowveld legend. He died in 1939.

Jock of the Bushveld
It was about Barberton and its neighbourhood that Sir Percy Fitzpatrick wrote his classic 'Jock of the Bushveld', describing the experiences of his dog and himself when he was a transport rider working on the wagon route to the gold fields there.

Gold Mines
Rimers Creek, where the first gold was found, is being turned into an open-air museum and there are several hiking trails that take in old workings. The Information Bureau has maps. Eureka City, the evocatively named settlement for one of the richest finds, is a romantic site now in ruins up in the mountains. The working Fairview mine, just off the R38 road north to Kaapmuiden, can be visited (telephone the General Manager's office on 23021). You may also notice an aerial cableway carrying buckets of ore down the mountains. Believe it or not, this brings asbestos from Havelock in Swaziland, a 20 km ride for the ore, crossing and recrossing the mountain road. The views from this gravel road at the Saddleback Pass are splendid, but it is an horrendous way of getting to Swaziland itself: far better to cross further north at Jeppe's Reef or further south at Oshoek.

The Songimvelo Game Reserve

The Komati river flows through the mountains on the Swazi border, south of Barberton. The hills, once the site of gold diggings too, were only marginal farmland and have been turned into a 56,000 ha (138,-000 acre) game reserve. A true wilderness, it has been restocked with giraffe, elephant, rhino and many other species, while the scenery is magnificent. Songimvelo is little-known, and the game is shy, but it's worth the effort. The only lodge, the Komati River Lodge, has luxury tented accommodation, but was closed at the time of writing. You reach the reserve via Badplaas and the R 541 towards Lochiel. After 20 km carry straight on, instead of turning right to Lochiel, and it is signed by a Total garage six km after the tar ends.

Cascades Hotel at Sun City

The North - West Province

A New Province

From 1977 to 1994 Bophuthatswana was a self-governing republic within South Africa. In 1994 it was re-incorporated into south Africa as part of a new North-West Province. This restored geographical coherence to a territory that had been ruled by Tswana chiefs in the 19th century when Robert Moffat, the distinguished missionary, obtained permission to found a mission near Kuruman in the 1850s.

Although the capital is Mmabatho, the best known part is around Sun City: South Africa's Las Vegas, where indeed Sinatra has performed and which has grown into an international attraction, originally made possible by Bophuthatswana legalising gambling, which was illegal in South Africa. However the province also stretches west a long way along the Botswana border into the former northern Cape, including Vryburg and Taung.

Information

The North-West Tourism office is in Mmabatho at Suite 101, Borekelong House, Lucas Mangope Highway (PO Box 4488; tel 0140 843040, fax 842524). South African travel agents have details of tours and hotels.

Communications

Mmabatho airport (information tel 0140 851130) is some 18 km (11 miles) from the town. Pilanesberg Airport (information tel 01465 21261) is ten minutes drive from Sun City. Both have daily flights to Johannesburg. The airline is Sun Air, which has offices at Johannesburg airport (tel 011 394 5555). Mmabatho is 290 km (181 miles) from Johannesburg on a fast road – roughly three hours drive. Sun City is only 167 km (104 miles) and has daily buses from the Johannesburg International airport hotel and from Lleyds Street, Johannesburg. They are operated by Welcome Tours (tel 011 442 8905). There are also buses to Pretoria. Various package return trips are offered.

National Parks

The Madikwe Game Reserve, the second largest in South Africa, was created in 1991 on the Botswana border. The Pilanesberg National Park is right by Sun City. Both are described later. The smaller Botsalano Game Reserve of wooded grassland is only 30 km from Mmabatho. The former Bop National Parks had a remarkable record of re-stocking wilderness areas with big game and persumably will become a North-West Parks Board.

Mmabatho

Postal code 8681. Telephone code 0140. Tourist Info 843 040.

The capital represents an architectural attempt to mix African with modern design, the government buildings being constructed in a horseshoe shape to remind one of a traditional Tswana village meeting place. Situated only 20 km (12 miles) from Botswana and in corporating Mafikeng, it grew up rapidly out of the bush with a University, TV station, convention centres, stadium, airport and all the architectural accoutrements of independence. Its Mega City is a maze of shopping malls and entertainments. There is a Lion Park on the outskirts.

Sun International have two luxury hotels here. The Molopo Sun in the capital and the Mmabatho Sun a few minutes drive away, with good sports facilities. Bookings for both through central reservations in Johannesburg (PO Box 784487 Sandton 2146, tel 011 783 8660).

Mafikeng

Postal code 8670. Telephone code 0140.

The name of Mafeking – today spelt differently – was known around the world during the Anglo-Boer war. It was besieged by the Boers for 217 days, yet 800 British soldiers and others, led by Colonel Baden-Powell, held it tenaciously. The night the news of the town's relief reached London the celebrations were so riotous that the word briefly entered the language as meaning 'creating an uproar'. The garrison was militarily less important than Kimberley's – besieged from October 1899 to mid-February 1900. However Baden-Powell's stratagems for its defence, coupled with the length of the siege, had made it seem the emotional lynch-pin of the British Empire. Subsequently Baden-Powell founded the Boy Scouts, instilling in them the value of the bushcraft he had learnt in Africa. He stayed in Africa too, retiring to the highlands of Kenya.

For many years it was the administrative capital of the Bechuanaland Protectorate (now Botswana), although a few miles outside that country. Today, except inside the Museum depicting the siege, it is difficult to feel the impact of Mafikeng's history. However, the cemetery tells its own story and out at Cannon Kopje from which the Boers shelled Chief Montshiwa's Kraal (the original town) there are still trenches.

Sun City

Telephone code 01465.

Situated alongside the Pilanesberg hills north of Rustenburg less than three hours drive from Johannesburg, this glittering pleasure-dome of a resort complex is not going to be everyone's idea of sophistication. However it does present its abundant facilities with considerable panache and it is worth visiting if only to be amazed at how this rather brash style of super-success is achieved. There are three hotels, laser shows, casinos, theatres, discos and cabarets. The fantasy world of constantly clattering slot machines and gaming tables attracts swarms, especially at weekends. The Gary Player Country Club hosts an annual $1,000,000 Golf Challenge, there is a 'tennis ranch' and other sports. Waterworld is a watersports lake, incongruous in the dry bush. Bookings through Sun International as above, or PO Box 7, Sun City; tel 21000. In 1992 the entertainment centre was doubled in size and the underground emporium of slots is now vast. A second golf course was constructed, beyond the Lost City.

The Lost City

In the valley above Sun City is the ultimate hotel fantasy, the Palace of the Lost City. Alive with monster statues of leopard and kudu, that springing from its towers, it could be an Indian Maharaja's concept of an

African Palace. Its 338 rooms are spaciously luxurious; and access to it is rigorously denied to anyone not staying there. Whereas Sun City is vulgar, the Lost City is not; just quite imaginatively extraordinary, with very good food and service. But you need a deep wallet to enjoy it. Bookings as for Sun City.

Pilanesberg National Park

Utilising a volcanic crater in the hills near Sun City is a 500 sq km (195 sq miles) game reserve, which has been stocked with elephant and white rhino, as well as buffalo, springbok and other game. It includes a lake and a wilderness area without roads. Guided vehicle tours are available from Sun City.

Three four-star lodges have been opened in the roughly circular area of the park. Kwa Maritane is a substantial hotel and conference centre, close to the Pilanesberg airport, though built in traditional thatched style. The Bakubung Game Lodge, by the Bakubung gate, is also quite large, though thatched and informal. It has a timeshare element. Tshukudu is much smaller and closer to the heart of the park, taking only 30 guests in cottages on a commanding setting among trees on a hill, with its own waterhole for game. All arrange game drives, bush barbecues, night drives and courtesy transport to Sun City. Bookings through Stocks Resorts and Hotels, PO Box 1091, Rivonia 2128; tel 011 806 4100.

Madikwe Game Reserve

This 75,000 ha (185,000 acre) reserve, four hours drive from Johannesburg on the Botswana border via the N4 road or direct from Sun City, is re-introducing 10,000 animals to desolate former grazing land. Farming had become unprofitable and tourism looked a better bet, but the reserve is being handled with sensitivity. Each lodge has its own exclusive 800 ha of territory. As yet the elephant are shy, but there is no problem seeing rhino, kudu, the relatively rare nyala, mountain reedbuck and many other species. A curiosity is an abandoned Jesuit Mission Station in the centre of the arid savannah and woodland. Founded in the 1880s, the Mission's last priest died in 1989 and its buildings are now the park headquarters.

At the Derdepoort end is the delightful Madikwe River Lodge (bookings PO Box 17, Derdepoort 2876; tel 014 778 891, fax 014 778 893). Moderately priced, its thatched cottages overlook a river and it is well run by the owners, Jan and Jaci van Heteren. The British agent is African Ethos, 13 Bowman Mews, London SW18 5TN; tel/fax 0181 875 1404.

Bloemfontein's twin-spired Church

The Orange Free State

The Free State's Character

To outsiders what made the Orange Free State so dear to the hearts of Afrikaners might seem to have been a political vision, now threatened by multi-racial government. When you skirt its borders going by train to Cape Town or drive down the N1 road all you see are the apparently limitless horizons of a vast savannah, where grasslands and maizefields stretch forever under a blue sky dotted with fluffy white clouds and lazy-looking small towns have streets wide enough to turn an ox waggon in. The artist who first illustrated this chapter in the late 1960s drew a cattle farm with a corrugated-roofed farm house, shaded by trees, a windpump and water storage tank prominent beside it. He might have added a few semi-domesticated besblok alongside the cattle. Until recently that and its industrial north characterised the Free State, where all one saw was the dust of other people's journeys, although the magnificent mountains on the eastern side of the province were always an attraction for visitors.

Boundaries of the Free State
Geographically the Orange Free State lies in the centre of the Republic, bounded to the north by the Vaal river, to the south by the Orange and to the east by the majestic Maluti mountains of Lesotho. It is all on the same high inland plateau as the semi-desert of the Great Karoo beyond the Orange river.

Climate
The days are sunny and warm, and the nights cool and crisp. Rain falls mostly in summer. In winter snow falls on the mountains. Average temperatures at Bloemfontein, 1,422 m (4,665 ft) above sea level, are 24°C (74°7F) in summer and 8°C (47°3F) in winter.

Gold
Gold was discovered on a farm near Welkom in April 1946: not that Welkom existed then, it was preplanned as a mining city when gold transformed the economy. Other towns rapidly sprang up. So did parks, dams, and recreation centres. Today the northern Free State's mines produce over a third of South Africa's gold, which means they are a force in the world's financial market places. They have generated wealth for Africans as well as whites and if Welkom has occasionally hit the headlines on account of racial tension as apartheid was dismantled, then it is fair to remember that this was once an independent Boer State, which the Voortrekkers had won for themselves.

Leisure
Recently great efforts have been made to open up remote parts of the Free State and improve its leisure facilities, both for locals and visitors. It is not easy for a landlocked, largely flat and arid province of 49,866

sq miles to compete with the beaches of Natal and the Cape. Nor, owing to the indigenous game having been all but exterminated in the 19th century, can the wildlife in the new reserves compete with the Kruger or the Natal Parks. But the eastern highlands have the assets of magnificent scenery, wildlife, fishing and an interesting modicum of history in their favour.

Communications and Itineraries
Bloemfontein is the commercial communications centre, with the only major airport and mainline trains. Long distance luxury buses, like Translux, also route through Harrismith in the east on the way from Johannesburg to Durban. Bloemfontein itself is off some tourist routes, which usually skirt the mountains from Harrismith round via Ficksburg and Ladybrand to Wepener and the Eastern Cape. So if you're not in a tour group the answer in a car. Happily there is little traffic and the roads are both good and well-signed. But security in laybys is poor. If you're broke try the black taxis - see under Bloemfontein.

Inheritance of the Voortrekkers

You cannot hope to understand the Free State, even under the new governments, without knowing something of its history. The Orange River itself was named after the Royal House of the Netherlands by a professional soldier, Colonel Robert Jacob Gordon, in the 1770s. When the Boers – people of Dutch, German and Huguenot origin at the Cape – trekked away from British rule in 1836 they crossed the Orange River and found vast uninhabited tracts of land suitable for stock breeding. Here they outspanned their ox wagons and built homesteads. They shot out the game, ploughed, cultivated, ranched: and soon claimed the whole area between the Orange and Vaal rivers.

Technically, however, these Voortrekkers were still subjects of the Cape Colony, though they disputed it bitterly and many went further, crossing the Vaal River to found the Transvaal. In 1854, after 18 years of continual conflict, the British decided to cut their losses and recognise the Orange Free State through the instrument of the Bloemfontein Convention. But this did not prevent eventual armed conflict in the Anglo-Boer war.

'Commandos' in the Boer War
During the Boer War at the end of the century much of the fighting took place in the Free State. The mobile Boer commandos, mounted on horseback and carrying their food and ammunition in their saddlebags, long outwitted the British infantry. They initiated the use of camouflage clothing in war and coined the word 'commando' to denote a small, tough striking force. They were only defeated by the

imprisonment of their families and the construction of long lines of forts that divided up the countryside into controllable zones, some still visible today. If you are interested in the Boer War, try to get hold of 'Goodbye Dolly Gray' by Rayne Kruger, the grandson of President Kruger, which is an excellent and impartial account of it.

Free State in the Union

In 1910 the Free State, having lost its independence in the Anglo-Boer war, regained it as part of the union. In recognition of its importance, Bloemfontein was made the South African judicial capital and houses the South African Court of Appeal, a classical sandstone building with fine stinkwood panelling inside.

National Parks and Reserves

The Free State has a scenically magnificent National Park, the Golden Gate, and eleven provincial Nature Reserves, some created to re-introduce species eliminated in the 19th century. They include the Willem Pretorius Game Reserve near Winburg, the Soetdoring Nature Reserve by the Krugerdrif Dam north west of Bloemfontein, the Franklin Nature Reserve on a hill above Bloemfontein, the Wolhutherskop near Bethlehem and the Gariep, formerly Hendrik Verwoerd, the largest in the Free State, in the south. Only the Golden Gate Park and the Willem Pretorius and Gariep Reserves have accommodation. Between Bloemfontein and Ladybrand is the small Maria Moroka Park. Brochures are available from the Conservator, PO Box 236, Memel 2970; tel 01334 40183.

Bloemfontein

Postal code 9300. Telephone code 051. Tourist Info 405 4980.

The capital of the Free State and judicial capital of the republic, Bloemfontein does not belie its name. It is a city of flowers and gardens, set among small hills, whose spires, old buildings and monuments testify to a pioneering past. The *bloemspruit* – the clover bordered stream by which Johannes Nicolaas Brits made himself a dwelling in 1840 –still runs through the city centre, feeding Loch Logan in Kings Park, while Naval Hill is a Nature Reserve within the city. Founded in 1846, it was the fastest growing centre in South Africa in the 1980s and now has a population of 250,000 of all races, with a large and active university, sports complexes, modern shopping malls, theatres, hotels and restaurants. Not surprisingly its inhabitants are proud of it: even if visitors are more likely to stop off as part of a round trip taking in the eastern Free State and Kimberley than to seek out the city as a destination in its own right.

The Orange Free State

Getting to Bloemfontein
Daily South African Airways services connect Bloemfontein with Johannesburg (one hour's flight) Cape Town, Durban, Kimberley and Port Elizabeth (reservations tel 481812). Airlink flies to Port Elizabeth. The airport is ten minutes drive from town (enquiries tel 33 2901). But there is no bus service.

The Orange Express train operates weekly between Cape Town and Durban, calling here and at Kimberley. Daily trains call on their way from Johannesburg to Cape Town (Spoornet enquiries tel 408 2111).

By road Johannesburg is 425 km (254 miles), and Cape Town 1,901 km (645 miles). Fast Translux buses (local tel 408 3242) connect Pretoria, Johannesburg, East London and Cape Town with the city. The terminal is in Cricket Street.

Information
The Tourist Information Office is on Hoffman Square (PO Box 639; tel 405 4980) and the SATOUR offices (PO Box 3515; tel 471362) are in the Sanlam Plaza on Charles Street.

Car Hire and Black Taxis
Car hire can be arranged through Avis or Budget. Conventional taxis, as elsewhere in South Africa, can seldom be hailed on the street. Get your hotel to call one. The mushrooming 'black taxis' business of minibuses operates from by the Fichardt Mall, close to Fraser Street. The taxis run all over the Free State, and are very cheap.

City Centre

Bloemfontein's hub has always been Hoffman Square, with its lawns, trees and its notable fountain. At night this is illuminated in ever-changing colours as a reminder of the city's name. The fountain is a favourite rendezvous. The Sanlam Plaza shopping precinct is on Hoffman Square and Middestad Plaza is on the corner of Charles and East Burger streets. You can get most things in either, although neighbouring streets have specialist shops. You will notice a mix of Afrikaner and very English street names in the centre, legacies first of the Voortrekker Republic and then of British rule after the Anglo-Boer war.

Security
Oddly, the city centre is probably safer in the evening than during the day. Be wary of public toilets and stopping in laybys when driving.

Accommodation
Among a fair number of hotels there is a City Lodge (tel 479888) and

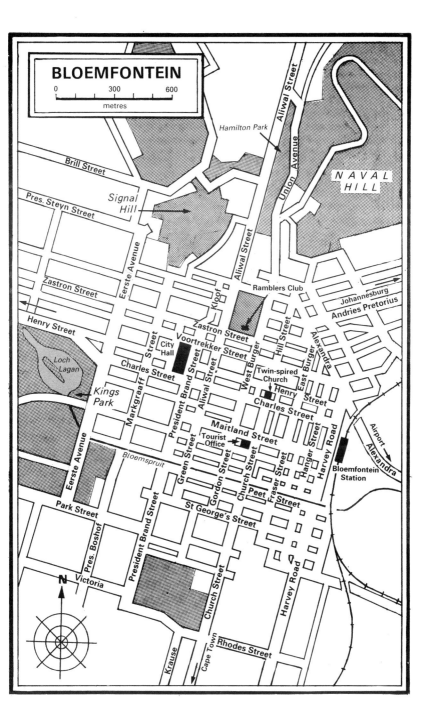

The Orange Free State

two impersonal Holiday Inn Garden Court hotels, both three star. The small three-star Halevy House, is a converted mansion on Markgraaff Street (PO Box 1368; tel 80271). The Cecil on St Andrew Street (PO Box 516; tel 81155) is recommended by locals. Guest Houses are being graded and the Tourist office has a list. A pleasant, restored Victoria one is the Hobbit House at 19 President Steyn Avenue (tel 470663). If you want to stay on a farm try De Oude Kraal near Kaffirriver 35 km out on the N 1 road (PO Box 8331, Bloemfontein; tel 05215 636).

Restaurants and Nightlife

There is no lack of restaurants. We enjoyed the Carousel on the 26th floor of the C R Swart Building on Elizabeth Street: good food and a panoramic view of the city. Nightlife is less dazzling, though there are excellent theatres. Nowadays you can make up for the lack of nightclubs by speeding out to the casino and strip shows at the Thaba 'Nchu Sun resort, though it is an 85 km haul each way.

Theatres

The 946-seat Sand Du Plessis Theatre on Markgraaff Street and its smaller companion Andre Huguenot Theatre (500 seats) form a contemporary theatre complex decorated with works of art. Both have performances not only of opera, ballet, drama and music throughout the year, but also other social events and exhibitions. Check the daily press for details. The Civic theatre is on the corner of Markgraaff and Charles Streets.

Places to See

The Old Raadsaal

Bloemfontein's most interesting building is also the least pretentious. This is the Old Raadsaal in St George's Street. It was originally a school, then served as a church, as Government offices and as the Free State Parliament. Within its whitewashed mud walls, surmounted by a thatched roof, were held the meetings that led to the signing of the Bloemfontein Convention and the recognition of the Free State in 1854. Naturally the Free Staters hold it in very special affection. The present Raadsaal, with its sandstone pillars, is in President Brand Street and is quite a notable piece of architecture.

The Old President's House

Some fairly splendid residences were built for State officials in the city. The Cape Dutch style Administrator's House on Signal Hill looks across at a similar mansion, the former residence of the State President, the *Oliewenhuis.* The latter was opened as an art exhibition centre in 1989: not to be confused with the Old Presidency in the city centre on President Brand Street, which is also open to the public.

Museums

The magnificent Military Museum of the Boer Republics on Monument Road houses a comprehensive collection of relics and antiquities of the war period, both military and domestic, including the first radio ever used in warfare. It has an extensive research library. The National Museum is worth visiting to see the fossil remains of the largest known dinosaur of the Triassic period, and the 'Florisbad' skull of primitive sapient man.

Historic Monuments

Other places of historic interest include the twin-spired church, the only one of its kind in South Africa, where Presidents of the Free State Republic were sworn in; the Fort, built in 1848; and the Women's National War Memorial, an obelisk 36.5 m (119 ft) high, commemorating the women and children who died in the Anglo-Boer War concentration camps. The memorial adjoins the Military Museum. Though many British people do not appreciate the fact, the South African War was one in which Boer families, men, women and children were totally involved. Many had their houses and farms burnt down by the British as reprisals: hence the monument, beneath which lie the ashes of a most courageous Englishwoman, Emily Hobhouse, who worked for the welfare of the prisoners alongside the Boer leaders, President Steyn and General de Wet.

Roses, Orchids and the Zoo

Of the many public gardens King's Park is the largest, and is a blaze of

The Fourth Raadsaal, Bloemfontein

colour all year round, while it also hosts a flea market on Saturdays. The lily ponds are particularly attractive and the Rose Garden covers eight acres and is one of the biggest anywhere in the world. There is an annual Rose Festival in October. President Swart Park adjoins King's Park – on maps they appear to be one entity – and encompasses the Free State stadium, a swimming pool, tennis courts and a caravan park.

The domed Orchid House, with a landscaped interior and over 3,000 specimens is in Union Avenue, beneath Naval Hill. The Zoo on Kingsway has the largest collection of primates (i.e. monkeys) in South Africa and also a cross between a lion and a tiger. It's called a 'liger' which presumably sounded better than 'tion'. The Zoo has night tours.

Franklin Nature Reserve
The flat topped Naval Hill is actually part of the Franklin Nature Reserve, overlooking the city centre and with a road circuit from it. The Reserve covers 500 acres and protects springbok, blesbok, red hartebeest, eland, giraffe, zebra, ostriches and various species of birds. The former observatory is now used as a theatre. Naval Hill is so-called because the British army set up naval guns on it during the Anglo-Boer war.

Observatory
Professor Lamont Hussey of the University of Michigan started an observatory on Naval Hill in 1925 to take advantage of the clear atmosphere, but it was moved to the Boyden Hill station at Mazelspoort some years ago because of increasing light from the city at night. One Bloemfontein speciality has been the study of double stars, a name given to two suns revolving around a common axis, and of the Milky Way.

Sports
In this climate you get more value out doors, and sporting facilities are numerous. The city has five bowling clubs, two golf clubs, 11 rugby clubs, horseracing, polo, archery and yachting. Temporary membership is available.

The Northern Free State

The Vaal river is the Free State's northern boundary and crossing it from the PWV on the N 1 road brings you into a territory that mixes industrial plants with extensive recreational facilities for the people who run them. Further on you come to the goldfields, while all round are wide expanses of maize guarded like sentinels by the towers of grain silos. If you are here on business, then the various resorts are more likely to be of interest than if you are on holiday, as they are pretty much for the locals. The name of one at Parys, the Smilin' Thru Resort, gives the flavour.

Parys

Postal code 9585. Telephone code 0568. Tourist Info 2131.

As you come south from Johannesburg on the N1 road, your first taste of the Free State is the resort town of Parys on the Vaal River. It is a bracing and popular place with several small hotels, including the one-star Echos Motel in Boom Street (tel 2752) and the two-star Riviera Protea.

The Museum has cultural exhibits and you can get brochures on the Maize Route, which starts here. However, one of the most interesting aspects of Parys is geological.

The Vredefort Dome

Parys is partly encircled by unusual hills. These are the rim of the Vredefort Dome, a cresent-shaped depression some 42 km wide caused by a meteorite hitting our planet 2,000 million years ago. It is estimated to have been a cubic kilometre in size. The Vaal river flows through the 'dome' and there is a scenic route. Ask at the Parys Museum.

The Vaal dam

The other main road from the PWV into the Free State, the N3 to Harrismith, passes the Vaal Dam, which has developed as an island resort with fishing for barbel and yellow fish, and golf. On the Transvaal side there is the four-star Riviera International Hotel and Country Club (PO Box 64, Vereeniging, 1930; tel 016 222861). Again, this huge man-made lake with its Nature Reserve is only of interest if you are staying locally anyway.

Kroonstad

Postal code 9500. Telephone code 0562. Tourist Info 22601.

From Parys 90 km (56 miles) south brings you to Kroonstad, a modern town nestling peacefully on the Vals River and a good base for a fishing holiday. Watch out for the traditional South African game called *jukskei,* very like pitching horseshoes, except that wooden yoke-pins as used on the Great Trek are pitched at a peg, instead of horseshoes. The players dress formally in white at tournaments. Although your first impression of the Free State will have been of mile upon mile of maize crops – not for nothing is it nicknamed the granary of the Republic – at Kroonstad you begin to see the influence of a different wealth. Suddenly the horizon is dotted with mine dumps as you near the towns of Welkom, Odendaalsrus, Virginia and Allanridge, all built on gold.

The Old Town Hall, a national monument, houses the Tourist Office (PO Box 302; tel 22601), which organises day trips on the Maize Route: basically a marketing scheme by the growers. There are several small resorts in the area.

Welkom

Postal code 9460. Telephone code 057. Tourist Info 3529.
The goldfields of the Free State were only discovered in 1946. Yet today they yield more than a third of South Africa's gold. Welkom was turned from barren veld into an imaginative town in under 20 years. In fact if you want to see what a boom town of the 1960s looks like you should stop there, then compare it with pictures of Kimberley or the Rand in the old pioneering days. Quite a difference! They have even achieved a traffic system without traffic lights. No longer does getting rich quickly involved making a shambles of the emvironment. There is a three-star Holiday Inn (PO Box 887, tel 7361) on the corner of Stateway and Tempest Streets. One extraordinary sight near Welkom is the water pans of the mines on which thousands of waterbirds, seagulls and flamingoes settle.

Willem Pretorius Game Reserve

Near the town of Winburg, 12,000 ha small reserve includes the Allemanskraal Dam lake. Animals to be seen include white rhino, buffalo, giraffe, springbok, eland, black wildebeest and impala. The scenery is striking, flanked by the rocky ridge of the Dorinberg, and drops from these mountain slopes through wooded gorges to open plains and the lake. You can reach the dam from the road between Winburg and Kroonstad and will find it to be a small masterpiece of game reserve planning, stocked with indigenous fish and attracting a lot of bird life: 200 species have been identified. Boats can be hired, which provide a good way of watching the animals coming to drink at the lakeside in the late afternoons. In the hills nearby are prehistoric beehive-shaped stone huts. A public resort and education centre (tel 05777 4003) overlooking the lake has fully equipped chalets, a supermarket, restaurant, petrol station, swimming, golf and watersports. Fishing is allowed within a limited area.

The Eastern Free State

The Eastern Free State is dominated by the mountains that ring Lesotho and which not only offer spectacular scenery and walks, but also wildlife, fishing, ancient rock painting sites, hill resorts and attractive small towns. Spring cherry blossom in October, autumn gold in April and snow in winter add colour and excitement to expeditions. If this sounds like a bran-tub of attractions, well, happily for the Free Staters it is, and they've capitalised on it by establishing the Highland Route.

The Highland Route

The Route is not so much specifically mapped as identified by places along it. The starting point is Harrismith, near the Natal border in the north east, presumably because the town is easily reached from Johannesburg and the PWV area by the N3 road. The route runs along the R26 road near the Lesotho border via Ladybrand to its termination at Zastron in the south, though the northern sections have the most to offer. A useful accommodation guide is 'Highland Escape' obtainable free from Highland Tourism (PO Box 927, Ficksburg 9730; tel 05192 5447).

Harrismith

Postal code 9880. Telephone code 05861. Tourist Info 23525.

Halfway between Johannesburg and Durban on the N3 road, the town is called after a former Governor, Sir Harry Smith, a man who believed in leaving his mark. His wife gave her name to Ladysmith in Natal and his horse to Aliwal North, just inside the Cape Province. Harrismith is in an extremely beautiful highland area and is a good base from which to look around the dramatic valleys of Van Reenen's Pass, or to strike out for the Drakensberg resorts of Natal in the opposite direction to the Highland Route.

There is a one-star hotel, the Grand National (tel 21060) though do not expect too much in small towns like this. For a meal try the Silver Rapids Spur at 100 McKechnie Street.

Harrismith was founded as a military outpost in 1846 and became a strategic point in the Boer War, many mementoes of which remain in the area. One is a blockhouse preserved in the Drakensberg Botanical Gardens by the river, another the annual Berg Marathon race, held every October 10. This originated from a British officer, Major Belcher, being rude about the diminutive size of the Platberg hill. He was bet that he could not run up it in less than an hour. He not only won, but donated a trophy for future runners. The handsome sandstone town hall was built in 1907, while the petrified tree beside it is somewhat older: 150 million years, give or take a millenium.

Local Attractions

The Drakensberg Botanical Gardens are at the foot of the Platberg and contain flora representative of the mountains. Just north of Harrismith is the Mount Everest Game Reserve, 1,000 ha of mountain and valleys with log cabin accommodation (PO Box 471; tel 21816), riding and fishing. There is excellent fishing at the Sterkfontein Dam, 25 km (16 miles) to the south west, with self-catering chalets and campsites. Piet Retief's rock, where his daughter wrote his name in 1837, is at the head of the Oliviershoek Pass, which is the most spectacular route to the Drakensberg resorts. An alternative route is through Bergville. Up here you should check the condition of roads before setting out, especially after rain.

Qwaqwa

High in the mountains, green in summer and snowclad in winter, Qwaqwa was a self-governing Homeland nestling high in the mountains on the OFS/Natal/Lesotho border. It has hiking trails (some more easily reached from the Natal side) and trout fishing at the Swartwater dam. The Berg Resort hotel complex is not up to the standards of the Drakensberg resorts in Natal. Details are available from Qwaqwa Tourism (PO Box 826, Witsiehoek, 9870; tel 058 7134444). Friends advise that if you do stay there you must ask for the brick-built accommodation.

Clarens

Postal code 9707. Telephone code 058. Tourist Info 256 1406.
Always called the 'Gem of the Free State' this is a village on a stream in the Caledon valley, famous for its spring blossom. It's right on the best route from the Harrismith – Bethlehem road to the Golden Gate Park and has an agreeable hotel, the Maluti Lodge (Box 21, tel 256 1422), with chalets looking at the mountains. Nearby is the somewhat crazy Cinderella's Castle, its battlements and walls constructed of 50,000 beer bottles. In the village the Sandstone art gallery does B & B (tel 2561051). There is fine upland scenery all around Clarens with hiking and riding, bushmen paintings and dinosaur remains.

Golden Gate Highlands National Park

The plum in the Free State's pie, from the visitor's point of view, is the Golden Gate Highlands National Park in the State's north-eastern corner. It is among the foothills of Lesotho's Maluti mountains, just around the corner from the Drakensberg resorts in Natal, and 58 km (36 miles) from Bethlehem. Scenically the best approach is via the little town of Kestell and through Qwaqwa. Being between 1,828 m (6,000 ft) and 2,743 m (9,000 ft) above sea level, the Park has very different vegetation from South Africa's other National Parks. In autumn the red, green and deep yellow of the indigenous trees – oudehout, protea, mountain sage and wild olive – are unrivalled. So are the sunsets, whose golden light on the sandstone cliffs gave the Park its name. Wind and water erosion have carved some of these cliffs into extraordinary shapes, thanks to their being capped with basalt and having dolerite sills where volcanic magma forced its way up through cracks in the softer sandstone.

Wildlife here includes eland, black wildebeest, blesbok, red hartebeest, mountain reedbuck, grey rhebuck, duiker, klipspringer and baboon. The Park is also the habitat of the rare black eagle and the lammergeyer, so it is worth bringing binoculars. The 26 km (16 miles) Rhebuck hiking trail through the Park is one of South Africa's finest: and less booked up than most. It takes two days to follow. You can walk freely or picnic in the park and could hike up the 2,378 m high Ribbokop mountain. For the less energetic a tarmaced scenic drive runs up among herds of game on the sourveld.

The magnificently sited Brandwag rest camp has a hotel-style main building with a restaurant, shop, a swimming pool, laundromat and Information Centre. Glen Reenen further on has rondavels and swimming in a natural rock pool. Petrol is available. You can hire horses. Reservations with the National Parks Board, PO Box 787, Pretoria; tel 012 343 1991.

Bethlehem

Postal code 9700. Telephone code 058. Tourist Info 303 5732.
Bethlehem is situated appropriately on the Jordon River, both names deriving from the devout farmers who established the settlement in 1864. The turn of the last century and the early years of this one saw the building of some of the finest sandstone houses in the province: this Clarens stone is characteristic of the mountains. Today the town is the unofficial capital of the eastern Free State and a small fortune has been spent on turning nearby Lake Athlone into a holiday resort. A reasonable hotel in the town is the two-star Park hotel in Muller Street (PO Box 8; 303 5191). The Information Office is in the Civic Centre.

Pretorius Kloof Bird Sanctuary
Within easy walking distance of Bethlehem's centre is the Pretorius

The Orange Free State

Kloof bird sanctuary, along both sides of the river, which winds through a forested mountain gorge.

Wolhuterskop Nature Reserve

Six km (4 miles) south of bethlehem is the Wolhuterskop Nature Reserve, with a variety of gazelle, antelope and bird species. There are also some beautiful old sandstone buildings in the reserve.

Bethlehem is rather off the Highland Route, which ought to be followed direct from Clarens to Fouriesburg and then Ficksburg.

Fouriesburg

Postal code 9725. Telephone code 058.

This small town is notable mainly for the Brandwater Hiking Trail, a five day, 60 km (37 miles) route past rock art caves, old farmsteads and up and down mountain valleys. It begins and ends at the Meiringskloof Caravan Park. There is a two-star hotel, the Fouriesburg at 17 Reitz Street (tel 223 0207), while the Wyndford Holiday Farm (PO Box 9725; tel 233 0274) is 8 km out on the Caledonspoort road and has tennis, riding and a pool.

The Joel's Drift border post with Lesotho and the mountain town of Butha-Buthe are not far away (see Lesotho chapter).

Ficksburg

Postal code 9730. Telephone code 05192. Tourist Info 5447..

Altogether larger, Ficksburg is an agricultural centre, known for its annual Cherry Festival in November, celebrating the fact that 90 percent of South Africa's crop comes from the district. The town has a golf course, fishing in the Meulspruit dam, a fine hiking trail starting from the dam and a game farm 13 km (8 miles) out on the Fouriesburg road, while the General Fick Museum has exhibits on local sandstone architecture. (Box 93, tel 2214). The Hoogland Hotel on Voortrekker Street (tel 2214) is quite attractive and there is a three-star holiday farm, the Nebo (PO Box 178; tel 3947) on its own estate. The Tourist office is on Market Square.

From Ficksburg the Highland Route continues hard up against the Lesotho frontier, then past Clocolan to Ladybrand.

Ladybrand

Postal code 9745. Telephone code 05191. Tourist Info 3205.

Ladybrand is just off the main route R64 from Bloemfontein to Lesotho, and is so close to Maseru that Lesotho gives it preferential phone call rates. Rather spread out, it has a few notable old sandstone houses and a handsome church dating from the 1870s. The archaeological collection at the Catharina Brand Museum is worth stopping for. Unusually for South Africa, local sports include polo and there is a Saddle Horse Show in February. There is a two-star hotel, the Travellers Inn at 23 A.Kolbe Street (tel 40191) and a much-recommended guest house, Cranberry Cottage at 37 Beeton Street (tel 2290).

In the mountains around there are a spectacularly sheer-walled river gorge and underground caves, while nearby at Modderpoort are excellent examples of prehistoric rock paintings and a famous cave church which dates from 1869 and is still used.

Ladybrand to Zastron
Although there are fine mountain scenery and rock formations on the rest of the Highland Route, a small game reserve at Wepener and Bushman art in caves near Zastron, you can skip the rest of the route. The Bushman caves, 19 km (12 miles) to the south east of Zastron, were a last Bushman stronghold in the area.

Thaba 'Nchu

Situated astride the Bloemfontein to Ladybrand highway, Thaba 'Nchu was one of the separate jigsaw puzzle pieces of the independent republic of Bophuthatswana. Although founded in 1673 and with an attractive church; the town became strewn with litter and abandoned vehicles: a monument to the lack of self-respect attendant on the homeland concept.

Thaba 'Nchu Resort
All the more exceptional, by contrast, is the Thaba 'Nchu Sun resort some 21 km (13 miles) south of the road. Following the signs across a wide plain, you eventually come into sight of the flattish topped Thaba 'Nchu mountain – the black mountain of Twsana legend – and there are the high conical roofs of the complex. Aside from the standard casino and slot machines, the Thaba 'Nchu Sun (international reservations tel 011 783 8660) is luxuriously furnished and has excellent facilities. These include two restaurants, a good pool, a gym, riding, fishing and daily expeditions into the Maria Moloka National Park.

Maria Moloka National Park
The impressive black mountain creates an amphitheatre with the Groothoek dam below which roughly delineates the 3,413 ha park. Springbok, blesbok, zebra and eland are among the game. There are two short hiking trails. You start both through a wooded ravine with abundant birdlife after being ferried across the dam lake. Game rangers can also take you on game viewing drives. On top of the

mountain there are the remains of Morolong tribal fortitications, constructed to save this important hill from invaders.

The Southern Free State

The southern part of the free State has frankly not much to offer. It is hard, dry, ranching country, relieved only by a few resorts around river dams and tends to be associated with the neighbouring Karoo which actually has considerably more fascination.

Historically, however the veld that the Voortrekkers of the 19th century opened up west of Bloemfontein is rewarding. Although Kimberley, the legendary diamond city, is in the northern Cape, many of the most frenetic events of the 1870s diamond rush took place in the Free State. Koffiefontein is where a transport rider found a diamond in June 1870, stimulating no less than 1,428 claims to be staked and the excavation of a 240 m (786 ft) deep hole that rivals Kimberley's. Jagersfontein to the other side of the Kalkfontein dam (see below) once held the record for a diamond. The 971 caret Excelsior was the world's largest until the Cullinan outpointed it.

Battlefields

A bare quarter century later the same wide-horizoned farming land reverberated to the guns of war and the Boer siege of Kimberley, where Rhodes directed the defence. By the end in 1902 Lord Roberts would fly the British Union Jack over Bloemfontein. Quite a number of battlefields sites lie between the two cities. During the war itself Thomas Cook, the London travel agents, sold battlefields tours in Britain, much to the annoyance of the British authorities. Sometimes, due to the constant movements of the campaign, they landed their clients in actual battle zones. Today interest in the subject is reviving, just as in the United States the Civil War battlefields have become tourist attractions, and sites are signposted.

Philippolis

Postal code 9970. Telephone code 017.

Further south is the Free State's oldest town. Philippolis was established in 1823. Five of its buildings are now national monuments, including three in the simplified Cape Dutch idiom known as Karoo-style. The church is especially fine and there are two Museums. The one-star Oranjehof Hotel is on Voortrekker Street.

Lakes and Nature Reserves

Huge water and hydro electric projects have created three large lakes in the southern Free State, all of which have been secondarily exploited for recreation and nature reserves. The Kalkfontein Dam north of Fouriesmith has a nature reserve with some game, plenty of yellowfish for sporting fishing and a camping resort. The Vanderkloof dam's long reservoir on the Orange river supports two reserves. The Doornkloof Nature Reserve is on its south eastern banks, with a small variety of game. The Rolfontein Nature Reserve on the other bank is larger, with hiking expeditions and overnight huts.

Gariep Dam
The lake contained by the high dam wall covers 374 sq km (146 sq miles). It is allied to the Lesotho Highlands Water Project, the biggest in Africa. Appropriately its nature reserve is vastly bigger than the others, covering 11,237 ha and climbing the largest springbok population in South Africa. A resort adjoins the reserve, with bungalows, shops a restaurant, tennis courts and a golf course. Another sanctuary near the dam is the Mynhardt Game Reserve, close to the town of Bethulie. This has a small resort.

Tussen-die-Riviere
Finally a 23,000 ha Nature Reserve called Tussen-die-Riviere has been established at the junction of the Orange and Caledon rivers, at the extreme eastern end of the Gariep dam lake. Gemsbok, kudu, eland, wildebeest and other antelope are numerous. The reserve has self-catering chalets. In winter there is a limited hunting programme.

Voortrekker Klaas Smit's wagon stuck in a drift.

The Voortrekkers

by Alison Whitfield

The six lane highway takes you north out of Johannesburg and as you near Pretoria a huge grey monolith rises out of the veld up ahead, growing bigger as you get nearer. By the time you reach it, it has become a blunt, hulking chunk of grey stone, virtually square and almost 15 stories high. This is the Voortrekker monument, symbolising the fundamental values and unshakable resolve of the Boer founding fathers, in origin both Dutch and Huguenot.

South Africans hold differing views on the Voortrekkers and the Great Trek. To the descendants of the Voortrekkers it meant freedom from British colonialisation and oppression, to the blacks it was a period of conquest and loss of freedom. I will attempt to briefly explain what occurred......

The Zulus were building their empire in present day Natal and Shaka's *impis* were forcing various groups away. The Shangaan, Matabele and Ndebele moved north and north west and the Xhosa south until they came into contact with the white migrant farmers at the Fish River.

The two groups clashed continually over grazing for their herds, but the Boers (Dutch farmers) seemed to be able to cope with the situation. Whenever their cattle were stolen they would cross the river and steal them back, often stealing a few more at the same time. The Xhosa then did likewise.

The British were increasing their empire in the Cape and therefore enforcing laws on the Boer farmers. The Boers were instructed not to cross the Fish River and retrieve their cattle and the British Government promised to police the region. However the situation deteriorated and a number of wars between the British and Xhosa resulted. Heavy losses were suffered, particularly during the sixth Frontier War of 1834-35.

The mounting conflict between the Xhosa and the white farmers, the growing political estrangement between the colonists and the British Government, and a feeling of insecurity are said to have been the main causes for the Great Trek.

The Great Trek

In 1835 the first two parties of Voortrekkers left the Cape and made their way into the Transvaal and Mozambique. The van Rensburg party were murdered by the Shangaans and most of the Trichardt party died of fever in Lourenco Marques.

However other individuals and groups followed their example, many deciding to settle in the uninhabited area between the Orange and Vaal rivers. Here they came into contact with the Matabele and Ndebele tribes and war broke out. But the Voortrekkers did manage to force the Matabele north of the Limpopo into present day Zimbabwe, holding the future territory of the Orange Free State for themselves.

Blood River and the Republic of Natalia

Another party led by Piet Retief, crossed the Drakensberg mountains into Natal. Here Retief met Dingaan, the Zulu king and negotiated land rights for the Voortrekkers. Retief and his advance party were massacred by Dingaan. The Voortrekkers retaliated and the Zulus were defeated at the Battle of Blood River (see Natal Battlefields article), allowing the Voortrekkers the opportunity of establishing the Republic of Natalia. Their capital was at Pietermaritzburg. But not long afterwards the British annexed the region and the Boers were forced to trek again.

The Voortrekkers move across the Vaal.

After the annexation of Natal, Andreas Potgieter, the leader of the Transoranje Voortrekker declared his republic independent of Natal. Not everyone in the territory favoured his claims to Transoranje and Potgieter was forced to move further north across the Vaal river, where he founded another independent republic beyond the Soutpansberg Mountains.

The Transvaal and the Orange Free State

In 1848 Sir Harry Smith, the Cape Governor, proclaimed Orange River sovereignty. Once again those who did not move away beyond its northern border, the Vaal river, became British subjects. In 1852, after numerous conflicts, Pretorius, the leader of the Transvaal Republic, met the British commissioners and signed a declaration. This gave trekkers north of the Vaal River independence from Britain.

At the same time the British Government at the Cape was having increasing trouble with the Xhosa on the eastern frontier; and Basuto raids north of the Orange River. They therefore found it convenient to give the territory of De Oranje Vrijstaat its independence in 1854.

After twenty years of hardship and danger, violence and the loss of many lives, the Voortrekkers had found their 'promised land'.

The Ampitheatre in the Drakensberg

KwaZulu-Natal

The Province

Though the smallest of South Africa's four provinces, KwaZulu-Natal is remarkably varied both culturally and in its landscape. Within a little over 85,700 sq km (33,500 sq miles) there are 71 Parks, Game Reserves and State Forests, ranging from the peaks and vast natural amphitheatres of the Drakensberg mountains to rhino sanctuaries in the sub-tropical bush of Zululand. Between the mountains and the coast lie the rolling grasslands of the 'midlands'. You can hike in the hills or visit Zulu *kraals* and the sites where Ceteswayo's *impis* fought the British army at Islandhwana and Rorke's Drift. On the Indian Ocean shore you can sample the mystery of the East in Durban's bazaars or laze on the beaches of the coastal resorts. Everywhere there are sports tp pursue, from bowls to scuba diving. Natal is both a playground and a rich area to explore. Furthermore the spectrum of hotels, lodges, self-catering apartments and cottages, camp sites and entertainments is unrivalled in the whole of Africa.

In our view the three most rewarding aspects of Natal, depending on your interests, are the pleasures of the coast, the historical sites and game reserves of Zululand and the crisp, sub-alpine scenery of the Drakensberg. So those are what this chapter concentrates on.

Maps
One of the best available maps, which shows historic sites and nature reserves clearly, is the 1: 1,000,000 Natal Minimap, one of a series published by Map Studio of Johannesburg, available in bookshops. There are smaller scale versions in the SATOUR publications.

Climate
The sun shines virtually all year round, with most of the rain falling in summer, when the days can be uncomfortably humid at the coast, especially from January to March. The winter months are cool and dry, with cold, clear nights and snowfalls in the mountains. Generally speaking the autumn (September and October) and the Spring (March to May) are the most congenial times for touring, although the coast is sometimes swept by gales in October.

History

Natal owes its name to Vasco de Gama, the Portuguese explorer who pioneered the sea route from Europe to India. Sailing up this sparkling – and then virtually uninhabited – coast on Christmas Day, 1497, da Gama christened the land 'Terra Natalis'. However, it was to be over 300 years before European settlement began – and in the interval great movements of Bantu tribes took place, bringing the Zulus and Xhosas down from central Africa. By the early 19th century the Zulus

KwaZulu-Natal

had been welded into a formidable fighting force by their famous leader, Shaka, whose aggression caused a migration of the Matabele and the Swazis to other areas. Eventual conflict with incoming European settlers was inevitable.

British Settlement
In 1700 the Cape Governor, Simon van der Stel, had despatched the crew of the brig 'Noord' to buy the area round Durban for the Dutch East India Company from the local Zulu chief Inkanyesi. The captain succeeded, but on the voyage back the ship was wrecked and the all-important deed was lost. Subsequent Zulu chiefs disclaimed the deal. A renewed attempt had to wait until 1823 when a small naval party, led by Lieutenants Francis Farewell and James King, came up from the Cape Colony in the brig 'Salisbury' to establish an anti-ivory poaching station in the natural harbour of the lagoon, which they named Port Natal, harking back to Vasco de Gama. They succeeded in obtaining a grant of land from Shaka and the next year returned as traders with their colleague, Francis Fynn, and 23 others. Thus began the long-lasting British connection with Natal, the control of which centred on the port re-named Durban in 1835 after the then Governor of the Cape, Sir Benjamin D'Urban.

The Voortrekkers Arrive
Next a group of Voortrekkers arrived in Durban in October 1837. They had travelled overland by ox-wagon and were warmly welcomed by the existing settlers. However relations with the Zulus rapidly turned sour after the Boer leader, Piet Retief, was treacherously murdered when parleying with Dingaan, Shaka's successor, over a grant of land. War followed and the Zulus were finally defeated at the crucial battle of Blood River on December 16, 1838. See our special article on Natal's Battlefields.

The Republic of Natalia
The Voortrekkers' victory led to their declaring a Boer Republic of Natalia, with its capital at Pietermaritzburg. For a while the British government disregarded this, until finally in 1842 a battalion was sent up from Umgazi to recapture Durban harbour and was defeated on May 23 at the battle of Congella. Their commander, Captain Thomas Smith, retreated to the fort, managed to ship the women and children out and was facing starvation when one of his lieutenants, Dick King, escaped and rode to Fort Peddie for help. On June 24 two British warships sailed into the bay, relieved the garrison and Natal became British again. In 1844 the province was annexed to the British Cape settlement and was subsequently created a separate colony in 1856.

The Anglo-Boer War
Natal was again fought over during the Boer War, the battles of which are commemorated at various places, notably the siege of Ladysmith. But apart from war memorials and evocative place names, like Colenso and Spioen Kop, there is little to remind one of Natal's stormy colonial past.

Natal Today
Natal remains the most British of South Africa's provinces in both atmosphere and language. In the 1980s KwaZulu became self-governing. In 1994 it was re-integrated with the Republic and the province became KwaZulu-Natal, gaining a little territory from the Transvaal in the north. At the time of writing it was uncertain whether Pietermaritz would continue to be the provincial capital, or if Ulundi would be. Either way the Inkatha Freedom Party of the Zulus dominates everyday politics, not least in its disagreements with the central government.

In recent years the growth of agriculture, industry and communications had been energetic and rapid. This owes some of its impetus to the third main racial grouping in a pot-pourri of peoples – the Indians. Indians workers were originally brought to help on the sugar cane fields by British landowners in the 1860s, because Zulus refused the menial labour of cutting the cane. Today their culture is firmly established throughout Natal, their bazaars and temples are a feature of Durban and many businesses are run by Indians.

Communications

Air
Durban is 500 km (312 miles) by air from Johannesburg and there are several flights a day by South African Airways (tel 031 305 6491). Other SAA flights serve Bloemfontein, Cape Town, East London, George, Kimberley, Maputo and Port Elizabeth. Comair serves Johannesburg and Cape town (reservations through SAA) and Airlink (local tel 031 422136) flies to Bloemfontein, Maputo in Mozambique, Nelspruit and Umtata. MAC Air (031 469 1959) connects Durban with Ladysmith, Newcastle and Vryheid. The Durban International airport enquiries tel is 031 426111. Avis, Budget, Europcar and Imperial have car hire desks.

Rail
A few express train services are excellent. Johannesburg is a 15-hour overnight journey, while the Trans-Orange Express achieves the 2,000 km (1,277 miles) to Cape Town in 40 hours via Ladysmith, Kroonstad, Bloemfontein and Kimberley, leaving on Thursdays.

Otherwise train services, though cheap, are limited and slow. The Natal south coast is served by local trains down to Port Shepstone.

Road
The main roads are mostly tarred and fast. If in doubt about driving and routes consult the Automobile Association offices or SATOUR's Tourist Map of the Republic.

Coach Services
Greyhound (tel 031 361 7774) Citiliner and Translux (tel 031 361 8333) are among operators running air-conditioned coach services linking Durban with all major cities. Connex buses run within the province, for instance to the Drakensberg. For information call the Durban Transport Management Board (D.T.M.B.) on 031 309 4126 or the Central Bus Terminal on 031 307 3053.

Telephone Numbers
Many Natal telephone numbers were due to change in 1995. For enquiries dial 1023.

Natal Parks, Game Reserves and Nature Reserves

Not to visit one or more of KwaZulu-Natal's reserves would be an omission you would regret, as they are unique in their scope and excellently maintained. The reserves most worth visiting are the Royal Natal National Park, 290 km (181 miles) from Durban and the Giants Castle Game Reserve in the Drakensberg; and the Hluhluwe Game Reserve (pronounced Shlush-shloowy) 290 km (181 miles) north of Durban and the Umfolozi Game Reserve in the same area, both famous for their rhino. They are open all the year round, have accommodation and are described further on.

The Natal Parks Board was created in 1947, but some of the reserves, notably St Lucia, date back to 1895 and are the oldest conservation areas in Africa. One of the aims of the Parks Board is to preserve and, if necessary, recreate the conditions in which the area's indigenous flora and fauna lived before human settlement began to affect the balance of nature.

Information and Camp Reservations
At the time of writing the Natal Board's headquarters were still at the Queen Elizabeth Park Nature Reserve, 8 km (5 miles) outside Pietermaritzburg, but it was being amalgamated with the KwaZulu Dept of Nature Conservation. Meanwhile free literature on the parks may be

obtained from the Information Officer, PO Box 662, Pietermaritzburg 3200 (tel 0331 471961). The Reservation office (PO Box 1750; tel 0331 471981, fax 471037) deals with bookings for all hutted camps, though not for hotels, which handle their own. Bookings may be made through travel agents. You normally have to bring your own food and cooking untensils to the hutted camps, and of course to caravan and camp sites: but check on facilities with the Board. Firearms and domestic pets are prohibited. Charges are very modest.

Wilderness Trails

You can footslog just about anywhere in KwaZulu-Natal, but we strongly recommend the recognised wilderness trails. These are treks on foot round otherwise inaccessible parts of the reserves. You need to be fit, especially in the high Drakensberg area. Some trails are only operated in winter, for example the Mkizi Trail linking St Lucia and Cape Vidal. It is always worth looking out for tropical flowers and birds as well as game.

Fishing

The Drakensberg mountain streams are excellent both for brown and rainbow trout. Largemouth and smallmouth black bass thrive in warmer waters. Bream are numerous in coastal waters and in Zululand. The best fishing seasons are September, October and March to May. You want to avoid the summer rains when rivers are in spate (November to February). For inland fishing, you need a licence, obtainable from resort hotels, sporting goods dealers or local Town Clerks' offices. No licence is needed for sea fishing, except in Durban Bay. Boats can be chartered for big game fishing.

Durban

Postal code 4000. Telephone code 031. Tourist Info 304 4934.

This internationally known maritime city was only ever rivalled on the Indian Ocean by Lourenco Marques in Mozambique – now, as Maputo, in a sad state of decline. Today despite – or perhaps because of – the high-rise hotels that have sprung up along the seafront Durban remains an inexhaustible holiday playground for 1,500,000 visitors a year, in a climate that is warm and balmy most of the time, while the hospitality of Durban people has long been a legend.

In the late 1980s the city began an imaginative face-lift operation. The seafront has been given elaborate swimming pools, tropical gardens and sunbathing lawns. In the city pedestrian malls, an exhibition centre and a performing arts centre have been created. Old buildings have been given new functions and life. The Victoria Front Embankment, around the Southern side of the harbour, is being developed with hotels and restaurants.

Quite apart from being a staggering measure of the city's prosperity, the face-lift has managed to emphasise rather than destroy the rather un-South African exoticism that is a key ingredient of Durban's attraction. In addition to wide-ranging cultural activities, you can find garish silks and silverwork in Indian markets, English roses competing with Japanese gardens, creole cooking vying with ostrich eggs on local menus and orchids in the botanical gardens being fertilised with milk. No wonder it is a regular port of call for cruise ships. Yet at the same time the city rivals Cape Town as a commercial centre, boasts the largest and busiest harbour on the African continent and has a population of 750,000 of all races (the total in the Greater Durban area is around 3,500,000).

How Durban Developed
All this began in 1823 with the historical events already described: events commemorated by the ornate da Gama clock on the Victoria Embankment – more usually known as the Esplanade – by the Dick King statue near it and by the streets named after Farewell and Fynn. St Paul's Anglican church was completed in 1859, the railway station in 1898, the City Hall (based on the one in Belfast, Northern Ireland) in 1910. And so the city grew. As recently as 1960 the area of the naval base on Natal Bay was a mangrove swamp and the shallow water glinted pink with wading flamingoes.

Today the low hills that used to enclose the city are rich residential areas like Berea. But beyond them the seemingly wooded landscape – cut through by the N3 Freeway – is actually the variegated sprawl of greater Durban, albeit set with trees and parks. Indian housing in Chatsworth and Kharwastan surrounds the Stainbank Nature Reserve in Yellowwood Park. Out to the west are the black township of Cato Manor, 'yuppie' social-climbing suburbs like Westville, while down the coast the suburbs have spread beyond the airport. Today the truly rich 'old money' families live way out in Kloof and Hillcrest, towards the Valley of the Thousand Hills.

Information
Before deciding on a plan of action call at the very helpful Durban Unlimited offices (PO Box 1044; tel 304 4934) on the corner of Pine Street and Soldiers Way or at the Information kiosk at 106 Marine Parade (tel 32 2595). Both have useful maps, hotel lists and brochures, while there is a tele-tourist information line working 24 hours a day (tel 32 8877 English language). The 'KwaZulu-Natal Vistors Guide' lists service from ambulances and Consulates to

theatre reservations, and the monthly 'Whats On in Durban' is very useful. Both are free. For national information go to the SATOUR office Shop 1, The Marine, 22 Gardiner Street (PO Box 2516; tel 304 7144).

Medical Care
The city has a number of good doctors and dentists, a large provincial hospital, Addington Hospital and many private nursing homes.

Personal Security
As elsewhere, muggings have increased in Durban, especially along pedestrian areas of the Golden Mile Beachfront.

Getting Around

For getting around the city centre you will find the three-wheeler motorised rickshaws called 'tuk tuks' invaluable. They can be hired at the beachfront, are cheap and ply anywhere within a three km radius from the City Hall. Conventional taxis are also plentiful, but they do not cruise the streets in search of a fare. You will find them at special ranks. Black taxis, or 'Zola Budds', are cheap and everywhere. The Mynah Shuttle buses provide frequent, cheap, services to the north and south beaches and the suburbs (tel 307 3503). The old Zulu-powered rickshaws, with their owners decked out in fantastical horned and beaded headgear, have their starting point opposite the Edward Hotel. If you want to be self-powered you can hire bicycles from beachfront shops.

Tours
Sightseeing tours range as far as the Wild Coast Sun casino in the Transkei or up to Zululand. Connex and Springbok Atlas Safaris operate first class coach tours to the game reserves and down the coast as far as Cape Town. Consult Durban Unlimited or the U-Tour Coach Company (tel 368 2848). Note that tours start from the Coach Tours Office opposite the Tropicana Hotel, as well as the central bus terminus at the new Durban Station. For long-distance coach services see Communications section above.

Air Services
Scheduled air services depart from the international airport, 20 minutes drive south of the city centre. The airport bus service leaves from the SAA terminal on the corner of Smith and Aliwal Streets. Charter services leave from Virginia airport, north of Durban on the way to Umhlanga Rocks.

Car Hire
Imperial, Europcar, Budget and Avis all offer cars for hire and arrange

special tours to various parts of South Africa with a uniformed driver/courier.

Shopping and Markets

The main shopping zone is along West Street, virtually slicing the city in two, and is a pedestrian mall at the beach front end, where there are a multitude of shops stocked with holiday clothing, curios, and souvenirs. (Don't forget to get certificates of origin for any skins you buy, as customs officers may want them when you leave the Republic). The Bazaar is a new market on the South Beach. Near the centre of the city are department stores like Garlicks, the OK Bazaars and Woolworths, plus some innovative entertainment and shopping complexes. One of these is The Wheel on Gillespie Street, combining stores, twelve cinemas and a supermarket. Visually more exciting is The Workshop, an imaginative refurbishment of the old railway workshops with their wrought iron pillars as a Victorian 'theme' mall, incorporating 126 shops and boutiques, cinemas and some quite classy restaurants (see below). Indian goods are a renowned local 'buy' and two of the most renowned establishments are Popatlall Kara for saris – five and a half metres of cloth go into a single sari – and Premjis jewellers, for gold bracelets, rings and earrings. The Pavilion is a 75,000 sq metre shopping and entertainment complex ten km out of town on the N3 road.

The Indian Market

You should not miss the large Indian market. In 1990 it moved back from a temporary location on Warwick Road to the Grey Street section of the city, among mosques and temples. Specialities are fine wrought jewellery, curios, leather work, subtle blends of curry powders, baskets of all shapes, brass, ivory and filigree silverware. You can buy anything from a hollow lucky bean with a tiny elephant carved inside to Chinese camphor kists. But never pay the first price asked – offer half and pay around three-quarters. After trying the market you ought to experience the bustling, jostling Madressi and Ajmeri Arcades. Run by descendants of the 1860s Indian settlers, the shops here sell mainly to black buyers, so prices are low. About 624,000 Indians live in Durban playing a large part in its trade. You will notice their influence in many places besides the markets.

African Crafts/Ethnic Markets

African stalls at many places in the city - especially along the Golden Mile - sell assegais, carved masks, miniature shields made of toughened cowhide, the ingredients for witchcraft potions, elaborate walking sticks and other curios. Here, too, a little good-natured wrangling will work wonders with the price. However you may not be able

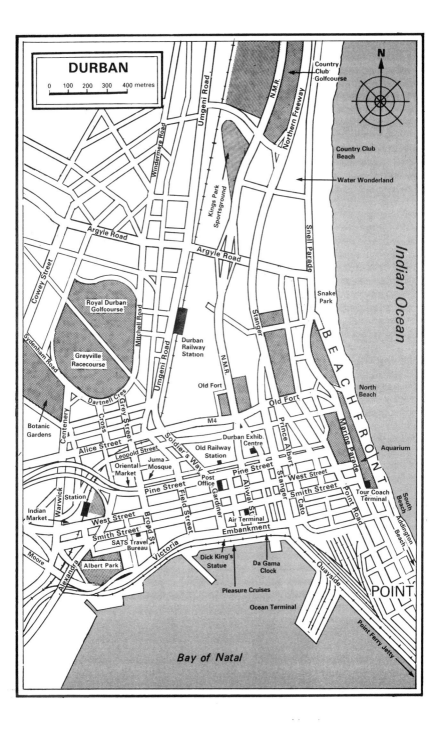

to bargain at the best place for African handicrafts. This is the African Art Centre in the Guildhall Arcade, 35 Gardiner Street. Handmade items here – baskets, beadwork, ceramics, sculptures, wool rugs and graphics – are much more akin to original works of art.

Flea Markets
These are held every Sunday on the south plaza of the Exhibition Centre and at the Ampitheatre on North Beach. There are numerous suburban markets - see 'Whats On in Durban'.

Hairdressers
There are good ladies' hairdressing salons at most of the hotels (like the Karos Edward and the Royal) and at the major department stores.

Hotels

Because of its year-round equable climate, Durban attracts visitors in spring, summer and autumn as well as during the fashionable winter season (mid-May to mid-August). For this reason, the hotels are of a higher standard and considerably cheaper than those at resorts depending on a seasonal trade.

Top Hotels
Durban's one five-star silver hotel is the Royal (PO Box 1041; tel 304 0331) five minutes walk from the beach at 267 Smith Street. The Royal is one of the very best hotels in South Africa. Another well known hotel is the four-star Edward on the Marine Parade (PO Box 105; tel 37 3681). The four-star Marine Parade Holiday Inn (PO Box 10809; tel 373341) is a towering white structure facing the sea and there are two other Holiday Inns. The City Lodge on the corner of Brickhill and Old Forts Road (PO Box 10842; tel 32 1447) is good value three-star.

Budget Accommodation
For somewhere cheaper, yet comfortable, try the two-star Lonsdale (PO Box 10444; tel 373361) also on Marine Parade. The YMCA is at the corner of Beach Road and the Victoria Embankment (tel 428106). The Durban Beach Youth Hostel (tel 324945) is at 19 Smith Street, behind the Four Seasons Hotel, while there is an unofficial Youth Hostel at 15 Cadogan Place. There is plenty of cheap yet clean accommodation, including many bed and breakfasts. Durban Unlimited will help you find and book it.

Holiday Apartments
Recent years have seen a rapid growth in timeshare apartment build-

ing on the coast around Durban. Some rental apartments are listed in the 'Accommodation Guide'. Among letting agents is H Lewis Trafalgar (tel 32 9471).

Restaurants

There is no lack of franchised fast food eateries and steak houses, especially along the seafront. Wimpey, Pizza Hut and Spaghetti Junction are here as they are everywhere else. However if you are not on a tight budget, then Durban rivals Cape Town as a gourmet's paradise with some excellent restaurants: and prices are not absurd. The St Geran at 31 Aliwal Street (tel 373 088) has long been among the city's most popular restaurants. For de luxe dining nowhere beats the Grill at the Royal Hotel on Smith Street (tel 304 0331): though the Causerie at the Edward Hotel, with its smorgasbord every evening, is a close runner-up (tel 37 3681). For eating with a view go to the Roma revolving restaurant (tel 372978) on top of the John Ross building, opposite the Vasco da Gama clock on the Esplanade.

Speciality Restaurants

For seafood try Skellini in the Beach hotel (tel 375511) or Langoustine by the Sea (tel 849768) in Waterkant Road, Durban North. And, of course, there are many Indian restaurants. The most individual of these merits the short taxi ride involved. It is the British Middle East Indians Sporting and Dining Club (tel 312717) at 16 Stamford Hall Road, just north of the city centre: 'a must for Indian food enthusiasts, with real old-fashioned courtesy and comfort' comments our local editor. Or else try Saagries (tel 32 7922) at the beach end of West Street. The latest, and very pleasing Indian idea, is to eat at a family's home. One possibility is The Houndee, 12 km out at 107 Varsity Drive (tel 825950); not particularly cheap, but a fine menu, or the Ulundi in the Royal Hotel for curries.

Nightlife

Durban's nightlife is energetic and most hotels have their own discos and cocktail bars with live music. The Bali Hai at the Elangeni is a diehard Durban favourite (tel 341321), while the Top of the Royal in the Royal Hotel (tel 304 0331) is both more elegant and more subdued. Some restaurants advertise 'dining and dancing', but the dancing bit may be only on Fridays and Saturday. A string of bars, topless bars, clubs disco and escort agencies advertise in the 'Durban for all Seasons' information guide.

Cinemas and Theatres

There are at least a dozen air-conditioned cinemas, while the stunning Natal Playhouse complex, created in 1987 from the Spanish-style Prince's Theatre and the mock-Tudor Playhouse, contains five performing arts venues for drama, music, dance and the arts. In their time Maurice Chevalier, Sophie Tucker and Cliff Richard have been on stage at the Playhouse. Check the daily press for details.

Things To Do and Places To See

Even so, Durban's most popular entertainments centre on a vast range of activities and places to see. Many of these are along the beachfront, which becomes a fairyland of lights at night, with fun fairs and amusement arcades in full swing. By day there you will find Minitown, a miniature city; Seaworld, South Africa's finest Marine Centre at the end of West Street; the Snake Park and the Water Wonderland, both on Snell Parade. Seaworld's dolphins give displays five times a day, while the fish in the Aquarium are fed at 1100 and 1500: and fearless divers hand-feed the sharks every second day. At the Snake Park you can see cobras, the deadly ringhals and fat, bloated puff adders by the score. Attendants stage four display sessions a day. Water Wonderland is the largest of the many swimming pools along the seafront, with cascades and slides for children.

Beaches
The city's greatest attraction is undoubtedly the 'Golden Mile' of beaches along the Marine Parade, though in fact a good five km of golden sands and warm Indian Ocean waters serve the city. The beaches begin with Country Club to the north and run down through North and South to Addington near North Pier, all protected by shark nets. Country Club and North are good for surfing.

Parks and Gardens
Durban's famous Orchid House, in the Botanical Gardens five minutes' drive from the city centre, houses the finest collection under one roof in the whole of Africa, with more than 3,000 plants and hundreds of exotic varieties. Among a staggering 423 other parks of one kind or another are the Japanese water garden, at Durban North; Jameson Park, famed for its roses; Albert Park with its jogging routes; Mitchell Park and the Botanical Gardens themselves. Depending on the time of year, you will find bougainvillea in profusion, azaleas, even daffodils in the spring. Further afield from the city are the Umgeni River Bird Park and the Beachwood Mangroves Reserve.

Museums
The city's 'Family of Museums' ranges from the Natural History

Museum and the Art Museum, both in the City Hall, to a working harbour tug. The Art Museum exhibits classic European art as well as native arts and crafts. The delightful Natal Settlers' Old House Museum on St Andrews Street is full of early settlers' furniture and memorabilia. A brochure on the museums is available.

The Harbour: Two Very Different Ladies

Harbours are always fascinating and the Port of Durban is no exception. The Point Road area behind the Ocean Terminal has been cleaned up, notwithstanding memories of Rosie Dry, a local lady of pleasure who got her name from tippling London gin mixed with Roses lime juice. Another lady is officially commemorated with a statue on the North Pier. Perla Gibson or 'The Lady in White', as she was known, was an opera singer who sang farewell to countless departing troopships during World War II. The megaphone she used is now in the Warriors Gate Museum. The departure of big ships from Durban used always to be a festive occasion; alas the ocean liners are gone, though cruise ships often call.

Sight-seeing Cruises and Deep-Sea Fishing

Operating from Dick King jetty, on the Esplanade, near Dick King's statue, are fast, fully equipped and very comfortable boats which can take you on sight-seeing cruises around the Bay and docks. Or if you prefer it you can go deep-sea fishing after salmon, barracuda or '74' – rod, line and bait are supplied. For information contact the Durban Charter Boat Association (tel 261 6010). Alternatively people have caught a wide variety of fish - even sharks - off the South Pier.

Indian Ceremonies and Temples

In March and April the Indian community holds fire-walking ceremonies and rituals near the Hindu temples and the Indian Quarter is always full of women in beautiful Benares silk saris and the smells of exotic cooking and incense. Various temples can be visited, notably the Shree Shiva Subrahmanya Alayam in Sirdar Road and the phenomenally vulgar Temple of Understanding of the Krishnas in the Chatsworth suburb.

Walkabouts

Guided morning walking tours of the city on weekdays - Durban Experience, historical and oriental - are bookable through Durban Unlimited.

Sports

Racing

The Durban Turf Club, at Greyville, encircles the Royal Durban Golf Course, not five minutes from the business centre of the city. It is here that the Durban July Handicap takes place each year on the first Saturday in July. Like Ascot in England, this is South Africa's most fashionable race meeting of the winter season and tens of thousands of people come from all over the country for the event. The Gold Cup meeting, four weeks later, is another elegant occasion.

Golf
Durban is a great golfing centre and was the home town of Gary Player. There are numerous courses near the city and along the coast, notably at the Durban Country club where facilities include eight tennis courts, croquet, numerous squash courts, a swimming pool and the best food in town. If you want to play as a visitor – and do not know a member – contact the Secretary (tel 238282).

Durban's Neighbourhood

Durban has several nature reserves in its immediate vicinity, as well as stretches of coast both north and south that are easily accessible for an outing, while the Valley of a Thousand Hills is a favourite day trip for coach tours.

Stainbank Nature Reserve
One of the most interesting reserves is the Kenneth Stainbank Reserve at Yellow Wood Park, only 14 km (9 miles) from the city centre, which not only has indigenous bush and flowers, but birds and several species of game, including rhino, giraffe and zebra.

Krantzkloof Nature Reserve
Near Kloof, 22 km (14 miles) out on the main road towards Pietermaritzburg, is the larger Krantzkloof Nature Reserve, a forested gorge on the Emolweni River. Bushpig, bushbuck, reedbuck and duiker are among the wildlife and there is an attractive picnic site immediately above the Kloof Falls. If you are driving yourself, don't be confused by the succession of townships along the National road, you will find both the reserve and Kloof all right.

Valley of a Thousand Hills
Further on again, if you divert on to the old Pietermaritzburg road beyond Kloof and Hillcrest, you reach the Valley of a Thousand Hills bordering KwaZulu. Traditional 'beehive' huts dot the hillsides. There are craft shops and restaurants around Botha's Hill, a Safari Park, and PheZulu kraals, where witch doctors throw the bones and Zulu dancers perform, not to mention dozens of roadside traders whose pestering announces that you have reached a major local tourist attraction. The Rob Roy hotel (tel 031 777 1305) on old Main Road, Botha's Hill, is a favourite stopping point.

Shembe Festival
Out in the valleys there is an annual religious spectacle of considerable interest, though you should only go if invited. This is the Shembe Festival, held on the Sunday nearest July 25 at Ekuphakameni village in the Inanda district by followers of a sect started by Isaiah Shembe. Zulu tribal rites have been adapted into Christian ceremonies.

Natal's Coastal Resorts

From the Tugela river north of Durban town to Port Edward on the border of the Transkei there is a string of seaside resorts, interrupted only by occasional headlands and river mouths. Tourist authorities have given them marketing names – 'The Dolphin Coast', 'The Sunshine Coast', 'The Hibiscus Coast'. But to the Transvaal families who swarm to them for holidays they are simply 'The North Coast' and 'The South Coast', divided by the central attraction of Durban. Their beaches – 42 in all – are protected by shark nets and shark guards, monitored by the Natal Anti-Shark Measures Board. Inland from the coast, both north and south of Durban, are extensive sugar plantations among the low hills. Many country clubs have golf courses, such as Mt Edgecombe, close to Umhlang Rocks.

Addicted visitors argue that the shorter north coast is less crowded and more like the beach cottage days of 30 years ago. It is true that more of its resorts are reached by quiet side roads off the main N2. But recent development has studded the entire 220 km (137 miles) with package tour hotels, timeshare and rental apartments, caravan parks, shopping centres and – of course – water sports facilities. Even when gales lash the coast and salt spray double-glazes the windows, as can happen in early summer, there is plenty to do. We deal with only a small number of the many places. Write to SATOUR (PO Box 2516, Durban 4000) for a copy of 'The KwaZulu-Natal Experience' and Durban Unlimited's extremely detailed 'KwaZulu-Natal Visitors Guide'.

North of Durban

Umhlanga Rocks *Postal code 4320. Telephone code 031. Info 031 561 4257.*
This attractive resort, pronounced 'Umshlanga', is only 16 km (10 miles) north of Durban and quite sophisticated in its shopping centres, holiday flats and villas. The attractions include golf, botanical gardens and the Scarlet Tanager Aviary, a remarkable collection of talking birds of the parrot and parakeet variety. Two hotels here, where many visitors to Durban prefer to stay, are the three-star Oyster Box (PO Box 22, Umhlanga Rocks 4320; tel 561 2233), which is renowned for its

food and the five-star Beverly Hills Sun (PO Box 71, Umhlanga Rocks 4320; tel 561 2211), with iced water on tap, three restaurants and a nightclub.

The Dolphin Coast

There is less development further north, though all the resort villages like Compensation Beach, Ballito Bay, Willard Beach, Thompson's Beach, Chaka's Rock, Salt Rock and Sheffield Beach have acquired timeshare apartments and caravan parks. All along there is good surf and rock fishing. The holiday beaches end beyond Stanger at the Tugela river mouth, where there is a waterbird sanctuary and the ruins of the British Zulu War forts of Pearson and Tenedos.

Shortens Country House

One of South Africa's best country house hotels is just inland from Ballito. This is Shortens Country House (four-star silver PO Box 499, Umhlali 4390; tel 0322 71140), a 1905 colonial-style homestead with guest cottages in its exotic gardens, adjacent to a country club golf course.

Shaka's Assassination Site

Stanger, now basically an Indian commercial centre, was once a major Zulu Kraal. A monument marks where the great King Shaka (also spelt Tsaka and Chaka) was murdered on September 22, 1828. His Indaba Tree, an old mahogany, still stands by the Municipal offices and so, outside town, does the cliff used for executions.

South of Durban

South of Durban, the road passes through the port and industrial area. Once clear of this, you come to several major resorts before reaching the Hibiscus Coast. Amanzimtoti, 27 km (17 miles) from Durban has many facilities, including a zoo and a golf course, but is spoiled by unending high-rise apartment blocks. The Ilanda Wilds Nature Reserve houses a bird sanctuary with wildfowl, peacocks, and aquatic birds. There are some interesting indigenous trees like oleander, wild banana and coral tree. Next are five small resorts, collectively known as Kingsburgh. Warner Beach offers good surfing, surf angling and swimming in a tidal pool. Illovo Beach is the nude sun-worshippers' paradise.

Umkomaas *Postal code 4170. Telephone code 0323.*
At Umkomaas there are several hotels, including the two-star Lido (PO Box 24; tel 31002) which has a good table, a championship golf course and a swimming pool heated in winter.

Further on, Scottburgh has a particularly good beach, with hotels, excellent camping sites and golf. Indeed most of the resorts on the south coast have golf courses. Inland, off the R612, is the Vernon Crookes Nature Reserve, with prolific birdlife and some game animals, such as eland and zebra.

Selbourne Country Lodge
There is another notable country hotel here. The Selborne Country Lodge (PO Box 2, Pennington 4184; tel 03231 51133) is furnished like an English country house and stands among azaleas and indigenous forest, adjacent to the Selbourne golf course.

The Hibiscus Coast

The Hibiscus Coast is one of the most popular holiday playgrounds in Southern Africa. It is considered to stretch from Hibberdene to Port Edward. The coastline is ruggedly attractive and, because of the warm Mozambique Current which flows down the coast, the sea is warm throughout the year and is ideal for water sports. There are many golf courses, in fact it is nicknamed 'The Golf Coast'.

The Sardine Run and Big Game Fish
Fishing is excellent, especially in late June or early July, when millions of sardines make their annual migration up the coast, hotly pursued by game fish. The sardines are forced ashore in their thousands by their pursuers and holidaymakers rush out to scoop them out of the sea in baskets, children's sand-castle buckets or any other receptacle that happens to be handy. Grilled over hot coals, or fried in butter, they are delicious! Meanwhile big-game fishermen are out after the tunny, barracuda, kingfish and shark that have followed them.

Hibberdene to Port Shepstone
Hibberdene is the first of a clutch of small family resorts on the N2 road – also served by the railway – before you reach Port Shepstone, the commercial centre of the south coast. Here the serious railway metaphorically hands over to the Banana Express. This narrow gauge steam train jolts and puffs its way along the beachfront and then inland among farms of the Oribi Gorge.

South of Port Shepstone
Many other resorts dot the coastline on the half-hour's drive down the R61 to Port Edward – St Michael's, Uvongo, Ramsgate, Southbroom, Shelley Beach, to mention just a few. A brochure description of Shelley Beach says it all: 'from a few sleepy cottages to a buzzing seaside resort in a few short years'. Hotels cater for all types of visitor and children are usually very welcome. One holiday complex deserves special mention. This is San Lameer near Southbroom (PO Box 78,

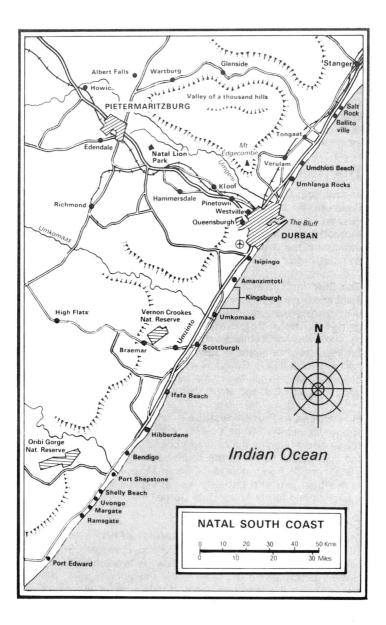

NATAL SOUTH COAST

Southbroom 4277; tel 03931 30011), a Protea resort with an extensive beach, 350 cottages, hotel accommodation, restaurants, golf, riding, bowls and watersports. It is definitely a cut above the accepted 'Queen' of the south coast, Margate.

Margate *Postal code 4275. Telephone code 03931. Tourist Info 22322.*
Anyone who knows the Margate in England will immediately recognise this town's beauty contest and paddling pool oriented, fun-for-all-the family, atmosphere. Every July an Hibiscus Festival elects its beauty queen. The South Coast Publicity Association (PO Box 1253, Margate 4275; tel 22322) is on Main Beach and can provide a full list of the many hotels, holiday flats, camping sites and well-laid-out caravan parks. Sports include tennis, golf and bowls. Car hire is available. The airport has scheduled flights on Comair to Johannesburg and Pietermaritzburg (information tel 21356). The Margate Mini Coach runs a daily return service to Durban (tel 21406).

The Oribi Gorge
Inland from Margate is the Oribi Gorge, an awesome chasm cut out of solid rock by the Mzimkulwana river over thousands of years. Altogether 24 km (15 miles) long and five km (3 miles) wide, its sheer sides dropping 364 m (1,200 ft) at some places, the gorge is an unforgettable sight, especially seen from the 'hanging rock' that projects over it. There are also good views from the one-star Oribi Gorge Hotel (PO Box 575, Port Shepstone 4240; tel 0397 91753) and along the four km drive to the Oribi Heads. A 1,800 ha Nature Reserve in the bed of the gorge protects indigenous forest and some wildlife. The gorge can be reached by car or bus, via a turn off the N2 road.

Port Edward *Postal code 4295. Telephone code 3930.*
The main beach of this small town is at the foot of Tragedy Hill, where in 1831 Zulus massacred a party of settlers, led by one of the founders of Durban, Francis Fynn. The Zulus believed Fynn's men had been rustling Dingaan's cattle. They had not: and Dingaan ordered the originator of the rumour to be shot by a settler. There is a golf course and a nature reserve, the Umtamvuna, which shelters small game and has walking trails.

The Wild Coast Sun
If you find Port Edward unexciting, then a ten-minute drive away in the Transkei you have the luxurious Wild Coast Sun hotel and resort (Sun International. Local address PO Box 23, Port Edward; tel 03930 59111). Here you'll find considerable luxury, a casino, live entertainment, several restaurants and numerous sports. You get there via the bridge across the Umtamvuna river, on which the hotel runs sundowner cruises.

The Drakensberg Reserves and Resorts

The Natal ranges of these majestic mountains are famous far beyond the borders of the Republic for their invigorating climate, summer sunshine, precipitous peaks and challenging hiking and pony trekking trails. The lower slopes are alive with crystal clear mountain streams, tumbling waterfalls, wild flowers, ferns and ancient yellow wood trees. Their resorts offer many kinds of sporting relaxation. You might say the Drakensberg is both very grand and very approachable, and particularly splendid in the tawny-gold colouring of autumn.

The Voortrekkers who came into Natal from the high veld thought that the vast basalt escarpment above the lush green hills of Natal resembled the saw-toothed spines of a dragon. So they named it the Drakensberg. The wall of the escarpment, in places a sheer drop of more than 1,000 m (3,300 ft), is the edge of the central plateau of Lesotho, the greatest watershed of Southern Africa. The Orange river flows west from near Cathedral Peak to the Atlantic, while the Tugela flows east to the Indian Ocean off the 3,248 m (10,763 ft) Mont-aux-Sources or 'mountain of springs', so named by two French missionaries in 1836.

Wildlife

Dinosaur footprints – they display three giant toes – reveal that those prehistoric monsters existed up here. Bushman paintings illustrate the herds of eland and buck that used to graze the slopes and which they hunted with bows and arrows for countless centuries. But European settlers almost eliminated Natal's game and the last Drakensberg lion and elephant were shot in 1872.

Today there are no predators – which makes life safer for mountaineers – just baboons, dassies (hamster-like rock-rabbits) and small regenerated herds of the eland and buck. Birdlife is more abundant. Eagles and the rare bearded vulture, or lammergeyer, with its two-metre wingspan soar around the cliffs. The largest predator bird in Africa, it has been cleared of a reputation for taking farmers' lambs, and become the symbol of the resorts. Vultures are unable to prey on domestic stock: they are scavengers, whose claws are not talons like an eagle's. But their numbers have all dwindled, whether they are bearded, white backed, lappet-faced or the particularly persecuted Cape species. Active measures to save them include persuading farmers to leave stock carcasses that are unfit for human consumption out on the ground at 'vulture restaurants'. You might see lammergeyers - so graceful in the air and so ugly face to face – feeding at one.

Fishing
Fishing is superb as both rainbow and brown trout were introduced into the rivers at the turn of the century and the streams are constantly being restocked. The rivers are 'open' from September 1 to June 1 and fishing licences are obtainable from hotels and Natal Parks Board offices in the reserves.

Getting to the Reserves and Resorts
A chain of nature reserves with camps and resort hotels runs along the escarpment from Royal Natal National Park in the north to the Sani Pass in the south. They are all signed off the N3 road with a distinctive shield-shaped emblem bearing a lammergeyer and either 'North' or 'Central' plus the road number. You can reach them via various towns in the valleys below the mountains; being so high up there are no direct routes between them, except hiking and horseback trails.

Hotels and Camps
Virtually all the hotels offer riding, fishing, swimming, tennis, bowls and other amusements, both indoor and outdoor. There are also a number of guest farms. For a complete list write to the Pieter-maritzburg Publicity Association, PO Box 25, Pietermaritzburg 3200; tel 0331 45 1348. All accommodation in the reserves is bookable through the Natal Parks Board Reservations Office (PO Box 1750, Pietermaritzburg 3200; tel 0331 471981).

Mountain Climate and Clothing
Because of their altitude the peaks are snow-covered in winter and subject to unpredictable storms. Summer temperatures are pleasant, though the coolness of the air is deceptive and you can easily get sun-burned. Remember that for hiking you need tents and warm clothing at night, as well as stout shoes. An accurate map and a compass are potentially vital if the weather closes in, and do not forget a torch.

Royal Natal National Park

The Royal Natal National Park, which includes Rugged Glen Nature Reserve, covers 8,094 ha (31 sq miles) of magnificent mountain scenery upwards of 1,500 m (4,700 ft) above sea level. Originally proclaimed in 1916, it became 'royal' when the British King George VI and Queen Elizabeth stayed here in 1947. The park is gradually being restored botanically to its primaeval state, which engendered the uni-que pink alpine protea, while its wildlife includes black wildebeest, various species of buck and baboon. There are many waterfalls, deep ravines and great mountain bluffs. Two of these mountains, the Sen-tinel and the Eastern Buttress, flank a huge natural amphitheatre (illustrated in our drawing), over the edge of which the Tugela river falls 948 m (3,081 ft) in three dramatic stages on its way to form the one-time boundary of Zululand. Roads inside the park are not tarred. A mile inside the gate there is a viewing site, where the main features are identified. The Visitors' Centre, half a mile further on, has a dioramic model of the park and sells a useful guide brochure.

Getting to the Park

Access is either from the north via Harrismith (see Orange Free State chapter) and the R615 through the Oliviershoek Pass, or via Estcourt and Bergville off the N3 from Durban, a total distance of 290 km (181 miles). The Midlands Mini Coach from Durban serves towns below the mountains like Bergville, but not the park. See the section on the Midlands. Our description of the park starts from the north.

The best country hotel stopping point near Harrismith is the small colonial-style Oaklands Country Manor (PO Box 19, Van Reenen 3372; tel 05867 883), just off Van Reenen's Pass on the N3. There are also Andrews Motels near the pass and near Ladysmith.

Bergville *Postal code 3350. Telephone code 036. Info 448 1557.*
This small town houses the Drakensberg Publicity Association (PO Box 325; tel 448 1557). It is at the one-star Walter Hotel (PO Box 12, Bergville 3350; tel 488 1022) There are a petrol station and a couple of stores. Further on, near Winterton, is the much-acclaimed Cayley Lodge, described under Central Drakensburg hotels two pages on.

Trails in the Park

The only way to travel in the park is on foot or horseback. There are 25 hiking trails and contributors to this chapter recommend the guided walks run by the Rangers. Groups are also formed to climb the Mont aux Sources – the summit is made accessible by a chain ladder. Ask at the Visitors' Centre and if you have a chance to chat to one of the Wardens, take it. They are very knowledgeable. The Warden's Office at Mont-aux-Sources adjoins the hotel.

Opening Times

Gates to the parks are open 0500 to 1900 in summer (October 1 to March 31) and 0600 to 1800 in winter. But there is 24 hour access to hotels in them.

Accommodation

The two-star Royal Natal National Park hotel (Private Bag X4, Mont-aux-Sources; 3353; tel 036 438 6200) has most rooms with private baths. It is essential to book ahead. At Tendele there is a hutted camp, three km (two miles) from the hotel and there are two attractively positioned camp sites. For details contact the Warden's office.

Just outside the park, adjoining Rugged Glen, is the three-star Karos
Mont-aux-Sources Hotel (Private Bag X1, Mont-aux-Sources 3353;
tel 036 438230). It offers riding, bowls, tennis and swimming
facilities. Also warmly recommended by people who have stayed
there is the three-star Little Switzerland Resort (Private Bag X 1661,
Bergville 3350; tel 036 438 6220). Jacarandas bloom among its
thatched cottages, many sports are available and it looks towards
the Ampitheatre.

Central Drakensberg Private Resorts

These resort hotels, situated between the Royal National Park and
Giant's Castle Reserve, all offer riding, fishing, tennis, golf and swimming. Their postal codes are Winterton 3340 and telephone codes
036. You pass them on the winding 34 km (21 mile) drive through
farmland from Winterton. They can be heavily booked and at peak
seasons it is worth having the Pietermaritzburg Publicity Association's
complete list. There are also self-catering holiday cottages to rent, like
Berghaven (PO Box 192; tel 036 468 1212), caravan parks and
holiday farms.

Cathedral Peak
Reached via Winterton, the two-star Cathedral Peak Hotel (PO Winter-
ton; tel 488188) is set in superb scenery with facilities to match.
There is also a camp site four km away. One worthwhile hike is to the
Sebeyeni caves to see a well-preserved 'gallery' of Bushman
paintings.

The Cathkin Valley: Cathkin Peak and Champagne Castle
The flat-topped Cathkin Peak of 3,149 m (10,234 ft) is a landmark
from way off as you approach the resorts of the Cathkin valley on the
R600 from Winterton – not the same road as goes to Cathedral Peak –
although Champagne Castle south of it is higher at 3,371 m (10,955
ft). Cathkin acquired its name from a Scottish settler longing for his
hometown, while Champagne Castle allegedly commemorates a
bottle of champagne lost by an explorer – obviously a well-heeled one
in all senses. The Sterkspruit river flows down the valley, with a spectacular waterfall up near the Forestry Station and there are delightful
walks in the fern forest of the Cathkin Forest reserve. On the way up to
the resorts, roughly 25 km (16 miles) from Winterton you could
pause to see the Mount Memory Sanctuary containing the Memorable Order of Tin Hats (MOTH) national shrine, honouring the dead of
the two world wars.

Hotels
Our choice of the hotels – there are others – starts with the well-known
Cayley Lodge (PO Box 241; Winterton; tel 468 1222). It is in its own

estate with a lake, organises forest and mountain walks, and has superb views. Natal people like The Nest (Private Bag X14; tel 468 1068), which has a fine bowling green and was recently renovated. It is about 20 km (12 miles) from Winterton. Past it you reach the Champagne Sports Resort (Private Bag X9; tel 468 1000) a time-share with tennis courts and some hotel accommodation. Then a kilometre beyond the Mount Memory shrine the road divides, with the right fork going to Cathkin Park and the left roughly following the course of the Sterkspruit to Champagne Castle.

Both the Cathkin Park (Private Bag X12; tel 468 1091) and the Champagne Castle (Private Bag X8; tel 468 1063) are well known, family hotels, the latter with accommodation in thatched cottages and rondavels. Before reaching it you pass the turn-off to the far larger and more glossily modern Drakensberg Sun (PO Box 335; tel 468 1000).

Giant's Castle Game Reserve

The Drakensberg's largest reserve is the 34,600 ha (135 sq miles) Giant's Castle Game Reserve, 70 km (43 miles) from Estcourt on a good road. Dominated by the escarpment and the Giant's Castle Peak 3,280 m (10,660 ft), it is mainly a grassland plateau intersected by many streams and valleys, where myriad sub-alpine wildflowers bloom in Spring. Gradually enlarged since its foundation back in 1903 – the reserve is one of Africa's oldest – it has, in an enthusiast's phrase, 'enough to keep one interested for a month'. Eagles and occasional lammergeyers circle overhead and malachite kingfishers perch attentively by the streams, while game includes around 600 eland, as well as blesbok, red hartebeest, mountain reedbuck, duiker, baboons and an occasional leopard. The fishing is excellent.

Bushman Life
Bushman paintings are a feature of the park, with around 5,000 visible in caves and under rock overhangs. The Main Caves are now a museum, with a tableau of Bushman life. Small communities of these San people hunted here for countless centuries, in particular following the herds of eland, until 19th century white settlers first forced them up here even in the cold of winter and then hunted them down because of their cattle raiding.

A Rebellion
In 1873 another local tribe's Chief named Langalibalele rebelled against colonial taxes. A British punitive expedition pursued him up the Bushman's river, but was defeated at the pass, now named after the chief, while the peaks on either side commemorate the four British and one African soldiers killed there.

Pony Treks
You can hire ponies for guided riding trails, which last two to four days, camping out. Book in advance with the Parks Board in Pieter-maritzburg. Half day trails can be arranged with the Camp Superinten-dent at Hillside Camp (see below), where the rides start.

Accommodation
The Main Camp consists of attractive two-to five-bedded thatched bungalows, with bathrooms, as well as self-contained cottages with kitchens. They are all in beautiful surroundings. Note that there is no shop, so bring plenty of your own food and drink, though at Main Camp permanent staff do the cooking and clearing up. The electricity is only on from 1630 to 2230, so you need a torch. Hillside, 30 km (19 miles) away in the north east of the reserve, is a camp site with an ablution block. There are various mountain huts for climbers, plus the large Injasuti hutted camp (where you do your own cooking) in the north. Injasuti is reached by a 30 km gravel road signed off the Loskop to Bergville road.

Kamberg, Loteni and Vergelegen Nature Reserves

The smaller Kamberg Nature Reserve of eight sq miles is situated among the Drakensberg foothills, by the Mooi River, with 13 km (8 miles) of trout fishing. The reserve is now the main home of the white Zulu Royal cattle – once numerous and from whose hides the shields

Mountaineering in the Drakensberg

of the Royal Regiments were made – and of reedbuck, eland, duiker and oribi. It can be reached either from Rosetta or from the road between Nottingham Road and Himeville, which also gives access to the Loteni Nature Reserve, 35 km (22 miles) from Himeville and the Vergelegen Reserve on the Umkomaas river beyond it. The wildlife in these is similar to that of Giant's Castle and the scenery in the river valleys is magnificent. All three have self-catering hutted camps. Hotels convenient for this area are described under 'Pietermaritzburg to Mooi River' further on.

Himeville

Postal code 4585. Telephone code 033.

This village is best known for its local trout fishing and for expeditions up the Sani Pass and into Lesotho. It has a Museum, a very small Nature Reserve, where the trout lake attracts wildfowl and the picnic site has toilets, and a pleasant, rustic two-star country hotel called the Himeville (PO Himeville; tel 702 1305), which makes a good lunch stop. Trout is the local speciality.

Routes Up

If you want to follow a little known route up here from Durban, drive via Richmond and the beautiful Byrne valley to the R617 and then through Underberg to Himeville, though this means missing the panoramic viewpoint on the Hella-Hella Pass. The very reasonably priced, one-star, Oaks at Byrne Hotel (PO Box 95, Richmond 3780; tel 03322 2324) is a possible stop in the Byrne valley.

Expeditions

Apart from the Sani Pass, other expeditions from the village are to the Coleford Nature Reserve to the south; to the Reichnau Mission on the Pholela river, with its blacksmith shop and Museum; and to Bushman's Nek, up in the mountains, where there is a resort hotel of the same name (PO Box X137 Underberg 4590; tel 033 701 1460).

The Sani Pass

This spectacular pass carries the only road from Natal into Lesotho and climbs 610 m (2,000 ft) in a mere three km up a series of tortuous and genuinely breathtaking hairpin bends, finishing 2,700 m (9,000 ft) above sea level. It seems incredible that the road can reach the top at all. People go up by jeep to enjoy the fabulous views and exhilarating air: and occasionally to ski, though it can be hazardous.

Remember to take your passport and warm clothes, ideally a tracksuit. If possible avoid exposing your own vehicle to the appalling road, even if you have got the necessary 4WD, without which the authorities will not let you through. At the top, perched almost on the cliff edge, is a mountain chalet. Though on the Lesotho side, it is bookable in Himeville through the Mokhotlong Transport Co (PO Box 12, Himeville; tel 702 1615), which runs 4WD trips up the pass. It can also be booked through the Sani Pass Hotel. Vehicles leave from Giants Cup Motors, one km from the Sani Pass Hotel. For a description of the chalet and what lies beyond read the Lesotho chapter.

Hotels
Many people never go further than the luxurious three-star Sani Pass Hotel (PO Box 44; tel 701 1435). Situated below the pass, the hotel is a sizeable complex of cottages and buildings, noted for its cuisine. Facilities include squash, tennis, swimming, horseriding, golf, fine walks marked by painted signs on rocks, and an airstrip. Note that 'smart-casual' dress is required in the evenings. Visitors can be met off the SARtravel bus from Durban at Himeville, as can guests at the 860 acre Drakensburg Gardens Golf & Leisure Resort, another popular holiday centre, with similar facilities, in the hills above Underberg (Bookings PO Box 10305, Marine Parade 4056; tel 031 374222).

Youth Hostel
The Sani Pass Youth Hostel (tel 033 7021615) is by the Hamakhakhe store about 16 km (10 miles) up the Sani Pass road beyond Himeville. A daily bus goes to it from the Durban Beach Youth Hostels.

Back Down to Pietermaritzburg
From Underberg you can drive via Bulwer down to Pietermaritzburg on the main R617 road, through country where many of the Africans cut fine figures riding their horses and down the glorious deep valley of the Umkomaas River. South of Bulwer are the Ixopo hills, the backdrop to Alan Paton's novel 'Cry the Beloved Country' about the tribulations of a black priest who travelled to Johannesburg to find his wayward sister.

Festival of First Fruits
Near Elandskop, at Majunza location, there is an annual Festival of First Fruits, (or harvest) at the time of the new moon, towards the end of March, with ceremonial African dancing at sunset.

The Historic Natal Midlands

Pietermaritzburg

Postal code 3200. Telephone code 0331. Tourist Info 451348.

The long-time capital of Natal, Pietermaritzburg, was founded in 1838 by Voortrekkers looking for a new home after the Battle of Blood River, and is named after Piet Retief and Gerrit Maritz. For a scant five years it was the capital of the Republic of Natalia, until in 1843 British troops took it over, built Fort Napier and made it the administrative centre of their colony. It is a pleasant Victorian city, given a colonial atmosphere by its many public buildings, full of parks and gardens and small compared with Durban, only 80 km (50 miles) away down the N3. Although at an altitude of 610 m (2,000 ft), Pietermaritzburg can get hot and sticky in summer, at other times it has a wonderful climate.

Information

The Pietermaritzburg Publicity Association (PO Box 25; tel 451348/9) is in Publicity House on Commercial Road and has an audio-visual centre for visitors. This is worth a visit, since the Association's material covers a huge area, including the Drakensberg, the battlefields of the north and the great Zululand game reserves. Maps cover local City and Green Belt walking trails.

Hotels

Frankly, there are few hotels worth staying at. The Imperial at 224 Loop Street (PO Box 140; tel 426551) and the Karos Capital Towers on Commercial Street (PO Box 198; tel 452857) are both three-star. The YMCA is on Commercial Road (tel 428106).

Things to Do and See

In the shops you can get just about anything a visitor needs. Every May a large open-air art exhibition is staged in Alexandra Park. Notable buildings are numerous. Pre-eminent among them historically is the simple, thick-walled Church of the Vow, built by the Voortrekkers to commemorate the victory at Blood River. It is at the corner of Church and Boshoff Streets. After being subjected to many lay uses – including being a store and school – it is now a Museum. Three blocks away at 333 Boom Street stands the oldest surviving Voortrekker house. British settler life is illuminated in the Macrorie House Museum, a small verandahed house in Pine Street, close to the Railway Station. By contrast the Natal Museum (a 'must' for its historical exhibits), Fort Napier, the Supreme Court and the City Hall are massive edifices.

Gardens

The city is noted for its annual Azalea Festival in early September and there are many parks. Alexandra Park, named after Princess Alexandra of Denmark in 1863, has rock gardens and a Chinese Pavilion and is close to the city centre. The Botanic Gardens display flowering trees and shrubs, especially azaleas, in the Exotic Garden; while there are indigenous plants in another section.

Queen Elizabeth Park and Natal Lion Park

Pietermaritzburg is also the headquarters of the Natal Parks Board, whose offices are at Queen Elizabeth Park Nature Reserve, 8 km (5 miles) north-west of the city on the way to Howick. This is particularly notable for its flora and has quite a few tame buck and a couple of rhino in an enclosure. The Parks Board publishes wildlife drawings that are well worth buying to have framed. The small lion park is 16 km (10 miles) from the city, off the main road to Durban.

Sports, Excursions and the Midlands Meander

Tennis, squash, watersports at the Midmar Public Resort and racing at Scottsville, organised by the Turf Club, are among recreations available. The 'Midlands Meander' is an arts and crafts route of studios hotels and guest farms extending to Mooi River. You can get a map of it from the Publicity Association.

One favourite excursion is to the Albert Falls Public Resort and Nature Reserve 22 km (14 miles) out on the Greytown road. The horseshoe-shaped falls are at their best in the rainy season of December to February. Greytown's Museum is devoted to the 19th century goldrush in the Tugela valley. At Wartburg, established by German pioneers, there is an attractive and very reasonably priced three-star inn called the Wartburger Hof, built in alpine style at 51 Noordsberg Road (tel 033 503 1482). It is not far from the Karkloof Falls (also accessible from Howick), while 25 km from Pietermaritzburg is the small attractive, Game Valley Lodge (PO Box 13010 Cascades 3202; tel 03393 787). Set in a lovely valley, well stocked with buffalo, antelopes and birds, it is signed off the Greytown road. Walks culminate at the Karkloof Falls and day visitors are welcome to drive around.

Pietermaritzburg to Mooi River

Diversions off the N3 take you to nature reserves and a few fine country hotels as you drive inland. The first, on a side road en route to Howick, is the timbered three-star Hilton Hotel (PO Box 35, Hilton 3245; tel 0331 33311), a popular stopping place.

KwaZulu-Natal

Howick Falls
According to the National Geographic Magazine, the Howick district has the second healthiest climate in the world (the most healthy is in Australia). The Howick Falls cascading down 110 m (365 ft) are a national monument. The Midmar Public Resort, on the Umgeni River 19 km (12 miles) west of Howick, is a much-frequented centre for yachting and fishing, with a nature reserve, an open-air museum and an historical village depicting early life in Natal.

Country Hotels
The fine scenery and climate of this area, plus easy access to the Drakensberg, have nurtured several remarkable country hotels. First, if you take the lesser R103 road from Howick to Mooi River, you will find the thatched complex of Granny Mouse's Country House (PO Box 22, Balgowan 3275; tel 03324 4071), a three-star delight overlooking the Lions river near Balgowan. Four-poster beds, three restaurants and a fine cellar complete the rustic luxury of this small hotel.

Then, further on near Nottingham Road (named after the Nottinghamshire Regiment) is another thatched landmark, the larger Rawdon's Hotel in the Old Main Road (three-star; PO Box 7, Nottingham Road 3280; tel 0333 36044). Rawdon's has its own trout lake, while other sports are available.

Finally, up on the downs past Rosetta, is the Hartford Country House, set in a 1,000 acre estate and once the home of Natal's first Prime Minister, Sir Frederick Moore. Well-restored, and furnished with Victoriana, this also offers country sporting activities (three-star; PO Box 31, Mooi River 3300; tel 0333 31081).

Mooi River to Ladysmith

Estcourt is an industrial town and trading centre for this agricultural district, with a small nature reserve around the Wagendrif Dam. North of the town is the Bloukrans Monument, a memorial to the Voortrekkers killed here in the lead-up to the Blood River battle in 1838 (see Historic Battlefields article). Here too, you are coming into the scenes of the Boer War's most dramatic incidents.

The Anglo-Boer Wars
The reason why this part of Natal featured so conspicuously in the fighting of both the seldom-remembered First Boer war of 1880-82 and the 1899-1902 battles is simple, though not obvious today. In those days Natal's territory tapered to a wedge inland, hemmed in by

the Orange Free State to the west and the upper Buffalo river border of the Boer South African Republic to the east. Dundee and Newcastle were only just inside Natal – and at Newcastle the colony was barely 50 km (31 miles) wide. So the line of road and rail up from Durban through Ladysmith was crucial to the British generals, and an immediate target for the Boers. The first present-day reminder of this is between Frere and Chieveley, where the Armoured Train memorial commemorates the young Winston Churchill, then a war reporter, being taken prisoner in a Boer ambush (he subsequently escaped). The town of Colenso was used by the British army as a base during attempts to lift the siege of Ladysmith.

Ladysmith

Postal code 3370. Telephone code 0361. Tourist Info 22992.
Ladysmith is emphatically worth a visit. Originally a transport riders' camp and now growing industrially, it owes its name to Juana, the Spanish beauty married to Sir Harry Smith. The town centre retains many of the pleasant old Victorian houses of the last century. However the town's fame derives from its 118 day siege during the Anglo-Boer War from November 2, 1899 until February 28, 1900, although the excitement in Britain over the relief of Ladysmith did not quite equal the Mafeking celebrations. Hotels include the colonial-style Royal at 90 Murchison Street (three-star; tel 22167), which has a pool and air-conditioning, though if you have a car the Andrews Motel (PO Box 1035; tel 26908) out on the Durban road is recommended.

The Siege
The war had only begun on October 12 and the Boers were determined to cut the British line of communications between their Dundee garrison and Ladysmith. The British Commander-in-Chief, Lt General Sir George White, had his headquarters at Ladysmith and held out despite lack of water and the attentions of a siege gun called Long Tom, mounted on the hills above by the Boers. An Indian was employed to stand on an adjacent part of the hill and wave a flag every time Long Tom was fired so that residents could take cover – there were no high velocity shells in those days.

Places of Interest
The Museum contains interesting relics and so does the Town Hall. At All Saints Church there are memorials to the British who fell, as there are at battle sites in the surrounding hills. Caesar's Camp and Wagon Hill are within walking distance of the town, others like Lombards Kop are further, while Spioenkop is out to the west by a nature reserve of

the same name. You can get more details from the Publicity Association in the Town hall.

Northern Natal Battlefields Route

The area north east of Ladysmith – and indeed up to Newcastle – is studded with names that are part of both Afrikaner and British folk history. The Anglo-Boer war actions centred here for the reason already described. Those of the Voortrekkers and the British against the Zulus arose because the Natal settlers had moved into territory which the Zulus under Shaka had earlier devastated, emptying them of Bantu in the migrations called the *Difaquane.* Some historians reckon a million were killed. Although Shaka welcomed the whites, his successors attacked them: and eventually Boer commandos and British troops in their turn pursued the Zulu *impis* across the traditional boundaries of Zululand, which were the Buffalo and Tugela rivers east of Ladysmith and Dundee. Recent interest in these historical events prompted the inauguration in 1990 of an official 'Northern Natal Battlefields Route'. The route starts at Dundee and you can find out about it at the notable Talana Museum, at the Talana battlefield site just outside the town. Our article about the wars by a military historian describes the main events, plus a simple map. All the local Publicity Associations provide maps.

Accommodation
The battlefields are all in the country east of Dundee, a coal mining centre, which has three hotels, including the two-star El Mpati (PO Box 15 Dundee 3000; tel 0341 21155) Fugitives Drift Lodge. However, if you want to be where the action was, try for on David Rattray's farm, West Kirkby (PO Rorke's Drift 3016; tel 03425 843), which is at Fugitives Drift on the Buffalo river. He knows all the sites and has lectured on them at the Royal Geographical Society in London. He and his wife feed their guests well.

Rorke's Drift Crafts
The Art and Craft Centre run by Swedish missionaries of the Lutheran Church at Rorke's Drift produces widely-acclaimed hand-printed fabrics and pottery.

Majuba
Further north, near Volksrust, is the extraordinary conical mountain Majuba, where the British General, Sir George Colley, fell. And at the foot of the mountain is another national monument, O'Neill's Cottage,

where the agreement to end the first Boer War was signed in 1882, a piece of history that is often forgotten.

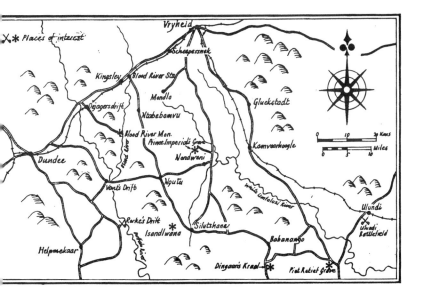

Bronze Replica Wagons of the Blood River Laager

Historic Natal Battlefields

Compiled with the assistance of Major Philip James

From the 1838 battle of Blood River, through the Zulu War of 1879 and the first Boer War of 1880-2, to the end of the Boer War in 1902, the greatest number of significant battles on South African soil took place in northern Natal. These battlefields all lay within a small stretch of rolling hills and stony veld between the Ladysmith to Newcastle road and the Zulu capital of Ulundi. Today it is farmland, attractively interspersed with small mountains, rock kopjes and rivers. Then it was a lot tougher, whether for Voortrekkers with their ox-wagons, Zulu warriors, or red coated British infantry with white helmets and muskets. A map is on page 154.

The Voortrekkers and Blood River, 1838

The Boer farmers who had trekked up from the Cape in 1834-36 split into two groups. Piet Retief's group crossed the Drakensberg towards Natal and were allotted land by Dingaan, King of the Zulus, successor to Shaka. But in February 1838 he and a party of trekkers were murdered near Mgungundlovu (north of Melmoth) at the end of a second visit to the King. Shortly afterwards Zulu *impis*, ranging west against Retief's followers and their families, killed and disembowelled 200 of the trekkers and 281 of their servants, many at Bloukrans (near Frere), though they were driven off from the settlement of Saailaager (close to Estcourt). The trekkers' situation remained insecure until in November 1838 Andries Pretorius organised a Commando to avenge their losses.

Pretorius' Commando
Known as the Wencommando, this group's strength was about 464 whites, including three English settlers, 123 Port Natal blacks, 64 wagons, some 650 oxen and 750 horses with 100 black servants and grooms. There was no standard firearm; each man provided his own. Most of the Voortrekkers had two muskets – muzzleloaders with a range of up to 250 m – and there were three cannon. At night they formed their wagons into a defensive circle, with fences between the wheels, and gathered the entire force and its mounts inside. Two moveable wagons created a 'gate' for forays out.

The Vow
Pretorius pursued the Zulus up past the present day towns of Ladysmith, Waschbank and Dundee. On December 9 the commando vowed that if God helped them defeat the Zulus, they would forever celebrate that day as a Sabbath, the Day of the Covenant. They reached the Ncome river on December 15, where they assembled the wagons in an oval laager, in the angle between the river and a deep donga. In those days the river banks were covered in reeds, with a marsh and several pools nearby.

The Battle
The Zulu regiments were later estimated to have numbered 15,000. Their warriors fought with a stabbing assegai, which had a long blade and short shaft, one or two throwing assegais, a knobkerry and an oval hide shield about 120 cm long.

Early on the Sunday morning they attacked, charging repeatedly for three hours against the gunfire with extraordinary courage and suffering heavy casualties. Around 1100 hours the attacks faltered. Pretorius charged out and drove a wedge through the Zulu's main force (the chest). As many as 1,000 Zulus were shot after leaping into the river to escape and the water ran red with blood. Altogether 3,000 Zulus were killed for only three Boers wounded; one being Pretorius himself, when he rode out in pursuit of the defeated *impis*. Dingaan was finally defeated in 1840. The trekkers built their simple Church of the Vow at Pietermaritzburg and December 16 has remained a day of national thanksgiving for Afrikaners.

The Blood River site is reached by the R33 north east from Dundee. After 27 km turn right on to a dirt road and go another 21 km to a stone ox-wagon monument. There is a diorama, pamphlets are available, and Pretorius' laager has been recreated with true-size bronze wagons.

The Anglo-Zulu war of 1879

At the end of 1878 the British sent an ultimatum to King Cetshwayo making nine demands, including the complete disbandment of the Zulu army. With very little delay the British forces then moved against this numerically far stronger Zulu force, which now had some firearms as well as assegais.

Islandhwana

Lt General Lord Chelmsford sent five columns from different directions towards Ulundi. Number Three crossed the Buffalo river into Zululand at Rorke's Drift, where there was a Swedish Mission Hospital, on January 11/12, 1879. The column quickly defeated the local Chief Sihayo and advanced to Isandhlwana, where the 24th Regiment established a camp of about 1,000 men commanded by Colonel Pulleine, close to the high rocks of the Islandhwana hill and Black's kopje.

The natural ford at Rorke's Drift led directly into the heart of Zululand – there were no good river crossings further south – and the Zulus had marched from Ulundi anticipating this route. Lord Chelmsford was unaware that 23,000 of them were in hiding beyond the Nqutu hills only five miles to the north. On January 21 cavalry reconnaissance discovered some 1,500 to the east. Chelmsford supposed this was the main force, ordered an attack, and led half his men east before dawn on January 22. Reinforcements under Colonel Durnford also went east.

Within a short time the main Zulu regiments attacked the camp. No trenches had been dug because of the hard soil. The British defensive line was L-shaped, with one end on the hill, but ill-organised (afterwards much of the ammunition would be found in unopened boxes). Durnford's force attempted to return but was pinned down. Then the Natal Native Companies, who held the crucial corner of the L, broke and fled. By 1400 hours it was all over; 858 British troops and 471 native troops had been killed, including Colonels Pulleine and Durnford. There were only 74 survivors. Estimates of Zulu losses ranged from 1,000 to 3,000, but it was still a crushing defeat for the British. Cairns now mark where the various companies of the regiment formed squares and were cut down.

Fugitive's Drift

The few British who escaped Islandhwana could not follow the road they had made to Rorke's Drift, since it was threatened by the Zulus. Instead they struggled direct across the swampy Impete hill to a lesser drift on the Buffalo river. Only 24 Europeans escaped and the graves of those who fell mark the route. Two displayed amazing heroism. Lieutenant Melville had been ordered to save the 24th Regiment's Queen's Colour, the standard symbolic of its honour. But the river was in spate and his horse slipped, throwing him into the water. Lt Coghill, who was wounded but had crossed successfully, rode back to help him. Although both officers struggled ashore, they were overtaken and killed. Ten days later a patrol buried their bodies – a cairn marks the spot – and recovered the Queen's Colour from the river. Both officers were posthumously awarded the Victoria Cross.

Rorke's Drift

Meanwhile part of the Zulu force had continued towards Rorke's Drift. At the Mission Station 128 soldiers, 28 of whom were under treatment in the hospital, were commanded by Lt Chard. News of the Islandhwana massacre reached him at 1515 hours. The Mission consisted of a thatched hospital building, a store room and a small stone kraal, roughly in a line. Chard immediately built four foot walls of mealie bags, supplemented by biscuit boxes, thus forming a defensive rectangle, with a mealie bag redoubt by the kraal. The Undi Corps of 3,000 Zulus attacked at about 1630 hours from the south, but were beaten off. Then they approached from the north west and fired the hospital thatch. Chard's men evacuated the sick through the windows. After dark the store was lost, but the defenders held the tiny area of the redoubt and the kraal. Around 0400 hours the Zulus withdrew, having lost some 400 dead. The defenders lost 15 killed and 12 wounded. Both officers and nine soldiers were awarded the Victoria Cross, the most ever won in a single action. Rorke's Drift is reached by a gravel road off the R68. Approaching from Dundee it is before the Buffalo river and 17 km after the turn-off.

Battle of Ulundi

After the disaster, Lord Chelmsford withdrew to Dundee, re-grouped and re-inforced his column. He advanced cautiously and was met by a 20,000 strong Zulu army in the valley of the White Umfolozi river, just east of Ulundi. This time Chelmsford formed a vast defensive hollow square, which the Zulus failed to penetrate. British lancers then charged and routed them. The Zulus lost 1,500 dead and were completely defeated. The battlefield is just south of the R66 road, close to Ulundi. Nearby at Ondini King Cetshwayo's kraal has been restored.

The Prince Imperial

A sad footnote to this campaign was the death of the Prince Imperial of France, last of the Napoleons. Educated in England, he had persuaded Chelmsford to allow him to serve as a lieutenant in the hope of gaining some military glory. He was killed when a small scouting party was surprised by Zulus on June 1, 1879 during the advance on Ulundi. The site where he was killed, marked by a monument, can be reached by a gravel road south from Vryheid, or via Nqutu from Dundee. From the turn-off seven km of rough road takes you to the Jojosi river. The monument is on the hillside across the (wadeable) river.

Northern KwaZulu-Natal

The coastal region of northern KwaZulu-Natal is a country of green hills, studded with beehive-shaped native huts. It stretches to the borders of Swaziland and Mozambique and is the ancestral home of the Zulus. In the twentieth century, Zululand's 20,425 sq miles have also become famous for the wildlife in its reserves, which were first set aside for conservation in 1895. So there is a double incentive to head up the coast from Durban and cross the historic boundary of the Tugela river into a quite different part of the province.

If you have any of the traditional preconceived ideas about Africa, this where you will find them justified. It is all feature-film material – long beaches, sub-tropical vegetation, wildlife and the Zulus themselves, tall handsome men, quite often decked out in their magnificently beaded tribal dress. Some of the dirt roads can be the making of travellers' tales, too. Despite an energetic programme of tarmacing there remain many gravel roads that can be impassable after heavy rains. Speeding happily up the N2 freeway this is something you easily forget, so consult the AA before you set out. What is more, alas, you have to reckon on everywhere north of the Tugela being malarial, so start taking prophylactics before you go. There are numerous coach tours to Zululand and the game reserves from Durban.

Historic Zululand

A few miles before the Tugela river bridge on the N2 you pass Stanger, once a haunt of ivory hunters and now surrounded by green sugar estates. There is a memorial to Shaka, the Zulu king, on the site of his great kraal, Duzuka – which means Labyrinth – where he lived with his regiments and his concubines and where he was finally assassinated by Dingaan. His career began about 1818 and under his cruel but militarily brilliant dictatorship the Zulus were welded into a nation. His warriors wore leopard skins and ostrich feather crests and could not marry until they had killed. Every *kraal* was effectively an army camp, until the British finally broke the Zulu power at Ulundi in 1879. The bloodshed and the bravery of the Zulu Wars seem a far cry from the women now working happily in the mealie fields, while their men tend cattle in the hills; although as recent tribal violence has shown the Zulus national pride is never far below the surface.

Much of the Tugela basin was developed as part of the plan under which KwaZulu became self-governing in the 1980s, before it amalgamed with Natal in 1994. The Zulus traditional capital is Ulundi, 160 km (100 miles) from Durban, inland from Eshowe. You should go in that direction, even if you only make a deviation to loop inland on the R68 at Gingindlovu and regain the N2 at Empangeni. There is a lot to see, though you may have to search for some of it. In the Zulu wars, by the way, British soldiers turned the name Gingindlovu into 'Gin, gin I love you.' There cannot have been much to laugh about in fighting the *impis* and it had been Cetshwayo's military Kraal.

Eshowe *Postal code 3815. Telephone code 0354. Tourist Info 74079.*
Eshowe, 150 km (93 miles) from Durban, is in the hills 500 m (1,700 ft) above sea level and derives its name from the gentle sighing of the wind in the forests that surround it. Part of the forests form a nature reserve. The area is steeped in violent Zulu history and Fort Nongqayo is a museum. However there is little point in basing yourself at Eshowe's one hotel; better to rough it slightly at a *kraal* lodge out in the hills where the history was made.

Shakaland
In fact you do not rough it at Shakaland (PO Box 103 Eshowe; tel 03546 912), 14 km (9 miles) north of Eshowe, signed off the R68. This is a well-organised, rather expensive fake. The emphasis is on learning about the Zulus in an understanding way, which is why a visit is worthwhile. The comfortable guest cottages adjoin a large *kraal,* which was meticulously constructed in the mid-1980s for the film 'Chaka the Zulu' starring Edward Fox. Lunches include talks on Zulu tribal society. Dinners are preceded by lectures, feature Zulu dishes and are followed by tribal dancing. If staying overnight you must arrive by 1530 for the full programme. The staff are knowledgeable and can point you towards all the significant sites. Shaka's main military *kraal,* KwaBulawayo, is 20 km (12 miles) away, for example. They can also arrange a two-day visit to a genuine *kraal,* which is what the less costly rival, nearby is anyway.

Kwaphekitunga Kraal
Kwaphekitunga Kraal (tel 03546 644) houses a Zulu community, making its living from handicrafts, where 40 guests can be accommodated in 'beehive' huts. You sleep on mats on the huts' earth floors, though there are 'mod cons'. You may well marvel at how Africans throughout the continent manage to keep themselves and their clothes so clean when having to fetch water from streams. The *kraal* is 16 km (10 miles) from Eshowe, off the R68.

To tour Dingaan and Cetshwayo's homelands you will have to travel further via Melmoth up the R68 (which briefly joins the R34 at Nkwalini). Dingaan's *Kraal* is south of Babanango and Cetshwayo's near Ulundi. You are now in the area already described under Natal Midlands.

KwaZulu-Natal

Empangeni and Richards Bay
Concluding our diversion inland the R34 going east from Nkwalini takes you back to the N2 at Empangeni, Zululand's largest town, a commercial centre for sugar growing and home of the University of Zululand. A short way away on the coast is Richards Bay, a port and industrial centre. There are good beaches, protected against sharks, but hardly worth coming this far for.

Beyond Empangeni you come into the region of game reserves, and game farms, hot arid woodland and scrubs, and untarmaced side roads: a dream if you like the bush, to be driven past if you don't. The N2 road strikes up through it to Johannesburg, along the Swaziland frontier.

Umfolozi and Hluhluwe Game Reserves

West of the N2 are two magnificent game reserves, Umfolozi and Hluhluwe, famous for their rhino and where elephant have been reintroduced: they had been shot out in the 1880s. The reserves are linked by a 'corridor' for the game to move along, which effectively makes the two total 90,000 ha (352 sq miles), though the R618 road runs between them, providing access to both. Together with St Lucia they were proclaimed in 1895 and are the oldest reserves in Africa. Thick bush has encroached on the grassland, so you may encounter controlled fires that check this process and improve the game viewing.

Accommodation
Both reserves are open all year round and the Parks Board publishes a joint booklet. Accommodation and trails are bookable through the Board (PO Box 662, Pietermaritzburg, 3200; tel 0331 471981). The speed limit is 40km/hr, though even that is too fast for spotting game easily. If you are not staying in the self-catering camps (where servants are available) then the nearest hotels are in Mtubatuba, while the more luxurious Zululand Lodge, further north, is described below. You definitely need a local base for at least two nights if you are going to get value from this trip. Forget the one-day tours from Durban.

Umfolozi Game Reserve
The larger Umfolozi Reserve is primarily a sanctuary for the largest herd of 'white' rhino in Africa, from which animals have been translocated to the Kruger Park, the Addo Park in the Cape, to Kenya, Zimbabwe and to zoos in London, New York and Germany. One of the Kenya shipments in the apartheid era produced what must be wildlife conservation's most ludicrous episode. The rhino were deported for having racialist South African origins. They are, of course, not coloured white; the word comes from the Dutch 'weit' meaning

broad, or square lipped. Other game include black rhino, leopard, buffalo and various antelope. The reserve is 270 km (169 miles) from Durban by road. Allegedly, poaching of the rhinos here has already begun; and these sanctuaries are where Africa's last big rhino populations survive.

A feature of Umfolozi are its self-guided walks and the hiking trails led by game rangers into areas where cars are not allowed. Each trail party consists of three to six people, providing their own food, though sleeping bags, tents, pots and cutlery are supplied.

Hluhluwe Game Reserve
Hluhluwe, which is pronounced 'Shlushshloowy', derivesits name from the Zulu word for the kind of monkey rope which grows by the river. It is 290 km (182 miles) from Durban via Mtubatuba. There is also an access road further up the N2 near Hlulhuwe village. which links the reserve to the False Bay Park. Hluhluwe has around 390 white rhino and 70 black, plus elephant, lion, leopard and cheetah, so you are no longer allowed to leave your car. Other game includes buffalo, zebra, brindled gnu, kudu, impala, bushbuck, waterbuck, steenbuck, reedbuck, duiker, giraffe, warthog, bush pig, leopard and baboon. Among the numerous birds are marabou stork, vultures, bateleur eagles, crested guineafowl, quail, sunbirds, fish eagles and ground hornbill.

The reserve's 89 sq miles consist of undulating bush, rising to 610 m (2,000 ft) above sea level, with a network of gravel roads. Game viewing is considered best on the northern loop roads and in the extreme south. Certainly entering by the northern Memorial Gate and idling down around the Hluhluwe river we saw plenty, including elephant. There are cottages and rondavels. Petrol is available. You could make a circuit by entering at Memorial and leaving via Gunjaneni in the south: or vice versa, if you're staying outside the reserve.

Zululand Safari Lodge
Between Hluhluwe's Memorial Gate and the N2 is the private 3,000 acre Ubizane Game Reserve, centred on the three-star Zululand Safari Lodge (bookings Southern Sun or PO Box 16, Hluhluwe 3690; tel 3562 63/64). A bare-breasted Zulu maiden greets you with a welcome drink, the thatched rondavel rooms are air-conditioned and the food is excellent. Game viewing drives, riding and walking trails and hunting are available in Ubizane, while the lodge is only 18 km (11 miles) from the False Bay Park.

The Greater St Lucia Wetland Park

East of the N2 road is one of the largest conservation schemes ever dreamt up in Africa. This is the Natal Parks Board's 289,376 ha (700,000 acre) wetland park stretching from St Lucia right up to the Lubombo mountains and incorporating the existing St Lucia complex, plus Mkuzi further north, Sodwana Bay, the Sibaya lakes, State forests and much of the land contained in this extended triangle, to which lion and elephant are being re-introduced. Five distinct eco-systems are protected, from sea and inland estuary to thorn bush. Dept of Nature Conservation contributed land and the park is being put forward (1995) to the International Union for the Conservation of Nature as a World Heritage Site. It may eventually link with the Maputo Elephant Reserve in Mozambique. Meanwhile it continues trying to buy out farmers and resolving legal disputes over the Richards Bay Mining Co's rights to extract rutile for the St Lucia dunes; to which conservationists are bitterly opposed. The park may eventually include quite a number of private game reserves, game farms and biosphere reserves adjacent to it.

St Lucia Game Reserve

From Mtubatuba it is a pleasant 25 km (16 miles) drive to the small resort of St Lucia on the estuary leading to the vast water wilderness of Lake St Lucia, the largest inland lake in South Africa. The lake and its perimeter form the 1,903 sq mile St Lucia Game Reserve, which extends some 72 km (45 miles) north from the estuary and was created to protect its hippos. They and crocodile abound, while there are pangolin, and red duiker and antelope on land. Birds of 367 species have been identified, a third of them waterbirds, including both pink-backed and white pelicans, goliath herons, white-bellied korhaan, saddlebill and spoonbill. The whole area is a fishing paradise, both in the lakes and the sea. However, to enjoy St Lucia you need to be a water wilderness emthusiast and willing to book months in advance. Swimming is not safe due to crocodiles and sharks.

The Lake System

The series of lakes, fed by several rivers whose flow affects the Mkuzi Reserve further north, is elongated like a tadpole with its tail at the estuary and an H-shaped head. From the estuary a long channel snakes up until it widens at Catalina Bay, with hutted camps at Charters Creek and opposite Fanies Island. The seaward part of the H-shaped head is a huge closed-off wilderness area of lake and reed-fringed islands, while the join of the H takes boats through into False Bay Park, with two campsites and a road connecting with

Hluhluwe on the other side of the N2. Finally there is a motorable track up the seaward side of the lake from the resort to Cape Vidal (huts and campsite) in the Eastern Shores Nature Reserves. There is also road access to Charters Creek.

Parks Board Facilities

The self-catering camps, where bedding is provided, are bookable through the Natal Parks Board Reservations Office (PO Box 1750, Pietermaritzburg 3200; tel 0331 471961) or through the local Parks Board office in the resort (see below). The staff here are very helpful, have brochures and maps and can arrange launch tours and guided wilderness trails (April to September only). The Mkizi Trail goes up to Cape Vidal. Trails from Charters Creek spend one of their three days moving around by boat, so you see a lot of wildlife. Boats can also be hired in the resort, which is the only source of food supplies.

St Lucia Resort *Postal code 3936. Telephone code 03592. Info 590 1143.*
The resort, with its shops, banks and numerous holiday cottages is on a spit of land between the river and the sea here; complete with a lingeringly acrid smell, apparently caused by bacteria in the swamps, though we were told it is not always present. Mackenzie Street has an Information Bureau in Mnandi's clothing store and the only hotel, the Boma (tel 590 1330). The Parks Board office is in a pleasant wooded area to which this main street leads and where there is a short nature trail. The opposite direction takes you to the Crocodile Centre, camp sites and walks down to the estuary channel, sometimes almost literally heaving with hippo. On a three-hour launch trip you could see up to 200 of them. Just south of the resort is the Maphelane Nature reserve – favoured by surf anglers – with camp sites and log cabin accommodation.

The St Lucia Holiday Resort complex (PO Box 2; tel 590 1091) is one of several with holiday apartments and cottages for rent.

The Remotest Reserves

Going further north you can drive all the way to the Swaziland border and see nothing except bush as you approach the distant hump of the Lubombo Mountains; while the wildest – and hottest – corner of Natal is on the Mozambique border. You need to go prepared, but there is a lot to reward the adventurous in the little-visited game reserves up here. Mkuzi has been incorporated into the Greater St Lucia Wetland

Park, so has the huge Sodwana State Forest and the little Makasa Nature Reserve between the two. Others may be brought in too and facilities are improving, though some parts have deliberately restricted access. Thus the northern road off the N 2 to Sodwana Bay is being tarmaced, while the dirt road further south, which runs between Mkuzi and the Phinda Resource Reserve, may be closed to allow freer movement of the game that is being re-introduced.

Maputaland

The area east of the N2 around Mkuzi is known generically as Maputaland and is the scene of both the Parks Board and private game farms re-stocking with wild animals. So successful has this been that the wildlife population is now back at levels not known since 1900. Elephant have been brought from the Kruger, cheetah from Namibia, rhino from the parks. It has been an amazing effort, though some of the re-introduced animals remain wary of humans.

Mkuzi Game Reserve

Mkuzi, was originally gazetted as a game reserve back in 1912. This 246 sq km (96 sq miles) area of arid bush protects black rhino, leopard and a wealth of other animals, among them the striped Nyala antelope. Game and birds are attracted to the Nsumu pan in the south during the dry season. In the centre there is a hutted camp (bookings through the Parks Board) and three-day trails are conducted twice a month. The best game viewing is in the winter and there are over 300 bird species, including emerald spotted wood doves and the relatively rare little bittern.

Phinda Resource Reserve

This privately run 17,000 ha (42,000 acre) reserve lies just east of Mkuzi on woodland and rangeland that had been very badly managed as farms. What with a river, it contains several eco-systems and is being sensitively restored to a wilderness state. Existing game has been added to with elephant, more rhino, cheetah, wildebeeste, impala and zebra: all species that were once indigenous. Run by the Conservation Corporation, its management principles include giving both employment and facilities like a clinic to local Africans. Phinda may eventually be linked with the Wetland Park. Road access is via either the Hluhluwe turnoff the N2 (from Durban) or the Mhlosinga turn off (from Johannesburg).

There are two exceptional lodges, the elegantly Japanese inspired Forest Lodge and the Nyala Lodge (reservations PO Box 1211, Sunninghill Park 2157; tel 011 803 8421, fax 011 803 1810). The food is excellent and the whole operation is intelligently managed and guests are well looked after.

Sodwana Bay National Park

Further up the coast is the tiny Sodwana Bay National Park. If you want to see magnificent dunes and like scuba diving on coral reefs, fishing and snorkeling - then this is for you. Whales and dolphin come inshore to calve, so do huge leatherback turtles to lay eggs. There is a first-class hotel, the Sodwana Bay Lodge and Hotel resort (reservations PO Box 5478, Durban 4000; tel 031 304 5977, fax 304 8817). Though not luxurious, the lodge is well set up for divers, with a training pool, a dive shop and offer good value diving packages. It is just outside the park.

Inside the park, which has a hiking trail, the simple and cheap Sodwana Dive resort and numerous campsites can take up to 7,000 visitors. This is not only the nearest beach to Johannesburg, it is an absolute mecca for divers. Boats can be chartered for big game fishing and surf fishing is allowed, but not bottom fishing. The park exists to protect the only break in dunes that stretch 150 km from Cape Vidal to Mozambique. So there are restrictions, especially when the turtles come ashore to lay eggs just below the high water mark from late November to late January. The gravel access road past Mkuzi can be bad in the rains, but the road to Jozini, close to the N2 and the Pongolapoort Dam, is being tarred.

Lake Sibaya

The largest freshwater lake in South Africa, this haunt of hippo and fish eagles is just north of Sodwana Bay. A camp on its southern shore organises boat trips. You need a Parks Board permit; ask for details at the Sodwana Bay office.

Rocktail Bay and Kosi Bay

This whole coast is noted for big game fishing, sometimes possible from the shore. There is a lodge at Rocktail Bay (details from Wilderness Safaris in Johannesburg (tel 011 884 1458, fax 883 6255).

Kosi Bay the most northerly fishing resort. Its Nature Reserve is a lake system sanctuary for waterbirds, where mangroves and swamp figs line the shore and Zulu fishermen build reed fish traps. For camping and self-help chalets there contact the Game Warden, PO Box Mkuzi 3956.

Tembe Elephant Park

From Kosi the road directly east to Jozini and the N2 goes past the Tembe Elephant Park. This was proclaimed to save the last elephant herds in this part of Zululand, but there no day visitors facilities, though there is an overnight camp site. Adjoining Tembe on a side road is Ndumu.

Ndumu Game Reserve

Right on the Mozambique frontier, around a floodplain, Ndumu has hippos, crocodile, rhino and antelope. The abundant birdlife includes many East African species. There are a hutted camp, curio shop and reference library. Land Rover tours are available, as well as guided walks, but you ought to have 4WD yourself.

Jozini

Jozini is a small trading centre for an agricultural area irrigated by the Pongolapoort Dam, round which there is private Reserve of the Biosphere. The Pongola river supports crocodiles and hippos. Over the west of it, reached along the R69 road, is one of KwaZulu-Natal's finest and least known wildlife sanctuaries.

Itala Game Reserve

Rolling hills and cliff outcrops feature in the lush green landscape of this 29,653 ha (73,000 acre) reserve, which protects the province's only herds of tsessebe (an antelope), as well as rhino, elephant and many other species. The rivers support some 100 species of amphibians and reptiles and there are 320 species of birds. But the statistics do not convey the idyllic quality of the area. There is a hutted camp with a restaurant, three bush camps, camp sites hiking trails, and picnic sites for day visitors. Details from the Parks Board.

The Zulus

'A very remarkable people, the Zulu,' remarked the British Prime Minister, Benjamin Disraeli, on hearing of a fresh disaster in the Anglo-Zulu war of 1879, 'they defeat our Generals, they convert our Bishops, they have settled the fate of a great European dynasty.' They had indeed just killed the Prince Imperial, the last of the Napoleons, who was attached to the British army, shortly after the inflicting the defeat of Islandhwana on Lord Chelmsford. In fact King Cetshwayo was totally defeated that same year at Ulundi. But British respect for the Zulus was such that when Cetshwayo was held captive in Cape Town castle he was allowed his own apartments, wives, and servants. So who are the Zulus, and how did they achieve their fame as warriors?

The Zulus came to South Africa early in the 17th century as part of Nguni migration from inland East Africa. The Xhosa and Dlaminis (Swazis) were part of the movement and they all settled north of the Tugela river, in what is now Natal. Each Nguni clan was independent. In about 1785 Senzangakhona became chief of the abakwaZulu (people of Zulu). He had an illegitimate son, who was called Shaka.

Shaka

Shaka fused the independent Zulu chiefdoms into a single Great Kingdom, which he dominated. He achieved this through a revolutionary military doctrine – for Africans – of inducting all young Zulu men into regiments (amaButo) and giving them strict military training. His regiments were armed with white cowhide shields, throwing assegais, short stabbing assegais, and knobkerries. They learnt to move at a jogtrot and to obey orders. Their tactics were those of the pincer movement. The regiment's 'horns' attacked the enemy's flanks; then the 'chest' made a frontal assault on the centre. The discipline and ferocity were devastating. The other tribes were either annihilated or fled, in what was known as the *difaqane*, or migration. The Xhosa went south. The Swazis retreated to the mountains.

Dingaan

In 1828 Shaka was stabbed to death by two of his half-brothers, one of whom, Dingaan, took over and came into conflict with the new white settlers at Port Natal. At first relations were amicable, then in 1838 he had the Voortrekker leader, Piet Retief, murdered. This led directly to the Zulu defeat at Blood river. Dingaan was assassinated in Swaziland in 1840.

Cetshwayo

The next king, Mpande, ruled until 1872, being succeeded by Cetshwayo, who created a new Royal Kraal (as was customary) at uluNdi, meaning the 'high place'. The Anglo-Zulu war of 1879 ended with the burning of Ulundi in July and Cetshwayo's defeat; but he insisted on being taken to Britain to meet Queen Victoria, and ended back in Zululand with limited powers under the British. In 1897 Zululand became part of Natal.

Traditionally the Zulu economy is based on livestock, agriculture, and hunting. Labour is divided according to sex, with the men herding cattle and clearing the fields, and women responsible for cultivation of crops, brewing beer, making pots and carrying out all menial tasks. Meat is considered a delicacy to be eaten only on ceremonial occasions. The nutritious beer, also drunk at ceremonial occasions, is socially and ritually important. Zulu kraals are ringed by beehive-shaped huts, while kinship plays a dominant role in society.

Today's Leaders

Today there is still a hereditary ruler, King Goodwill Zwelithini, although politically Chrief Mangosuthu Buthelezi is more influential as leader of the Inkatha Freedom Party. Chief Buthelezi is the great-grandson of Cetshwayo and was born in 1928.

Zulu carver at Eshowe

Cape Dutch farmhouse

The Cape Province

Diversity of the Cape's Three Provinces

To most people 'The Cape' summons up a vision of Table Mountain towering above the city of Cape Town, of warm beaches and vineyards around whitewashed Cape Dutch homesteads. This is the historic vision. But in reality the three provinces into which the old Cape Province was divided in 1994 encompass an extraordinary diversity of landscape and peoples in a territory whose overall 240,000 sq miles is substantially larger than France.

The Western Cape is centred on the vibrant life of Cape town itself, with the adjoining winelands, but also takes in 300 km of the west coast, past beaches and fishing ports to flower-strewn Namaqualand, while eastwards it extends through the forests and resorts of the Garden Route and the ostrich farms of the Little Karoo to the Storms river.

The Eastern Cape includes numerous resorts, the historic settler country around Grahamstown and the former Transkei homeland of the Xhosa people, while the former Ciskei's capital, Bisho, is now the 'capital' of the province.

The Northern Cape is both dramatic and harsh, stretching from the diamond mining city of Kimberley inland to the wild shores of the Richtersveld and up into the sandy wilderness of the Kalahari Gemsbok Park on the Botswana border.

However, these administrative boundaries may seem artificial to visitors. The arid sheep farming country of the Great Karoo is still an identifiable region, even if split between the three provinces. So, although generally speaking our headings follow the new tourism areas, they do not run counter to commonsense.

History

In fact the Dutch started the Cape colony, not the Portuguese, even though Antonio da Saldanha gave Table Mountain its name in 1503. During the 16th century the bay became a place where ships stopped for fresh water on their way to the Far East. One of them, the 'Haarlem', foundered there in 1647 and the shipwrecked sailors grew vegetables and bartered with the Hottentots for meat. This led to a Dutch

---

Opposite: In the Swartberg, (top left). Cape Town market (top right)
                    The National Gallery on the Gardens, Cape Town (below)
Overleaf: Church at Prince Albert in the Karoo (top)
                    'Mon Bijou' in Church Street, Tulbagh (below)

expedition, commanded by Jan van Riebeeck, founding a settlement that would provide the Dutch East India Company's merchant fleet with regular supplies of fruit and vegetables and combat the dreaded seafaring ailment, scurvy.

The Dutch Colony
The first colonial governor was Simon van der Stel. The vines he planted at Constantia produced wine in 1659, and the vineyard is still doing so. In 1688 Huguenot refugees from France brought their viticultural skills to a district they named Franschoek. For another hundred years the colony expanded as Boer farmers pushed their way into the interior and also up the west coast, belatedly following an expedition sent by van der Stel to search for rumoured copper deposits in Namaqualand in 1685. The Hottentots had forced the ancient inhabitants, the Bushmen, out of the Cape; now they themselves were driven up the west coast and further squeezed by the pressure of Bantu peoples moving down from central Africa.

British Rule
Then in 1795 the British claimed the Cape in the name of the Prince of Orange, exiled in England after France had invaded Holland. The Dutch regained their colony in 1803 – but only for three years. The British valued this staging post on the route to India too greatly to let it go and British settlement began. The 1820 settlers founded Grahamstown in the Eastern Cape. By 1835 the first Boer farmers were trekking away from British domination across the Orange River, until the Cape Governor, Sir Harry Smith, annexed the Orange Free State too.

Diamonds
But what really transformed the Cape Colony's power was the discovery of diamonds near Kimberley in 1867 and the resultant wealth. In 1872 the colony achieved self-government, with Cecil John Rhodes becoming its most noted Prime Minister. Next came the Anglo-Boer War in 1899 and, eventually, the formation of the Union of South Africa in 1910. The Cape Province then retained its size until after the landmark elections of 1994, when it was divided into three provinces, where names may yet change.

National Parks and Game Reserves

Few big game animals remain in the three provinces, except in the

Previous page: Ostrich racing at Highgate farm, Oudtshoorn (top)
                      The Karoo National Botanic Garden (below)
Opposite: On the road near Hotazel (top left). The Big Hole at Kimberley (top right). Kimberley Mine Museum (below)

National Parks, and even those have nothing like the Kruger's abundance of wildlife although the elephant in the Addo Park now number over 200, while the Kalahari is famed for its dark-maned lion. But you will most certainly come across smaller animals such as springbok. There are some 75 reserves either under the control of the province or of local authorities, while the Cape's 10 out of the Republic's 17 National Parks protect a very great variety of wild life – animals, birds and reptiles – and of landscape and flora. The Parks are described in the text and indexed.

Accommodation and Information
Most parks have rest camps with chalets, except for the Bontebok Park, which only has a camp site. They are open all year round. Bookings can be made through the National Parks Board offices in Long Street, Cape Town (tel 22 2810) or through the Pretoria (tel 012 343 1991).

The Western Cape

Climate

Around the Cape Peninsula the climate is Mediterranean with low humidity. Summer temperatures from November to February are warm, averaging from 13°C (55°F) at night to 26°C (77°F). Winter temperatures in June to September range from 8°C (48°F) to 18°C (65°F). In winter mountain tops are snowclad in the wine country. Most of the rain falls between May and September and in spring the countryside is aflame with wild flowers. All in all the Western Cape climate is one of the healthiest in the world.

Getting to the Cape

Air
South African Airways (tel 021 25 4610) operates frequent daily flights direct from Johannesburg to Cape Town, while East London, Port Elizabeth and George are also served. National Airlines serves the north-west Cape mining towns (tel 021 943 0350). The airport is 22 km from the city centre and a bookable shuttle bus (tel 021 794 2772) leaves from behind the Tourist Rendezvous in the station complex. The flight enquiries number is 021 934 0407.

International airlines serving Cape Town include British Airways, KLM, Lufthansa, Olympic, South African Airways, Swissair and UTA. See also General Information at the start of this book.

Rail

The prestigious Blue Train and Trans-Karoo Express link Cape Town with Kimberley and Johannesburg in 26 hours (enquiries tel 021 405 2991). For Rovos Rail see General Information.

Coach

Greyhound Express coaches run overnight from Johannesburg to Cape Town via Kimberley, Beaufort West and Worcester. For information tel 011 403 6463 (Johannesburg) or 021 418 4312 (Cape Town). Translux (tel 021 405 3333) runs daily overnight from Johannesburg/Pretoria via Bloemfontein, with another route stopping at Garden Route resorts, and a mountain route through Robertson, Worcester, Paarl and Stellenbosch. InterCape (tel 021 934 4400) runs a similar coastal route and a west coast route from Cape Town to Windkoek via Springbok.

Information

Information centres have been regionalised, although the Tourist Rendezvous in the railway station complex in Cape Town's Adderley Street (tel 021 418 5214) is well-organised to handle queries on the province with the SATOUR office close by (tel 216274).

Cape Town

Postal code 8000. Telephone code 021. Tourist Info 418 5214.

The classic introduction to Cape Town is to arrive by sea, still possible on cargo ships, though you get the same view from the Bloubergstrand beaches. Ahead of you rises Table Mountain, its deceptively flat-looking top sometimes shrouded by cloud, which people call 'the tablecloth'. On either side of it stand two peaks, Devil's Peak to the east and the lower Lion's Head to the west, with Signal Hill forming the lion's rump.

It's not easy to get oneself orientated in Cape Town, but the maps in this chapter should help, as would the panoramic aerial view postcards on sale locally. The city and the harbour face north. Signal Hill separates the city from the resort suburbs of Sea Point and Clifton, on the Atlantic. Round to the east, on the far side of Devil's Peak, are the snobbier residential areas of Newlands, Claremont, Kenilworth, Bishopscourt, Constantia and Wynberg. The suburban sprawl around the city, much of it deprived black townships, has taken the metropolitan population close to 3,000,000. Furthermore the removal of racially restrictive laws has led to an increasing influx of blacks seeking jobs. and the central business district is beset with 'informal traders'. Nonetheless the dramatic, ever present, mountain makes Cape Town visually one of the world's most exciting cities.

The Western Cape

The Company Gardens – now the city centre's park – were the Cape settlement's original vegetable patch. Although some of the fine old buildings have been preserved, like the castle which replaced the first mud-walled fort, Jan van Riebeeck might have problems finding his way around. The foreshore near the harbour was long ago reclaimed, the city centre has been partially transformed by pedestrian malls, and freeways snake right into Cape Town's heart. Most recently the waterfront officially begun by Queen Victoria's second son, Prince Alfred, in 1860 has been transformed into an exciting and sophisticated centre that is eclipsing the city's traditional facilities.

Information

The Tourist Rendezvous Travel Centre in the main railway station on Adderley Street is the focal point for a network of organisations. The Captour bureau (PO Box 1403, Cape Town 8000; tel 418 5214, fax 418 5228) can provide a goldmine of brochures and book accommodation. It is open seven days a week. Its publications include comprehensive guides to hotels, guest houses (becoming popular) and restaurants, as well as the monthly 'What's On in the Cape.' Many helplines numbers are listed in the invaluable 'Cape Explorer' booklet, from rape emergencies onwards. Captour has subsidiary offices in the Tygervalley Centre, Bellville (tel 940 2498) and on Atlantic Road, Muizenberg (tel 788 1898). The SATOUR bureau (tel 216274) is in the same complex.

Other useful addresses:
American Express has branches in the Tourist Rendezvous, on Thibault Square, and in the Victoria and Alfred Waterfront. British Airways, BP Centre, Thibault Square (tel 252970). International telephone and fax at the Main Post office on Parliament Street, seven days a week. South African Airways on Thibault Square (tel 254 610). Thomas Cook at branches of Rennie's Travel, including the Tourist Rendezous and the V & A Waterfront. Weather forecast tel 934 0450.

Getting Around Locally

Trains
An efficient, electrified, train service runs round to Wynberg, Fishhoek and Simon's Town, but there are no trains to Sea Point, Clifton and Hout Bay on the Atlantic side, which depend on buses. For train information tel 4052991.

Buses and Taxis
Local buses leave from the Golden Acre Bus Terminus (telephone 4614365). Conventional taxis do not cruise the streets. Two num-

bers to call are Marine Taxis on 4340434 and Sea Point Taxis on 4344444.

The big recent additions to local transport are the black-owned minibuses that stop if you wave them down, run defined routes but to no schedule, and charge a flat rate. These serve the suburbs as well as the townships and depart from the trading area above the railway station, reached by stairs from the concourse.

Tours

Countless tours vary from a four-hour city tours to Connex's seven-day trip up the west coast to Namibia. The largest tour operator is Springbok-Atlas (tel 448 6545). Details of hiking tours on Table Mountain, wineland tours, motorcycle tours and others are available from Captour. Tours to the black and coloured townships, such as Khayelitsha and Langa, are run by Otherside Tours (tel 531 8528). Among the best tailor-made itineraries are those of Specialised Tours (tel 253259, fax 253329), which also does standard ones. For a helicopter view of the Peninsula calls Court Helicopters (tel 252966).

Cruises/Harbour Tours

Boat trips, from evening dinner cruises to serious big-game fishing, are an attractive alternative to conventional tours. Sealink at 5 Quay on the V & A Waterfront is one firm (tel 254480), or ask Captour.

Car Hire

Avis, Europcar and Imperial are represented. Various cheaper firms compete, for instance Tempest (tel 245 000) and Pride (tel 934 0430). Hire firms will meet clients at the airport or station at no extra charge. Parking your car is, of course, something else. Unoccupied parking meters are hard to find and costly. There are indoor and outdoor parking venues, like that on the Parade.

City Centre and Shopping

The focal business thoroughfare is Adderley Street, at the Table Mountain end of which are the Gardens, with grouped around them the cool, white classical South African National Gallery and the Parliament Buildings, largely designed by Sir Herbert Baker. The Gardens are a delightful refuge from the streets and the tame squirrels and doves an attraction to children.

Malls, Concourses and Curios

Shopping malls are a big thing in South African everyday life and Cape Town has its share. Extensive underground concourses beneath Strand Street link the Golden Acre with the Station, the Cape Sun hotel, and the car parking in the Picbel Parkade. The St George's Street pedestrian mall often has groups of musicians, while dancers stomp

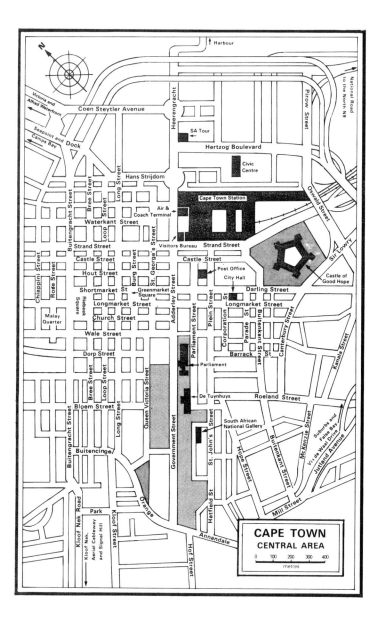

CAPE TOWN
CENTRAL AREA

0   100   200   300   400
metres

174

to authentic – and sometimes not so authentic – African music. Saturday mornings are especially lively. You can sit at a pavement cafe and just soak up the atmosphere, or more actively prowl around in search of oriental jewellery, diamonds or Zulu crafts. The Link and Cavendish Square out in Claremont have quite a few unusual boutiques. And, as befits a great city, you stumble on small dealers, like the Wandel Street Shop near the Gardens, whose sign announces 'Purveyors of Antiquities, Curiosities and High Class Junk.' However, the big news is the Waterfront, while the city centre has suffered an invasion of 'informal traders' whose stalls clutter the pavements.

The Victoria and Alfred Waterfront
This continuing development must be one of the most imaginative anywhere in the world, combining a working harbour with a brilliantly conceived mix of entertainment, speciality shopping malls and boutiques, hotels restaurants and bars, theatres and festivals, boat trips and helicopter flights. Forget the impressive statistics, the Waterfront produces its own restaurant guide and calendar of events (tel 418 2369) It also has abundant parking and its own security staff; which means no 'informal traders' or muggers. It is located two km from the centre and is well-sign posted.

Shopping Hours
Conventional shopping hours are 0900 to 1700 Monday to Friday and 0900 to 1300 on Saturdays. However supermarkets and shopping malls now stay open all day Saturday and on Sundays, while liquor shops (bottle stores) stay open all day Saturday. There are also numerous 'cafes' which are open long hours and where you can buy groceries and household goods.

Markets
Cape Town's street markets are more entertaining than most. The flower market held daily on Grand Parade opposite the City Hall vividly illustrates the Cape's wealth of flora. Others, usually exhibiting crafts and oriental jewellery, include daily ones in Greenmarket Square and by the railway station. There is a Sunday market in Greenpoint. For details of craft markets in the suburbs buy 'What's On' or get the 'Arts and Crafts' map from Captour.

Hotels

Although Cape Town and its suburbs have a mass of hotels, you still need to make reservations well in advance during the November to March holiday season. Do not assume that hotels in the suburbs will be inferior, the reality is the opposite. Some of the most delightful are in the semi-countryside east of the mountain and easily reached by car or train. A full list, from five-star through budget accommodation right down to guest houses, is published by Captour. Our selection is, a tiny proportion of the total.

City Centre
The near-legendary five-star Mount Nelson (PO Box 2608; tel 231000), in its own eight-acre grounds above the Gardens, is back to its former glory. The Cape Sun (PO Box 4532; tel 238844) is a five-star skyscraper on Strand Street. The Town House (PO Box 5053; tel 457050) on Corporation Street, behind the City Hall, now has four stars while the three-star Mijlof Manor in Military Road, Tamberskloof (tel 261476) is a restored Victorian villa close to town and good value. The four-star Victorian and Alfred (PO Box 16157; tel 419 6677) is in Edwardian Style on the Waterfront, the other luxury hotel there being the Portswood (tel 418 4733).

Atlantic Coast
Sea Point is the main hotel area, with value for money at the one-star Carnaby on Main Road and the Three Anchor Bay (tel 497410). For luxury try the four-star Peninsula on Beach Road (PO Box 17188, Sea Point 8060; tel 439 8888), while beyond Sea Point is the really first class five-star Bay Hotel on Victoria Road at Camps Bay (tel 438 4444).

Behind Table Mountain
In the other direction from the city, round behind Table Mountain, are three excellent country hotels, namely the Vineyard (four-star, PO Box 151, Newlands; tel 642107) in Newlands; the four-star Alphen (PO Box 35, Constantia; tel 79450), a former Cape Dutch farmhouse in the lovely Constantia Valley, which is more expensive; and in the same valley the four-star Cellars-Hohenort (PO Box 270; Constantia; tel 7942137). You need a car if you stay out at Constantia.

Youth Hostels/Budget Accommodation
Cape Town is well-equipped with youth hostels. The Youth Hostel National Office is at 101 Boston House, Strand Street, (tel 419 1853) if you need advice. The YMCA is at Louis Botha House, Burham Road, Observatory (tel 476217) and the WYCA at 20 Bellevue Street Gardens (tel 233711). Out of town there are the Abe Bailey Youth Hostel on the corner of Westbury and Maynard Roads in Muizenberg (tel 7884283) and the Stan's Halt Youth Hostel at Camps Bay (tel 4389037).

Restaurants

You can eat well both expensively and quite cheaply around Cape Town and many of the best places are out of town. The cuisine often takes advantage of Malay dishes, like *bobotie* – a mild curried mince with raisins – and of the abundant sea food. One Cape pudding is baked *malva*, which looks like gingerbread, but is made with apricot jam, is light and sweet and is served with a gluttonous sauce of cream, orange juice and brandy. The Argus newspaper's 'Tonight' section lists most restaurants. Many are unlicensed so it is best to check beforehand as this can make a big difference to the price of the food. Restaurants that are licensed sometimes do not mind if you bring your own wine, but charge corkage. Such a wealth of wine is available that it is often advantageous to take one's own. Remember that bottle stores close at 1830 weekdays and 1700 on Saturdays.

City
The following are some reasonably priced places in central Cape Town. The Old Colonial (tel 454909), at 39 Barnett Street near the Gardens, is small and has a friendly atmosphere. Kaapse Tafel (tel 231651) at 90 Queen Victoria Street serves traditional Cape food and also vegetarian dishes. The Perseverance Tavern, at 83 Buitenkant Street (tel 461 2440), has a pleasant beer garden and serves German dishes. At the other end of the price scale, Floris Smit Huijs (tel 233414), on the corner of Loop and Church Streets, has the reputation of being one of South Africa's top ten restaurants. Champers (tel 454335), on Deer Park Avenue, serves *nouvelle cuisine* in a formal atmosphere. The Grill Room of the Mount Nelson Hotel has game dishes in season. The V & A Waterfront has numerous eating places, including a floating restaurant, the Alabama 2000.

Sea Point
Out at Sea Point the restaurants change often, with Italian and Greek predominant. Main Street is crowded with them and it is simplest to consult Captour's 'Wine and Dine' Guide for Suburban restaurants. That said, at Delmitchies, 78 Main Road (tel 434 6500) the hors d'oeuvres includes smoked angel fish and there is a set price for the whole seafood buffet.

Southern Suburbs
Behind the mountain you will get excellent, though expensive, food at the Alphen Hotel, already mentioned; while the restaurant at the Cellars - Hohenort Hotel is renowned. The Fisherman's Cottage at Plumstead (tel 797 6341) also serves excellent food.

Nightlife

The top hotels grill rooms provide music and dancing, as do quite a number of restaurants. Places on the Waterfront stay open late. But, although there are plenty of discos, there is a dearth of good nightlife, and like all cities, Cape Town has its clip-joints. Try the Argus newspaper's 'Tonight' section or the official 'What's On' listings.

Concerts and Theatres

The Cape Town Symphony Orchestra gives concerts in the City Hall on Thursdays and Sundays. There are two well-known theatre complexes, the Baxter out at the university, and the Nico Malan on the foreshore, hosting opera and ballet as well as plays. At Baxter's Stagedoor venue you can watch a show whilst having a drink and something to eat; but it is not large and you need to book (tel 685 7880). The Dock Road Theatre on the Waterfront is a smaller, privately-run, theatre. Standards of performance are high in all the theatres. Performances are detailed in 'What's On'.

Places to See

Culturally, historically, and indeed botanically, Cape Town has more to interest a discerning visitor than most cities in the southern hemisphere. We have already mentioned the Company's Garden – or the Gardens – which have many varieties of plants, flowers and trees, plus an aviary and a restaurant. The oldest cultivated tree in the Republic, a saffren pear, stands down from the restaurant. Around the Gardens are the Cultural History Museum, the South African Museum, the National Gallery, and Parliament. The State President's house, the Tuynhuys, is very handsome architecturally, but not open to the public.

Houses of Parliament

Situated by the Gardens, the Parliament buildings deserve a visit. They contain many relics of British rule, such as the solid gold mace, and there is a statue of Queen Victoria in the grounds. Members convene here only from January to June; the other sessions are held in Pretoria, where all the sessions may eventually take place. When Parliament is sitting gallery tickets can be booked by telephoning 403 2460. From July to December there are daily guided tours at 1100 hours. You should bring your passport with you for identification.

Cultural History Museum

The Cultural History Museum, at 49 Adderley Street, close to the Gardens was originally built as a slave lodge for the Dutch East India Company and later became the Supreme Court. Today it houses, *inter alia,* exhibits on the early history of man, a reconstructed 19th century chemist's shop, weapons, stamps and coins. The Museum has six satellite buildings, which between them illustrate the main life styles of the Cape's civilised history. Governor Simon der Stel's manor, Groot Constantia, is described later. The Bo-Kaap Museum at 71 Wale Street was built in 1763, though it is furnished as a late-19th century Muslim home. The Koopmans de Wet House, at 35 Strand Street, was completed in its present neo-classical style in 1793 and contains one of the finest collections of colonial Dutch antiques anywhere. The Bertram Museum, on Government Avenue, is the city's only surviving red-brick Georgian town house, with period furnishings. The Stempastorie out at 2 Church Street, Simon's Town, is a Dutch Reformed Church parsonage, where the national anthem was written in 1921. Finally – and rather oddly – there is a Maritime Museum of two vessels at West Quay.

South African National Museum
Founded in 1825, this is the Republic's oldest museum and holds Bushman paintings among its many exhibits of *Africana,* archaeology and the natural sciences. Adjoining it is the recently-built Theatre of the Sky, a most imaginatively designed Planetarium, with displays originally invented for training astronauts.

Castle of Good Hope
The castle is South Africa's oldest building. It was begun in 1665 and its five-pointed star shape made it virtually impregnable. You should look for the contemporary stone relief of an East Indiaman ship on the staircase of the Katzenellen Bastion. The elegant Kat Balcony is one of various 18th century additions. Lady Anne Barnard's ballroom enlivens the former Governor's residence, dating from the brief 1795 to 1806 period when the British Governors lived here. The castle's eventful history saw the internment of the Zulu King Cetewayo, after his defeat in 1879. He was allowed to bring servants and four of his wives with him. Today the Castle houses the HQ of the Western Province Command of the South African army, together with Military and Maritime Museums. There are guided tours hourly from 1000 to 1500 and the Changing of the Guard ceremony is at 1200.

Malay Quarter
The Malay quarter on the slopes of Lion's Head, also known as Bo Kaap, is the home of descendants of the slaves brought to the Cape from the East in the 17th century by the Dutch East India Company. Its veiled women, minarets, narrow streets, and the dilapidated elegance of its old houses, all give it a special atmosphere. Unfortunately it is safer to go there on a guided tour than alone.

Walking Tours
Two and a half hour city walks start from the Cultural History Museum every Saturday from September to May at 1500. There are many smaller city attractions – for instance, the Michaelis Collection of Dutch paintings in the old Town House on Greenmarket Square. Captour's 'Tourist Guide' is a handy reference. But features you must not miss are Table Mountain itself and the Kirstenbosch Gardens, described under 'Excursions' and the Victoria & Alfred Waterfront.

Township Tours
Several firms run tours to the sprawling black and coloured townships around the city notably to the much-publicised Crossroads, Langa near Pinelands, Gugulethu and Khayelitsha on Mitchell's Plain. Try One City Tours (tel 387 5351). The tours are safe.

Table Mountain
There is nothing to beat the mountain top for a view of the city. The highest point at Maclears Beacon (1,087m/3,533ft) is easily reached by a seven-minute ride in the cable car, which starts from the station in Kloof Nek Road, followed by an hour's walk along a signed footpath. You can pre-book a place on the cable car. There is a restaurant at the cable car's top station and panoramic view points, where hyraxes (rock rabbits) seem as unconcerned about the precipices below as are the birds. The mountain can be climbed from the bottom, but some of the ways up are dangerous and need a guide. Camp and Climb at 6 Pepper Street (tel 232175) are experts. There is one signposted walk up a deep cleft in the Platteklip Gorge. If you get lost, try to return to it. Other magnificent views, particularly of the lights at night, can be had from the road that winds up Signal Hill, where a noonday gun is fired every day (except Sundays). Signal Hill's name derives from its having been an observation post since the first settlement. If the mountain is too much of an effort, then look down on the city from the Observation Tower in the Sanlam Building in the Heerengracht, open weekdays 1015 to 1515.

Fairs and Festivals

Annual events start with the Minstrel Carnival on January 1, when bands of gaily costumed Cape Coloured people go singing and dancing in street processions, continuing in a stadium. The Cape Coloured people are a centuries-old mixture of Hottentots and Asians, with a small addition of African and European blood.

In February the Cape Show is held. This is an agricultural and industrial exhibition which includes galloping mule and horse team competitions, wine tastings, and sporting events. Easter sees the Two Oceans Marathon race for long-distance runners. Fairs are held all year round in many suburbs. August has spring flower shows in the city. September hosts the Double Cape Ocean race for yachts. The Christmas season brings carol singing in Greenmarket Square.

Sports

Numerous sporting facilities around the Cape include fishing, about which there is a daily report on Radio Good Hope; golf, with 18-hole courses at the Royal Cape Club in Wynberg, Clovelly, Milnerton, Mow-

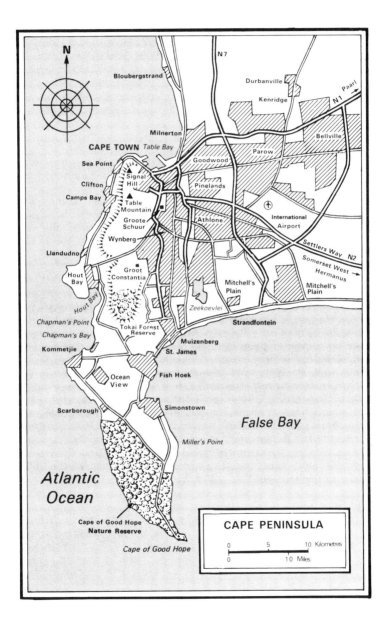

N

Bloubergstrand

Durbanville

N7

Kenridge

N1 Paarl

Milnerton

Bellville

CAPE TOWN *Table Bay*

Parow

Sea Point

Goodwood

Signal
Hill

Pinelands

Clifton

Camps Bay

■ Table
Mountain

Athlone

Groote
Schuur

⊕

International
Airport

Wynberg

Settlers Way N2

Llandudno

Somerset West
Hermanus

Hout
Bay

Groot
Constantia

Mitchell's
Plain

Mitchell's
Plain

Hout Bay

Zeekoevlei

Chapman's Point

Strandfontein

Chapman's Bay

Tokai Forest
Reserve

Kommetjie

Muizenberg

St. James

Ocean
View

Fish Hoek

Scarborough

Simonstown

False Bay

Miller's Point

*Atlantic
Ocean*

Cape of Good Hope
Nature Reserve

Cape of Good Hope

CAPE PENINSULA

0   5   10 Kilometres

0   10 Miles

bray and also out at Hermanus and Stellenbosch; riding; and scuba diving. For big-game fishing contact Charles Day Bluefin Charters in Kommetjie (tel 783 1 756) or Deep Sea Angling (tel 782 3889). The South African Turf Club holds race meetings at Kenilworth and the Cape Turf Club at Durbanville and Milnerton. The racing season starts two days before Christmas and ends in mid-March.

Local Excursions

Kirstenbosch
Outside Cape Town you should try to see the world-famous Kirstenbosch Botanical Gardens, which shelter 6,000 of South Africa's 20,000 species of flora. They are open from sunrise to sunset, with tea and refreshments available. From December to March there are Sunday evening Concerts from 1 730 to 1 830 and listeners bring picnics. On the way you pass near Groote Schuur (Great Barn), the property which Cecil Rhodes presented to the nation and is now the home of the Presidents of South Africa.

Constantia
Another splendid example of a Cape farm house is Groot Constantia, former home of the Dutch Governors, in the charming Constantia Valley. The manor was faithfully rebuilt after a fire in 1925 and is now a satellite of the Cultural History Museum. The wine cellars behind were untouched and you can now buy the produce of Constantia's own vineyards in them, notably Cabernet Sauvignon and Sauvignon Blanc. Both Napoleon and Bismarck were admirers of Constantia wine, Napoleon having it shipped to him when he was in exile on St Helena. Governor Simon van der Stel began planting this land in 1685 and, although the vineyards are smaller than they were, a Constantia Wine Route has been devised, encompassing Groot Constantia, Klein Constantia and Buitenverwachting. There are cellar tours and wine tastings daily, walks in the valley and restaurants at Groot Constantia and at Buitenverwatchting. The vineyards are reached via the M41 road, from either Hout Bay or Wynberg.

Bird Sanctuary and Crocodiles
Further on towards False Bay is the Ronde Vlei Bird Sanctuary, where 170 species have been identified, pelicans and flamingoes being among the most easily recognised. Bordering this *vlei* or marshy lake, is the largest of the fresh-water lakes out here on the Cape Flats. Called Zeekoe ('hippopotamus') Vlei, it is a favourite location for sailing. At Strandfontein, in the African Reptile Park, crocodiles eye you lazily; a misleading laziness, since they can snap up an unwary buck by a river with amazing speed – or a human.

However, most visitors come this way as part of a circular tour of the Cape Peninsula, more spectacularly reached if you approach it via Hout Bay on the Atlantic side.

Ostriches
North of the city, on the way to Bloubergstrand, is the West Coast Ostrich Farm.

The Cape Peninsula

The rest of the peninsula, which stretches 51 km (32 miles) south of Cape Town, is skirted by a series of resorts amid magnificent bays and mountains. When Sir Francis Drake, the Elizabethan navigator, sailed by in 1580, he called it 'the fairest cape we saw in the whole circumference of the earth'. The most impressive way to see it today is via the Chapman's Peak Drive. You leave the city past the white high-rise clusters of Sea Point and the beaches of Camps Bay, drive above Llandudno at the foot of the Twelve Apostles, which buttress Table Mountain, and then reach the beautiful curve of Hout Bay. The secluded beach before Hout Bay, called Sandy Bay, is South Africa's only nudist beach.

Hout Bay
The name 'Hout' derives from the fir trees cut for timber here in the

The Cape Peninsula, Cape Town in background

early days of settlement and the remains of two forts guard the bay. Hout Bay is both historic and a delightful fishing port, where crayfish and snoek are sold on the quayside. The Hout Bay Museum, out in a valley, reflects this dual ancestry. In fact mining came into it too and you can buy polished semi-precious stones at the Hout Bay Mining Company's shop on Beach Crescent. Up on the hill is a fine Cape Dutch mansion, Kronendal, dating from 1677, which is a national monument and houses a noted restaurant (tel 790 1970). However the most lively eating places are at the harbour, such as the Mariner's Wharf Bistro (tel 790 1100), and specialise in lobster. Cruises to nearby Seal Island are run by Drumbeat Charters (tel 438 9208).

From the bay the Chapman's Peak Drive continues, snaking past the peak itself to intersect with the M65 road to Kommetjie, where there is a glorious beach that is little frequented because of the cold Atlantic water. From Kommetjie you continue to the Nature Reserve, also reachable from Simon's Town, on the False Bay side.

Cape of Good Hope Nature Reserve

The tip of the peninsula is a 77 sq km (30 sq miles) nature reserve, which surprisingly includes wetlands, as well as the *fynbos* type of vegetation. The plants and shrubs of 'fine bush' include heather and ericas. You will also find proteas – South Africa's national flower – and orchids here. The reserve has been stocked with eland, springbok and bontebok, plus zebras and baboons and there is a Nature Conservation Centre. Until 1939 this was farmland and one of the former homesteads is now a restaurant. If you have not got a car one way of reaching the reserve without hassle is to come by train to Simon's Town and then hire a chauffeur-driven minibus at the station from Rikkis Taxi Service (tel 786 2136). or take a full day tour from the city.

The entrance road ends at a parking area, from which the little 'Flying Dutchman' bus plies the short distance along the old military road to the original lighthouse of 1857 (the present one is at the foot of the cliffs); or, if you're feeling energetic, walk up. There is new route up, as well. The views are panoramic – you can see way beyond False Bay and Cape Hangklip on a clear day. Cape Point itself is often thought to divide the Atlantic from the Indian Ocean and the waters to the east of it are several degrees warmer than those to the west. But Cape Agulhas, 200 km (125 miles) to the east, is the real dividing point of the two oceans.

A Different Route Back

After leaving the reserve you can vary your return to the city by initially following the same route as far as Red Hill, but then taking the road to the right. Crossing the hump of the peninsula, through scenery that could be in the Mediterranean, the hillsides scented with shrubs and herbs, the M4 road leads to the recreation area of Millers Point. After this you go back towards Cape Town past Simons Town, on the False Bay side of the peninsula.

Simon's Town to Fish Hoek

Simon's Town is an attractive fishing town with cobbled streets and buildings dating from 1687. It is the headquarters of the South African navy. From there you follow the curve of False Bay to Fish Hoek. False Bay's name originates from the first settlers' belief that it would provide a deep anchorage; and their disappointing discovery that it was shallow (even Simon's Town has limitations). There is a very good surfing beach, a caravan park, and a golf course at Fish Hoek. Tunny and big-game fishing can easily be organised in the summer months in False Bay and the boating of a 272 kg (600 lb) blue fin is not unusual. Yachting and other water sports are popular, while within a few miles of Fish Hoek are many glorious stretches of safe beach, though there are muggers around and the safest is at Fish Hoek itself.

Kalk Bay to Muizenberg

Kalk Bay is the next suburb-cum-resort along False Bay. It has an attractive harbour for fishing boats, you can savour seafood at the waterfront Brass Bell restaurant (tel 788 5455), with a lively pub atmosphere and good food.

Leaving Kalk Bay along the coast road to Muizenberg you pass St James, a holiday resort as well as a rich residential area. Muizenberg is a popular town with a long sandy beach and many entertainment facilities. The sea is safe for children. The Information Bureau is in the Municipal Offices, Atlantic Road. (tel 788 1898) and there is a Treasure Coast Art Route of galleries. Reputedly the best Indian food in the Cape is served at Gaylords (tel 788 5470). The main road from Muizenberg leads to the suburb of Wynberg and on to Cape Town. All these seaside villages are served by the train.

The Winelands

Whichever way you go from Cape Town you'll find the diversity of the scenery so characteristic of this most stimulating of South Africa's provinces. Directly inland takes you to the mountains and the wine country. The west coast leads past long beaches to the rugged beauty of Namaqualand. Directly east from the city by some 100 km (60 miles or so) lies the Overberg - the country beyond the mountains - with sophisticated resorts, fishing villages and the southernmost point of the African continent, Cape Agulhas. The Overberg leads in turn to the celebrated coastline of the Garden Route.

The Boland

Inland from Cape Town lies the Boland district beyond the Jonkershoek mountains and some of the most lively, and most productive, countryside in the Republic. These valleys, watered by clear streams from mountains that are dusted with snow in winter, shelter orchards – some planted when the wine trade was in recession – and vineyards. Often estates sell their wines direct to visitors and their histories make appealing tales, like that of the Swartland vineyard Allesverloren – 'all is lost' – so named because it was ravaged in succession by Hottentot attacks and fire. The climate is pleasantly warm in summer, but can be cold in winter.

Cape Wines

The Cape vineyards were originated at Constantia by Jan van Riebeeck in 1685 and the date when the first of his wines was tasted is on record; Sunday February 2, 1659. In 1688 Huguenot refugees arrived from France, bringing their own vine seedlings and skills with them and settling inland. By the 1820s Jane Austen was mentioning Constantia wine in her novel 'Sense and Sensibility' and Napoleon, in exile not so far away on St Helena, asked for some.

Harvesting grapes in the Cape Winelands

The different soils and climatic variations in the many valleys enable a very wide range of wines to be pressed, from exquisite sweet whites from the hanepoot grape, through dry whites to fruity reds. Excellent sherries and ports are also produced. The present high degree of sophistication in Cape wines is due both to strict quality control – half the grape crop is not considered good enough for table wine at all – and to long experimentation with different varieties of vine stock, or cultivar. The finest Cape wines come from the Franschoek, Paarl and Stellenbosch areas.

The Most Successful Cultivars

For red wines the most successful cultivars have proved to be Cabernet Sauvignon, Shiraz and a cross between the Pinot Noir and Hermitage stock, christened Pinotage (Hermitage is the South African name for the Cincault grape from the Rhône valley in France). The classic French Chardonnay and Sauvignon Blanc, and the German Riesling, have produced fine white wines; not identical to their European counterparts, but recognisable, yet with a South African character. Although the limited vintages of estate wines – such as those from Fairview, near Paarl or Vlottenburg near Stellenbosch – are the finest, some more widely marketed ones are reliably enjoyable. Two that you find all over the Republic are Fleur du Cap Pinotage and Nederburg Cabernet Sauvignon, plus the light white Cape Nouveau, while Simonsig wines are worth seeking out.

Cape Dutch Homesteads

Architecturally the wine estates whitewashed homesteads are of a distinguished vintage too. In its simplest form the Cape Dutch house is a single storey, thatched structure, dignified by a high decorative gable over the front door, which holds a single upstairs room. Another of its features is a *stoep,* a verandah that sometimes runs the length of the house. Back in Holland this was a small space for sitting by the front door. Transplanted to the African sun it has expanded into an open-air living room, though you do not see it so often on the older houses.

Wine Routes

The gentle marketing ploy of promoting wine routes to visitors has expanded steadily. The original two centred on Stellenbosch and Paarl. Now they are numerous. Among the best are Constantia (already described) and Franschoek, Wellington, Worcester and Robertson in the Boland. All have their publicity offices and brochures that are also obtainable from Captour in Cape Town. Their estates and co-operatives participate with guided tours and tastings. Many run restaurants. Our account only gives the highlights, plus some side-trips; you could profitably explore further.

Stellenbosch

Postal code 7600. Telephone code 021. Tourist Info 883 3584/9683.

One easy and enjoyable drive from Cape Town is to Stellenbosch, only 41 km (26 miles) from the city and centre of a wine producing area with many other attractions. The simplest route is out by the N2, then turning north on to the R310, at exit 33, although you can make it part of more scenic drives via Somerset West, as described in a moment.

The Architectural Inheritance

The town itself, the second oldest in the Republic and now the home of a famous University, was founded in 1679 by Simon van der Stel. The name Stellenbosch means 'van der Stel's wood'. Later he planted the originals of its oak avenues. Many of the town's historic houses have been restored under the patronage of Dr Anton Rupert and the best way to see them is on foot. The Visitor's Bureau is an historic house at 30 Plein Street (tel 883 3584) with free parking outside. It is open Saturdays and publishes a walking tour pamphlet. Key streets to see are Dorp Street, where the mansion La Gratitude has a fine frontage and there is a traditional general store called Oom Samie; the Braak, or village green, with the Old Powder magazine; Old Strand, where the labourers' cottages were designed by Sir Herbert Baker and the house Libertas has a Rembrandt art collection, while its wine cellars have become the small Wine Museum; and Ryneveld Street, where four houses constitute the Village Museum. Then there is the perfect little Burger's House, by the Post Office. One could go on, because 60 of the town's buildings are national monuments. The Brandy Museum deserves looking at. October is a festival month with the Stellenbosch Festival in the first week, then the van der Stel Festival and finally the Food and Wine Festival.

Hotels and Restaurants

In the town there are several old-world hotels, all reasonably priced, all within walking distance of the centre of this architecturally delightful town. Three-star D'Ouwe Werf at 30 Church Street (tel 887 4608) is a near-perfect classical house built in 1802, with a pool and a garden. The three-star Stellenbosch Hotel at 162 Dorp Street (tel 887 3644) is a Cape Dutch house, while the Dorpshuis at 22 Dorp Street (tel 883 9881) is an elegant town house, as is three-star guest house at 110 Dorp Street (tel 883 3555). For a list of both larger hotels and guest houses write to the Tourist Bureau.

A short way out to the east is the famous and much larger Lanzerac Hotel (PO Box 4; tel 887 1182), a superbly modernised and furnished old manor house, noted for its food. Or you can stay in some luxury on a working wine route estate at L'Avenir Farm (PO Box 1135; tel 889 5001) on the R44 road, but it only serves light meals.

Restaurants are numerous and often inexpensive, this being a University town. Two of note are Le Chameleon Bistro (tel 887 2776) at 102 Dorp Street and Doornbosch (tel 887 5079) on Old Strand Road. Both serve French/Italian cuisine. Lanzerac's restaurant is also excellent.

The Stellenbosch Wine Route

Officially the wine route comprises 25 estates and three wine co-operatives, all within 12km (seven miles) of the town and situated on one or other of the four main roads leading into the town. The wine route office (PO Box 204; tel 886 4310) provides a descriptive brochure with a map. It is just outside the town on the R44 road at the Doornbosch restaurant. In fact eating well has become almost as much a part of the wine route as the tastings, so it is advisable to book in advance. The distinguished Neethlingshof estate, off the R310 road, has an excellent restaurant (tel 883 8988). Pleasant picnic basket lunches are served on the lawn at Morgenhof, and Eikendal Vineyards (tel 024 551422) on the way to Somerset West does a Swiss country lunch. Others, such as Hartenberg, offer 'vintners platters'.

Die Bergkelder
Before leaving the town you must visit the cellars of Die Bergkelder, near the railway station. They are cut into the mountain rock and 22 huge oak wine casks, made in Germany, all have their ends carved with scenes illustrating the history of South African viticulture. Each vat holds 2,700 litres. The size of the vat affects the colour of the wine, while the constant temperature in the rock cellars helps bring the wines to maturity. There are guided tours at 1000 and 1500 (not Sundays).

The Franschoek Wine Route

The valley of the Huguenots, first settled in 1688, is just across the mountains and – if you are short of time – can form part of a rewarding circular tour back to Cape Town, via the 'Four Pass' drive. Leaving Stellenbosch eastwards on the R310 you cross the Helshoogte Pass (Hell's Heights) – with memorable views – and come down through the Banhoek valley to this 'corner of France'. Well before you reach the village you pass two famous estates on its 16 member route, described in detail in a booklet obtainable from the Vineyards Wine Centre on Main Road, Franschoek, or from Captour.

The Western Cape

Boschendal
Boschendal is an historic manor house, its lofty rooms as cool and still as a 17th century Dutch painting. The restaurant is notable both for its decor and its splendid buffet lunches (tel 02211 41031, open every day except Sunday). Picnic lunches are served in summer. The vineyards, almost in the shadow of the Simonsberg mountains, occupy part of the land where Cecil Rhodes started fruit farms to alleviate wine farmers' problems. The fame of its wines derives from the celebrated winemaker and cellarmaster Aachim von Arnim, who used to supervise the estate.

Bellingham
After turning on to the R45 in the Franschoek valley you pass Bellingham, another name to conjure with, where South Africa's first Premier Cru wines were produced – a rosé and a shiraz. The Grand Cru white is also notable.

Other Estates
Names like Chamonix and La Provence reflect French origins. Clos Cabrière Pierre Jourdan produces champagne-type wines which are worth tasting.

Franschoek

Postal Code 7690. Telephone code 02212. Tourist Info 3603.
In the village there is a monument to the Huguenot settlers and a Memorial Museum, devoted to their origins and descendants. The Information Centre is in the Museum. Stopping-places for a meal include Le Quartier Francais (tel 3201) at 16 Huguenot Street and, La Petite Ferme (tel 2151), up in the Franschoek Pass, where smoked trout is a speciality. The two-star Huguenot Hotel (PO Box 27; tel 2092) is on Huguenot Road.

The Four Pass Drive to Somerset West

From Franschoek you continue along the R45 across the Franschoek Pass and so to the R321, turning right to reach Viljoen's Pass and, finally, Sir Lowry's Pass on the N2 towards Somerset West. A few hours spent quietly observing this magnificent scenery in the Hottentots Holland mountains will be well spent. The mountains are so called because in the early days the Dutch always talked of going home to Holland and the Hottentots adopted the word for *their* home territory in these hills. From the mountain drive along the eastern side of False Bay you have a magnificent view of the Cape Peninsula across the water.

Somerset West

Postal code 7135. Telephone code 024.Tourist Info 514022.
Just off the N2 is Somerset West, with the small Helderberg Nature Reserve adjoining it, prettily placed in a U-shaped valley of the Hottentots Holland Mountains, the highest point of which is Sneeukop (Snow Peak). The town was the home of the authors Stuart Cloete. During the 1980s it expanded vastly as a dormitory town for Cape Town and has a five-star hotel, the Lord Charles (PO Box 5151 Helderburg; tel 551040) in extensive grounds. Five km (three miles) further is the Strand, a major holiday and sea-bathing resort, past which the coast road leads to Cape Hangklip and a series of delightful beaches, described in a moment. The Stellenbosch wine route starts a short way up the R44 road and the local Vergelegen estate is worth visiting.

Paarl

Postal code 7646. Telephone code 02211. Tourist Info 23829.
The N1 takes you through fruit orchards, to the busy country town of Paarl, 57 km (36 miles) from Cape Town. Set under the Drakenstein Mountains, Paarl is named for three smooth granite outcrops, which glisten after rain like huge pearls. Although this is the largest inland town of the Cape Province, it is not as architecturally attractive as many of the others. The Oude Pastorie Museum, with its collection of antiques and Huguenot relics, merits a visit. Culturally, Paarl was the home of the Afrikaans language and there is also a Museum devoted to that. Otherwise its principal interest lies in wines; unless you are a canoeing fanatic and want to enter for the Berg River Canoe Marathon, which starts here.

Hotels and Restaurants
The area has several first class small hotels. On Paarl's 11km lonf Main Street is Zomerlust (193 Main St; tel 22808, fax 25239) a restored merchant's house with airconditioning, a pool and notable food. Mooikelder (PO Box 7266, North Paarl; tel 638491, fax 638361) is an 1835 manor house, comfortably modernised (B & B only). Another manor house is the Mountain Shaows (PO Box 2501; tel 623192, fax 626796) in the Klein Drakenstein valley, while perhaps the best is Roggeland Country House (PO Box 2710, Paarl North 7623, tel 682501, fax 682113) also in the lovely setting of the Klein Drakenstein and noted for its regional cuisine. More expensive and a five-star estate hotel is Grande Roche (PO Box 6038; tel 632727, fax 632220) on the slopes of Paarl Mountain.

Paarl's best restaurants are those associated with the Wine Route, about which details can be had from the Paarl Publicity Association∕

Paarl Wine offices at 216 Main Street (tel 23829). Among them are Bosman's at Grande Roche and Roggeland. Main Street has several places, not least Zomerlust.

The Paarl Wine Route

Seventeen estates are linked with the Paarl route and are usually open Monday to Friday and Saturday mornings. You must start with the largest wine and brandy cellars in the world, those of KWV on Kohler Street. Only a fraction of every crop is pressed by farmers themselves; most goes to co-operatives, among which KWV is dominant, taking grapes from all the Cape's vineyard areas. Tours of the extensive 'cellar' buildings, conducted in English, are held twice daily.

Estates Restaurants
Estates on the route include KWV's Laborie, where the firm's Wine House has a well-known restaurant (tel 73095); the prestigious Fairview Estate in South Paarl, which offers wine tastings and sales; Nederburg to the north of the town; and Villiera on the way to Stellenbosch. Villiera's restaurant is known for its cold buffet lunches (tel 021 8 822003, open November to Easter only).

Onwards from Paarl

From Paarl you go north through Wellington, either branching north east to Tulbagh and the Breede River Valley, or north west to the Swartland. We take the latter first.

Malmesbury

Postal code 7300. Telephone code 0224. Tourist Info 22996.
Malmesbury, 56km (35 miles) from Cape Town, was laid out in 1745 round hot sulphur springs. It was then known as Het Swarte land (the Black Country) on account of the local rhinosceros bushes, which turn black in summer, but was renamed in honour of the Earl of Malmesbury in 1829. Today it is the centre both of a huge grain-growing region and of a Wine Route. Malmesbury's wild flower reserve deserves a visit in spring.

The Swartland Wine Route

This very dispersed 'route' starts at the Swartland Wine Cellar outside Malmesbury on the way to Riebeek-Kasteel. For information telephone 0224 21134. About 10,000,000 litres of Swartland wines are sold annually. The magnificent Allesverloren estate, set against the Kasteel mountain at Riebeek West, was founded in 1780. After surviving the disasters which gave it the name 'All is Lost', it has become noted for its red wines and port (sadly not sold on the estate).

Riebeek West was the birthplace of General Jan Smuts, South Africa's internationally respected World War II leader, who helped found the United Nations. The Mamreweg Cellar is near a Moravian Mission that is a national monument, on the way to Darling.

Paarl to the Breede River Valley

Another diversion beyond Paarl is on to the glorious fruit and wine growing country round Wellington, Ceres, Tulbagh and the Breede River Valley. All three towns are in truly magnificent scenery, with the mountains snow-capped in winter, the most rewarding aesthetically being Tulbagh. The Blue Train goes slowly through these valleys in daylight and passengers stand glued to the windows. If you are driving up from Paarl you will also get extraordinary views back across the flat countryside to Cape Town, with Table Mountain standing out on the horizon.

Wellington

Postal code 7655. Telephone code 02211. Tourist Info 34604.
Wellington lies at the foot of the Hawequas and Drakenstein Mountains. It has a fine old church, an Anglo-Boer war blockhouse, several co-operative wineries and a couple of small hotels notably the Klein Rhebokskloof farm hotel (PO Box 270; fax/tel 34115). From here the Bain's Kloof Pass takes you through high mountains to Ceres. However, the star-turn of this district is definitely Tulbagh and that is where you should head for.

Tulbagh

Postal code 6820. Telephone code 0236. Tourist Info 301348.
This town, all but encircled by mountains, is about as perfect an example of an old Cape Dutch settlement as you could hope to find. First settled in 1699, it suffered a serious earthquake on September 26, 1969, since when 32 buildings in Church Street have been meticulously restored. The Tourist Information office (tel 301348) is in the Museum Annexe. Houses to look for include the 18th century Mon Bijou, designed by the architect Thibault, and now a private museum associated with the Old Church Museum at 14 Church Street. This church, with its fine gable decorations, was built in 1743 and has an interesting collection of antiques. It is open every day, as is the beautiful old Drostdy four km out of town on Van der Stel Street, where you can taste local sherries, or go to the nearby Drostdy Wine Cellar to sample wines.

A Lodging House and a Restaurant

De Oude Herberg, at 6 Church Street, is a pleasant and reasonably priced bed and breakfast lodging house (tel 300260); while number 23, actually a short walk off the street, is the first-class Paddagang restaurant (tel 300242). Specialities are traditional Malay dishes and the owners have their own vineyard in the valley, producing 'boutique' wines. The label shows a frog in a bow tie with glass in hand; in the evenings you will hear the frogs in the river croaking. Wines from a longer-established local vineyard, called Twee Jongezellen, are worth asking for too. The dry white is particularly palatable.

Ceres *Postal code 6358. Telephone code 0233.*

From Tulbagh the Bain's Kloof Pass takes you through high mountains to Ceres, where in winter there is skiing and the air is crisp, fresh and invigorating. The region produces South Africa's best peaches and pears. The two-star Belmont Hotel in Porters Street (tel 21150) is comfortable and there are several holiday farms in the vicinity. A wild flower show is held in october, to which excursions are run from Cape Town.

Worcester

Postal Code 6850. Telephone code 0321. Tourist Info 71408.

From Paarl the N1 cuts in a toll road tunnel through the Great Drakenstein range, partially missing the exciting old route through the Du Toit's Kloof Pass, to Worcester. This elegant town, a little over 100 km (62 miles) from Cape Town, dates from 1820 and is the focal point of a great fruit and wine growing area, with its own wine route, only an hour from Cape town.

The town centre has an unforgettable greensward, dominated by a fine white church with a most curious combination of tower and spire. The mountains rearing up behind are snow-topped in winter. Commercially Worcester is the 'capital' of the Breede river valley, which runs down past Robertson to Swellendam. From a visitor's point of view its Karoo Botanic Garden and Kleinplasie Museum are outstanding. The Publicity Association (tel 71408) is in the historic Stofberg House at 23 Baring Street, where there is a permanent exhibition on Worcester's history. Of several hotels, the best is the three-star Cumberland (tel 72641) at 2 Stockenstrom Street. Or try the attractive and less expensive Church Street Lodge (36 Church Street; tel 25194, fax 28859) in the well-preserved old town.

The Karoo Botanic Garden

This mountain garden is not just stunningly colourful in season, it nurtures some 400 species of indigenous arid-area succulents and so has a living collection that is one of the world's finest. Within the 154 ha plants are allocated territory climatically, so that the ones in the cultivated gardens near the entrance respond to winter rains, while those further up the hillside flower after summer rainfall. Among them are the gorse-like 'Karoo Gold' (*rhigosum oboventum*), Namaqualand flowers such as the purple and white *dorotheanthus bellidiformis*; many flowering shrubs; euphorbias; the Kokerboom, or quiver tree *(aloe dichotoma)* and its variant the Maiden's Quiver; the bladderbush (*nymania carpensas*), with blooms like Chinese lanterns; and even examples of the grotesque and ancient *welwitschia mirabilis* of the Namib desert. The scenery is magnificent and there are several walking trails. The garden lies three km north of Worcester, off the N1, and is open from 0800 to 1700.

The Kleinplasie Open Air Farm Museum

A working blacksmith, ladies making soap and bread, and other activities – mostly yielding edible or usable items for sale – combine to give this innovative outdoor museum a real breath of life. It reveals many quirky facets of the early settlers existence. They used everlasting flowers to stuff their pillows, exchanged sheep for rolls of tobacco the length of a sheep, and discovered that leaves of the bush *artemisia* cured stuffy noses. They drank a fiery home-distilled brandy – made here by the old methods – called witblitz, or 'white lightning', and when someone died they said he had 'stuck his spoon in the roof'.

The Worcester Wine Route

In 1989 Worcester was honoured as a champion white wine district. Some 20 estates and co-operatives form the wine route, details of which can be obtained from the Worcester Winelands Association (PO Box 59; tel 28710) at the Kleinplasie showgrounds on the road out towards Robertson. KWV runs a Wine House at Kleinplasie, where all the wines of the valley can be tasted and bought. It is open 0900 to 1700 Monday to Friday and on Saturday mornings. You ought also to visit the KWV Brandy Cellar. The town has two wine festivals, the Food and Wine in May and the Young Wine Festivals in August. And there is a Wine Route Canoe Adventure on the Breede River from October to March (tel 021 76 2935).

Robertson

Postal Code 6705. Telephone code 02351. Tourist info 4437.

Just under 48 km (30 miles) east of Worcester, and only two hours drive from Cape Town, is Robertson, on the lovely Breede River where the winter climate is particularly pleasant. There used to be an industry making fishing rods from bamboo, but fibre-glass killed that. Today Robertson has become known for high-quality muscadel wines and has joined with neighbouring villages of Ashton, Bonnievale and McGregor to form a wine route. Details are available from the Wine Trust at 3 Constitution Street (tel 3167). The place to eat locally is the Wine Trust's Branewyndraai Restaurant, while the most agreeable hotel is the Old Mill Lodge 21 km (13 miles out) at Mc Gregor (PO Box 25 Mc Gregor 6708; tel 02353 841). There is an unexpected resort outside the town, where a mile-long stretch of river beach is known as Silwerstrand, with holiday accommodation. For information about Robertson and the resort contact the Publicity Association in Church Street (tel 4437). The area's other great asset is the scenery along the river and the climbing possibilities in the Langeberg mountains.

Montagu

Postal code 6720. Telephone code 0234. Tourist Info 42471.
Montagu, a short and scenically splendid drive from Robertson past the oddly coloured rock formations of Cogmanskloof, is the gateway to the Little Karoo (described later). It is a most attractive small town, where 23 of the old buildings are designated as national monuments. Long Street is particularly noteworthy. The medicinal springs outside the town are both hot and mildly radioactive. Since the 1981 floods the springs resort has been reconstructed, with a three-star hotel, the Avalon Springs (PO Box 110; tel 41150). Right in the town are the small one-star Montagu Hotel (PO Box 338; tel 41115), and the old colonial Mimosa Lodge (PO Box 323; tel 42351) by the church. The Lodge, though ungraded, is respected for its excellent country cooking.

Overall, Montagu is an excellent alternative to the Garden Route resorts as a base for exploring the Little Karoo with walks and hiking trails in the surrounding Langeberg. The area produces both white table wines and sweet muscadel dessert wine.

The Overberg

Between the wine country and the sea, and including Cape Agulhas, is the coastal plain called the Overberg; the land beyond the Hottentots Holland mountains. Many delightful seaside villages, such as Arniston, the fashionable resort of Hermanus, the old town of Bredasdorp, and –depending on how finicky you are about definitions – Swellendam and the Bontebok National Park are all in the Overberg. From Cape Town you head east on the N2 towards Sir Lowry's Pass through the Hottentots Hollands with a choice of ways when you pass Somerset West.

The Coastal Road
If you are in no hurry then swing along the coast on the R44 through the attractive fishing village of Gordon's Bay, and the small resorts of Betty's Bay and Kleinmond, to rejoin the N2 at Botrivier on the other side of the Hottentots Hollands. It will be a rewarding diversion.

Gordon's Bay and round Cape Hangklip
Gordon's Bay has a three-star hotel, the Van Riebeeck (PO Box 10, Gordon's Bay 7150; tel 024 561441) where the lunch-time carvery is supplemented by ostrich steak. Then the cliff road goes on towards Cape Hangklip, like a wilder version of a Cote d'Azur corniche, giving views across False Bay that reveal the true length of the Cape Peninsula. The rock formations at Cape Hangklip itself are said to be geologically unique. More prosaically, one wonders at anyone daring to build houses among the gigantic boulders that have fallen from the mountain. The hillsides are covered with natural vegetation called *fynbos,* scented with herbs and heathers, and including many varieties of protea which grow wild along the road, (remember that picking wildflowers is illegal). The Harold Porter Botanical Reserve has a concentration of Cape flora.

Sandown Bay
Along towards Sandown Bay there are wide sandy beaches, thousands of water birds, the Kleinmond Coastal Nature Reserve, and the inshore spectacle of whales playing with their young during the Winter/Spring calving season. Dolphins and seals come here too, while in summer the Kleinmond resort's human population swells from 800 to 8,000 as people 'bail out' of city civilisation into holiday cottages. The Beach House hotel (tel 02823 3130) has been completely renovated, if you need a meal stop. Watch out if you swim; there is a vicious undertow, or 'rip tide' as the South Africans say.

Houw Hoek
The R44 ends at Botrivier. If you have not turned off on the R43 to continue along the coast, you might stop for lunch at the old coaching inn at Houw Hoek, (PO Box 95 Grabouw 7160; tel 02824 49646) just off the N2. The inn was founded in 1834 and though it is only rated one star, has good cuisine, riding, tennis and swimming. The farm stall opposite has fruit and food goodies worth stopping for as well. From here it is 48 km (30 miles) to Hermanus.

Hermanus

Postal Code 7200. Telephone code 0283. Tourist Info 22629.
This one-time fishing village has become a most fashionable resort, blessed by safe bathing on white-white beaches, Mediterranean-looking pines, picturesque walks in the Fernkloof Nature Reserve on

the mountains lying behind the town, and a championship golf course. The yacht club is eight km (five miles) away on the Kleinrivier lagoon. So there is plenty to do, plus antique and art shops in the town and the Old Harbour Museum. The Information Bureau (tel 22629) is on Main Road.

Whales
Hermanus is one of the best places to observe whales and dolphins. Whales come inshore to calve all along this coast from June to November. In fact a 'Whale crier' parades the streets, sounding a kelp horn, to announce where they have been sighted. The cliff paths provide good viewing points. The three main species seen are Bryde's Whale, the Humpback and the Southern Right. For whale watching walks contact the Publicity Association.

Hotels and Restaurants
The three-star Marine Hotel (PO Box 9; tel 21112) now belongs to the renowned hotelier David Rawdon. He has filled it with antiques, created luxurious suites, and serves extensive table d'hote meals. 'By any yardstick it should be five-star' comments one British hotel owner 'except that it does not have an *a la carte* menu'. The prices head that way, although officially it is not. The other notable hotel is the Windsor (PO Box 3; tel 23727). For eating out we strongly recommend the Burgundy Restaurant near the old harbour, where we had a memorable crayfish salad out in the garden; doubly memorable, in fact, because a school of about 200 dolphins leaped and curvetted past in the bay while we ate.

From Hermanus you could either take a partly untarmaced road through Shaw's Pass to Caledon or follow the R326 inland and then the R316 to Bredasdorp and Cape Agulhas. The coast road to Cape Agulhas is laborious and tough going.

Caledon to Cape Agulhas

Caledon, inland just off the N2, is best known for its hot springs, and its wild flower garden outside the town. South Africa's first mission station was established by the Moravian Mission Society 32 km (20 miles) away at Genadendal (Valley of Grace) in the mountains in 1737. Only four km further is Greyton, with its notably elegant small country hotel, the Greyton Lodge (PO Box 50, Greyton 7233; tel 02 825 49876). The country cooking is recommended and you need to book in advance.

Bredasdorp   *Postal code 7280. Telephone code 02841.*
Bredasdorp, founded in 1838, has a Nature Reserve, a museum devoted to shipwreck momentoes, and is the gateway to Cape

Agulhas and Arniston. It has a two-star hotel, the Victoria (PO Box 11, tel 41159).

Cape Agulhas

Cape Agulhas ('Needles') is the most southerly point in Africa. The worst disaster on its saw edged rocks occurred when the troop ship Birkenhead struck the reef at Danger Point in 1852 and 337 soldiers and 57 of the crew lost their lives, although their self sacrifice saved all the women and children. The lighthouse, dating from 1848, has been restored.

Arniston *Postal code Bredasdorp 7280. Telephone code 02847.*
The thatched and whitewashed fishermen's cottages here, restored as national monuments, feature in many tour brochures.There are glorious whitesand beaches. The village is also known as Waenhuis-kraus, meaning 'Wagon House Cliff' due to a huge cliff cavern nearby. The three-star Arniston Hotel (PO Box 126; tel 640) is on the seashore and enjoys a high reputation for its cuisine.

Swellendam

Postal code 6740. Telephone code 0291. Tourist Info 42770.
Architecturally, historically and because of its location at the foot of the Langeberg, Swellendam has great attractions. The early farmers used the peaks as natural sundials, calling them Ten O'Clock, Eleven O'Clock, Twelve O'Clock and One O'Clock. From the start the burgers were an idiosyncratic bunch, living as they did on the frontier of the Cape colony. When they became too difficult to control from Stellen-bosch, the Dutch East India Company appointed a Landdrost,or administrator, for them. That was in 1745 and Swellendam's establishment as South Africa's third oldest town followed.

Memories of an Independent Republic
Nonetheless, the burgers eventually rebelled and declared a Free Republic on June 17, 1795. As luck would have it, this co-incided with a British fleet attacking the colony. The burgers then loyally rallied to the overall defence, sending a mounted force, and joined in the Dutch surrender after the defeat at Muizenberg. Their indepen-dance had lasted only 91 days. Those events give the exhibits in the Drostdy Museum a special interest, since the building dates from 1746 – though later it was enlarged – and was taken over by the burgers. It stands at the end of the wide Swellengrebel Street, planted with ancient oaks.

Notable Buildings

The old jail and the Victorian house called Mayville are part of the Museum complex. Another building to look for is the Oefeningshuis, constructed as a church for freed slaves in 1838, on the gable of which a plaster 'clock' stands permanently at 1215, reminding people of the time to gather. A real clock ticks away beneath.

Amenities

The Publicity Association is at 36 Voortrek Street (PO Box 369; tel 42770). There are three hotels, hiking trails in the Langeberg, and sports including bowls, golf, tennis and gliding. There is a base for Breede river canoeing near the town (tel 021 762 5602). The town is 225 km (141 miles) from Cape Town.

The Bontebok National Park

The bontebok, a large brown and black antelope, with white under-parts and a white blaze on its face, had been in danger of extinction. As long ago as 1779 the traveller Borrow commented 'they are seldom seen in herds of more than a dozen', whereas they had been as common as springbok. By 1930 only 20 animals were surviving on farms near Bredasdorp, where a park was proclaimed to protect them. In 1960 it was relocated to the lushly vegetated banks of the Breede river, seven km (four miles) south of Swellendam. Now there are around 200 bontebok on the 2,740 ha (11 sq miles). Other antelope include grey rhebuck, Cape grysbok and mountain zebra. Wild olives and yellow woods grow along the river, and flowering plants dot the veld. There are picnic sites, a camp site and a small shop.

The West Coast

Exploring the West Coast

These are the wilder shores of the Western Cape, much less sophis-ticated than the Garden route, but more varied and leading to the rugged wildflower paradise of Namaqualand. Seabirds and seafood, fishing villages, wrecked ships and the sea kept cold by the Benguela current from the Antarctic, characterise the coast. just inland lie the Swartland vineyards and fruit farms, already described, reached up the N7 road. This is a completely different landscape to explore, dot-ted with old Mission Stations.

Namaqualand itself has been administratively divided between the Western and Northern Cape Provinces. From a visitor's viewpoint it is really one area. But we have made the break north of Bitterfontein and you will find Springbok in the Northern Cape section.

From Cape Town to the Sandveld

Driving directly north out of Cape Town on the R27 road up the coast you pass Paarden Island, no longer an island, where once Dutch settlers kept their horses. The small white-washed house of Wolraad Woltemade is a national monument, open to the public. In 1865 he rode out into the surf to rescue passengers from a storm-wrecked ship. After bringing 14 safely to shore, the remainder panicked, drowning themselves, Woltemade and his faithful horse. The Cape flats here were planted extensively with 'Port Jackson' bushes from Australia, which are able to survive in a sandy soil and stabilise it (Port Jackson became Sydney). Beyond the flats the sandveld begins.

Bloubergstrand

Bloubergstrand's long white sands are the star turn of a succession of beaches which reach to the Orange River and Namibia, though the Atlantic rollers are always cold. The classic view across the bay to Table Mountain is much photographed and there are several seafood restaurants, but as a resort Bloubergstrand is sadly ugly. Robben Island, a jail for long term convicts where Nelson Mandela was held, lies seven km off shore. Only one prisoner has ever escaped, utilising a warden's pedalo. The abandoned pedalo was found, the convict never. The island is to be a Nature Reserve eventually. Past Melkbosstrand, near which there is an ostrich ranch, the R27 continues to Saldanha Bay.

Inland are mile upon mile of rolling fertile hills, intensively farmed both for dairy products and grain, and still called 'The Granary of South Africa', despite the increasing value of the eastern Free State's wheat.

Langebaan and Saldanha Bay

The R27 takes you to Langebaan and Saldanha Bay. If there had been fresh water available Saldanha Bay could have been a major port. As it is, all that is shipped out is iron ore from the northern Cape, fortunately for the prodigious marine life.

Langebaan is a holiday resort on a 26km (16 miles) long lagoon which forms the West Coast National Park. A little further on is the Club Mykonos resort village and yacht marina. Both benefit from watersports allowed in parts of the park. To charter a boat for serious deep-sea fishing safaris contact Schaafsma Marine at Vredenburg (PO Box 172, Vredenburg 7380; tel 02281 31571. You can sail out 500 nautical miles to fish on the undersea volcano of Vema for trophies, or just take a weekend trip around this area. Crayfish is the popular catch and dishes at the local hotels and restaurants feature that and snoek pate, made from a species of barracuda.

The Western Cape

A popular seafood restaurant is Die Strandlope (tel 02287 51611), right on the beach at Langebaan. Incidentally this stretch of coast is good for viewing whales from June to November.

The West Coast National Park

The long lagoon, several islands, and the Postberg Nature Reserve on the spit of land enclosing the lagoon, comprise 18,000 ha (70 sq miles). In summer the salt marshes and the clear, shallow waters of the lagoon attract as many as 55,000 waterbirds; cormorants, flamingoes, curlews and gannets among them. Many birds migrate here from the Arctic. The Park has good bed and breakfast accommodation at the Langebaan Lodge (bookings tel 012 343 1991).

Saldanha Bay *Postal code 7395. Telephone code 0221. Info 42088.*
This small fishing town and naval base 20 km (12 miles) north of Langebaan is fairly nondescript, as is Vredenburg nearby. However the Protea hotel (PO Box 70; tel 41264) on the waterfront now rates three stars. A short drive away there is a pretty fishing village called Paternoster by Cape Columbine.

Further north, on St Helena Bay, Velddrif has a welcoming small one-star hotel, the Riviera (PO Box 26, Velddrif 7370; tel 02288 31137). This is where the Great Berg river flows into the sea, and the Berg River Canoe Marathon in July from Paarl ends. You will see pelicans, sacred ibis and herons along the river; and also a small fish called 'bokkom', a type of mullet, for sale, dried and salted. Vasco da Gama anchored in the bag in 1497, naming it. There is a monument to him.

Beyond St Helena Bay the saltbush heathland of the sandveld stretches up into Namaqualand. You now need to drive the 65 km (41 miles) to join the N7 road at Piketberg, near which is the excellent Noupoort Guest farm (tel 0261 5754). For information and advice call 0261 31261.

Namaqualand

North of St Helena's Bay you begin to enter a new landscape, shaped by the Atlantic receding 60 million years ago, its sandveld and mountains enabled to bloom prodigiously in spring by the cool, moist wind off the sea, Namaqualand is justifiably famous for its Spring profusion of wild flowers, its birdlife, its rugged scenery and – thanks to irrigation in southern Namaqualand – its citrus fruits and vineyards. Less visited than the Western Cape, parts of it are well worth the journey and many tours go there. But the nearer you get to the Orange river, the bleaker it becomes. Originally the area between the Olifants river and the Orange, bounded to the east by the high plateau of the Karoo, was inhabited by Bushmen, but they were displaced by Hottentots. The elephant herds seen by early explorers in the 18th century, which gave the river its name, have long since gone as well.

Climate
In January temperatures reach 40°C, the further north you go the hotter it gets by day, and fall as low as -3°C at night in winter. Rainfall is miniscule at 160mm annually, it is the moist ocean air that nourishes shrubs in the sandy soil, as it does all along the west coast desert of Namibia in this unique climate environment. By far the best time for a visit is when the flowers are blooming in August and September.

Topography
Experts divide Namaqualand into four regions. The 30 km (19 miles) wide coastal strip of the Sandveld, effectively starting at St Helena Bay, is a wind-scrubbed plain where cattle survive on saltbushes. Inland of this are the hills of the Knervslakte, littered with white quartz pebbles and bounded by the Bokkeveld mountains. North of Bitterfontein you reach the bizarre granite rocks and hills of the aptly named Klipkoppe. Finally in the extreme north are the barren mountains of the Richtersveld, west of the main road, inaccessible without 4 WD and now partly protected as a National Park. The area is named after a German missionary priest.

Flora
In spring the best known flowers are the orange/yellow Namaqualand daisies. Many varieties of annuals, from tiny yellow 'goose eyes' upwards, carpet the veldt. They flower and seed very quickly during the moist Spring and, because each kind has its own germination temperature, continue to germinate through to July. Herbs and shrubs burst out in purple. Succulents range from the smallest to the flowering aloes, like the kokerboom, or quiver tree, capable of attaining a 9 m (29 ft) height. The season starts in the north and moves south as the weather warms up. By October and the approach of the searing summer the flowering cycle is over. Removing plants is illegal and anyway few survive transplanting. Seeds, succulents and some plants can be bought at the Clanwilliam Wildflower Garden, also at Vanrhynsdorp and in the north at Nababeep. Two illustrated books on the flora are 'The South African Wildflower Guide', published by the Cape Department of Nature Conservation, and 'Namaqualand in Flower', published by Macmillan.

Driving from Cape Town
Driving up the main N 7 road – as already described – from the wheatfields around Piketberg, you come first to Citrusdal and the unexpec-

tedly green and fertile valley of the Olifants river, locally called 'The Golden Valley', because its wheatfields shine like brushed gold.

The Golden Valley

You enter the Olifants river valley via the dramatic Piekenierskloof Pass through the Olifants Mountains, 519 m (1,687 ft) above sea level, and with fine views both back across the sandveld and into the valley itself. The Piekenier, or pikeman, was a look-out stationed here by the Dutch East India Company in the early days to watch for Hottentot cattle raiders. They killed him and his ghost is said to haunt the pass at night. Ghost or not, there is a pleasant wayside restaurant called the Vanmeerhof Farmstall, looking down on Citrusdal. It offers home made pies and scones and has a craft shop.

Citrusdal *Postal code 7340. Telephone code 022. Info 912 3210.*
Famed for its orange groves, Citrusdal's earliest farm dates from 1725 and there is a 200-year-old orange tree at Groot Hexriver. Vineyards have become a strong competitor, however, and there is a Golden Valley Wine Route. Both the citrus and the wine co-operatives can be visited. The town's other attraction is the hot springs spa 12 km (seven miles) away. The Cedarberg Hotel (tel 921 2221), at 57 Voortrekker Street, is two-star. Nonetheless, Clanwilliam, further up the valley, is a more rewarding place to stay.

The Cedarberg Mountains
The best side-trip from Citrusdal is into the Cedarberg Mountains where there is fine hiking. The indigenous cedar forests are protected, there are curious rock formations and waterfalls, and on the higher ground – often snow-covered in winter – you can find the rare snow protea, its fluffy white centre surrounded by crimson petals. A permit is needed to enter the Wilderness Area. Apply to the Government Forester, PO Citrusdal 7340; tel 921 2289.

Bushman Paintings
There are rock paintings in the Cedarberg and at many other places along the Golden Valley. Some depict early European settlers as well as animals.

Clanwilliam

Postal code 8135 Telephone code 027. Info 482 2024.
One of South Africa's ten oldest towns, though still very small, Clanwilliam is a good base for seeing the spring flowers, or exploring the Wine Route. The notable 19th century church is now a national monument and the tiny Georgian jail a Folk Museum. The local hero was the doctor and poet Louis Leopoldt, while the botanist Nortier first

promoted the delicately-flavoured 'rooibos' herbal tea. This is made from the leaves of a most unpromising-looking small bush, now grown all around. The period Clanwilliam Hotel (PO Box 4; tel 482 1101. Two-star) has a pool, gymnasium, squash court, and Reinhold's Restaurant, serving well-prepared country dishes.

Flowers and Excursions

There are various attractions in the neighbourhood, in addition to Cedarberg hikes. Great expanses of wild Namaqualand daisies flower in season, there is a Wildflower Garden on Main Road, while many varieties grow in the Ramskop Nature Reserve on the banks of the Clanwilliam Dam. This dam, incidentally, feeds irrigation channels that run as far as Lutzville, making cultivation possible all the way. You can fish in the Olifants river, as in the Cedarberg streams, or make an excursion across the rugged Pakhuis Pass to visit the 1830 mission station village of Wuppertal, with its pretty Cape-style thatched cottages and a very old-established Coloured community. The making of South African 'veldskoen' shoes originated here.

Towards the coast from Clanwilliam the R364 road leads 58 km (36 miles) to Lambert's Bay, while the N7 continues up the Wine Route to Vanrhynsdorp.

Lamberts Bay

Postal code 8130. Telephone code 027. Info 432 2335.

Frankly, unless you are a birdwatching fanatic or planning a novel about pilchard canning, you can safely miss this stretch of coast, despite the whitesand beaches. Lamberts Bay is known for the Cape gannets that congregate in a screeching, malodourous multitude on Bird Island, reached along a causeway round the trawler harbour. True, there are also cormorants and the endangered jackass penguins. Even so, the three-star Marine Protea Hotel (tel 432 1126) deserves to be in a better resort. Crayfish are a speciality in the season of November to mid-May.

Clanwilliam to Vanrhysdorp

The rest of the Golden Valley Wine Route takes you through fine scenery, vineyards and uninteresting towns, all with small hotels, banks and adequate shops. Klawer is a road and rail junction, where you can board express buses of the Namaqualand Busdiens back to Cape Town or on to Springbok. But, as the assistant in the general store put it, 'We don't depend on tourists here at all'. The same goes for the other towns. However at Vredendal, on the R362 road down a well-watered and lush valley, the Co-operative Wine Cellar merits a visit. Palatable vintages here include Chardonnay, Chenin Blanc and Sauvignon Blanc. You can get export-quality KWV brandy too. Further on Lutzville marks the end of the Wine Route. The R362 then takes you to the Olifants river mouth, where the lagoon is a waterbird sanctuary, and next to the tiny angling and scuba-diving resort of Strandfontein. Offshore a special rig dredges diamonds from the seabed. A dirt coastal road continues south to Lambert's Bay, making a circuit back to Clanwilliam possible.

Vanrhynsdorp

Postal code 8170. Telephone code 02727. Info 91552.
One of the most important centres of the Olifants river valley this small town was founded in 1751, although the area had become known much earlier in the searches for copper. There is a local museum in the old prison and a large nursery of succulent plants. This is where the stony semi-desert of the Knersvlakte begins, many of the stones being small pieces of quartz, and the distant views become more craggily mountainous. So the apparent miracle of thousands of tiny plants bursting into flower in July and August is all the greater. The town has various guest houses. Inland lies sheep farming country around Calvinia, with a quite spectacular round-trip drive via mountain passes on the R27 and R364 back to Clanwilliam.

Bitterfontein to Springbok

Mining for copper opened up the north of Namaqualand, though the term 'opened up' remains relative. The further you go, the tougher the terrain. The Knervslakte ends beyond the small township of Bitterfontein, which has a simple one star hotel, the Bitterfontein (PO Box 1; tel 02752 ask for 42). Then you come into the more interesting and rugged Klipkoppe, with extraordinary piles of jumbled rocks and bare, whaleback granite hills rearing out of the sandy plain. They form one edge of the great African continental plateau, extending from the Karoo to the Sahara.

A curiosity by the N7 road 15 km (ten miles) south of Kamieskroon is the iron-fenced grave of a British officer who died in 1902 during the Boer War. Lt C J Darter's resting place is the smallest registered piece of land in South Africa. It is beneath a tree on the right as you drive north.

Springbok is described in the Northern Cape section on page 250.

The Garden Route

The name 'Garden Route' is slightly deceptive. The route runs along a beautiful strip of land between a series of mountain ranges and the sea, basically following the N2 freeway from Riversdale through Mossel Bay, George, Knysna, and Plettenberg Bay to the Storms River at the Tsitsikamma Coastal National Park. This coastal plateau has a temperate climate, thick indigenous forests, lush green river valleys, cliffs, lagoons and long clean beaches excellent for surfing. It has become one of South Africa's most famed holiday coasts, but it is a 'garden' only by comparison with the aridity of the Karoo further inland. The most rain falls in August to October, and the Mossel Bay end is relatively dry, while at Tsitsikamma there are showers all year round, which produce near-tropical vegetation.

Various passes through the mountains to the dryer and hotter landscape of the Little Karoo offer panoramic views without long journeys. Consequently, by convention and the itineraries of coach tours, the Route has come to include Oudtshoorn's ostrich farms and the Kango Caves in the Little Karoo, which we deal with separately, and sometimes the attractive town of Prince Albert in the Great Karoo (see Karoo section). The local Publicity Associations produce a positive surfeit of brochures, as do tour companies, so our description is confined to the highlights. equally there are a mass of hotels and guests houses, of which we mention a few. For selective lists contact Hotelogue or Portfolio; address in the South African Factfile.

Just about every Cape Town tour firm offers coach tours, notably Specialized Tours (tel 021 25 3259), Hylton Ross (tel 021 438 1500), and Springbok Atlas (tel 021 455468). Via the N2 road George is 432 km (270 miles), or five hours drive, from Cape Town. Translux (tel 021 218 3871) and Inter-Cape (tele 021 419 8888) run express coach services, taking anything from five and a half hours to seven hours. Inter-City (tel 021 419 6038) runs from Johannesburg overnight to George and Mossel Bay. There is no longer a passenger railway service, but there are flights to George.

The Overberg to Mossel Bay

After traversing the Overberg you come to Riversdale, a farming town with several hotels and an Africana Museum. Down at the coast there is good fishing at Still Bay East and surfing on the long beach of Still Bay West; the two sides of the resort being divided by the Kafferkuils river. More information from the Town Clerk (tel 02934 41577).

The Western Cape

Back on the N2, Albertinia has the curiosity of an ochre mine, which supplies the Xhosa tribe with their traditional red ochre 'make up'. The local reeds are used for traditional Cape roof thatching.

Mossel Bay

Postal code 6500. Telephone code 0444. Tourist Info 912202.
Mossel Bay has several sides to its character. It is a commercial seaport on the slopes of Cape St Blaize, which enjoyed a boom in the 1990s due to the discovery of offshore oil; a holiday centre for watersports, rock angling and big game fishing (especially black marlin); and a town with a niche in history. This bay is where the Portuguese navigator, Bartholomeu Dias, made his first landfall after rounding the Cape in 1488. The Museum has a replica of Dias' caravel, an astonishingly tiny ship for a voyage that was scientifically as adventurous then as exploring space is now. The Information Office is in Church Street.

The Post Office Tree
Because the bay has a spring which never runs dry, it became a provisioning stop for sailing ships on the way to India. The Post Office tree is a venerable milkwood to which a seaboot was nailed for many years. Seafarers collected letters from, and posted them in, the boot. Today the tree is part of the Bartholomeu Dias Museum complex and letters posted in a boot-shaped postbox next to it are specially franked.

Hotels and Restaurants
The town has quite a few hotels. The three-star Rose and Crown at 3 Matfield Street (tel 911069) is central. The three-star Santos Protea (PO Box 203; tel 7103), on the Santos beach, is a large and well-equipped holiday hotle. A good guest house is Huis te Marquette (tel 913 182). For seafood try the Camelot restaurant, or the Gannett Guest House (tel 913738) by the Post office tree. Mussels –which gave the town its name in the 17th century – are a speciality.

Beaches, Expeditions and a Mountain Inn
There are fine beaches for watersports at Santos and Die Bakke and you can also swim at the long rock pools and the little beach below the lighthouse, which is the best place for angling. But beware being caught by the tide in the tunnel caves. Offshore is Seal Island, the home of penguins and many seals. Boat trips run out there from the harbour. A longer expedition is up through the Outeniqua mountains to Oudtshoorn on the R326, via the Robinson Pass. Near the pass is the recommended three-star Eight Bells Mountain Inn (PO Box 436 Mossel Bay; tel 951544), some 32 km (18 miles) from Mossel Bay, with Swiss-style log chalets, swimming, horses for riding in the forest and hiking trails on its own estate.

George

Postal code 6530. Telephone code 0441. Tourism Info 744000.
This is a quiet inland town, founded in 1811 and named after King George III, with a fine white 1840 church and streets lined with ancient oaks. Behind it rises the 1,698 m (5,562 ft) Cradock Peak of the Outeniqua Mountains, which form the backdrop to the Garden Route and in whose foothills stand forests of yellowwoods, stinkwoods and other indigenous trees. There was a forestry station here as early as 1778 and George's timber-oriented history is displayed in the Museum in the handsome Old Drostdy.

Today George is more of a commercial centre and the best shopping buys surprisingly include diamonds from the Schuster Diamond Cutting Works in the Industrial Area. However there is an active sports centre, an excellent golf course and the 137 km (86 miles) Outeniqua Hiking Trail starts nearby at Witfontein. The Tourist Information Office is in York Street. The airport is ten km (six miles) south of the town.

Hotel and Restaurants
The best hotels are the King George III (PO Box 9292; tel 74 7659, fax 74 7664), overlooking the Country Club fairways, and the elegant Fancourt (PO Box 2266; tel 70 8282, fax 70 7605), with its own 27 hole golf course designed by Gary Player. if you want to stay outside the town in less expensive comfort try the Hoogekraal Country House (PO Box 34; tel 791277) at Glentana. The Old Townhouse Restaurant (telephone 743663) on Market Street specialises in seafood and grills. Another reliable eating place is the Copper Pot.

George to Wilderness and Knysna

Easily the most entertaining way of travelling the next stage of the Garden Route is aboard the Outeniqua Choo-Tjoe, which steams once a day on weekdays through the splendid scenery of lakes and lagoons from George to Knysna and back, via Wilderness, and will stop at any station you want. The trip, of 65 km (41 miles) or so, takes three and a half hours, one way. For reservations phone (0441 738202). A more adventurous driving route than the N2, not all tarmaced, is the old Seven Passes road, higher up on the plateau, which climbs in and out of river valleys and forests.

Wilderness

Postal code 6560. Telephone code 0441. Tourist Info 770045.
The resort town of Wilderness is on a spit of land with a glorious long beach (though beware the current). Behind it are a series of salt-water lakes, set among forested hills, that are a fisherman's and birdwatcher's paradise. They extend almost to the Knysna lagoon and are partly managed by the National Parks Board. So you have two quite distinct opportunities for relaxation; watersports and nature-watching.

The Lakes

The first lake, the Serpentine, leads from the river estuary to Island Lake where there is a yacht club. Further east Langvlei and Rondevlei are protected. The much larger Swartvlei has a channel to the sea at Sedgefield, where regattas are held. Finally the freshwater Groenvlei, beyond Sedgefield, has a small nature reserve where you can walk. The lakes are a sanctuary for waterbirds, the forests protect the scarlet-winged Knysna lourie, and there is good fishing in the Swartvlei for leerfish and for black bass in the Groenvlei. Riding in the forests can be arranged through Cherie's in Sedgefield (tel 04455 31575). There are self-catering cottages and campsites in the National Park. For information contact the Cape Town office (tel 021 222810). Tourist Information is handled by the George office.

Hotels

The three-star Holiday Inn Garden Court (PO Box 26; tel 91104) overlooks both the lagoon and the sea. The Karos Wilderness Hotel (PO Box 6; tel 91110), has its own private nature reserve. The old-established Fairy Knowe (PO Box 28; tel 91100) is two-star.

Knysna

Postal code 6570. Telephone code 0445. Tourist info 21610.
Knysna has a lot to offer; historically, recreationally and in its delightful setting. It was founded by one of the most intriguing characters ever to set foot in South Africa, George Rex, who arrived at the turn of the 18th century and in 1817 was the first man to sail a ship safely into the lagoon, establishing a timber port. Why the Cape Governor treated him as a VIP was never recorded, but the belief is that he was the illegitimate son of George III and a London Quakeress called Hannah Lightfoot. The town's Millwood Museum has a collection of his belongings. He certainly chose an attractive spot to settle.

The Lagoon

The lagoon now protected as the Knysna National Lake Area runs out to the sea between the two sheer red sandstone cliffs called the Heads, whose perils Rex defeated. The eastern of the two is easily accessible by land and gives splendid views and good rock fishing. Pleasure boats do trips up the lagoon and to the Featherbed Nature Reserve on the Western Head, so called because the anchorage offshore is so calm. On the way out is Leisure Island, facing Knysna across the lagoon. An oyster hatchery makes oysters a local speciality in season. Sadly, the new N2 road is routed along the lagoon.

The Town
The town is proud of its semi-French atmosphere, with pavement cafes, markets and sophisticated shops. Being among thousands of acres of hardwood forests, Knysna's craftsmen have become expert at making South Africa's highly prized traditional stinkwood furniture. The wood's hard, fine grain gives it a satiny finish, usually oiled rather than polished. Yellowwood furniture is also attractive, similar to pine and light yet strong. The Publicity Association is at 40 Main Street (tel 21610) and can provide details of local excursions and organised walks, as well as accommodation. A big new shopping mall has replaced the old mill, complete with flea markets.

Hotels
There are numerous small hotels, bed and breakfasts, and holiday complexes. The three-star Knysna Protea (PO Box 33, tel 22127) is in the town, and the elegantly luxurious Belvidere Manor House (PO Box 1195; tel 871055), across the lagoon bridge on the road to George, while the small Knysna Lodge (PO Box 1245; tel 825401, fax 825265) has delightful thatched cottages near the lagoon. The Ashmead Resort (PO Box 109; tel 23172) has well-furnished apartments for rent.

Local Activities
You can swim either in the lagoon or on the beaches at Buffalo Bay and Noetzie, where eccentric seaside houses have been built like castles, and there is every conceivable watersport available. Interesting excursions could be to the Homtini Gorge, a natural bird sanctuary; to Belvidere – on George Rex's former estate – with a pretty Norman-style sandstone church built by Cornish masons; to Noetzie beach; to the abandoned goldmines inland at Millwood, which were South Africa's first; or to the Knysna Forest.

Knysna Forest
This dense primeval forest in the hills harbours a few extremely shy antelope and elephant. The 18 km (11 miles) Elephant Trail, and two shorter variants, are signed from the Diepwalle Forest Station. No permits are required. Take the R339 off the N2, just beyond Knysna Lagoon, signed for Prince Albert's Pass, and soon becoming gravel. Various picnic sites are located by monster yellowwoods, the only sur-

vivors of earlier logging. At 22 km (14 miles) from Knysna you come to the Forest Station and nearby is King Edward's Tree, standing 46 m (150 feet) high and reckoned to be 700 years old. The Elephant Trail starts here, and it is also the end of the eight day Outeniqua Trail from George. Further on a precipitous and rough road off to the left leads to superb panoramas from the Spitzkop viewpoint. Back on the R339 you can branch east for Kransbos and Plettenberg Bay.

Plettenberg Bay

Postal code 6600. Telephone code 04457. Tourist Info 34065.
Plettenberg Bay has some of the finest and safest beaches in South Africa. This one-time village, on a promontory, was founded in 1778 by the Dutch East India Company. Remains of the 1787 timber yard, rectory and chapel still exist, off the road to Beacon Island. However the resort has become immensely popular. So if you want the unsophisticated atmosphere of old you'll have to try the small resorts beyond East London. That said, every kind of watersport is available, and there is a country club with golf and tennis. Sea and rock fishing are particularly good off Robberg Point. Fishing tackle can be hired in the town and boats from the Angling Club Marina on the Keurbooms river. The Publicity Association is on Main Street (PO Box 894; tel 34065).

Hotels
The small Plettenberg (PO Box 719; tel 32030, fax 32074), on the Lookout Promontory, has become four-star and is one of the Cape's best, while the Arches Hotel (PO Box 115; tel 32118 two-star) is much less expensive but well situated. The small Hunter's Country House (PO Box 454; tel 7818) is an exclusive four-star retreat between the mountains and the resort. Finally the Plettenberg Park (PO Box 167; tel 33067) is a fastidiously elegant hotel overlooking the sea some way from the town. The peak season here is December-January, and you must book ahead.

The Tsitsikamma Coastal and Forest National Parks

These two parks respectively protect a small area of untouched natural forest inland of the N2 and a 100 km (72 miles) length of magnificent coastal plain, cliffs, foreshore and sea. 'Tsitsikamma' comes from a Hottentot word meaning 'clear water'. The Coastal Park begins around the Nature's Valley Reserve, just east of Plettenberg Bay, is cut through by the Storms River ravine and ends at Groot River. Proclaimed in 1964, it is unique in safeguarding both mammal and marine wildlife, not to mention countless birds. So you could conceivably see bushbuck, clawless otters and dolphins on the same walk, while the scenery where various river gorges cut through the cliffs to the sea has made the park's four-day Otter Hiking Trail about the most popular in South Africa. The trail must be booked through the Parks Board Headquarters (PO Box 787, Pretoria 0001; tel 012 343 1991).

Accommodation
You reach this park by a road turn-off nine km (five and a half miles) from the strikingly graceful Paul Sauer bridge on the N2. At the bridge there is a National Parks restaurant and a track to the Storms River mouth where a swaying suspension bridge takes walkers across the gorge. There are self catering beach cottages and apartments at the Storms River mouth and a shop, plus log cabins, in the forest (Bookings National Parks). Nearby accommodation includes the Tsitsikamma Forest Inn (PO Storms River 6308; tel 042 5411711) and the Tsitsikamma Lodge (PO Box 10, Storms River 6308; te; 04230 702). Both are in the forests, rustic, and not expensive.

The Forest Park
The ancient trees, shrubs, creepers and ferns of the Forest Park, encouraged by a rainfall of 1,200 mm (47 inches) a year, crowd the sides of the Storms River ravine. Very short trails lead past fine specimens of trees, ferns and proteas. You turn off into the Forest Park from the N2 three km (two miles) before the bridge. There is no park accommodation.

The Little Karoo

This valley behind the Garden Route, running from Montagu in the west to Oudtshoorn between the Swartberg and Outeniqua ranges, is a place of unexpected contrasts and curiosities. The surrounding mountains are high enough to be dusted with snow in winter, while their streams provide the irrigation for farms and vineyards in what would otherwise be arid veld, although when it does rain around October the shrubs and herbs burst out into pink, yellow and purple flower. The climate is hot in summer, reaching 45°C, and cold in winter. The R62 runs the length of the Little Karoo, with north-south roads down to the coast and several scenically-magnificent passes through to the Great Karoo inland. Montagu has already been described in the Western Cape section. We start at the other end with the 'capital' and most visited town, Oudtshoorn.

Oudtshoorn

Postal code 6620. Telephone code 04431. Tourist Info 22 2221.
Oudtshoorn is synonymous with ostriches, because the district made its fortune from ostrich farming in 1860-85 and 1905-14, when ostrich plumes were ragingly fashionable in Europe. The Great War and then the windswept nature of early motoring killed the fashion, not that it has ever completely died.

The town is named after an 18th century Dutch Governor of the Cape, who never even reached Africa, let alone the Little Karoo. The Baron Pieter van Reede van Outdtshoorn died on the voyage out. One of the main streets is named after him, on which the C P Nel Museum has illuminating exhibits both on ostrich farming and on what the town used to be like, with meticulously reproduced turn-of-the-century shop interiors and dress fashions. Mauve flowering jacarandas and blue gums grow along the River Grobbelaars, which divides the town, and the old suspension bridge across it is preserved. Overall, Oudtshoorn is quite spread-out, with wide streets and some handsome sandstone and ornate Victorian houses, notably around Baron van Reede Street, where most of the hotels are located.

Hotels
There are several three-star hotels, including a very ordinary Holiday Inn Garden Court (PO Box 52; tel 22 2201). The Kango Protea (PO Box 370; tel 22 6161), also on Baron van Reede Street, is virtually in the countryside, with thatched rondavels – which shows how very long the street is. The older two-star Queens Hotel (PO Box 19; tel 222101) is in the town's historic centre, but Oudtshoorn is best seen for a day and left.

Ostrich Farms

Of the world's 150,000 ostrich population, roughly 120,000 are in the Little Karoo, the only place where they have been successfully ranched. Indeed it is an offence to remove eggs or chicks from this district. Two of the big farms make a business of showing visitors their operation and have well-organised tours of about an hour and half, plus the chance of riding an ostrich yourself or watching a miniature 'Ostrich Derby'. The Safari Ostrich Farm and the Highgate Ostrich Farm are both on the Mossel Bay road outside the town and are open daily 0730-1700. The Safari farm's Feather Palace, called Welgeluk, is a national monument, illustrated in our drawing.

Feather Palace on the Safari Ostrich Farm

The Ostrich Business

Queen Nefertari of ancient Egypt adorned herself with ostrich plumes, plumes are the three feathers in the Prince of Wales' crest, and in the Edwardian era they fetched as much as their weight in gold. The fortunes they made built 'Feather Palaces' like Welgeluk, illustrated above. The feathers still sell today. Where would fan dancers be without them, indeed? Farmed ostriches are plucked every nine months. The largest plumes are main wing feathers, which are not hooked together as other birds' are, so ostriches could never fly, even if their wings were large enough. The tail feathers are utilised for dusters.

A female ostrich scrapes a hollow in the ground for the 14 to 16 eggs she lays, which she and her mate take it in turns to incubate for 42 days. Each egg weighs one and half kilos, or one fiftieth of a grown bird (whereas the tiny hummingbird's egg is one eighth). If scrambled it would provide 20 breakfasts. Although strong, the shell is translucent enough for the egg's fertility to be assessed by holding it up to a light. The parent birds stay together for life, but while 'widows' find new mates, 'widowers' do not.

Ostriches can run at well over 60 kph, their kick can kill a man, and they do not hide their heads in the sand, although their brains are very small. On farms they mainly eat alfalfa, but will pick up and swallow almost anything. Ultimately farm ostriches' skins become expensive leather, distinguishable by the quill sockets; their meat sells as ostrich steak, known in Switzerland as 'African turkey'; and their exceptionally clear corneas are used for human eye transplants.

The Western Cape

The information in the adjoining special article was provided by Highgate, founded in 1850 and now in the hands of the fourth generation of the Hooper family. They run a very pleasant restaurant in their house, serving scrambled ostrich eggs, ostrich steaks – which taste like stewing beef – and exotic pumpkins cooked in butter, with estate wines to wash the meal down. The coloured staff, in period print dresses, sing songs afterwards, making the standard tour much more of an event.

The Ostrich Express
This special train runs from Oudtshoorn to Calitzdorp where you are met by Coon Carnival singers, shown a wine estate, dined and accommodated overnight before returning.

At Calitzdorp the Boplaas and Die Kranz vineyards produce prize-winning ports, as well as dry white and light red wines, using Merlot and Sauvignon cultivars, though the Karoo climate and the fertile alluvial soil favour their sweet wines better. Both estates offer tastings and tours.

Kango Caves

These calcite caves 26 km (16 miles) from Oudtshoorn on the R328 have extraordinary coloured formations of stalactites (growing downwards) and stalagmites (growing upwards). A series of 80 caverns extend for three km (two miles) underground, the first so large that concerts are held in it, the smallest requiring you to slither through on your stomach. Guided tours last two hours, there is a restaurant, a curio shop, and a creche. On the way from Oudtshoorn you pass the Kango Crocodile Ranch and Cheetahland.

The Swartberg Pass to the Karoo

Beyond the Cango Caves the road to Prince Albert declines to gravel and climbs through the near-red rock formations of the Swartberg range, strangely folded and twisted by the forces that created the mountains. Clear streams cascade down the slopes and in Spring a myriad of wildflowers come out. There are frequent roadside picnic spots. The top of the pass is at 1,585 m (5,150 feet), where there is a memorial to Thomas Bain, this road's constructor. Near the summit a turn off goes down to Die Hell, where a solitary Boer community farmed before the Anglo-Boer war. The road reached it in 1960, but only one farmer remains. The main road continues to Prince Albert. The pass is liable to be closed by rain or snow; we found ourselves slipping and sliding and had to turn back and go via the easier Meiringspoort Pass to the east, which is often used to make a tourist circuit with this one.

The Great Karoo

To most city living South Africans the Karoo is nothing more than a drab, hot, semi-desert plain, criss-crossed by mountain ranges, which they have to drive through on the way from the Transvaal to the Cape. No-one has attempted to invent a Karoo tourist route. Its ash grey and olive coloured scrub is monotonous, with the only signs of life being isolated farmsteads, merino sheep and an occasional springbok, where in the 18th century there may have been three million. The impression of desolation is understandable, but misleading. These thousands of square miles of upland plateau – which were an inland sea 280 million years ago, and whose transformations are illustrated in the Karoo National Park – conceal a few treasures.

The Karoo's Character
If you take the trouble to explore you will discover attractive small towns, with a distinctive Karoo adaption of Cape Dutch and Georgian architecture; hidden valleys; eagles and mountain zebra in the National Parks; plus other unexpected wildlife and plants. The air is clear and crisp, while the apparently dull landscape has moments of great beauty. The word 'Karoo' is Hottentot for 'arid' and in places it takes five acres to support a single one of either those valuable merino sheep or the black headed 'dorpers' which provide Karoo lamb. Yet, when it does rain, the scrub changes overnight to a rich green and wildflowers bloom everywhere. Majestic storms create vivid rainbows. In winter the mountains are snow-capped. One of the most delightful towns, Prince Albert, reached from the Little Karoo via the reddish rock scenery of the Swartberg Pass, has become an extension of the Garden Route. Beaufort West, on both the N1 road and the main railway, is the 'capital'.

The Karoo Divided
Perhaps because of the Karoo's apparent desolation it has been carved up administratively between the Western Cape and the Eastern Cape. To the traveller this makes not a blind bit of difference. So this section describes the Karoo as a whole, starting with its principal town of Beaufort West, which is reached from the Little Karoo by a scenically splendid road through the Swartberg mountains.

Beaufort West

Postal code 6970. Telephone code 0201. Tourist Info 51160.
This is the 'capital' of the Karoo, a stop on express train services from Johannesburg, and has a variety of hotels. So, although it is not an outstanding town, many tourists stay here over night. Its most famous son, the heart transplant pioneer Chris Barnard, is honoured by an

exhibition of his dozens of international awards in the City Hall. Barnard himself lives in Cape Town. The Publicity Association is in the Barnard family home, the restored Sendingpastorie at 91 Donkin Street.

The Karoo National Park

This is the place to gain an understanding of the Karoo's diverse and unusual ecology and geology. Scant though the Spring rainfall is, fauna and flora derive moisture from winter snowfalls and mists. Many of the larger mammals which used to inhabit the area have been re-introduced, including mountain zebra and red hartebeest. Caracals and wild cats are indigenous. Reptiles include rock monitors and strange tent tortoises. Bull frogs may wait three years in their underground holes for it to rain, when they come up and breed. There is actually a profusion of life in this harsh environment.

Driving the short distance from Beaufort West you come into the Nuweveld mountains. These are all that is left of two levels of volcanic plateau ridges, which pushed up through the floor of the Karoo 150 million years ago, when the earth's continents divided. The cliff 'battlements' of these mountains are hard dolerite, which has survived the erosion that cut the valleys and created the parks lowest level of the plain. The upper level is sour grassveldt, where otters and water mongoose live in pools; gemsbok and other plains game frequent the middle level, where various streams rise; and the plain includes riverine bush, supporting kudu, reptiles, brown-headed kingfishers and many other birds. The park's uplands have 18 breeding pairs of black eagles, which largely feed on rock rabbits, which would destroy the vegetation, if fear of the eagles did not check the distance they feed from their hides.

Accommodation and Hikes

The park has a large rest camp. There is a restaurant, a shop, and an excellent Information Centre. The 'fossil trail' illustrates the abundant life the Karoo supported 240 million years ago. There are few roads, although you can reach the top escarpment via the R381 at the Molteno Pass. Walkers are encouraged and there is a three-day Springbok Hiking Trail. The Park Warden can provide information (PO Box 316, Beaufort West; tel 0201 3342), but reservations are made through the Parks Board in Pretoria (tel 012 343 1991).

Prince Albert

Postal code 6930. Telephone code 04436.
This little town, named after Queen Victoria's consort, and nestling in fruit farming country at the foot of the Swartberg mountains, dates

from 1762. It has a mild climate, beautiful local mountain walks and drives, and is architecturally appealing. Many of its Cape Dutch and Karoo houses bear a characteristic 'Prince Albert' gable, on which the extravagant plaster curves are alternately convex and concave, with a distinct resemblance to those at Tulbagh, where the master mason came from. They also have horizontal mouldings and upright pilasters. Good examples are on the lengthy main street, Church Street, at numbers one, five, 52 and 56, with others at four and 12 De Beers Street. Other houses have delicate front door fanlights. The church itself has a striking white Norman-style tower, with palm trees looking strange alongside. All the old buildings were originally thatched and had no verandahs.

The Gold Rush
The great moment in Prince Albert's history came with a gold rush in 1890. A tent town sprang up, but the alluvial finds were soon worked out. There are souvenirs of those hectic days in the gracefully furnished museum, at 16 Church Street, halfway between the church and the hotel. The Seven Arches House, opposite has a private mineral collection, which the owner will show to visitors. Information is available from the Town Clerk (PO Box 25; tel 320). The best local shopping buys are rugs and mats, woven from Karoo wool.

Hotel
The two-star Swartberg Protea at 77 Church Street (tel 332) has a history too, having had a licence since 1865, and being a national monument. It has a pleasant old-world atmosphere and is adequately comfortable.

Local Expeditions
If Prince Albert is pretty quiet in the evenings, at least there is plenty of scope for daytime sightseeing. The watermill outside the town is an historic landmark, there is tennis, golf, sailing and fishing, plus some magnificent hikes and drives. The Swartberg Pass offers one drive, provided it has not rained or snowed. Another is along the side of the hills to Klaarstroom and Meiringspoort, where weeping willows and poplars line the valley. At Meiringspoort – the other pass through to Oudtshoorn – there is a 200 ft waterfall.

Matjiesfontein

Postal code 6901. Telephone code 02372.
You cannot leave the Karoo without stopping, if only for a drink, at a hotel that has made itself legendary twice in its history; and which owns a village halfway between Beaufort West and Cape Town. Matjiesfontein is on the main railway line 312 km (195 miles) from Cape

The Western Cape

Town, where an enterprising young Scot named Jimmy Logan opened a hotel in 1884. The whole village is now a National Monument.

Logan's Fortune Hunt
Shipwrecked as a teenager on the way to Australia, Logan progressed from being a station porter at 17 to District Superintendent at Touws River at 21. At that time the dining car had not been invented. Streams of speculators were passing by train and ox-wagon to the Kimberley diamond fields. Logan obtained refreshment room concessions here, 3,000 ft above sea level, where the dry air suited his health, and ended up turning Matjiesfontein into a wildly fashionable resort. Royalty, Cecil Rhodes and the Sultan of Zanzibar were among his guests and he was elected to the Cape Parliament. After his death the hotel declined.

Restoration
In 1968 the hotel (and the village) was brought by David Rawdon, restored, furnished with period pieces, and re-opened as the Lord Milner (PO Matjiesfontein; tel ask for 5203). The atmosphere is of a distinguished country house, there are quiet lounges and a library, courtyards and a pool. Because of a few deficiencies the hotel is only graded two-star, but the food is excellent and you are unlikely to stay anywhere as individual again.

The Lord Milner hotel at Matjiesfontein

Local Interest
Alongside on Logan Street the General Store has become a coffee house. The Laird's Arms is a Victorian pub. There is a small museum, a Court House and a Police Station, although restoration is not complete. A red double-decker London bus takes guests sightseeing. One curiosity, visible to the left on a farm ten km down the N1, is the grave of a British General killed at the battle of Magersfontein, near Kimberley. The British authorities subsequently confused the names and had the stone obelisk erected here. The town of Sutherland, to the north, has a Planetarium, where some of the best observations of Halley's Comet have been secured.

The Karoo in the Eastern Cape

Just over 200 km (125 miles) east of Beaufort West on the R61, and administratively in the Eastern Cape, is one of the most attractive and architecturally distinguished towns in the whole Republic : Graaff-Reinet, which is three hours drive from Port Elizabeth.

Beaufort West to Graaff-Reinet
Initially the R57 takes you through Aberdeen, where you join the N9. Aberdeen itself is a pretty town, with some nice Victorian and Karoo-style houses, a fine church and craft shops. Beyond it you head almost dead straight across a dry and stony plain. Low trees clustered with white thorns look like clouds of spray, but the land has been overgrazed and farms have had to be consolidated to make them viable. One reason for the creation of the Karoo National Park was to preserve plants which this denudation destroys.

Graaff-Reinet

Postal code 6280. Telephone code 0491. Tourist Info 24248
This delightful and historic town, where over 200 buildings are now national monuments, comes as a complete surprise in the harsh Karoo landscape. You drive across the plains south of the Sneeuberg mountains, and there, studded with trees such as one has not seen for hours, situated on a horseshoe loop of the Sundays River, is one of the most perfect towns in the Republic, strangely enough born of turbulent conflict between advancing Dutch settlers and both Bushmen and Xhosas.

The Republic's Fourth Oldest Town
The Dutch had settled this area, the Camdeboo, in the early 1770s. In 1778 the Great Fish River, far to the east, was proclaimed a frontier

and on July 19, 1786, Graaff-Reinet was established as the local seat
of administration. The name derived from the Cape Governor Cornelis
van der Graaff and his wife Reinet. But by 1793 the frontier situation
had become so bad that the burghers overthrew the Landdrost and, as
at Swellendam, made themselves briefly independent until the British
seized the Cape late in 1795. Subsequently this intransigent-minded
town provided several leaders of the Great Trek of 1834, among them
Andreas Pretorius. In the 1840s many Boer houses and farms came
into the possession of English 1820 settlers.

During the Anglo-Boer War the Coldstream Guards were stationed
here. The map their Commanding Officer drew shows the Dutch
town, the coloured town and the black township, all separate. It hangs
in the Graaff-Reinet Club and the illustrious regiment has kept up its
connections with the town. For a clear view of a layout that will now
change, drive up the tarmac road to the valley of Desolation (see
below).

Restoration
Restoration of the town's historic houses began in 1952 with Reinet
House, once the Parsonage, and really took off in 1981 with the 'Save
Reinet Foundation' under the leadership of Dr Anton Rupert. The
architecture of the town is a combination of elegant Cape Dutch, like
Reinet House and the Drostdy (see below); and various Victorian and
Karoo-style flat-roofed buildings. The Victorian houses reflect what
had been fashionable in Britain a few years earlier. You will notice that
high ceilings reflect the need to keep rooms cool in summer, while
fireplaces counter winter cold.

Museums
The Museums complex includes Urquhart House, a fine piece of restoration; Reinet House with a collection of early settler furniture and,
in the basement, of dolls; and the Old Residency. When Reinet House
was the Parsonage both Livingstone and Moffat stayed there. Its garden has a famous vine, planted in 1870. For fuller information consult
the Publicity Association (PO Box 153; tel 24248) in the Old Library
Museum in Church Street, itself worth seeing for the fossil, clothing
and photographic collections. The Association organises conducted
tours. You can buy attractive colour prints of the town, from water-
colours by Philip Bawcombe, who drew some of our illustrations.
Finally the Hester Rupert Museum has a collection of modern South
African art and sculpture.

Accommodation
The three-star Drostdy (PO Box 400; tel 22161) on Church Street is

exceptional. Designed by Louis Thibault in 1806, and turned into an hotel in 1878, it was totally restored in 1977. The little houses behind it in Stretch's Court, reputedly slaves' quarters, were converted into bedrooms. It has great atmosphere and excellent food. Furthermore it has a swimming pool, which is a real asset in the hot summers, and log fires in winter. We rank it among South Africa's best country hotels.

There are other ungraded hotels and the Publicity Association has a list of private accommodation, displayed in the porch of the Old Library.

The Valley of Desolation
The standard local sightseeing trip is to view the Valley of Desolation in the Karoo Nature Reserve, west of the town. Here a grouping of sheer-sided basalt pillars rise to a height of 455 m (1,478 ft) in dramatic confusion. The valley has been the backdrop to various films there are panoramic views over both it and the town from the top, and there is a hiking trail.

Nieu Bethesda
A very different excursion is to Nieu Bethesda, an hour's drive away in the Sneeuberg mountains via a dirt road off the R9 towards Middleburg. You descend from the arid plains past a red tower of rock, like a sentinel, and find a completely unexpected lush, green, well-watered oasis among barren hills. A lovely white wedding cake of a church decorates the village, there are trading post shops and old houses line the unpaved streets. One is the Owl House, described in the adjoining article. The playwright Athol Fugard has a home here.

The village has several guest houses (ask the Publicity Association in Graaff-Reinet) and Egbert's Village Inn serves simple meals.

On to Cradock and Eastern Karoo
Just beyond the Nieu Bethesda turn off the N9 the R61 takes you east across a typical Karoo landscape to the Mountain Zebra National Park and the pretty town of Cradock. These are described further on, after Grahamstown.

Helen Martin's Owl House at Nieu Bethesda

The Owl House

Biblical and prophetic figures raise their arms in salutation before a shrine of bottles, while camels watch. Perched on an arch, a flapping owl presides, flanked by screeching peacocks. Miniature church spires bearing silver stars and an Egyptian obelisk rise against the backdrop of the Sneeuberg's barren slopes. All the sculptures are of grey cement and this is the 'Camel Yard' at Helen Martin's tiny cottage in Nieu Bethesda, the inspiration for Athol Fugard's play 'The Road to Mecca'. It would be a weird and moving expression of an artist's life to find anywhere, let alone in a small Karoo village.

Inside the house bright suns are painted on the windows, imitation snow crusts doors in defiance of the heat, waves wash the walls and there is a confusion of exotica. Candlesticks crowd a table, the single leg of which is a snake's tail, coiled on the floor. Tiny segments of glass glitter from unexpected places. Helen Martins was born here around the turn of the last century, left for Graaff-Reinet to become a teacher, married unsuccessfully, and eventually returned to nurse her ailing parents. During the 25 years after she inherited the house until she herself died in August 1978, she devoted all her resources of physical labour and money to transforming it according to her own intense personal vision. The house is now widely recognised as a work of art and is maintained by The Friends of the Owl House, attracting regular visitors. It is open daily.

The Eastern Cape

Climatically, in landscape and vegetation, and historically, you enter a different territory as you approach Port Elizabeth from the Garden Route. The coast changes. The high dunes and long sandy beaches that run up to St Lucia in Natal begin, with a string of small resorts. Gradually the vegetation becomes sub-tropical, while the climate is near-perfect, with temperatures at the coast rarely falling below 9°C or rising above 30°C. April to July are the best months.

If you strike inland you drive through indigenous forests and fertile valleys to the Great Karoo, just described, while the settlers' country behind Port Elizabeth is studded with late-Georgian and Victorian towns, as well as forts, towers and other mementos of much turbulent history. Beyond lie the Xhosa lands of the Ciskei and Transkei, with the magnificent and unexploited beaches of the Wild Coast. Resorts further north up against the Drakensburg mountains offer fishing, hiking, and even skiing in winter.

History
Algoa Bay – now Port Elizabeth – was one of several places where Bartholomeu Dias landed in 1488. More lastingly significant was the arrival there of 4,000 British settlers escaping the slump that followed the Napoleonic wars. Unbeknown to themselves, as well as opening up the Albany district, around Grahamstown, they were to act as a buffer between the rest of the Cape Colony and the Xhosas. The Great Fish River was then the colony's eastern frontier, a boundary inherited from the Dutch, which lasted until the 1834 war between the British and the Xhosas.

In 1835 Sir Benjamin D'Urban and Colonel Harry Smith fought their way further to the Kei River and proclaimed the Province of Queen Adelaide, renaming the former Buffalo Mission Station as King William's Town in May. But the British government promptly gave it back to the Xhosas! It must have been a burden, since it could only be supplied by sea. After the 1846 War of the Axe it was re-taken, however, and given a new name, British Kaffraria.

British Kaffraria
Kaffraria is derived from the arabic word *caffres*, meaning 'unbelievers', which the Portuguese explorers had used. The region lay between the Keiskamma and Kei Rivers. Missionaries returned to convert the natives, military pensioners were offered land, and in 1857 ships brought 3,000 mercenaries of the British-German legion to East London. They had originally been recruited to serve in the Crimea and the idea was both to provide them with a living and have a military force to

hand. Although their Colonel became an MP, they were not a success as settlers. Some deserted to the Free State. The crime rate soared. The second influx of German civilians in 1858-59 fared better, as the many German-named villages testify. By then the great cattle-killing of 1857 (see the Transkei section) had broken the Xhosa's power and in 1865, its buffer function concluded, British Kaffraria was annexed to the Cape Colony. It re-emerged in the shape of the Ciskei, where Bisho has become the Eastern Cape's official capital.

Communications

Access to the Eastern Cape and Border is excellent. The N2 road runs up from Cape Town and on to Durban. South African Airways (local tel 041 344444) links East London and Port Elizabeth with Johannesburg, Durban and Cape Town. Airlink (tel 041 512310), National Airways (tel 041 514194) and Atlantic Air also serve Port Elizabeth.

By rail the Amatola Express links Johannesburg with East London and the Algoa Express runs from Johannesburg to Port Elizabeth, both overnight.

Express coach companies serving the region are Inter Cape from Cape Town, Translux from Cape Town and Durban, and Greyhound from Johannesburg (addresses in the 'Useful Facts'). Additionally the Whippet Express (tel 041 334052) runs from Graaff-Reinet to Port Elizabeth and the Leopard Express (tel 0461 24589) between Grahamstown and Port Elizabeth.

The Garden Route to Port Elizabeth

The Coast between Cape St Francis and the Eastern Cape's capital has become renowned among surfers the world over. The best time to exploit the smooth-breaking rollers is May to September. They also bring in a harvest of sea shells for collectors.

St Francis Bay and Jeffreys Bay *Telephone code 0423. Info 940076.*
Cape St Francis itself was named in 1575 by the Portuguese after the patron saint of sailors and has a small nature reserve, protecting sea otters. The resort of St Francis Bay is fairly exclusive, with a golf course, a marina on the Komme river estuary, and watersports, but accommodation is b & b or self-catering, except for the pleasant Thatchwood Lodge at 63 Lyme Road (tel 940082). The houses are attractively thatched and whitewashed. At Paradise Beach there is a lagoon bird sanctuary, with many flamingoes. The best-known resort on the great sweep of sands, and allegedly the place to find the perfect

surfer's wave, is Jeffreys Bay. Originally a fishing village, this now has a couple of hotels and many holiday apartments. For a list contact the Publicity Association (PO Box 36, Jeffreys Bay 6630; tel 9 32588). There is an exceptional collection of sea shells in the C J Langenhoven Library on the beachfront.

Van Staden's Pass
On the way to Port Elizabeth you pass the Van Staden's river, now crossed by a great bridge, but more scenically traversed through the old Van Staden's Pass. There is a flower reserve close to the pass, and good fishing for steenbras on the lagoon at the river mouth.

The Long Kloof and the Apple Express
Inland, between the Tsitsikamma and Kouga mountain ranges, is the fruit growing country of the 'Long Valley', stretching way west behind the Garden Route to Uniondale. A 283 km (177 miles) narrow gauge railway, opened in 1906, freights out the apples, apricots, pears, plums and other produce to Port Elizabeth. Short passenger excursions run on the steam-hauled Apple Express to and from Lorie, inland from Jeffreys Bay. For details contact Spoornet (tel 041 507 2777). The Long Kloof is watered by many streams, with hiking trails through the wilderness in the Kouga hills. The main town is Joubertina, which has a hotel.

Baviaanskloof Nature Reserve
The Kouga-Baviaanskloof wilderness in the Gamtoos valley has ancient rock paintings, mountain tortoises, hundreds of birds and rare vegetation, including 17 types of protea. There are tourist cottages. For information tel 04232 30437.

Port Elizabeth

Postal code 6000. Telephone code 041. Tourist Info 521315.
The 'Friendly City' is the commercial capital of the Eastern Cape, as well as a resort, and is blessed with a mild sunny climate. It lies on Algoa Bay – the name being a corruption of Bahia da Lagao (Bay of the Lagoons) – for the protection of which the British built a simple stone fort in 1799. Even so, all else that the 1820 settlers found here was a huddle of fishermen's huts, a few dwellings, and military storehouses. Sir Rufane Donkin, the acting Cape Governor, named the settlement in memory of his wife, who had died of fever in India. The first cottages on Castle Hill Street were built in the 1830s, and gradually others followed, like the pretty terraced houses of Donkin Street. At that time the Market Square was the heart of the town. In 1923 the 52m (169 ft) high brick Campanile was erected at the entrance to the docks in commemoration of the 1820 settlers (of whose landing there is a mural on the wall of a house in Upper Hill Street).

The Eastern Cape Province

City Centre

Although Port Elizabeth is the home of many industries, the centre is compact with attractive parks and gardens, and is being revitalised by a substantial waterfrom development, Cape Town style. Mainstream shopping has moved out to Greenacres near Newtown in the suburbs and the centre's shops are speciality ones. The City Hall, restored after a fire in 1977, is on Market Square, with two crosses outside it. One is a replica of that erected by Dias at Kwaaihoek in 1488; the other an Ethiopian Coptic cross, dedicated to the seamen who searched in vain for the legendary Christian African priest-king, Prester John. An informal market is held every first Sunday of the month in St George's Park.

Travel Information

The Publicity Association is by the lighthouse in the Donkin Reserve on the hill (PO Box 357; tel 521 315) and the SATOUR regional office in an historic house at 23 Donkin Street (PO Box 1161; tel 557761). The South African Airways office is out at the Greenacres Centre (reservations tel 34 4444) and the airport is ten km (seven miles) south of the city (enquiries tel 512984). For express coach information tel 507 2777. The mainline railway station is by the harbour entrance (telephone 520 2975), but Humewood Station is the terminus for the Apple Express. Car hire firms include Avis, Budget, Europcar and Imperial.

Hotels and Accommodation

The city has a substantial number of hotels, including two Holiday Inns and a City Lodge. About the best is the three-star Marine Protea (PO Box 501; tel 532101), on the beachfront at Summerstrand. These hotels are all air-conditioned, which others are not. The Publicity Association can provide a list, which includes holiday apartments, and makes bookings through the Leisureplan computer system. The YMCA is at 31 Havelock Street (PO Box 12007; tel 29792), which runs off Rink Street on Central Hill; and the Youth Hostel at 4 Roseberry Avenue.

Restaurants

There are at least 90 restaurants and prices are reasonable. The best include the Bella Napoli at 6 Hartman Street Central, the delightful Lemon Tree at 58 Pearson Street for light lunches, and the Sir Rufane Donkin Room (tel 25534) in a restored cottage on Upper Hill Street. The South African Restaurant Guild publishes a discriminating list obtainable free from the Publicity Association.

The Oceanarium Complex

The Museum, Snake Park and Oceanarium at Humewood form a complex worth at least half a day's visit. The Snake Park has a fine collection of exotic and indigenous reptiles, including crocodiles and iguanas. The Tropical House forms part of it, where birds reptiles and fish live in lush tropical vegetation, which visitors can walk through. Nocturnal animals and birds may be seen under simulated moonlight conditions in the Night House. Performing dolphins and seals in the Oceanarium give daily displays at 1100 and 1500. Finally the Museum itself has an Historical Costume Gallery, a Marine Hall and a Children's Museum.

Monuments
Three monuments deserve special mention, as they are landmarks in Port Elizabeth. The first is the Campanile at the harbour entrance. The 204 steps to the observation floor give a panoramic view of the city. Then there is the pyramid next to the lighthouse on the Donkin Reserve, which commemorates Lady Donkin with the words 'To the memory of one of the most perfect human beings'. The lighthouse itself now houses the Publicity Association. But the most famous is the Horse Memorial in Cape Road, which commemorates horses killed in the Anglo-Boer War. It has a particularly moving inscription.

Historic Buildings
Domestic houses worth noting on a walk around the town, many of them national monuments, though not open to the public, include the Regency ones in Cora Terrace, off Bird Street; houses in Upper Hill Street; Donkin Street; and Castle Hill Street. Number seven Castle Hill Street, built around 1830 by the town's first rector, is open to the public. The Feather Market Hall was built in 1883 for ostrich feather auctions and has been skilfully adapted as a concert hall and conference centre. Fort Frederick, named after the Duke of York, is at the end of Belmont Terrace and is open daily. The Publicity Association has mapped out a Donkin Heritage Trail, and a rewarding Art Walk, covering galleries, restaurants and speciality shops.

Beaches
Only a ten-minute bus ride from the city centre an 11 km (seven mile) stretch of golden beach, starting at King's Beach where the British Royal Family's train was parked there during their 1947 visit. You can go by rail too; the Dias Express is a narrow-gauge steam train operating from the Campanile to the beach, with a stop at Humewood for the Railway Museum. A garden valley runs inland from the promenaded Humewood Beach, midway along the seafront. Hobie Beach with the Boardwalk Leisure complex, is the main boating area. There are no security problems on PE's beaches.

Sports
The city has numerous recreational facilities, among them four golf courses, Humewood being one of South Africa's finest (tel 532137);

underwater sports and wreck diving are popular and there are race meetings at St Albans Fairview and Arlington.

Expeditions from Port Elizabeth

Settlers Park is a striking wild flower reserve in the Baakens valley, between Port Elizabeth and the neighbouring municipality of Walmer, where a representative collection of indigenous buck and waterfowl has been introduced and there are 160 varieties of trees and shrubs. There is a three-hour walking trail. The Marine Drive is a winding, 24 km (15 mile) coastal road, through the picturesque village of the Driftsands Forest Reserve, leading to the village of Schoenmakerskop (Shoemaker's Head). Still visible on the rocks is part of the rusted hull of the 'Western Knight', wrecked in the 1920s. From Schoen- makerskop the Sacraments beach walking trail leads into the Sardinia Bay Sea Reserve. Beyond Sardinia on the way to Van Staden's river mouth is the Island Forest Reserve of indigenous sub-tropical forest.

For yachting and river fishing enthusiasts, a visit to the Swartkops river is a must. This wide, slow flowing tidal river has the villages of Swartkops and Amsterdam Hoek on opposite banks near the mouth, and is a photographer's paradise in early morning, and towards even- ing, when the harsh African sunlight is mellowed. Further upriver is the village of Redhouse. Boats can be hired locally.

The town of Uitenhage, inland by the Swartkops river, is known for its gardens, jacaranda avenues and historic buildings. The old Drostdy houses an Afric Museum, the Cape Dutch Cuyler Manor is a craft centre, and the old station a Railway Museum.

Further afield from Port Elizabeth the N2 leads to Grahamstown, with an easy deviation to the Addo Elephant Park.

The Addo Elephant National Park

The story of the Addo elephants is a minor classic of wildlife preserva- tion. They once roamed the Sundays river valley in large herds, but ran foul of farmers and had been almost entirely shot out by 1930. The few remaining were given protection in 1931 in the Zuurberg foothills. Old tram tracks and steel cables were employed to keep them there. They had adapted already to the low bush and trees of the area and have slowly multiplied in numbers to about 250. One of their peculiarities is that the females have no tusks. There is a road around the area, with viewing ramps, and the herd can be viewed throughout the year; see our cover photo.

The 11,000 ha park also supports black rhino, buffalo, eland, kudu and other antelope, down to tiny steenbok, as well as some 170 species of birds. The park has accommodation in chalets with bedding supplied, a restaurant, pool and shop. Bookings through the National Parks (012 343 1991). The park is 72 km (45 miles) from Port Elizabeth on the R335 road.

The Zuurberg National Park

This small area of veld and forest valleys is in the Winterhoek mountains, just north of the Addo park. The primary interest is in flora and vegetational zones, with very rare plants like the Zuurberg cycad and the cushion bush in the veld, and forest trees higher up. Black eagles breed in the forests and there are some small mammals. As yet there are no tourist facilities, except for two short hiking trails. But there is an adjacent one-star hotel, the Zuurberg Inn (PO Box 12, Addo 6105; tel 0426 400583).

The Amatole Region

This often beautiful, sometimes rugged, country between the Karoo and the coast up to East London is studded with small towns of both historic and architectural interest, like Fort Brown, Fort Beaufort, Bathurst, the early Methodist Mission station of Salem, and the centres of Grahamstown, King William's Town the modern capital of Bisho. Although the Ciskei divides the settler country the background of its Xhosa people is part of the same story, which began in 1812 with a British soldier, Colonel John Graham, riding up to an abandoned farm in what was then the frontier zone near the Great Fish river, and deciding to build a defended settlement there.

Grahamstown

Postal code 6140. Telephone code 0461. Tourist Info 23241.
The blood-curdling war cries of Xhosa warriors and the African sun glistening on spears were regular threats to Grahamstown as late as the 1870s, though that seems as unbelievable now as the high hats and ladies' bonnets of the settlers themselves. Colonel Graham, originally of the 93rd Highlanders, wanted to populate this area with Scottish crofters after the Napoleonic Wars, although in practice more Scottish soldiers than settlers came and many stayed in death. Seaforth Highlanders killed at De Bruyn's Drift in 1819 lie in the botanical garden near the Old Provost. Men of the 28th Iniskilling Regiment built St Patrick's military church in 1839. The few Scots immigrants among the 1820 settlers moved further inland around the Baviaans river valley, while English farmers built Grahamstown's

small houses, no doubt for security during a half century when the 40 churches were regularly used as a refuge from warfare for women and children.

Town Centre, Information, Hotels

With this legacy Grahamstown has matured into a charming, rather old-world cathedral city, centred on Church Square (actually a triangle) and with broad streets and fine houses. Set among green hills it stands at a climatically agreeable 535 m (1,740 ft) above sea level. Rhodes University, dignified behind the old Drostdy Gate – constructed by the Royal Engineers in 1841 – makes it a lively academic centre and the helpful Publicity Association at 63 High Street (tel 23241) is keenly interested in the British connections. Among hotels the two-star Cathcart Arms on the Market Square (tel 27111) is one of the oldest hotels in the Republic, while a former Jesuit College has been turned into a Gothic-style luxury hotel called St Aidan's Court (PO Box 237; tel 311188, fax 311140). A recommended guest house, itself a national monument, is The Cock House at 10 Market Street (tel/fax 311287). Outside the town the Settlers Inn (PO Box 219; tel 27313), in 14 acres of gardens, is reasonably priced. For a meal try Guido's restaurant off Hill Street.

Places to See

Get a map from the Publicity Association, and explore! Victorian shops opposite are preserved as national monuments. The cathedral (on the site of the original farm) was begun in 1825, enlarged in 1853, given its spire in 1879 by Sir Giles Gilbert Scott, and finished in 1952. Just along in Bathurst Street is an unusual classical house, the Observatory Museum, the most interesting building in the town. It belonged to a jeweller, Henry Galpin, whose premises are reproduced inside and whose Victorian roof-top *camera obscura* projects activity on the street outside on to a screen, using solely natural light and an arrangement of lenses. The house is open weekdays and Saturday mornings. Further down there are attractive early settler cottages in Cross Street. You ought also to see the 1820 Settlers Memorial Museum on the corner of Somerset Street and Lucas, with the Albany Museum opposite, both next to the botanical garden. The Old Provost in the garden was a military prison and now has a craft centre in its tower while the whole of this slope is part of the 1820 Wildflower Reserve around Gunfire Hill.

Gunfire Hill and the 1820 Settlers Monument

The hill is so named because of the daily gun fired from Fort Selwyn, which commands the town. The main Port Elizabeth road passes near both the fort and the massively ugly 1820 Monument building on top of the hill. Internally, however, the monument is imaginatively equipped with conference halls, a theatre and a restaurant. It is the venue for the annual Arts Festival at the end of June, which also attracts many fringe events, and has acquired national Status.

Inland from Grahamstown

The Kudu Reserve and Fort Brown

As you progress inland towards the Karoo the landscape becomes dramatically more rugged and dryer. The more rewarding of the two main roads from Grahamstown is the R67 towards Fort Beaufort. This takes you within striking distance of the Andries Vosloo Kudu Reserve in the Great Fish river valley, where black rhino, buffalo, ostriches and duiker share the bush with the kudu. There is a campsite on the river (information tel 0461 27909). Fort Brown, on the R67, dates from 1817 and still has its gun tower.

Fort Beaufort *Postal code 5720. Telephone code 04 634. Info 32094.*

Georgian houses, wide streets, and one of South Africa's two defensive Martello towers characterise Fort Beaufort. The town was founded in 1823. The round tower is a Corsican design, widely used in England's defences against Napoleon and then copied here. Alongside it is a former Officers Mess, now a Military Museum, where if you order in advance you can eat in the officers' dining room. There is a two-star hotel the Savoy (tel 31146), though a more agreeably private-feeling and not expensive place to stay is the Yellowwoods Hotel (PO Box 432, Fort Beaufort; tel 04662 1131) 21 km (13 miles) out on the R63 to Adelaide. Originally an 1841 coaching inn, it has a sunny, country atmosphere and good cooking, though officially only two-star, with tennis and a pool as well. You are out in magnificent veld here and there are several game farms up towards Tarkastad.

Adelaide to the Karoo

Adelaide, further on, is a pleasant small town with a charming Heritage Museum in the old parsonage. But Bedford, at the foot of the Kaga mountains, is uninspiring. From there you can continue to the Karoo, and the Mountain Zebra Park, described next, or return on the R350 to Grahamstown.

Game Reserves

Out of five reserves, the Tsolwana Game Park of 10,000 ha is the most rewarding. It is up by the Tafelberg mountains on the Karoo border, where savannah, semi-desert and hill country meet. There is a wide variety of game, with accommodation in self-catering chalets (contact PO Box 1424, Queenstown 5320). Some hunting is permitted in the July 1 to July 31 season. The most curious reserve is a tiny one protecting giant earthworms, near Debe Nek. The worms grow to three m (ten ft) long and a scary science-fiction girth.

Cradock

Postal code 5880. Telephone code 0481. Tourist Info 2383.
This pleasant small town, close to the Winterberge and Bankberg
mountains, originated as a military post in 1813. Some handsome
buildings in the centre include the sandstone church, built in 1868 as
a replica of St Martin's in the Fields in London, with the nice
incongruity of typical Karoo aloes and succulents sprouting sharp-
edged and colourful in the adjoining garden. Olive Schreiner, the
author, had a single storey, yellow-painted, period cottage in Cross
Street. It is a national monument. Among hotels there are the
excellent, small Tuishuise (36 Market Street; tel 5098), actually a
series of 14 restored houses, each different, all furnished with period
pices. You must book dinner in advance. The Publicity Association is
on Market Square (tel 2383). Although there is a small spa near the
town at the Karoo Sulphur Springs (tel 2709), the outstanding local
attraction – with an agreeable restaurant and accommodation into the
bargain – is the Mountain Zebra National Park, 27 km (17 miles) away
to the west, off the R61 road.

Onwards from Cradock
After seeing the park, the most rewarding route into the Karoo is to
continue on the R61, across the satisfyingly dramatic Wapadsberg
Pass, and so via the R57 to Graaff-Reinet, described earlier.

The Mountain Zebra National Park

These 6,536 ha of dry grassland valley and rocky hills are on the
northern slopes of the Bankberg in a typically vast Karoo landscape,
interrupted by flat topped mountains and granite outcrops. (There is
more about these rock formations under the Karoo National Park). The
highest outcrops in the park reach 1,975 m (6,420 ft), shelter many
small animals and eagles, and are snow-capped in winter. Indeed the
valley itself, only 4,100 ft above sea level, can be under snow. As well
as the zebra, there are herds of eland, springbok, blesbok and
wildebeest, and at least 206 species of birds. The roads are good and
you do not need 4WD in the park.

The Mountain Zebra
The park was created in 1937 to save the few remaining mountain
zebra of the southern Cape. Today there are over 200, with 150 having been translocated elsewhere, out of a world population of 500.
They are smaller than the common Burchell's zebra, with a dewlap, a
reddish brown nose, a white belly, and no 'shadow' stripes between
the markings. You will be lucky to get close enough to spot those dif-
ferences without binoculars, but you will see how much woollier and
less sleek they look. The park authorities can identify them individually

from their shoulder stripes, which are always different, like finger-prints.

Accommodation

The a la carte meals at the restaurant are worth booking in advance. There are a shop, fully equipped two-bedroomed chalets and, much more appealing, an old farmhouse up the valley, which can be rented. Called Doornhoek, it was built in 1836, is furnished in period style, sleeps six, and comes complete with a maid (though not a cook). The house was the location set for the film of Olive Schreiner's book 'The story of an African farm.' A three day hiking trail is served by simple overnight huts. Bookings for all facilities should be made through the National Parks Board.

Grahamstown to Port Alfred

The Settlers' country merits a detour through Bathurst, down to Port Alfred with several good places to stop for a meal or the night. It is only 57 km (36 miles) on the R67 from Grahamstown to Port Alfred.

Bathurst *Postal code 6166. Telephone code 0464. Info 250832.*
This was the original administrative centre for the 1820 immigration. The settlers had their new farms pointed out to them from Thornridge nearby, where a toposcope monument shows the 57 locations. Practically wherever they were sent they suffered calamity: drought, flood, wheat rust, and Xhosa stock raids. Both the strongly handsome stone church of St John – which could be in an English city – and the Wesleyan chapel doubled as forts on occasion. The country around is full of reminders of those wars, like Kaffir Drift, once a vital pass; and Cuylersville church, near Shaw Park, used as a refuge in both 1846 and 1851. Today what you see is prosperous cattle farming and pineapple plantations, with a forest reserve on the muddy Kowie river and a good old English pub in Bathurst. This is the one-star Pig and Whistle (PO Box 123; tel 3673), built by a blacksmith from Nottingham in 1831, and with a few bedrooms.

Port Alfred and the Coast

Postal code 6170. Telephone code 0464. Tourist Info 41235.
At the mouth of the Kowie river, and a 45 minute drive from Grahamstown, is Port Alfred. Named after Queen Victoria's second son, Prince Alfred, it is the centre of the 'Sunshine Coast', with beaches, a tidal lagoon, miles of river boating in beautiful scenery, fishing, an 18 hole golf course, and a first-class hotel. The Kowie Nature Reserve stretches along the river, protects waterbirds, and has

The Eastern Cape Province

a popular canoe trail. A steam train called The Settler Express makes the scenic – and slow – ascent to Grahamstown. The Publicity Association (PO Box 63; tel 41235) has details of other excursions and in the small Kowie museum, there is a card index of all 4,000 of the 1820 settlers. The reasonably-priced, three-star, Cape Cod style Halyard's Hotel (PO Box 208, tel 42410) is on the marine waterfront and there is a three-star Protea hotel.

Smaller Resorts, the Alexandria Trail, Kariega Park
The coast on either side of Port Alfred is well sprinkled with minor resorts, undisturbed beaches, nature reserves, and attractions of historic interest.

Inland to the west of the Kenton-on-Sea resort is Alexandria, with an indigenous forest that has a two day hiking trail, which takes in beaches and the largest shifting dune field in South Africa, running 50 km from the mouth of the Sundays river. Also inland from Kenton is a private game reserve called Kariega Park, with 20 self-contained small lodges (PO Box 35, Kenton-On-Sea, 6191; tel 0461 23040).

George river mouth, commonly called the Riet River (Reed River), has a fine beach and a lagoon. Nearby are the Three Sisters Rocks, originally named Fountain Rocks, by Bartholomew Dias in 1488, because of the spectacular way waves smash against them. Further along is Cawood's Bay, where the lagoon and beach are a holiday resort.

However the big resort deal is at the Fish River Sun, a possible north of Port Alfred and focal point for a 56 km round trip excursion along this attractive coast. On the way to the bridge, across the 19th century frontier, you pass the ruins of Fort D'Acre built by men of the Royal Navy in the Kaffir War of 1846 to protect the crossing. At the mouth of the Great Fish river is a small wetland nature reserve, a sanctuary for many birds. Dias made his last anchorage here before turning back to Portugal.

The Great Fish River to Hamburg
Crossing the bridge over the Great Fish River, where there is a tourist centre brings you to the Fish River Sun (PO Box 323, Port Alfred 6170; tel 0403 612101). Very well designed and luxurious, the hotel's access to the dunes and beaches is actually poor, though transport is provided to the beach ten km away at the sister establishment, the Mpekweni Marine Resort (PO Box 2060, Port Alfred 6170; tel 0403 613126), which is between a lagoon and the beach and close to hiking trails in the Mpekweni Reserve.

From Mpekweni you could footslog on the Shipwreck Hiking Trail to the other resort of Hamburg, or take a road inland. Shipwreck is a reasonable title for this coast where seven ships went aground on the single day of May 26, 1872. Hamburg, at the mouth of the Keiskamma river, has watersports and fishing in a get-away-from-it-all atmosphere. There is one hotel, the Hamburg (PO Hamburg; tel 0403 611501).

Grahamstown to King William's Town/Bisho

The N2 road takes one through what was the Ciskei (described below) and past several places of interest. The Dr Lennox Sebe Game Reserve is in rugged country on the Great Fish river. At Peddie the original stockaded fort no longer exists – this was a key frontier post – but the stone watch tower of 1841 does, together with ruins of the cavalry barracks. The town is named after Colonel John Peddie of the 72nd Highlanders. Further on the road crossed the Keiskamma river close to Line Drift, in its day a vital crossing.

The Eastern Cape's new capital, Bisho, formerly the Ciskei's capital, is so close to the old settlement of King Williamstown that they are becoming a single entity. This district used to be called Border, because it was the Cape Colony's ultimate frontier district, defined by the Kei river.

King William's Town

Postal code 5600. Telephone code 0433. Tourist Info 952115.

King William's Town, the one-time capital of British Kaffraria, was a garrison town until 1870, a status to which its 35 inns pay tribute. Its first royal visitor was Prince Alfred in 1860 and its last the present Queen Elizabeth II in 1947, with her parents. However, its importance declined in the present century until the short-lived independence of the Ciskei and laws making businesses in neighbouring Bisho tax-free brought a resurgence in the 1980s, while Bisho becoming the Eastern Cape's capital has created a further boom and the town has livened up considerably. There is a touch of irony in this benefit since the imposing Grey Hospital was built to counter the influence of Xhosa witchdoctors. There are a number of one-star hotels, and the three-star Grosvenor Lodge at 48 Taylor Street (PO Box 61; tel 21440). The East Cape Accommodation Network is at 3 Mount Street (tel 23369). The best source for historic information and walking tour guides is the Kaffrarian Museum.

The Kaffrarian Museum

Standing in the town centre, allied with the Missionary Museum and the Natural History Museum, the Kaffrarian is the place to start. Over 25,000 exhibits illustrate wildlife, and the cultural background of all

The Eastern Cape Province

the people who have made the district what it is; British, Germans, and Xhosas alike. Six leaflets give different walking tour routes around the town's many historic buildings. The Museum also contains one of Natal's most famous citizens, Huberta the hippo. In 1928 Huberta left Zululand on wanderings south, via Durban, which made her a national heroine. The Hindus of one village even deified her. Alas, in April 1931 this quite unaggressive lady was shot by farmers at the Keiskamma river, near Line Drift.

Historic Sites in the Region
These are too numerous to list. No less than nine frontier wars were fought across this territory. Some forts have been used as local stone quarries, but Fort Armstrong, Fort Cox, Fort Hare, Fort Murray and Fort Peddie survive, and battlefield sites are marked. Get the Tourist Map. In Xhosa history several leaders had great influence and their graves have memorials. Chief Ngquika, who lies in the Amatola mountains, co-operated with the colonists and brought about a split in the Xhosa nation. By contrast, Chief Sandile led his people in three frontier wars, being killed in 1878, and is buried near Keiskammahoek. Something that is easily forgotten today is that when the frontier struggles were over the Cape Colony gave black Africans the vote, this area had a black African newspaper in 1884. Fort Hare University dates from 1916. Many sub-Saharan African leaders are among its graduates, including President Mugabe of Zimbabwe.

Bisho

Poatal code 9999. Telephone code 04023. Tourist Info 952115.
Visually interesting modern architecture, a stadium, and African markets alongside shopping centres, plus a casino resort, make Bisho a worthy capital and it is humming with activity. The Eastern Cape Tourism Board is in CONTOUR house (PO Box 186; tel 952115, fax 92756). It publishes a very informative 'Tourist Map', with details of all the historic sites. Hotel rooms are at a premium. The glossy Amatola Sun (PO Box 1274, King William's Town 5600; tel 0433 22516) is just outside Bisho, providing a wide range of sports and excursions to the Amatola mountains, as well as its slot machines and gaming tables. There is a large, but seldom-used airport; a monument to the self-importance of the former homelands.

The Ciskei
In 1981 all the white farmers in a narrow strip of land running from the coast almost to Tarkastad were bought out to create the self-governing Ciskei, as part of the Xhosa people's homelands. The far

238

larger part was the Transkei, independent since 1976. Both were re-incorporated into South Africa after the 1994 elections. The Transkei and Xhosa history are treated with a few pages further on.

German Settlements and Mountains

North of Bisho the R346 road takes you through undulating farmland to Stutterheim and the Amatola mountains, with many rewarding drives and hikes. Braunschweig, Frankfort and Wiesbaden are reminders of the 1857 German settlers origins –or perhaps of their ambitions. Some telling verses, if laboured, are displayed in the bar of the Eagles Ridge Forest Resort.

'And so they came and tilled the soil
They tilled from morn 'till night.
They grew onions and potatoes
Like all good Germans might.'

Stutterheim is not inspiring, but the forests around the mountains are.

The Amatola Mountains
Magnificent drives through the mountains to Fort Beaufort are possible, either through Keiskammahoek in the Ciskei, or going north via Cathcart. The latter route passes Gaika's Kop as it approaches the Hogsback Pass. The distinctive, sheer-sided, lump of mountain is where the warrior and Xhosa chieftain Gaika lived and – by repute – dispatched his enemies to their deaths from the top. The two-star Hogsback Inn (PO Box 63, Hogsback 5721; tel 045 642 and ask for 6) is a well-known mountain resort of thatched bungalows, with tennis, riding, hiking and fishing. The trout owe their presence in these streams to the 19th century Frontier Acclimatisation Society, a soft name for a tough task.

Eagles Ridge
Reached by a turn off from the R352 road from Stutterheim to Keiskammahoek, the Eagles Ridge Forest Resort (PO Box 127 Stutterheim; tel 0436 31200) looks across a valley to the slopes of the Kologha State Forests, where the two-day Kologha Hiking Trail takes walkers past cliffs, where eagles do indeed nest. The hotel is rustic and warmly German. Bookings for the hiking trail, which has a large overnight hut, are through the Forest Region office in King William's Town, tel 0433 23445.

East London

Postal code 5200. Telephone code 0431. Tourist Info 26015.

Coming from King William's Town on the N2, past a series of villages named Berlin, Potsdam and so on by German settlers you reach East London, the fourth biggest seaport on the South African coast. The city came into being as a result of its natural harbour when the Cape Colony was seeking a quicker, safer way of bringing in troops and supplies to the border than the hazardous overland route. Lieutenant John Bailie, an 1820 settler, formerly of the Royal Navy, who was on board George Rex's brig the 'Knysna', climbed what is now Signal Hill in November 1836, hoisted the Union Jack, and claimed the port as British. However the settlement which followed was arduous. To boost progress the German Legionaries were brought in 1857: and in the same year 153 Irish girls, all prospective brides, arrived on the Lady Kennaway. A few actually did marry settlers! There are tableaux and pictures of these early occasions in the Museum.

Today East London is a thriving industrial city that also makes a point of catering for tourists. Its surfing and swimming in the warm Indian Ocean are excellent. There are white sandy beaches right on the city's beachfront, separated from modern hotels only by the broad Esplanade. The main shopping streets are Oxford Street and Terminus Street, while there is an intriguing group of small craft business in The Hives, on Lock Street; originally the cells of a prison, still with its gallows.

Information and Travel

The Metropolitan Tourism Association (PO Box 533; tel 26015) is at 35 Argyle Street. For rail and tour information go the Connex Travel bureau on Terminus Street. Airlink flies to Johannesburg, Port Elizabeth and Cape Town. The airport is 11 km from the city and the enquiries telephone is 4460211. Long distance bus services are run by Translux (tel 442333) to Johannesburg, Port Elizabeth and Cape Town. Avis, Budget, Europcar and Imperial all have car hire offices both in the city and the airport. A free 'What's On' booklet is published monthly, which lists entertainments.

Hotels and Restaurants

The city's hotels are more businesslike than vacation-minded, even when they face the sea. Protea hotels are reliably comfortable and the three-star Kennaway (PO Box 583; tel 25531) is no exception. The Majestic on Orient Road (tel 437477) is a safe two-star bet. The Port Rex Youth Hostel is at 128 Moore Street, Eastern Beach. For a feeling of holiday relaxation you could try the two-star Dolphin (PO Box 8010; tel 351435) five miles out in Harewood Drive, and only two minutes walk from Nahoon beach. The Tourist office can provide a list of guest houses and holiday flats. Air-conditioning is desirable, since in summer it can be sticky, in spite of the wind. One of the best restaurants is Le Petit (tel 353685), 54 Beach Road, Nahoon, where the extensive French menu also extends to kingklip, prawns peri-peri and grilled steenbras. And there are restaurants in the complex by the Aquarium. Fish is naturally a local speciality.

The Museum and its Coelacanth
Locals are fond of saying their museum houses 'the best fishing story in 50,000,000 years'. They are talking about the coelacanth, a fish that was known only through fossils and presumed extinct. Then, at Christmas 1938, one turned up in the nets of a trawler fishing off the coast. Miss Marjorie Courtenay-Latimer, the Director of the Museum, realised what the fish might be, was refused help by the government, but trundled it in a barrow to a taxidermist. Because of its four slightly leg-like fins it is associated with the theory that land animals evolved from fish. But even when it had been indisputably identified people refused to believe it had been a brilliant blue. Certainly it is a sad, dark brown now. However another was caught off the Comores in 1952, where in 1987 scientists from Grahamstown filmed live ones underwater; and the lady was proved right. The fish is blue. Although the coelacanth is the museum's star, the rest of the marine collection is superb. So are exhibits of native Xhosa life, which include a section on witchdoctors and fertility dolls, and of early German and English settlers' costumes.

Sports
There are three sandy beaches right on the city's waterfront, divided from the hotels only by the broad esplanade. Nahoon beach has some of the world's finest surfing on its short reef and there are shark guards; sharks, by the way, only come close to the shore when the sea is murky and the temperature over 21°C (70°F). 'Pretty cloudy water today,' one guard remarked to us cheerfully 'and the temperature's around 22.'' In fact, thanks to them, the bathing is safe. Watersports, of course, are plentiful and you can hire boats for fishing on the Buffalo river. Deep sea fishing, riding, and tennis are available.

Mpongo Park
Among several nature reserves in the area, Mpongo Park is the liveliest, with lions and many other species. It is 30 km (19 miles) from the city towards Macleantown.

East London's Wild Coast

This stretch of long beaches, with high dunes sheltering them, is among the least spoilt and most secluded holiday resort areas in South Africa. East London, like a mini-Durban, is at the centre. The resorts to the south – known as the west coast – extend to Kidd's Beach and culminate at Hamburg. The 'east' coast runs up past Beacon Bay to Kei Mouth, where the true Wild Coast begins. The resorts are reached by dirt roads off the N2. Most of them are at river mouths, where the Indian Ocean rollers build up sand bars, which both create lagoons and also allow one to walk across. The climate is sub-tropical, and becomes hot and humid in January. The best months are April and May, though the season is January to July. December can be windy. From our observation these small resorts cater for two definite groups, families with young children and the over-40s. Either way, the long sands and high dunes behind them make for real get-away-from-it-all holidays in simple conditions.

Glengariff and Buccaneers Retreat

The rock fishing is excellent at Glengariff Bay. Further on, 35 km (22 miles) from East London, is an example of what a more sophisticated approach can produce. The Buccaneers Retreat (PO Box 13092, Vincent 5217; tel 0431 383102) is a cluster of very well appointed cottages among lawns and bouganvilleas, served by an excellent restaurant and bar, overlooking Cintsa lagoon and some 12 km of beaches. Run by the owners, Lee and Anne Price, it has a pool, tennis and sailing.

Morgan's Bay

Then at Morgan's Bay, a resort with a golf course, is the Morgan Bay Hotel (PO Morgan Bay 5292; tel 043272 62). Nicely situated on a bluff alongside wide beaches, this larger hotel deserves two stars, though it only has one. Morgan's Bay itself has most of the qualities one wants in a small resort too, with plenty of coast to explore, river fishing, and occasional minor treasures to be found from Portuguese wrecks. It has a bus service from East London and the hotel will fetch guests from the airport, though not cheaply. There is a 40 km (25 miles) gravel road up to the N2, which snakes inland to cross the Great Kei river into the Transkei. There is also a car ferry at the Kei river mouth.

Transkei

The Transkei – meaning 'across the Kei river' – was created as an independent Xhosa state in 1976, with its capital at Umtata. In 1994 it was re-incorporated into the Republic as part of the Eastern Cape, bringing with it a small enclave of land in Natal. During those 'independent' years the Transkei acquired a reputation for backwardness and insecurity, so that although the N2 road from East London to Durban runs past Umtata, many people preferred to fly. With luck security will be restored, since this ancestral land of the Xhosas is scenically lovely, with a magnificent and largely undeveloped coastline, always known as the Wild Coast and still deserving the name.

Communications

Transkei Airways operate scheduled flights to K D Matanzima Airport, 17 km (nine miles) outside Umtata, from Johannesburg and Durban. The airport telephone is 0471 360115. There are helicopter services to the Wild Coast Sun hotel. South African Airways offices will make bookings. There is no public transport from the airport to the town, but there are taxis and an Avis car hire desk.

Local hire cars get heavily booked. It would be better to fly SAA to East London or to Margate (depending which side of the Transkei you want to visit) and hire a car there.

Umtata's Legislative Building, the Bunga

The Eastern Cape Province

The N2 road is tarmac; so is the road from Umtata to Port St Johns. Most other roads are gravel and can be extremely bad; some are little more than tracks.

Information
The Eastern Cape Tourism Board is on the corner of York Road and Victoria Street in Umtata. Address Private Bag X5029, Umtata; tel 0471 312885, fax 312887.

Hotels
There are a number of smallish coastal resort hotels – plus the giant Wild Coast Sun – and plenty of inland hotels. They are not yet classified, but the Tourism Board's list quotes their facilities. You can book direct with them, through the Tourism Board, or through Wild Coast Holiday reservations (PO Box 8017, Nahoon 5210; tel 0431 58003). High seasons are Easter, June-July and December-January.

The Xhosas

This is the homeland of the Xhosas, whose rhythmic 'click' songs were made internationally famous by Miriam Makeba. President Mandela is a Xhosa. Xhosa itself is pronounced 'Kosa' with a click in the 'Xh'. The tribe originally came from central Africa, along with the Zulus, but were driven down here by Shaka at the time of the Difaquane in the early 19th century. They remained comparatively strong, however, until in 1856 an episode occurred which was extraordinary even by the standards of primitive superstition.

A Prophet's Disastrous Vision
A young girl called Nongqawuse, claiming to be a prophet or a medium, announced that she had been visited by ancestral spirits, who told her that if the Xhosa slaughtered their cattle and destroyed their crops, then the white man would be driven out. A gigantic storm would blow them into the sea, while old Xhosa heroes would be reborn and new cows and crops be created. One has to remember that there were continual frontier wars at that time and although the Xhosa had defeated the British at Boma Pass in 1850, they had also suffered savage losses in the 1850 – 53 frontier war that followed. At all events, they did as Nongquawuse ordered; and on the appointed day in February 1857 nothing whatever happened. Despite aid from the Cape Colony nearly 60,000 Xhosa out of 105,000 either died or became refugees. The tribe's power was broken. Nongquawuse is buried on the Glenshaw farm, near Kenton-On-Sea. The definitive account is in 'The Dead will Arise' by J B Peires, published by Raven Press, Johannesburg.

Up to that time the Xhosas had achieved many victories in the frontier wars, utilising a guerilla-style of fighting that was totally unlike that of the Zulus. And, unlike the Zulus, they never harmed women and children. In some ways they had much in common with the Boers: all five of the Boers great treks away from the British (whom the Xhosa were fighting) originated in the Eastern Cape.

The Transkei's People Today

Today the population is nearer three million and the rolling hills of the Transkei, dotted with groups of huts and villages, reveal a way of life with a dignity and a happininess all its own. You will notice that north of the Umtata river the Pondo people wear blue clothes, whereas south of it the Xhosa women – who like to smoke pipes – prefer reddish-orange, their full skirts embroidered with black and wear huge turbans, as well as an assortment of beadwork. In fact the colours and the bead designs all have significance; sometimes indicating special occasions, or age groups. They are on sale to passers-by at craft centres near Umtata. If you want to know more read 'Red Blanket Valley' by Joan Broster. Alas, the other thing one cannot fail to see in the Transkei is the erosion of farmland that accompanies overgrazing, is pitiful in so potentially fruitful a country and is likely to get worse as the population increases. The authorities are trying to increase earnings from tourism, meanwhile families remain heavily dependent on pay sent home by their men-folk working in the gold mines.

Umtata

Postal code 5100. Telephone code 0471. Tourist Info 312885.
Situated 698 m (2,290 ft) above sea level, Umtata has a pleasant climate. It is an obvious stopping place, since it is smack on the N2 road in the middle of the country and the Port St Johns road leads down to the coast from it. However facilities are fairly limited, though there are eight hotels. The best is the Holiday Inn (PO Box 334; tel 22181), with a pool, air-conditioning, gambling and 24-hour room service. The hotel is one km south of the town. The Savoy Hotel (PO Box 175; tel 23391) is near the golf course. The air-conditioned Windsor (PO Box 111; tel 25654) is more of a businessman's hotel, with conference rooms, and a hairdresser. Recommendable restaurants are the China, La Piazza and the Jimz.

There are various local crafts, about the best being the hand-woven mohair tapestries and carpets produced by Hillmond Weavers, five km (three miles) off the Kokstad road. For traditional beadwork go to the Wonk'umntu Centre a similar distance south on the N2.

The Eastern Cape Province

Umtata to KwaZulu-Natal
Past Qumbu the N2 passes through Mount Frere, where there are two hotels and good fishing. You cross the Natal border shortly before Kokstad, which the road skirts. The town sits 1,283 m (4,210 ft) up on the slopes of Mt Currie and is named after Adam Kok III, the last of the Griqua chiefs. It has two hotels and offers tennis, bowls, polo, golf, swimming and fishing. There is a useful cafe at the turn off from the main road. From Kokstad you can either drive down to the coast at Port Edward or Port Shepstone, both in Natal, or continue through another part of the Transkei to Ixopo, also in Natal.

The Wild Coast

The coast's rocky and dramatic length is arbitrarily divided half way along its 250km (156 miles) shore, from near East London to Port Edward in Natal, by Port St Johns, and enthusiasts talk about the south and north wild coasts. A series of small nature reserves line the coast. From north to south they are Mkambati, Silaka (near Port St Johns), Hluleka, Cwebe and Dwesa. They have self-catering chalets bookable through the Department of Nature Conservation (PO Private Bag X5002, Umtata; tel 0471 24322). If you want detailed descriptions then get hold of Duncan Butchards 'Guide to the Coast and Nature Reserves of Transkei', published by the Wildlife Society of Southern Africa. Or one of the AA's publications.

Overall the coast's fame is based on its rock fishing, its unspoilt nature and its unfrequented beaches; which is another way of saying they are often pretty inaccessible. Roads along the coast are non-existent, because of the 20 rivers that cut down to it, so access is always off the N2.

Qora Mouth to Coffee Bay
On the southern coast is the Dwesa Nature Reserve, with self-catering huts, situated by the mouth of the Bashee river. It lies between Qora Mouth and Coffee Bay. Qora Mouth has the thatched Kob Inn (PO Box 20, Willowvale; tel 0200 9901). Willowvale is a very small inland town, through which the gravel road from Umtata passes. It is also on the way to the Haven Hotel at Bashee Mouth (PO Elliotdale; tel 0020 1/3). The Haven has golf, tennis and boats for hire. But to reach Coffee Bay, a larger resort by Wild Coast standards, you would follow the N2 to 18 km short of Umtata before turning off on a tarmac side road.

Coffee Bay
There is a tidal lagoon here, with two hotels close to it, the Lagoon (PO Box 9054, Umtata; tel 0020 50), with tennis, fishing and boats; and

the Ocean View (PO Coffee Bay; tel 0200 59), which is slightly smaller. Both organise the seafood feasts that are a feature of Wild Coast holidays. There is a golf course and exciting cliff walks are near it. Just north of Coffee Bay are the Anchorage rondavels, while to the south is the Hole-in-the-Wall Hotel (PO Box 54, Umtata; tel 0471 23857), with a lot of activities and excursions, only reached by going inland again.

Hiking Trail
A fairly tough coastal hiking trail runs from Coffee Bay and past St Johns up to Mzamba, near the Natal border. It passes Cathedral Bluff and Waterfall Bluff and also where the treasure ship 'Grosvenor' was wrecked – of which more in a moment.

Sights near Lusikisiki
The easily-accessible Magwa Falls near Lusikisiki tumble 125 m (466 ft) into a gorge, while the old gravel road from Umtata to Port St Johns passes a precipitous rock called Mlengana, or Execution Rock. The theory is that local chiefs used to have their enemies thrown off the top. However experts say this was not so: the real execution site was a different cliff on the Umngazi river. The name Lusikisiki, incidentally, is an onomatopoeic word, deriving from the sound of the wind blowing through the reeds.

Port St Johns   *Telephone code 04752.*
This is the largest resort on the coast, with tropical gardens, excellent beaches at Umagazi and some inspiring scenery, notably the two forested headlands called 'The Gates'. An ancient fig-tree is where a Norwegian captain lost his ship's bell in a gambling session – the bell is in the Town Hall. But recent visitors report that St Johns is slowly falling apart. The neighbourhood was used for the filming of Wilbur Smith's 'Shout at the Devil'; appropriate for that colonial adventure, although notionally the ramshackle setting was Tanzania. The Protea Cape Hermes (PO Box 20; ask exchange for 35), is about the best on the coast after the Wild Coast Sun. There are a golf course, fine cliff walks and nearby is the Silaka Nature Reserve, which protects some indigenous buck, plus introduced species, such as zebra, while green parrots feast on yellow wood fruits.

Port St Johns to Port Grosvenor
The access to the coast north from Port St Johns can be tough going, and 4WD is definitely useful. You have to drive through Lusikisiki, then branch off to the sea again. Two of the Transkei's most arresting sights are along here; namely Waterfall Bluff, where the Mhlambom-kulu river plunges over a cliff into the sea, and the arch of

Cathedral Rock.

Further north is the so-called Port Grosvenor – barely a landing place among rocks, let alone a port, and hard to find since there is only a track some 25 km (15 miles) from Lusikisiki on the way to South Sand Bluff. The 'port' is where the 'Grosvenor' was wrecked on the rocks on August 4, 1782. Plenty of merchant ships have foundered on this coast, but this British owned East Indiaman was allegedly laden with £6 million worth of gold and – which is certainly untrue – the Peacock Throne of the Moghul Emperors. Many attempts have been made to locate the treasure and some gold coins have been found, but not the ship itself. Of the 136 crew and passengers who managed to clamber ashore, only 17 survived the long struggle south through thick bush and across rivers towards East London.

Mkambati Nature Reserve
Further north, reached via Flagstaff, is the largest of the Transkei's reserves, where a walking trail gives spectacular views of the Msikaba gorge. Accommodation includes a lodge and cottages. A scheduled helicopter flight goes in from Umtata on Tuesdays, a lot less boneshaking then the five-hour drive.

Port St Johns to the Wild Coast Sun
To reach Mzamba and the Wild Coast Sun you have to drive in a wide arc inland via Lusikisiki, Flagstaff and Bizana. According to 'Getaway' magazine, whose coverage of the more remote parts of Southern Africa is unrivalled, Russian submarines used to surface here on the way to Port St Johns in the 1960s. They were bringing back Pondo freedom fighters from training in Moscow to struggle for the Transkei's independence. Ironically, the 1990s decided the Xhosas to rejoin South Africa. Be that as it may, the Wild Coast Sun (Sun International or PO Box 23, Port Edward, Natal 4295; tel 0471 59111) has skilfully utilised what were deserted beaches, palm groves and the river estuary into a casino resort, with all the beach and watersport activities that the Wild Coast makes possible, plus a golf course. There are evening cruises on the Umtamuna river and the hotel is only ten minutes drive from Port Edward, across the D F Mitchell bridge (see KwaZulu-Natal chapter).

The North East

Way inland of the Transkei and the Settler Country is a region well-known to South Africans for its small resorts, fishing, hiking, scenic splendour and even skiing. It runs 300 km (185 miles) from the high backdrop of the Drakensberg mountains on the Lesotho border to the dry plateau of the Karoo. The Orange river divides it from the Free State.

Aliwal North

Postal code 5530. Telephone code 0551.

Aliwal was where Sir Harry Smith defeated a Sikh army in India in 1846. He named this settlement on the Orange river after the battle, and also his charger. It is 'North' because Mossel Bay once had the name too. Sir Harry was so shrinking violet as regards recognition. Today the town is a mineral spa, where pools and baths draw on a spring delivering two million litres a day at around 35C (95 F). It is the main base for exploring the North East and has two hotels, both two-star, Thatcher's Spa (tel 2772) and the Umtali Motel (tel 2400).

Resorts

The clutch of resorts in the Witteberg mountains and the Drakensberg, close to Lesotho, include the artist's colony village of Rhodes, home to skiers in winter; Barkly East, which has a Trout Festival, and maclear, known for its hiking trails and the Tsitsa waterfall. Near Elliot there is a 32m long 'gallery' of bushman rock art, on the farm Denorbin.

A zigzag mountain railway, with eight places where the train reverses, links Barkly East with Lady Grey.

Hiking Trails

Numerous designated hiking trails, with simple overnight accommodation, explore the foothills. For details write to Cape Tourism in Port Elizabeth (PO Box 1161; tel 041 557761).

Northern Cape Province

Character of the Region

The vast northern half of the Cape Province stretches 750 km (470 miles) from the Namaqualand coast, where giant orange and yellow daisies carpet the ground in Spring, to the diamond city of Kimberley, its 'capital'. Much of it is the classic Africa of dry bush and migrating game animals; a harshly beautiful landscape through which flows the Orange river, the greatest watercourse of southern Africa, making citrus estates and vineyards possible in what would otherwise be sun-scorched veld. It edges into the Great Karoo, a desolate yet often spectacular semi-desert plateau which was once – incredibly enough – an inland sea and which, springs to life with wildflowers after rain.

Copper, Missionaries and Diamonds

At the coast Dutch settlement slowly followed Simon van der Stel's expedition in search of copper in 1685, although most towns date only from the 1800s, or the 1850's copper discoveries. Inland development was even slower. There were no fertile valleys to attract farmers and the impetus came from missionaries. The first of these arrived at the start of the 19th century, notably at the request of the Griquas, in whose country Griquatown was established west of Kimberley. A little further north the Tswana chiefs accepted a Mission Station in 1814. Trade followed the gospel. By the mid-1840s, a decade when the explorer David Livingstone spent much time with Dr Robert Moffat's family at the Mission near Kuruman, settlement was proceeding rapidly. A this time a large territory north of Kuruman was ruled by Tswana chiefs.

Then in 1866 the first diamond was found near Hopetown on the Orange river, followed by the 21.25 carat 'Eureka' in 1867, followed by an 83.5 carat stone in 1869. When diamonds were found on the Colesberg kopje in 1871 Kimberley was born. Thereafter events became tumultuous. Adventurers swarmed in from all over the world. The diamond rush brought about the financial transformation of South Africa. Roads and bridges were built; and with the wealth came economic development, which was only temporarily disrupted by the Anglo-Boer War of 1899-1902. At this time the northern frontier with Bechuanaland (Botswana) was still undefined.

The Anglo-Boer War

Some of the Boer-War's most significant battles were fought in the northern Cape, the unsuccessful sieges by the Boers of British garrisons at Mafeking and Kimberley amongst them. Magersfontein, 30 km from Kimberley, was the scene of a crushing British defeat at the hands of the Boers in December 1899, but only two months later General Cronje surrendered to Lord Roberts at Perdeberg. When the war was over the northern boundaries of the Cape Province were at last defined and thirty years later, in 1935, conservation of what was left of the once-abundant wildlife began with the proclamation of the Kalahari Gemsbok National Park.

The Province Re-defined
In the declining years of apartheid a Tswana speaking, independent homeland was created out of seven jigsaw pices of the northern Cape and the northern Transvaal. This was named Bophuthatswana and achieved some commercial success. After the 1994 elections a new province was created called the North West, which included both it and the contiguous country. The Northern Cape became a separate province too. Even today, however, it is the Republic's outback.

Getting to the Northern Cape

Kimberley has daily SAA flights from Johannesburg and Cape Town and is on the main railway line for both the Blue Train and the Trans-Karoo Express. However if you are visiting the Kalahari Gemsbok Park it is easier to fly to Upington, or take the Inter Cape bus there from Johannesburg. For the much-favoured tours of Namaqualand in the Spring the usual starting point is Cape Town, although you could travel from Upington to Springbok and drive, or take a bus, south from there. All three areas have very different characters.

Kimberley

Postal code 8300. Telephone code 0531. Tourist Info 806264.
Kimberley is a living legend. Its heart is the old mining town around the incredible amalgamation of individual diggings called 'The Big Hole'. Although fine Edwardian residence decorate the suburb of Belgravia and modern Kimberley is a city of parks, jacaranda trees, and office blocks, the centre retains a Victorian air. Streets still wind to avoid the original diggings. The old offices of de Beers on Stockdale Street, with their two-tiered cast-iron verandahs and corrugated roof, are faithfully maintained in use. Even the old wooden shacks of the prospectors and merchants, which used to crowd the perimeter of the Big Hole, have only moved a short distance to within the grounds of the Mine Museum, though they have given way to an ugly circular road. This preservation of an historic past reflects the lives of many international famous Kimberley citizens. Some of them were flam-boyant, like the young actor and boxing promoter from London's Whitechapel, Barney Barnato. Others, such as Alfred Beit, a clerk from

The Northern Cape Province

Germany and – later – Ernest Oppenheimer were more reserved. They all became multi-millionaires and the chief among them was, of course, Cecil John Rhodes.

Cecil Rhodes
Kimberley was Rhodes' town. He personally helped direct its defence against the Boer siege in 1899. Mementoes of him are everywhere. At the Kimberley Club there is a brass arrow set in the path to remind him which direction was north. In one barber's shop there is an old red leather chair with the invitation 'Have your hair cut in the same chair as Mr Rhodes'; just as if he were alive today, instead of having died far away at Muizenberg in 1902, at the early age of 48.

Information
The Tourist Information Office (Private Bag X 5030; telephone 806264) is in the City Hall and the SATOUR office (Private Bag X 5017; tel 31434) at 2 Market Square. There is also an Information Kiosk at the entrance to the Big Hole. The Computicket office is on Elliott Street (tel 24264).

Transport
The airport (information tel 851 1241) is seven km (four miles) out on Oliver Road. There are no airport buses, but car hire firms have offices at the airport. The railway station is close to the centre on Florence Street (information tel 882631). Regular steam trains take passengers to de Aar on a vintage ride. There is a taxi rank at City Hall, or telephone 614015 for a cab. Buses are usually crowded. Finally, restored open-sided trams run from the City Hall to the Big Hole and the Mine Museum every two hours starting at 0900.

Shopping
The main shops are around the Market Square, Old Main Street, Jones Street and Du Toitspan Road, with an Indian market in Stockdale Street. Diamond jewellery can be bought tax-free, provided you produce your passport and airline ticket, while several shops on Jones Street specialise in discount diamond sales. The Post Office is on Market Square.

Hotels
A large number of hotels are headed by the three-star Holiday Inn Garden Court (PO Box 635; tel 31751) conveniently located on Du Toitspan Road, close to the pleasant Oppenheimer Memorial Gardens and a short walk from the centre. The two-star Diamond Protea Lodge (PO Box 2068; tel 811281 is near it. The three-star Savoy (PO Box 231; tel 26211) on de Beers Road has historical associations and remains good. The Tourist Office can provide a list of cheaper one-star

hotels. On the way out of town on the Bloemfontein road there is a 120-bed Youth Hostel (PO Box 777; tel 28577), where tourists are welcome.

Hostelries
In the diamond rush era there were a host of bars, close on 130 of them. The Star of the West, on North Circular and Barkly Roads, dates from the 1870s. The Diggers Rest in the Mine Museum, with its piano, shows what others were like. But the Halfway House (tel 25151) is where it always was, half way to the Bultfontein mine. Rhodes used to ride in for a drink on his trips between the Big Hole and Bultfontein, and because of that there is still a drive-in bar. Kimberley is not lively at night, although the locals know how to make up for it. Fly-posters appear with day-glo messages like 'Late Night Beach Party. Grand Hotel. From 7.30pm 'till late. Dress – Beach Wear.' The nearest beach is 600 km away.

Places to See
There is no lack of these. The Public Library has a famous collection of Africana, while the Duggan Cronin Bantu gallery is worth a visit. So is the MacGregor Museum on Atlas Street, built at Rhodes' orders in 1897 as a sanatorium and where he spent the siege from October 12, 1899 to February 15, 1890. It has tableaux and mementoes of those sleepless weeks. Very close by is Lodge Road, one of the most distinguished residential streets. The Oppenheimers lived at number seven. Number ten, a delightful Edwardian house called Dunluce, can be seen by appointment (tel 32645). In the same district 'The Bungalow' at 5 Loch Road was built for the mining magnate D C Rudd. A huge house, it can also be visited (tel 32645). All these give a vivid impression of the old Kimberley life-style. If you are interested in flying you should visit the National Monument to the Pioneers of Aviation, with its early aircraft replica, outside the city.

The Big Hole
The Colesberg Kopje, where the first Kimberley diamond was found in July 1871, was the top of a kimberlite 'pipe'. Kimberlite, or 'blue ground', is hard rock, pushed up from the depths of the earth volcanically and bringing with it diamonds that have been formed by extreme heat and pressure. Sometimes the ground and the gems with it are washed away by rivers. The source of the Orange River's alluvial diamonds has never been found, though it must have been a similar 'pipe'. The Colesberg Kopje was intact; and was gradually transformed from an outcrop 30 feet high into a steep-sided pit by hundreds of diggers working individual claims, while the mining camp grew up round it. As the separate diggings reached deeper, with narrow walkways between them and each with its own ropes and pulleys to

the top, they became chaotic and dangerous. The miners amalgamated into combines, from which two major groups emerged – de Beers, controlled by Cecil Rhodes, and Kimberley Mine run by Barney Barnato. Both men were millionaires before they were thirty.

However, Rhodes realised that the market had to be managed or the price would fall, and won overall control, bringing all Kimberley mining under the aegis of de Beers Consolidated Mines Ltd. Subsequently it was from here that the development of Johannesburg and the Rand was planned and modern South Africa sprang. When working in the Big Hole ceased in 1914, it was 457 m (1,485 ft) wide, 183 m (3,600 ft) deep, and had yielded 14,500,000 carats of diamonds. Today its sheer sides still take one's breath away, even though it is partly full of murky green water. The observation post for visitors is inside the Mine Museum.

The Mine Museum
The great point about the open-air Mine Museum is its actuality. Here is the tin shack which Alfred Beit used as a buying office, complete with his wide desk. Here is Barney Barnato's Boxing Academy, which he opened in 1878 as a way of increasing his income when he was a 'kopje-walloper', buying stones from diggers and selling them to merchants (a 'profession' later banned). Here are houses, shops, and the mahogany panelled railway coach of the de Beers Directors.

Active Diamond Mining
By contrast, Bulfontein Mine is still working and can be visited. Or if you want to watch old-style alluvial diggings you can do so 32 km (20 miles) away at Barkly West, where from June to September prospectors are out panning for diamonds in the river. One Kimberley mining curiosity is that a company still prospers on the concession to search all local building sites for diamonds. Its men start crushing and sieving the debris after any house is demolished.

Routes from Kimberley

To the west the 'Kalahari-Namaqua Route' starts with a mere 440 km (275 miles) drive to Upington by the R31/R385/R27, before continuing to the Kalahari Gemsbok National Park or–alternatively – northern Namaqualand. This road goes through Posmasburg, which has a 'big hole' open diamond mine of its own. Or you can follow the R31 all the way to the park via Kuruman. The fastest route to Upington is by the N8, though the old mission centre of Griquatown, which continues to Springbok. Any route to the Kalahari is going to take you a day, and to Springbok longer. The N12 goes to Cape Town.

The R31 takes you near the diggings at Barkly West, already mentioned, and then past the Vaalbos National Park.

The Vaalbos National Park

Proclaimed in 1986, the Vaalbos is protected because it is where three ecosystems meet, namely the vegetation of the Karoo, of the Kalahari and of the grassveld. Game indigenous to all three kinds can thrive here and the species re-introduced include springbok, red hartebeest, eland, kudu, buffalo and black rhino. 'Vaalbos' is camphor bush, of which there is plenty, as well as camelthorn. The park covers 22,697 ha (89 sq miles) on the Vaal river.

Kuruman

Postal code 8460. Telephone code 01471. Tourist Info 21095.
The town is a pleasant enough place to stop for a meal, being near the Kuruman hills and made fresh and green by the continual flow of the 'eye', which rises from a dolomite cave in the town centre and yields 18 million mitres a day, irrigating the district. As an attraction, however, the 'eye' is over-rated. The Information Office (tel 21095) is in the municipal building and there is a two-star motel on the main street, the Eldorado (PO Box 313; tel 22191), as well as two one-star hotels.

In the early 1800s this area, on the edge of the Kalahari's southern extension, was in Bechuanaland (Botswana). In 1814 Chief Mothibi of the Batlhaping tribe agreed to accept priests from the London Missionary Society. By far the most distinguished was a Scot, Robert Moffat, who arrived in 1824 and built the unusual T-shaped stone church, with its mud floor, five km (three miles) north of the town off the road to Hotazel. Timber was donated by King Moselekatse and transported 350 km by ox-wagon. The roof is thatch. The church and Moffat's unpretentious cottage, still the incumbent's residence, are the Republic's oldest buildings north of the Orange river. They stand in a grove of giant syringa trees by a stream cut by Moffat from the 'eye', which nurtures gardens planted with pears and pomegranates. Moffat translated the Bible into Tswana, printing it here in 1583, made this the focal point of missionary activity for Southern Africa and stayed here until 1870. He also, during the only visit to Britain of his tenure, persuaded David Livingstone to come to Africa instead of going to China. Livingstone eventually married his daughter here, though Moffat himself outlived them both.

Kuruman to the Kalahari Park

Beyond Kuruman you come into the low-ridged dunes of the Kalahari, although because vegetation has stabilised them they are not so noticeable here as further on. This is cattle ranching country and there is lot of game too, especially kudu. Past Hotazel – christened by two sweating surveyors in 1917 – the R31's surface becomes shimmering gravel and eventually follows the Kuruman river. The characteristic red dunes of the Kalahari rise on the other side and as you progress west the landscape becomes more arid with fewer trees. You will pass donkey carts labouring along, but very few service stations. And remember that when driving on gravel you should reduce your tyre pressures by at least ten percent. We came across a French couple up here who had not done so, got out of control at speed and rolled their car. From Hotazel to the R360 road from Upington to the Kalahari Park is 317 km (198 miles), with the first mealstop available at the Molopo Motel, just north of the junction – see below.

Entry to Botswana

From near Hotazel the R380 goes up to Tshabong in Botswana, where there is a ranger camp. Self-contained expeditions can go into Botswana, but the roads are bad and you should be with another vehicle. The other border post is at Bokspits, close to where the R31 eventually joins the R360.

Upington

Postal code 8800. Telephone code 0541. Tourist Info 26911.
Originally a railway town on the Cape Town-Windhoek line, Upington is now the commercial, social, and educational centre of a region made fruitful by the massive Orange river irrigation schemes. As well as cotton, citrus fruit, lucerne, wheat and other crops, there are Orange River wines, among the more palatable being the dry white *Grand Cru*. The Orange River Wine Co-operative has even become the largest in the southern hemisphere. The area is also noted for Karakul sheep and semi-precious stones, of which there are collections in the Oranje Hotel and the Municipal Library.

Transport and Tours

However, for most visitors, Upington is the a starting point for visits to Augrabies and the Kalahari. The town is served by passenger trains and the very reasonably priced Mainliner bus takes roughly seven hours from Johannesburg, with meals included in the fare. South African Airways links Upington to Bloemfontein, Cape Town, Johannesburg and Kimberley. The airport is only seven km (four miles) out (tel 31 1364). If you want to charter a light plane to go to the Kalahari Park (where vehicles can be hired at Twee Rivieren) contact Walker Flying Services (PO Box 335; tel 23283). Avis hire cars and combis are available at the airport, as well as in Upington. There are no airport buses or taxis.

Tours to the Augrabies and Kalahari Parks are run by Spitskop Safaris (PO Box 1788).

The Town
The town straggles a full eight km (five miles) along the Orange river, on which one island has been turned into a pleasure resort. The wide streets have banks and well-stocked shops – they serve a huge hinterland. The Tourist Information Office (tel 26911) is on Mutual Street. There are two two-star hotels in mid-town, the small-windowed bedrooms of which are somewhat cell-like, and the Oranje (PO Box 100; tel 24177). Both are air-conditioned, which is most necessary, because the months October to March are very hot, though not humid. The most pleasant spot to dine out is Le Must in Schroeder Street, which is gratifyingly like a French bistro and exhibits South African artists' work on its walls. It is close to the Protea Hotel.

Upington to the Augrabies Falls

This is an interesting 120 km (75 miles) drive along the banks of the Orange river, passing the two small towns of Keimoes and Kakamas. At both there are giant waterwheels, formerly used to turn this valley into pasture in the middle of semi-desert. The river spreads out to be as wide as a small lake and there is a little nature reserve, the Tierberg, noted for its aloes. The wild-growing Kakamas peach, once cultivated with huge success, originated here. The fertile valley is in great contrast to the dry, rocky country around it, where karakul sheep are ranched. Karakuls, from whose pelts Persian lamb derives, are nicknamed 'black gold'. They can survive on very little; and they need to with the region's tiny rainfall.

Upington to Springbok
Past Kakamas the N8 road continues through Pofadder and near the wild flower area of Aggeneys to the main town of northern Namaqualand Western Cape chapter, Springbok. This section of the book should be read in conjunction with the Namaqualand part of the Western Cape chapter.

Augrabies Falls National Park

The much-photographed Augrabies Falls cascade down a 56 m (182 ft) drop into an 18 km (seven mile) granite gorge, its grey-black sides eroded into strange formations. The falls are the fifth largest in the world and liable to dramatic increases in their flow from rains far away in Lesotho. Indeed the viewing bridge was washed away in the

1980s. Prospectors believe the deep pool beneath the main fall must be lined with diamonds – after all this is the river which carried diamonds to the Namibian coast – not that anyone would stand much chance of retrieving gems from the onslaught of water (for more about Orange river diamonds see the Namibia chapter).

The park around the gorge supports klipspringer, springbok, kudu and many smaller arid environment mammals, some 52 species of reptiles, and nearly 180 species of birds, while the succulents and trees include kokerbooms and other aloes, camel thorn and wild olive. You need shoes suitable for scrambling over rocks even if you are not embarking on the Park's three-day Klipspringer Hiking Trail, a fairly easy 33 km (21 miles) signposted walk with overnight stops at two trail huts. It can be very hot during the day, and conversely cold at night. Reservations are through the National Parks (tel 012 343 1991), which run an excellent rest camp, with air-conditioned chalets, a shop, a restaurant, and also a camp site. The small one-star Augrabies Falls Hotel (PO Box 34, Augrabies 8874) is good too.

Upington to the Kalahari Park

The Kalahari Gemsbok Park's entrance at Twee Rivieren is 320 km (200 miles) from Upington and the R360 is being completely tarmaced. It takes you through karakul farming country, with the vegetation becoming more sparse and the soil reddish brown until you find yourself going up the wide riverbed of the Nossob on to the plateau of the Kalahari.

Molopo Motel and Game Reserve
Just after the junction with the R31 is the welcoming Molopo Motel (PO Box 32, Askham 8814; tel 916213), worth more than its one-star, especially right out here. Accomodation is in attractive thatched chalet rooms, each with its own bath, there is a pool and prices are very reasonable. Petrol is available too. Being only 60 km (37 miles) from Twee Rivieren the motel is a useful base if you are not staying in the park itself, while the owner, Christe Koortzen, maintains a 7,000 ha game farm near the Botswana border, where she can organise game-viewing and trophy hunting.

The Kalahari Gemsbok National Park

The Kalahari is unlike any other park in South Africa, being semi-desert where local variants of many species of fauna and flora have adapted to survival in an almost waterless environment. it is still supervised by members of the same family, the Le Riches, who alerted a government Minister to the extermination of the wildlife up here in 1934, provided the first Warden, and ended being 'godparents' to one of the largest conservation areas in the world. The real-life saga of the Le Riches' fight to save the wildlife is worthy of a novel. Including the Botswana park, the area totals 204,610 sq km (79,000 sq miles), greater than the State of Oklahoma. Rainfall is scant. The Nossob river flows perhaps once in 30 years, the Auob once in three. The present Warden, Elias Le Riche, is also an Honorary Warden in Botswana and there are no fences between the two parts, a fact of enormous importance not only because they form one eco-system, but for a further tragic reason. The anti-foot and mouth disease fences across the central Kalahari – unthinkingly financed by the European Economic Community to assist Botswana's cattle raising – have cut the ancient game migration routes and led to the deaths of hundreds of thousands of animals. Soon this could be the main sanctuary for the entire Kalahari's wildlife.

Wildlife
The wildlife is astonishingly varied and exploits the indigenous vegetation in unexpected ways. Dark-maned Kalahari lions, leopards and cheetahs doze in the shade of pale-barked shepherd trees, where the temperature of the sand can be 21°C lower than that of the open sand. Lionesses give birth beneath these trees, the orange-yellow fruits are edible and the lives of smaller animals and insects revolve around them. Springbok shelter beneath the Kalahari's other notable trees, the grey camelthorns, which dot the dry riverbeds, though in the dunes they only grow to shrub height. They, too, are centres of life. Animals feed on their leaves and seed pods. Sociable weaver birds attach communal nests to their branches, creating a vast bundle of grass, where 50 families may live and within which temperatures are much lower than outside. These nests are often shared by pigmy falcons. The falcons, far from attacking the weavers, kill their mutual enemies, the snakes.

Sustenance in the Desert
Unexpectedly there is food in the desert. When it does rain – usually between January and April – the seeds of annual plants germinate very rapidly. The gemsbok, whose straight V-shaped horns can spear a lion, feeds off tsamma melons and wild cucumbers, both containing a very high percentage of water. Herds of eland, hartebeest and springbok do the same, often disregarding the windpump-filled drinking places provided by the Parks Board along the riverbeds as a protection against prolonged drought. Even the wildebeest have adapted themselves to managing for long periods without drinking water; while the elephant and buffalo which were here in the early 1800s - when there was permanent water – have vanished.

The Northern Cape Province

Roads in the Park

Because the sand dunes are so treacherous, visitors are restricted to the roads along the Auob and Nossob valleys, plus one connecting road between the two, although new roads are planned. Even so it is amazing how many animals you can see, especially those already mentioned. Ostrich, kori bustards, eagles and that strutting snake-killer, the secretary bird, are among 150 bird species. Bat-eared foxes hunt in the dunes and meerkats, a species of mongoose, sit on their haunches to watch passers by.

Accommodation

Park accommodation has been hugely improved. The rest camp at Twee Rivieren, by the entrance to the park, has air-conditioned cottages and a good restaurant and shop. At both Nossob camp and at Mata Mata (on the Auob by the Namibia border game fence) there is comfortable accommodation and a shop, but no air-conditioning or restaurant, so you must provide for yourself. Groceries and tinned food are sold, but only Twee Rivieren has fresh meat, eggs and frozen food. A new camp is planned at Veertiende Boorgat. Diesel and petrol is available at all the camps. Car and combi minibuses can be hired at Twee Rivieren and credit cards are accepted. The park address is Private Bag X5890, Gemsbok Park 8815. For reservations 'phone 012 343 1991. Since distances are considerable – Mata Mata is 121 km (76 miles) from Twee Rivieren and Nossob further – it makes sense to stay several days, possibly spending two nights at Nossob. Note that you can no longer drive through into Namibia from the park and that there is a small park entrance fee.

The best times to visit are March to May and August to October, especially the latter as the herds are then in the riverbeds. In December and January it can be very hot, reaching 48°C or 49°C. In winter at night the temperature can fall far below freezing.

Springbok

Postal code 8240. Telephone code 0251. Tourist Info 22071.

The only town of any size in the north, Springbok sits in a narrow Klip-koppe mountain valley, dotted with kokerboom trees, where explorers found both a fresh water spring and copper. The Blue Mine nearby was the first commercial mine of any kind in South Africa. It opened in 1852, 167 years after Simon van der Stel proved the presence of copper ores up here. Old furnaces and chimneys betray the Cornish origin of many of the early miners. Today, Springbok thrives on various mines. Although not exactly sophisticated, it has banks, shops and two reasonably priced and clean hotels. The two-star Springbok Hotel (PO Box 46; tel 21161) is on Van Riebeeck Street, while a short way out of town is the Kokerboom Motel (PO Box 340; tel 22685).

Communications and Information

The airport has scheduled services from Johannesburg daily, except Saturday, and to Cape Town on Mondays to Fridays. For information call 22061. The daily express bus goes down the N7 to Cape Town and Jowell's express bus runs overnight to Johannesburg, via Upington, taking 15 hours. The Visitors Information Bureau is in the Muncipal Offices (tel 22071) and there are some unexpected local attractions in addition to spring flowers, not the least being white-water rafting and canoeing up on the Orange river.

Mining Relics

The stock visit is to where Simon van der Stel made his exploratory copper working in 1685, after copper ore dug by Bushmen had been reported. The site is uninspiring. Far better to visit the Mining Museum at the real, live O'okiep Mine at Nababeep - once the richest copper source in the world - where there are demonstration models of how a mine is operated and, outside, the last of seven mountain railway trains. The engine 'Clara' continued hauling copper through the Richtersveldt to Port Nolloth until 1946. Other mining relics and historic sites are listed in a pamphlet produced by the Cultural Histori-cal Society of Namaqualand and obtainable locally.

Nature Reserve

The Hester Malan Nature Reserve, 15 km (ten miles) east of Springbok, protects the rare mountain zebra, oryx, springbok and other plains game. Its 7,000 ha is in exciting country, with a hiking trail.

Springbok to the Orange River

From Springbok rough country descends to the impressive valley of the Orange River, the frontier post and the bridge into Namibia. On the way the road frequently intercepts the embankments of the abandoned Port Nolloth railway. You will also see traditional Nama huts, round reed mat constructions like upturned bowls, said to be cool inside.

Richtersveld National Park

This is near Steinkopf, on the Port Nolloth road. The Richtersveld's barren-looking mountains appear forbidding and require 4WD. In reality the rocky slopes harbour an extraordinary range of plants, including an unparalleled variety of succulents. The park extends over 750 sq km (293 miles). At the time of writing there was no accommodation and there are restrictions on entry.

Orange River Expeditions

Canoeing and white-water rafting on the stretch of the river between

Vioolsdrif, on the N7 road at the frontier, and the junction of the Orange and Fish rivers takes you through starkly splendid Richtersveld scenery, while blazing sunshine is guaranteed! Nights are spent camping by the river, with traditional camp fires and barbecues. Among Cape Town firms organising five-day canoe trips are River Runners (PO Box 583, Constantia 7848; tel 021 732135). Rafting is done by The River Rafters (PO Box 14, Diep River 7800; tel 021 725094), whose four-day adventure uses rubber rafts to negotiate the rapids.

Among Cape Town firms organising five-day canoe trips are River Runners (PO Box 583, Constantia 7848; tel 021 732135). Rafting is done by The River Rafters (PO Box 14, Diep River 7800; tel 021 725094), whose four-day adventure uses rubber rafts to negotiate the rapids.

The Upper Karoo

From Kimberley the N12 road, or from Upington the N10, lead south to the vast sheep farming lands of the Upper Karoo. Little visited by outsiders, much of this country is semi-desert, cut through by basalt capped hills that remind one immediately of a Western movie.

Towns

Rhenish missionaries were partly responsible for opening up the area in the 19th century and towns' names like Calvinia bear witness to them. In the east de Aar is on the main Cape Town-Johannesburg railway and was once the home of the author Olive Schreiner.

From de Aar you can drive on the N10/R63 right through this intriguing landscape, which becomes strewn with flowers in Spring, to Carnavon, founded in 1860 as a Mission, and on to Calvinia. You can then continue through the hills to Vanrhynsdorp in Namaqualand. brochures on this remote area are available from the Northern Cape Tourism office in Kimberley (see above) or from SATOUR. There are small hotels in the towns.

Brochures on this remote area are available from the Northern Cape Tourism office in Kimberley (see above) or from SATOUR. There are small hotels in the towns.

Factfile

Many points relating to South Africa are covered in the General Information and its Regional Air Services sub-section.

Getting There

Air
The major carrier to Johannesburg, and the only carrier to Cape Town, is South African Airways. The airline has British offices at St George's House, 61 Conduit Street, London W1R 7FD; tel 0171 312 5000 (reservations) and 5001 (fares), at Heathrow airport (tel 0181 897 3645) and 4th Floor, 1 St Ann Street, Manchester M2 7LG (tel 0161 834 4436).

British Airways flies direct to Johannesburg, Cape Town and Durban (London reservations 0181 897 4000, from other parts of Britain 3345 222111 at local rates). for other carriers see the General Information.

In the United States SAA offices are at 900 Third Avenue, New York (tel 212 826 0995, or toll-free 800 722 9675) and in Miami at 901 Ponce de Leon Blvd, Coral Gables, Florida 33134; tel 305 461 3484.

International Airports
Johannesburg International Airport is 24 km (15 miles) from the city centre, with an airport bus service. The information tel is 011 9216911. Cape Town's airport is 22 km (14 miles) from the city centre, with an airport bus. The information tel is 021 934 0444. Durban's airport is 14 km from the city and the information tel is 031 42 6111. A new airport is being built north of the city. Departure taxes are payable when buying your ticket. The airport banks open for two hours both before and after the departure and arrival of international flights.

Sea and Rail
See General Information.

Road
The principal road routes into the Republic are from Zimbabwe at Beit Bridge; from Botswana near Gaborone; and from Namibia at Nakop, near Upington, and Noordoewer on the Orange river. For exact border

post hours tel 011 314 8911. Basically posts open from 0600 to 2000.

Internal Travel

Air
The domestic network covers all the main cities and is detailed in the General Information on pages 12-13 and under individual cities. SAA has a car hire/flight ticket link-up with Avis.

Rail
In addition to the celebrated Blue Train between Pretoria and Cape Town there are several long-distance expresses. The Trans Karoo runs daily from Johannesburg to Cape Town, via Kimberley; the Trans Natal runs from Johannesburg to Durban, via Newcastle, Ladysmith and Pietermaritzburg; the Trans-Orange runs from Cape Town to Durban, via Worcester, De Aar, Kimberley, Bloemfontein, Bethlehem, Ladysmith and Pietermaritzburg; the Amatola runs from Johannesburg to East London via Bloemfontein and the Algoa runs from Johannesburg to Port Elizabeth, via Pietermaritzburg. All these services also run in the other directions. They are operated by Spoornet, with offices throughout the network. The Johannesburg telephone is 011 773 2944.

Train information and bookings are available in Britain through SAR-travel, Regency House, Warwick Street, London W1R SWA; (tel 0171 287 1133) and in the United States at 1,000 East Broadway, Glendale, California 91205 (tel 800 727 7207; or toll-free nation-wide).

Although there are city commuter rail services, the train is not a popular form of transport and few white South Africans think of going by train, except in Cape Town. With the 1990s the system has been partly privatised. South African Railways operations have become Spoornet and the SARtravel bureaux within South Africa re-named Connex.

Long Distance Coach and Road Tours
An efficent network of long-distance luxury coaches links the main towns. These are listed under 'Communications' in each chapter. In

Opposite: Bushman rock painting of hunters and gemsbok (top left)
          Kalahari Bushman hunter (top right)
          Black - maned Kalahari lions (below)
Overleaf: The Magistrate's house, Luderitz, Namibia (top)
          The 2,000 ft deep Fish River Canyon, Namibia (below)

1995 typical inter-city fares were R110 from Johannesburg to Durban and R260 to Cape Town. The major coach tour operators include Connex and Springbok-Atlas. The Connex central reservations office is at 6 Sandown, Sandton (PO Box 1111, Johannesburg 2000; tel 011 884 8110, fax 884 3090). The Springbok-Atlas head office is at Tramway House, 183 Sir Lowry Road, Cape Town (PO Box 819, Cape Town 8000; tel 021 448 6545). There are many others.

Taxis and Black Taxis

Taxis do not cruise and must be called from a rank. Waiting time is often limited. Long distance fares can be obtained on a quotation basis and are usually lower.

If you don't mind sharing a ride, then the 'black' minibus taxis of the SA Black Taxis Association (SABTA) cost a fifth of the price. They will stop if hailed at bus stops, are crowded, but very useful in cities and are nicknamed 'Zola Budds' because they are so speedy. If the rest of Africa is anything to go by, they will rapidly become an informal national network, though without printed timetables.

Banking

City banking hours are 0900 to 1530 on weekdays and 0830 to 1100 on Saturdays. Elsewhere weekdays hours are 0900 to 1245 and 1400 to 1530. There are banking facilities at Johannesburg, Durban and Cape Town airports. The First National Bank and the Standard Bank have branches throughout the Republic.

Business Hours

Shops are usually open from 0830 to 1700 on weekdays and 0830 to 1300 on Saturdays. Bookshops, and the small provision shops called cafes stay open later. Supermarkets in city shopping centres are open Saturday all day and Sunday mornings to 1300.

Car Hire and Driving

Avis, Budget, Europcar and Imperial have countrywide operations. For example, Europcar's competitive 1995 tariffs run from around R79 a

Previous page: Herero women in missionary - inspired dress (top left)
                      Kokerboom - the Bushman's quiver tree (top right)
                      Elephant in the Chobe National Park Botswana (below)
Opposite: Mokoro - dugout canoe - in the Okavango (top)
                      Cheetah on a kill (below)

day, plus 84 cents per km, for a small car to R199, plus R1.99 per km, for a Mercedes 230. Unlimited mileage rates are no longer offered, but there are three days upwards packages with 300 km free. VAT is added to all charges as is accident and theft insurance. The latter is high at R33 per day upwards. There are usually no 'drop off' charges between different offices and cars are delivered within cities at no charge. However there is a charge for rentals starting at airports. Cars cannot be taken out of South Africa without prior permission, which theoretically means you need it for Lesotho and Swaziland.

N.B. Most hire cars have manual gearshifts, not automatic transmissions, and all are right hand drive.

The head offices are Avis, PO Box 221, Isando 1600 (tel 011 974 2571; fax 011 974 1030); Budget, PO Box 1777, Kempton Park 1620; (tel 011 392 3907; fax 011 392 3015); Europcar, Royal Beamish Centre, Block C, Modderdam Road, Airport Industria, Cape Town (Reservations 021 934 4750, fax 934 9771, toll-fee 0800 10 1344). Imperial, PO Box 260177, Excom 2023 (tel 011 337 2300, fax 8695). Europcar is cheaper than the others and is rapidly expanding. The minimum age for hiring is 23. You must have a licence with a

Europcar inter rent

gets you going

BRANCHES THROUGHOUT SOUTH AFRICA

CAPE TOWN	GEORGE	PORT ELIZABETH	EAST LONDON	DURBAN	JOHANNESBURG	PRETORIA
(021) AIRPORT 9342263 SEA POINT 4399696	(0441) AIRPORT 769070	(041) AIRPORT 513878 DOWNTOWN 511547	(0431) AIRPORT 463093	(031) AIRPORT 4690667 DOWNTOWN 320540	(011) AIRPORT 398832 DOWNTOWN 3946605	(012) DOWNTOWN 3263715

photograph (eg an International licence issued by the AA). For driving advice see General Information. Petrol is available 24 hours a day, though some smaller service stations may be closed at night and on Sundays.

Automobile Association
The AA of South Africa assists visiting AA members. The address is AA House, 66 de Korte Street, Braamfontein, Johannesburg 2000 (tel 011 403 1000; fax 011 339 2058).

Maps
SATOUR can provide free maps. Petrol companies print useful road maps. Automobile Association maps are not only accurate, they give a great deal of basic information as well. The AA also publishes an excellent book 'Off The Beaten Track', which illustrates a series of day drives, and is sold by bookshops.

Credit Cards

Most business houses, tour operators and hotels accept major credit cards, such as Access, American Express, Diners' Club, Mastercard and Visa.

Churches

The predominant church is the Dutch Reformed, but there are churches of other denominations, including Catholic and Methodist.

Currency

The basic unit is the Rand, divided into 100 cents. There are R50, R20, R10, and R5 notes, and nickel R2 and R1 coins. Other coins are for 50, and 20 cents with copper ten, five, two and one cent coins. See also General Information. For exchange rates see page 17.

Customs

All valuables must be declared on entry and as personal effects are duty free. Duty free allowances include one litre of spirits, including liqueurs and cordials; two litres wine; 50 ml perfumery; 250 ml toilet water; 400 cigarettes, 50 cigars, 250 gr tobacco.

Diplomatic Representation

South Africa has missions in the following countries: Argentina. Australia, Austria, Belgium, Bolivia, Brazil, Britain, Canada, Chile, China, Denmark, Finland, France, Germany, Greece, Guatemala, Hong Kong,

Iceland, Israel, Italy, Japan, Kenya, Luxembourg, Malawi, the Nether-lands, Paraguay, Portugal, Reunion, Spain, Sweden, Switzerland, the USA and Uruguay. This representation is set to expand.

Electricity

City and town power systems are 220/230 volts AC. The Pretoria power system generates 250 volts and Port Elizabeth 220/250 volts. Adaptors for shavers and hairdryers are available for computers.

Fishing

A nation-wide licence is cheap and is obtainable from Receivers of Revenue and Magistrates' offices.

Gratuities

Ten percent is an average tip. Porters and room servants are usually given R1 or R2. Service charge is rarely added to restaurant or hotel bills (but VAT is included).

Health

Visitors arriving from areas where yellow fever is endemic must have yellow fever vaccination certificates. Only passengers on scheduled airlines passing through African yellow fever areas are exempt, pro-vided they have not left the en-route airport buildings. See the General Information, pages 21-2.

Sun preparations are essential – even in winter when the cooler day temperatures can be deceiving. Moisturising is also of great impor-tance due to the dry air. Local preparations are of a high standard manufactured with these conditions in mind.

You should obtain travel insurance as there is no national health welfare scheme; again see page 21. Doctors are listed under 'Medi-cal, or Mediese' in telephone directories.

Hotels, Lodges and Rest Camps

In 1993/94 a new hotel grading the classification scheme was introduced, by SATOUR, whose protea plaque adorns hotel entran-ces. The five levels are one star, 'comfortable and standard'; two star 'very good'; three star 'excellent'; four star 'outstanding' and five star 'luxury'. Establishments that have passed a deeper assessment of quality are graded 'silver' in addition. They are very few. These gradings are quoted in our descriptions. Additionally hotel guide symbols show whether they accept credit cards, have air-conditioning and so on. Virtually all hotels have restaurants.

At the time of writing the grading was not complete and many places are missing from the National Accommodation Guide. Furthermore, although it now lists many private country lodges, it omits even the most famous private game reserve lodges. The brochure gives a tariff guide and is available from SATOUR offices.

Rest Camps
A detailed list of National Park rest camps and facilities, with tariffs, can be had from the National Parks Board (PO Box 787, Pretoria 0001; tel 012 343 1991, fax 343 0905). It maintains a Foreign Desk for international reservations (tel 012 343 2007, fax 343 2006). The Natal Parks Board's facilities list is obtainable from it at PO Box 662, Pietermaritzburg 3200; tel 0331 47 1981, fax 47 1837. Accommodation details at the many local game reserves and resorts can be had from the relevant Publicity Association, whose numbers are in the text.

Hotel Chains, Publications and Reservations
The principal hotel chains are City Lodge (good accommodation without luxuries); Holiday Inn, usually three-star; Karos, three and four-star; Protea, nearly all two and three-star; and Southern Sun, three to five-star. All have central reservations systems. Protea's British telephone is 01789 20 4269, fax 41 4420. Holiday Inn belongs to Southern Sun, whose British offices are at Bray Business Centre, Weir Bank, Bray on Thames, Berkshire SL6 2ED; tel 01628 778722, fax 23908 and American ones with PRI at 1,100 East Broadway, Glendale, California 91205; tel toll-free 800 421 8905, fax 818 507 5802. Karos is represented in Britain by African Ethos, 13 Bowman Mews, London SW18 5TN; tel 0181 875 1404, fax 0181 874 8394.

Sun International runs four and five-star resort hotels in the North-West and Ciskei, Lesotho, Swaziland, Transkei and Venda. Their British reservations office is at Badgemore House, Gravel Hill, Henley-on-Thames, Oxfordshire RG9 4NR (tel 01491 574546; fax 01491 576194). Their American office is with Southern Sun, as above.

Additionally Three Cities Hotels in London (PO Box 673, London SW3 6SE; tel 0171 225 0164) represents the Carlton in Johannesburg, the Royal in Durban, the Plettenberg Park on the Garden Route and the Peninsula in Cape Town, as well as the Sodwana Bay Lodge. The famous Mount Nelson in Cape Town is represented by Orient Express Hotels, the Thameside Centre, Kew Bridge Road, Brentford,

South Africa Factfile

Middlesex TW6 OEB; tel 0181 568 8366.

Bed and Breakfasts/Country Retreats
Bed and Breakfast South Africa, a fairly comprehensive listing of private homes and farms offering reasonably priced B & B, is represented in Britain by Safari Consultants, Orchard House, Upper road, Little Cornard, Suffolk CO10 0NZ; tel 01787 228494, fax 228096, who can make bookings. So can the Retreats Collection of larger country houses (see below), represented by Collineige, 32 High Street, Frimley, Surrey GU16 5JD; tel 01276 24262, fax 27282.

Publications/Reservations in South Africa
There is such a variety of accommodation in South Africa, most of which never features in standard tour brochures, that it is well worth writing for whichever of the lists suits your budget or purpose.

The Portfolio Collection (PO Box 52350, Saxonwold, Johannesburg; tel 011 880 3414, fax 788 4802, covers Bed and Breakfast, Town and Country Retreats, Country Places (more upmarket), and Conference Places. The Hotelogue and Secluded Country lodges are detailed on page 28. Finally there is the more impersonal Leading Hotels of Southern Africa (Po Box 78291, Sandton 2146; tel 011 884 3583, fax 884 0676).

Youth Hostels
Youth hostels are also open to anyone travelling by car, although they are few. The Youth Hostels Association is at Room 101, Boston house, 46 Strand Street, Cape Town 8001 (PO Box 4402, Cape Town 8000; tel 021 419 1853, fax 021 216937).

Restaurants
Some of the very best restaurants are not licenced to sell any alcoholic drinks. If so, you can bring your own. Always check when making a table booking. The best impartial restaurant guide is the American Express Gold Card magazine 'Style', but it is confined to the main cities and surrounding areas.

Language

There are 11 official languages, including, English and Afrikaans, which are spoken throughout the Republic.

Passports and Visas

Visitors to South Africa require valid passports. Visas are not required by bona fide holiday visitors from the United Kingdom, the Republic of

Ireland, Switzerland, Lichtenstein and Germany. United States citizens no longer require visas as tourists unless they work for the media, or religious organisations, or are visiting as members of a sporting group. Visas are issued by South African diplomatic missions. Apply well in advance. Transit visas are issued to people travelling by air, road or rail through South Africa to adjacent territories. If you are visiting other countries and then returning to South Africa you will need a multiple entry visa. You must have proof of funds to support yourself, plus a return ticket. If you have no onward ticket the Immigration Officer may want a cash deposit of R2000, which is refunded when you leave.

Public Holidays

In 1995 these were New Year's Day (January 1), Human Rights Day (March 21st), Good Friday, Family Day (April 17), Constitution Day (April 27), Workers' Day (May 1), Youth Day (June 16), National Women's Day (August 9), Heritage Day (September 24), Day of Reconciliation (December 16), Christmas Day (December 25), Day of Goodwill (December 26).

Telephones

Virtually the whole of South Africa is now on the direct dialing system, resulting in many numbers having been changed. The International direct dialing code is 09, followed by the country code e.g. 1 for North America and 44 for Britain. The Directory Enquiry number is 0123.

Value Added Tax

A Value Added Tax (VAT) is levied at 14% on accommodation, meals, goods manufactured within the Republic, and imported goods. Goods consigned or delivered overseas are exempt at the point of sale. Foreign Visitors can claim VAT refunds on departure at airport Customs offices on production of shopping bills, but only if total purchases exceed R250.

Tourist Information

The South African Tourism Board's headquarters are in Pretoria with an Information Centre in the Tourist Rendezvous in Pretoria (tel 012323 1430). There are regional offices in all large cities and a well-equipped bureau in the arrival hall at Johannesburg airport. Virtually every town has its Publicity Association or Visitors Bureau. The literature provided by them is usually first class, but some apparently independent private publications are mainly 'advertorial'.

Mokoro in the Okavango

Botswana

The Country

Botswana is one of those few parts of Africa where game sanctuaries have remained unspoilt by so-called civilisation and where you have the feeling of being truly in the wild.

Wildlife and Tourism
The expanse of the Kalahari semi-desert, covering 82 percent of the country; the unique inland river delta and lagoons of the Okavango; the almost equally vast salt pans of what were once the lakes of Makgadikgadi; and the swamps and flood plains of the Chobe river collectively constitute an ecosystem unparalleled in Africa. Here over countless thousands of years a remarkable variety of animals and birds have evolved their own way of living.

Inevitably, the freedom of the wild has been affected by the needs of man; specifically by game control fences protecting new cattle ranching areas. Against this, 80,000 sq km (30,000 sq miles) have been designated as permanent game sanctuaries, or 17 per cent of the whole country, and some of the best known international safari companies have built small, unobtrusive – and expensive – lodges designed to blend with the natural surroundings. There are also some camp sites in reserves, although, Botswana would like to attract low volume and, let it be frankly admitted, high cost tourism. This is reflected in high National Park fees. Nonetheless it is possible to travel cheaply and even explore the Okavango on a tight budget, as we explain where relevant.

Combined with these natural attractions, Botswana has rich nickel and copper deposits, gold, three of the most important diamond mines in the world and a thriving beef export trade to the European Union. So the country is one of the most prosperous and economically self-reliant on the African continent.

Topography
Physically, Botswana covers 581,730 sq km (227,238 sq miles) of tableland, a huge chunk of Southern Africa about the size of France, which is entirely landlocked and bordered by South Africa, Zambia, Zimbabwe and Namibia. It lies on the Tropic of Capricorn and has a mean altitude of 1,000 m (3,300 ft) above sea level, being basically the Kalahari plain, bordered by low hills. The differerce in elevation between Gaborone and Maun, 600 km (375 miles) away, is only 100 feet.

The Kalahari stretches right across the country and down into the northern Cape Province of South Africa. The Chobe river forms the border between Botswana and Namibia's Caprivi Strip. To the east the Limpopo divides Botswana from South Africa. The best agricultural land lies along these eastern borders, although cattle are also ranched in the west and north. The diamond mines of Orapa in the Central District, and of Jwaneng in the south, are relatively near Gaborone, the capital.

Climate

The climate is generally sub-tropical but varies considerably with the latitude. The northern part of the country is in the tropics, and liable to heavy thunderstorms. The southern and western areas vary between being savannah with summer rains, to desert or semi-desert climates. The winter days are warm, and the nights cool to cold, with occasional frost in the north and heavy frosts in the semi-desert areas. In July and August the nights can be very cold. The summer is hot, but tempered by a prevailing north-easterly breeze.

The rains generally begin in late October, ending in April. May to September are usually dry months. Average rainfall is 450 mm (17 inches), though less than 225 mm falls in the Kalahari.

History

In the decades since Independence historians have utilised oral traditions and archaeological techniques to reconstruct an African past which left no written records; and to reconcile it with the observations of early European explorers and missionaries. Late Stone Age tools of about 25,000 years ago have been found in several parts of Botswana. They were made by ancestors of the Bushmen, or San, who were hunters, and the Khoi, the latter being cattle herders. As elsewhere in Southern Africa, they tended to be displaced by more powerful tribes, including Europeans. See also the Tuli Block text.

In the north east geologists, investigating primitive gold workings, have found fragments of third century oriental glassware. Explorers from the Orient who penetrated East Africa apparently reached as far as here. The coming of Bantu people is more recent. Folklore has it that they arrived from the north and historians believe the Tswana are a branch of the Sotho (see Lesotho), who moved down into Southern Africa during the great Bantu migrations of the sixteenth to eighteenth centuries. Those centuries were ones of continual tribal movement and conflict, too complicated to detail here. It is enough to say that the influence and rule of the Twsana chiefs extended way down into what is now the Cape Province of South Africa. Indeed the celebrated missionary Robert Moffat received his first grant of land for a church near Kuruman from the Tswana in 1817.

From Protectorate to Independent State
Effectively this was the Tswana's first contact with Europe, continued later by Moffat's son-in-law, the famous David Livingstone. In 1885, as a result of conflict with the Boers across the border in the Transvaal, the Tswana chiefs appealed to Britain for protection, and the Bechuanaland Protectorate was proclaimed. In 1895 Britain incorporated the southern part of the territory, including the capital, Mafeking, into the Cape Colony. However, Mafeking continued to be the administrative centre until, as independence neared, a new capital was built at Gaborone. The country became independent as Botswana on September 30, 1966. It is a Republic in the Commonwealth with an Executive President, Dr Quett K J Masire. The first President was Sir Seretse Khama.

The People

Some 80 per cent of the 1,200,000 population lives in the east, while the average density is under two people per sq km. The vast majority are Batswana, consisting of eight main tribes; the Bamangwato, Batawana,Bakgatla, Bakwena, Bangwaketsi, Batlokwa, Barolong, and Bamalete. Administratively the country is divided into ten districts, which follow tribal boundaries.

Towns
The capital is Gaborone, close to the South African frontier in the south. The other principal towns are Francistown in the east, Jwaneng in the Southern District, Lobatse near Gaborone and Selebi Phikwe in the north east. The diamond town of Orapa is closed to visitors. Semi-urban areas include Kanye, Mochudi, Maun, Molepolole and Serowe. Maun and Kasane, in the north, are the safari centres.

Communications

The country's huge size means the starting point of your visit should be determined by where you are coming from. Air and rail links are detailed in the Factfile. Maun is the starting point for the Okavango and Kasane for the Chobe Park. Many visitors fly to Harare and go to Maun via the Victoria Falls or fly in from Windhoek. This is detailed further under Maun. Generally speaking the north is for more accessible from Victoria Falls than from Gaborone, which is convenient for Khutse in the Kalahari. Air charter is possible at Gaborone through Kalahari Air Services (PO Box 41278, Gaborone; tel 351804). Several firms operate at Maun, see the Maun section.

Posts and Telephones
There are no postal or telephone codes - see the Factfile.

National Parks and Game Reserves

Botswana's game areas are among the finest in Africa and are less spoiled by tourism than most. The Chobe National Park of 11,007 sq km (4,250 sq miles) around the Chobe river includes the Savuti Channel, which is closed from January to March.

The Central Kalahari Game Reserve, a vast area in the centre of Botswana, is home both to large herds of game and to the Bushmen, though not open to the public. Roads are poor, there are no campsites, and expeditions require permits either from the Department of Wildlife in Gaborone (PO Box 131; tel 371405) or the District Commissioner in Ghanzi. But the Khutse Game Reserve next to it is accessible.

Moremi Wildlife Reserve is some 3,000 sq km of mainly dry land north of Maun in the Okavango delta, protecting elephant, buffalo, antelope and lion.

The Kalahari Gemsbok National Park has no water or campsites and is not open to visitors, but the Mabuasehube Reserve adjoining it can be visited.

Lesser parks are the Nxai Pan National Park east of the Okavango delta, and the Makgadikgadi Game Reserve (also known as the Makarikari) on the Boteti river between the delta and Lake Xau.

The Parks are administered by the Department of Wildlife and National Parks, PO Box 131, Gaborone. Information about them is not easy to obtain outside Botswana, except through safari firms. Lodges are privately owned and are listed in the guide published by the Tourism Division (see below). The best known are mentioned in this text. Park fees are deliberately set high to discourage 'Do it yourself' South African visitors.

Safaris and Tours

Hunting has already been covered in the 'Safaris' section at the beginning of the the book. The two principal safari centres are Maun and Kasane both in the north. Basically Maun is the starting point for safaris into the Okavango and the Moremi Reserve, while Kasane is the base for the Chobe National Park, the Savuti channel and the Linyanti swamps, which are just outside the Chobe Park. Kasane become more important that Maun, due to its new airport. A substantial number of safari firms, many Johannesburg-based, operate in northern Botswana, normally using light aircraft to ferry clients to their camps. Their operations may appear casual, but that is deceptive.

They are actually very professional. If you are making your own arrangements it is best to contact the South African, British or American offices, when they have them, rather than the Maun ones.

Safari Firms
Three first class safari firms with offices in America, Australia, or Britain, are the following - listed alphabetically:

Gametrackers was founded by the veteran Jon Panos and now belongs to Orient-Express Hotels, who have both upgraded three lodges in the Okavango and taken in two Savuti camps in the Chobe National Park. They operate their own aircraft under the name Sesovane. The Maun address is PO Box 40 Maun; tel 660302, local reservations through their Mount Nelson Hotel in Cape Town (76 Orange Street, Cape Town 8001; tel 027 21 231000, fax 247472). The British reservations office is Orient-Express Hotels, The Thameside Centre, Kew Bridge Road Brentford, Middlesex TW8 0EB; tel 0181 568 8366, fax 568 6782.

Ker & Downey Botswana established the first Okavango camps many years ago and have extensive adjouring private concession areas. They originated elephant-back safaris too. One of the best-known names in the safari business, they share offices in Maun with the hunting firm Safari South (PO Box 40, Maun; tel 260211, fax 660379). Their US offices are at 13201 North West Freeway, Suite 850, Houston, Teaxas 77040-6096; tel 713 744 5260, toll-free 800 423 4236, fax 713 744 5277. Their British office is at 18 Albemarle Street, London W1X 3HA; tel 0171 629 2044, fax 491 9177. Their rates are higher than Gametrackers'.

The third company, less expensive, is Okavango Explorations, who specialise in mokoro trails (mokoros are dugout canoes). Their address is Private Bag 48, Maun; tel and fax 660528. The South African office is Hartley's Safaris, Po Box 69859, Bryanston 2021; tel 027 11 708 1893, fax 708 1569. In Britain Hartley's Safaris are at 3 Bailgate, Lincoln LN1 3AE; tel 01522 511577, fax 511372.

Obviously you can make arrangements on arrival. One reliable local tour organiser is Okavango Tours and Safaris (PO Box 39, maun; tel 260220; or (PO Box 52900. Saxonwold 2132, South Africa; tel 011 788 5749). Their British tel is 0181 343 3283, fax 343 3287. Another is Wilderness Safaris in Maun (tel 660086). Cheaper minibus and Land Rover expeditions are run by Afro-Ventures (PO Box 2339, Randburg 2125, South Africa; tel 27 11 8861524, fax 886 1524) and its associate Desert and Delta Safaris. They have a

Maun base as does another firm that organises budget overland camping trips into Botswana, Karibu Safari (tel in South Africa 031 839774).

South-eastern Botswana

The capital, most of the few towns, and the country's industrial and agricultural heartland, are in the south east.

Gaborone

Gaborone is the capital of Botswana and the seat of government, which locals irreverently call 'Gabs'. Originally designed in 1962 as a new city for 20,000 people, it now has a population of at least 200,-000 and is expanding. It is on the line of rail in the south-east of the country close to the South African border. The city is centred on a traffic-free pedestrian shopping precinct, called the Mall, where airline offices, banks, shops, the President Hotel and one or two restaurants are located. Good local buys are karakul jackets, tapestries and ceramic jewellery. The Mall stretches between the National Assembly and government ministries at the western end, and the Pula Circle at the eastern end. The National Museum, the Library and the Town Hall are on the Pula Circle. Outside this area the city spreads out in a way confusing to strangers and is encircled by what amounts to highway, off which main roads lead. The railway station is south west of the Mall.

Information
The Tourism Division (Private Bag 0047; tel 353024) is away from the Mall. Its brochures are available from hotels. The American Express representatives, Manica Travel Services (tel 352021) in Debswana House on the Mall is the best informed travel agent among several. The airport is 15 km (nine miles) from the town. The Air Botswana telephone is 351921 and the Comair number 372397. There is no airport bus, but the main hotels meet flights.

Hotels and Restaurants
The best hotel is the Gaborone Sun (Private Bag 0016; tel 351111) on Nyerere Drive, five minutes by taxi from the centre. Entirely air-conditioned, it has well-appointed rooms, a casino, a swimming pool with an outdoor restaurant, shops and a bank. The golf course is adjacent. The Cresta President (PO Box 200; tel 353631) is on the Mall, also has air-conditioned rooms, and incorporates a lively terrace restaurant called the Pergola, which serves simple, inexpensive meals. The Sheraton Gaborone and Towers (Private Bag BR 105; tel 31299, fax 312989) is four km west of the town in attractive surroundings,

but hardly the 'gateway' to the Okavango that it claims to be, since Maun is 300 miles away. In truth these are all businessmen's hotels, comfortable, even luxurious but more expensive than their South African equivalents. A small and reasonably priced hotel outside town on the Zeerust road is the Morning Star Motel (PO Box 1509; tel 352201). or try the Cresta Lodge on Samora Machel Drive (tel 375375). In general prices are higher than the equivalent in South Africa. Among restaurants, the Savuti Grill at the Gaborone Sun is reliably good; the Pergola has been mentioned already; and the Bull and Bush, off the Francistown road, is the only English-style pub and serves steaks and barbecues.

Things To Do Locally
Amenities include a wide range of shops, the Capitol cinema on the Mall, the museum, the library, and sports and recreational facilities at National Centres including tennis, and squash. The golf course is well kept and has a pleasant clubhouse. Gaborone Dam, five km (three miles) from the town centre, offers a site for water sports such as yachting and water-skiing, while the Gaborone Game Reserve has zebra, kudu, white rhino and many birds. There are picnic sites and a Visitors Centre.

Short of flying up to Maun or the Tali Block, one answer to being stuck over a weekend is to hire a 4WD vehicle and gear locally and take off on a do-it-yourself safari. You could do this in advance through Avis or the Manica Travel Agency. The nearest major game reserve, Madikwe, is just across the frontier in South Africa, far closer than any Botswana ones.

Madikwe Game Reserve
We fully recommend the Madikwe River Lodge (local bookings through Manica Travel). It is only an hour and a quarter's drive, first along the 18 km to the border on what becomes the R 505 to Zeerust. Shortly after take a left down a gravel road towards Deerdepoort and the reserve is signed. You could do this without 4WD and the lodge has game viewing vehicles.

Francistown

Francistown lies close to the Zimbabwe border on the railway and is only 192 km (120 miles) from Bulawayo. The traditional industrial centre, with a shopping mall, it has good air connections to neighbouring countries and has become a staging post for the game parks in the north as well as for businessmen. There are several hotels, The Marang (tel 213991) is set in attractive gardens just outside the town. The Thapama Lodge (Private Bag 32; tel 213872) at the south end of the Mall has air-conditioning and a pool.

Lobatse

Lobatse is a small, but attractive, town situated amidst a range of low hills, almost midway on the railway line between Mafikeng and Gaborone, and 45 minutes by car from the capital. It is the seat of the High Court and also home to the Botswana Meat Commission, one of the largest meat processing plants in Africa. The Cumberland Hotel (PO Box 135, tel 330281) is air-conditioned.

The Tuli Block

Along the Limpopo river, on the South African border, there stretches a segment of country unique in Botswana, because it is all privately owned freehold land; most of it dedicated to game conservation.

Mashatu Game Reserve

In the north east of the Tuli block the Mashatu Game Reserve claims to be the largest private reserve in southern Africa and certainly has the largest herds of elephant on any private land, with over 700 animals. In the 19th century there were great herds along the Limpopo. But they were locally shot out and refugee elephant only began returning in 1947 to this 90,000 acre sanctuary, which is bounded by the Limpopo and the Shashe rivers. All the major predators are there too, in a landscape of real primeval bush, cut through by the Majale river. Main Camp has luxurious thatched bungalows, a pool and air-conditioning and conference facilities. The tented camp has more feel of the wild. Rates include all meals, game drives, and transfers from the border post at Pont Drift. The ownership is the same as Mala Mala described in the Eastern Transvaal Chapter, and the style of operations the same Rattray Reserves (PO Box 2575, Randburg 2125, South Africa; tel 011 789 2677). Clients normally arrive from South Africa because the 350 km (219 miles) of roads up from Gaborone demand 4WD. You can fly on the scheduled airline to Pietersburg, or drive to Pont Drift, and be met. Charters are available to the Tuli airstrip. British office is at 185-187 Brompton Road, London SW3 1NE; tel 0171 584 0004.

The Tuli Lodge (bookings in Johannesburg 011 788 1748) is west of Pont Drift on the banks of the Limpopo and situated in the same overall reserve, but is not as in the same class.

Other Tuli Lodges

Further places in the Tuli block, but not in Mashatu, are the Stevensford Safari Lodge and the Jwala Lodge. They are bookable through Phuti Travel (PO Box 40534, Gaborone; tel 314166).

Prehistoric Peoples

The Limpopo Valley was the home of Stone Age communities before either the whites or the Bantu blacks arrived. Their implements remain, as do relics of the Iron Age people who began to replace them around 300AD. They made pottery, domesticated animals, and grew crops. One site is at Pont Drift. This civilisation was linked with that of Greater Zimbabwe (see Zimbabwe chapter), and by the 11th century they were defending settlements with stone walls. However, as Dr David Price Williams notes in a historical survey written for Mashatu, by the mid-14th century the Limpopo communities declined, probably as a result of Greater Zimbabwe itself dominating the important trade with arab merchants at the coast.

The Kalahari

Although the Kalahari – sometimes called the Kgalagadi – occupies 82 percent of Botswana's land, safari veterans argue about its northern boundary. One accepted definition is the Francistown to Maun road and the Okavango delta (see map). From there the desert runs to the South African border on the Molopo river, and beyond. Many books have been written about this great wilderness, notably Sir Laurens van der Post's 'Bushmen of the Kalahari'. There is also controversy over the way large tracts of it are being turned into ranchland, even though – in theory at least – this does not affect the vast Kalahari Game Reserve in its centre, nor the Kalahari Gemsbok National Park in the south west, nor the Okavango (most of which is not protected officially). The easiest parts to visit are the Khutse Game Reserve, south of the Kalahari Game Reserve and the Mabuasehube Game Reserve, adjoining the Gemsbok Park.

The Bushmen

The Bushmen, or San (which means 'person') are among Africa's few indigenous peoples and took refuge from more aggressive tribes in the Kalahari, because here they could continue their life as hunter-gatherers undisturbed. The Botswana government calls them the Basarwa, regarding the name 'Bushmen' as demeaning, and is actively settling these 'Remote Area Dwellers' into reservations, with compulsory schooling for their children. They are despised by the Batswana, whose leaders have always been cattle owners. Of 55,000 Bushmen perhaps 3,000 are still living in small bands, wandering in the heart of the Kalahari, hunting with bows and arrows, spears and snares, and searching for edible roots. They can survive because this is not a true desert. It is sandy and dry, but its vast undulating spaces are covered by thorn bushes, grassland and strange trees. Among the latter are the shepherd tree, where lions find temperatures 21°C

Botswana

lower than in the open, and camelthorns under which springbok huddle. When the Spring comes many trees burst into bloom and the infrequent rains bring the whole desert to flowering life. The perceptible ridges across the Kalahari are reckoned to have been formed by the prevailing winds 3,000,000 years ago, when it was much dryer. Today, herds of gemsbok, eland, greater kudu, wildebeest, Cape hartebeest, springbok and ostrich live here while predators include lion and leopard.

The Cattle Threat
Unlikely as it may seem, due to aridity and disease, Kalahari ranching has been made possible by deep borehole water and spraying against tsetse fly; and encouraged by the European Union. The EU both pays well above the world price for Botswana beef and has financed game fences to prevent buffalo spreading foot and mouth disease. The fences are a source of bitter concern among conservationists, because they have cut the aeons-old migratory route of the game from the Okavango to the Nxai pan, then to the Makgadikgadi Pan, and south into the central Kalahari. And, of course, back again, according to the rains. In 1963 an estimated 300,000 wildebeest perished along the fences near Lake Xau, unable to reach water and grazing. Whereas conservationists claim few wildebeest are left, the government says there were still 300,000 in 1979, and plenty today. However the government is sensitive about international concern for the wildlife and aerial spraying against tsetse fly on the Okavango's boarders has been stopped.

Bushmen hunters in the Kalahari

Kalahari Gemsbok National Park

This park, combined with its South African counterpart constitutes the largest conservation area in Africa. However, although there is remarkable co-operation between the two nations' park authorities, there has been no tourist development on the Botswana side since it was declared a park in 1940 and there is no access for visitors. The Park's characteristics are described in the Northern Cape section of the South Africa chapters. However, the adjoining game reserve can be visited.

Mabuasehube Game Reserve

This 1,800 sq km (703 sq miles) reserve is focussed on three large salt pans among the sand dunes, with their associated areas of grassland and woodland. Herds of gemsbok and other game migrate in from the Gemsbok Park between May and October, since there is no dividing fence. Some 170 species of birds have been recorded. After rain even waterbirds fly in to the pans, which make the reserve quite different to the visitable (ie South African) parts of its neighbour. It is generally not as dry as the wilderness further west and there are higher trees. The largest pan is Bosobogolo. There is a campsite at Mabausehube Pan, but the Wildlife Department warns that there may be no-one around and you should enquire in Gaborone or at Tsabong before going there. The fact that the police use camels as transport gives some idea of the terrain. The access 'road' from Tsabong, which goes out again to the north to Tshane, can be deep sand and demands 4WD. It is wise to drive in company with another vehicle.

Ghanzi

The only hotel in the western Kalahari area is at Ghanzi, a small town in the desert with a hospital, two Air Botswana flights a week from Maun, a few shops and an agency of Barclays Bank International. Ghanzi is where the roads from Namibia, Maun and Lobatse meet. The 640 km (400 mile) drive from Lobatse needs four wheel drive. The Kalahari Arms hotel (PO Box 29, Ghanzi; tel 296311) is very small but offers good hospitality. Horse riding and visits to cattle ranches can be arranged.

Khutse Game Reserve

Since the Central Kalahari Game Reserve can only be visited with special permission. Khutse and the Makgadikgadi Salt pans are two of the few accessible places to experience the wilderness of the semi-desert. All Kalahari game have been recorded in Khutse, which may look small on the map, but actually covers 2,500 sq km (976 sq miles), protecting springbok, hartebeest, gemsbok and blue wildebeest. Lion, leopard, cheetah, caracal and wild dog are among predators. A number of pans attract the wildlife, though the animals can be very shy. 'If they see a human being they're over the horizon' comments one safari leader. Access to the reserve from Gaborone is via Molepolole, a total of 240 km (150 miles). The road is tarred through Molepolole to the village of Letlhakeng, or two-thirds of the way, but then deteriorates. The Department of Wildlife maintains a camp at the entrance, where guides can be hired. Details are obtainable from the Department in Gaborone (PO Box 131; tel 371405). It is advisable to have 4WD transport and you must come fully equipped, as apart from the campsite, there are no facilities. Petrol is available at Molepolole, as well as food supplies. It is best to set off with a water supply. A firm operating trips to Khutse is Holiday Safaris (Private Bag 0016, Gaborone; tel 353970).

Makgadikgadi Pans Game Reserve

The Makgadikgadi salt pans (Makarikari), once a large lake, began benefitting from a new wet period in 1989. Even so their vast white expanses are only ephemerally under water. When they are large flocks of flamingoes line the shore. Massive herds of springbok, gemsbok, zebra and wildebeest are to be found on the grasslands north and west of the pans, which are best visited from May to September. They lie just south of the Maun to Francistown road.

For the extraordinary experience of seeing the pans and the annual movement to them of gemsbok, zebra and wildebeeste from the water system of the Okavango and Linyanti - and doing this on horseback - you should pitch in at one of the two camps run on the western edge of the pans by Ralph Bousfield, Jack's Camp and the Sand Camp. Although his transfers are from Maun, his address is PO Box 173, Francistown; tel 212277, fax 213458. He is also represented by Wilderness Safaris in Maun and in britain by Safari Consultants (see page 27). The animals are around the pans from December to March.

The North

The majority of visitors head either for the Okavango delta or the wildlife around the Chobe National Park. Together with their associated safari areas they are the stuff of travellers' legends, Chobe for the greatest herds of elephant remaining in Africa and the Okavango for its complex system of inland waterways, creating a superb environment for game of all kinds.

Getting There

The town of Maun serves the Okavango, with flights in from Johannesburg, the Victoria Falls and Windhoek, while the ease of getting to the town of Kasane and Chobe from Zimbabwe is described in a moment. It is more economic, if you are coming from Europe, not to route yourself through Gaborone, as the north of Botswana is now part of a circuit taking in the Zambezi and the Victoria Falls.

Maun

Maun, the administrative centre of the Ngamiland District and the organisational centre for the Okavango, is 499 km (312 miles) from Francistown on a good gravel road. The airfield is close to town and has scheduled flights from Gaborone, Johannesburg and the Victoria Falls. Although the housing sprawls across the bush, there is only a single tarred road, along which just about everything you need is concentrated. There are shops, safari firms (see below), garages, banks and the Cresta Riley's Hotel (PO Box 1; tel 660204), which is comfortable and air-conditioned. The near-legendary meeting place of the Duck Inn at the airport has been closed. There is a good and friendly feeling about Maun. Local Africans include tall, dignified Hereros, whose wives wear magnificent full length robes and turban headdresses, derived from early German missionaries' styles. Their ancestors fled here from Namibia between 1904 and 1907, when the Herero rebellion was put down by the Germans with great loss of life (see Namibia chapter). You also see Bushmen, lean and small people with almost apricot-coloured skins.

Places to Stay

Apart from Riley's Hotel, there are several lodges a short distance from Maun, along the Thamalakane river, notably the Crocodile Camp (PO Box 46; tel 660265), the Island Safari Lodge (PO Box 116; tel 660300), and the Okavango River Lodge (PO Box 32; tel 660298). All have thatched huts or bunglows, are not wildly expensive, and can arrange game viewing and fishing. The River Lodge is a good place for making useful contacts.

Good Buys

If you have time in Maun for souvenir shopping, then among the best buys are reed and gameskin mats, karosses, and Bushmen's *majumboro* shirts, fringed with bright beadwork. There is a dusty shopping mall off the main road, where you can get ordinary clothing and safari gear.

Safari Firms

One hunter remarked of Maun that it's 'more a bunch of frenetic dreamers than a boom town'. Nonetheless the safari business is

Botswana

booming, with the 300 or so European residents including safari organisers, light aircraft pilots and others serving the 42 or more camps lodges of the Okavango. The leading firms with international reservations offices have already been mentioned under Safaris' and we do not repeat their addresses. Local firms are numerous. Any might fix you up with an impromptu trip. Okavango Tours and Safaris is prominent in this field. You could also look for Okavango Wilderness Safaris. Or hire a guide, a canoe and a tent yourself and set off.

Transport
Hire of 4WD vehicles is available through Avis Safari Hire (tel 660258, reservations in Gaborone 313093), through Island Safari Lodge (tel 660300), or and possibly at Riley's Garage. payment is required 30 days before your safari starts. But the normal way of reaching Okavango is by boat or light aircraft. If you want an unscheduled ride to one of the camps call Northern Air (tel 660385), which is associated with Safari South, or go to the airport and look for Sesofane (the Gametrackers company) or Aero Kavango. The latter basically serve their own clients, but may have spare seats. Flights around the Okavango, or up to Savuti, are not cheap. Maun Office Service (PO Box 448; tel 66022) could help find transport too. You can hire boats at both the Okavango River Lodge and the Island Safari Lodge.

The Okavango Delta

In the north west is the Okavango delta, 320 km (200 miles) wide at its greatest and covering more than 18,000 sq km (7,000 sq miles). This complex of waterways and wetlands is one of the ecological miracles of the African continent. Inland river deltas, where a river fails to reach the sea exist elsewhere. But nowhere else is there such a diversity of wildlife in a still partly unexplored wilderness.

Why the Delta Exists
The reason for the delta's existence is simple. The great Okavango river, rising in the highlands of Angola, flows south east away from the Atlantic and towards the Kalahari. There it is channelled by a geological fault into a fast flowing waterway that becomes blocked and lost in the semi-desert, on account of two other faults. The most important of these runs north east to south west along the line of the Thamalakane river past Maun and prevents water going further. You can see the low ridge the fault created when you are in the town. Consequently the Boro, the main river of the delta, has to be dredged and channelled to let it through this barrier. Aeons ago, the Okavango is thought to have formed one vast river with the Chobe and the Zambesi and to have reached the Indian Ocean via the Limpopo. But the earth movements

that created the Great Rift Valley hindered its flow. Today it falters 1000 km (600 miles) from its source, impeded by the fault and the millions of tons of sand it carries with it, and spreads out across the northern Kalahari like the fingers of a giant hand. Sometimes water does reach Lake Ngami, south of Maun and supplies the Boteti river. However the Boteti never reaches the Makgadikgadi and Nxai Pans to the east, once a vast lake, which only have water briefly after rain.

The Okavango's Geography

If you intend visiting the Okavango it is essential to understand something which few of the magnificently illustrated books about it make clear. This is that for wildlife viewing the Okavango has three distinct regions; the Panhandle, the Delta waterways, and the Moremi Wildlife Reserve (plus the hunting concessions north of the Khwai River and the Reserve). Some 42 camps and lodges are dotted around these areas. Nor, although they can look close on a map, are the Savuti Channel and the Chobe Park part of the system for human visitors, though they are for elephant and buffalo migrating in search of food.

The Panhandle

The Okavango river's normal course between the Angolan border and Serouga is known as the Panhandle. There are fighting tiger fish in the river and several small fishing camps, notably Nxamaseri (Private Bag 23, Maun; tel 660 205) and the more expensive Okavango Fishing Safaris (PO Box 12, Shakawe; telex 2487 BD). Nxamaseri organises horse trails and both firms offer excursions to the Tshodilo hills to the west, described later. The Panhandle is rich in birdlife, one of its more unusual birds being the African Skimmer, which nests in the sand by the river.

Around March, rain in Angola brings a flood to Shakawe. The river rises, carrying small floating papyrus islands with it and sweeps into the delta. But the difference in altitude between the Panhandle and Maun is only 14 feet; so the flood takes until late June to percolate the whole way. Its serpentine patterns are responsible for the vegetation and grasslands of the Delta's wetland environment. When the rains come the game spreads out and moves back into the Delta from the surrounding bush.

The Delta

This is a meandering network of narrow waterways and lagoons, surrounding islands that are often substantial, though barely ten feet above the water level and only identifiable among the papyrus and reedbeds because of their palms and other trees. Even the main rivers are reduced to a few metres width by the luxuriant vegetation, while the lesser channels are half blocked by water lilies. Only from the air can you appreciate that there are huge stretches of grassland on the islands.

Watching the Wildlife
The wildlife is fascinating, but not always easily seen. Carnivorous plants trap mosquitoes. The 200 or more species of birds include herons, storks, pelicans, sacred ibis and handsome, white headed, fish eagles. Hippos emerge at night from the channels to munch grass. Crocodiles slip through the shallow, sandy bottomed streams; as do bream and small pike. On the islands are elephant, lion, buffalo, giraffe, and comparatively rare marsh antelopes like the red lechwe, the shy sitatunga, and the reddish-brown sessebe. You can best observe birds by boat, either from the canoes fashioned from African ebony trees called *mokoros* or from shallow-draught motorboats. The canoes are easily the best, if you do not mind slow progress. The water slaps gently on your canoeman's paddle, reeds rustle against the wood as you glide through narrow openings, and you are part of the general quietness, able to watch for the alert ears of red lechwe on the banks and get close to pelicans and herons. By contrast the motorboat drivers all too often churn at speed through the channels, sending all other forms of life into hiding, on the way to specific islands or bird sanctuaries. 'Great for a ten year old' one client commented wryly.

The Delta Way of Life
The *mokoros* are part of a delta way of life, which was established over many centuries by River Bushmen and other hunting tribes, the Bayel and Bambukushu.They practise a small amount of agriculture, but live in harmony with the delta's ecology, which is fragilely balanced. The greatest threat to its existence would be if the cattle farming on its perimeters was allowed to extend in to it. Except for Moremi, it is not officially protected.

Delta Camps
These are usually tented, with solid foundations, flush toilets, showers and electricity. Addresses already given are not repeated. The best include Pom Pom and Shinde Island (Ker & Downey), the greatly improved Xaxaba (Gametrackers), the new Tchau (Wilderness Safaris and Xugana (Okavango Explorations). Clients are always flown in to island airstrips. There are some campsites, where you can hire equipment, such as Oddballs (PO Box 39, Maun). It is not practical for newcomers to attempt driving in on the very few roads. Camps maintain daily radio contact with their Maun offices and aircraft take back mail.

Mokoro Trails
All camps provide conventional boats or *mokoros* for their clients, but

a few firms, including Ker & Downey and Okavango Explorations organise water channel trails of up to six days, usually overnighting in 'fly camps' - tented, but more basic than permanent ones.

Elephant and Horse Riding Safaris

It used to be said that African elephants could not be trained for riding. But it was done in the United States with four young ones orphaned in the Kruger Park and used in the film 'White Hunter, Black Heart'. They are now based at Abu's Camp in the south western Okavango. A safari lasts five days and is expensive. You must book ahead through any of the specialist agents recommended earlier, or Ker & Downey.

Horseback safaris were pioneered by P.J. Vesterlink. He keeps the mounts at Gumare in the west of the Delta. Again, you must book in advance.

Boat from Maun to Shakawe

It is also possible to hire a boat from Maun through the narrow water-ways for 640 km (400 miles) and come out at the north west corner of Shakawe, taking four days, unless you camp longer on any of the islands en route. This could be a most exciting and rewarding trip, culminating with a fishing camp stay on the Okavango River, with 200 miles of river and lagoons for fishing, and bird watching. One organiser is Okavango Fishing Safaris, already mentioned. The most luxurious boat trip is on the African Skimmer, built for these water-ways, with cabins, a lounge and a high viewing deck. She is run by Okavango Explorations. But there is no problem simply asking around in Maun about boat hire and camp sites, which is the budget way.

Moremi Wildlife Reserve

The Moremi Wildlife Reserve lies some 144 km (90 miles) from Maun. Completely wild and unspoilt, this 3,000 sq km (1,171 sq mile) reserve set in the north east corner of the Okavango Delta is one of the most beautiful and spectacular of all African reserves; as well as the first in Southern Africa to have been created and administered by an African tribe on their own land, namely the Batswana. Here, among mopane woodlands, you will find the big game that most people want to see, and which are not so easily spotted elsewhere in the Delta; herds of elephant, lion, leopard, cheetah, buffalo, a profusion of antelopes, and hippo in the Khwai river. Moremi is also an ornithologist's dream, with virtually every species of Central African bird life represented. The heronry in the Reserve is a major nesting site of the Marabou stork. An excellent reference book is 'Birds of Botswana' by Kenneth Newman, available locally.

Botswana

Broadly, Moremi has three areas. The eastern land mass, bounded to the north by the Khwai river, the central areas of flood and waterways and the dry land of Chief's Island on the west. The first is accessible by road, though demanding 4WD. The north gate on the Khwai River is a 170 km (106 mile) drive from Maun and the south gate at Maqwe is 100 km (62 miles). You are not allowed on foot or to leave recognised tracks, because the meagre grass in the woodland is so easily eroded. Chief's Island is only accessible by plane or boat and visitors are allowed to use boats for game viewing and fishing. There are government campsites, but they are not well maintained.

Moremi Lodges

Except for camps Moremi and Xakanaka, which are inside the Reserve in the north, all the lodges are just outside the boundaries. The best for the mainland area are the upgraded Khwai River Lodge (Gametrackers) and Machaba (Ker & Downey), both delightfully situated on the banks of the Khwai river, near the north gate, plus Camp Moremi (Private Bag 10, Maun). Santawani (Gametrackers) is near the south gate, has been completely rebuilt, and has a waterhole to attract game. West of Chief's Island is Xaxaba Camp (Gametrackers), a larger camp than the others. Both it and the Khwai River Lodge have swimming pools. The atmosphere in all these camps is much more Kenyan than South African, and the standards are very high, though do not expect hotel-type luxury; you are in the bush. The Khwai River Lodge was the Okavango's first. Harry Selby came down from Kenya in the mid-1960s and built it, paying the labour with maize and buffalo meat.

Seasons to visit the Delta

The delta has two seasons, as a result of the seasonal changes in the levels of the water. May to August, when the river floods the channels, is best for fishing and exploring. But if you are interested in big game specifically, go anytime from September onwards and swap the canoe or dug-out you used in July for a 4WD drive vehicle in October. Many lodges and camps close in January and February because of the heat and the rains.

Tshodilo Hills

A ridge of micaceous quartzite schist, the Tshodilo Hills, rise 378 m (1,260 ft) above the surrounding desert 56 km (35 miles) west of the Okavango Delta. The San call them 'the bracelets of morning'. On their towering cliffs are over 2,000 Bushman rock paintings of wildlife dating from AD 1800. The two roads to the hills are very poor.

Lake Ngami

Situated 72 km (45 miles) south west of Maun, on the edge of the delta, Ngami is one of the finest bird areas in Africa. Sometimes the flocks of flamingoes number more than 20,000 and there is an abundance of pelican and other waterfowl. This lake, however, can be quite dry on occasions; it all depends on the rainfall. There is no accommodation, but camping is permitted.

Nxai Pan National Park

One of the most interesting parts of the former Makgadikgadi lake is the complex of pans around the Nxai Pan (or Paradise Pan). Lying 32 km (20 miles) north of the main road to Maun, the park covers about 155 sq km (60 sq miles). It is known for its large herds of giraffe and from February to April, when the rains produce fresh grazing, eland, gemsbok, springbok, zebra and wildebeest come in. And, of course, lion, cheetah and other predators accompany them. The Kanyu Flats, between Makgadikgadi and Nxai, have a group of ancient baobab trees. See the earlier description of Makgadikgadi for camps.

The Chobe Area

Chobe is much more accessible than the Okavango, especially if you have been visiting the Victoria Falls. There are two routes by road. One is to drive 80 km (50 miles) from Livingstone in Zambia to Kazungula at the confluence of the Chobe and the Zambezi Rivers, where four countries meet – Zimbabwe, Zambia, Botswana and the Caprivi Strip of Namibia. You then take the ferry across the river, landing in Botswana's borders close to the great Mazungula Tree (Sausage Tree) where David Livingstone first sighted the Zambezi, and 13 km (eight miles) further on is Kasane. Better, there is a one and a half hour drive from the Victoria Falls, following the south bank of the Zambezi, which avoids the ferry. The United Touring Company runs morning and afternoon bus services between the Falls, Kasane and the Chobe Game Lodge. Coming up from the south there is a good gravel road from Francistown and Nata.

Kasane

Kasane, once only a village straggling along the Chobe river's southern bank, lies close to the Zambian and Zimbabwe borders and the entrance to the Chobe National Park. It is becoming a safari centre in its own right and the new airport, with customs and immigration, and scheduled flights to Livingstone and Victoria Falls, will speed this process, although most ordinary European travel agents will never have heard of it. If you need local arrangements made, contact Kasane

Enterprises (Box 55; tel 650234; fax 650223). They liase with all the safari companies. Barclays Bank International is open every morning. At the Kasane store you can buy frozen and tinned foods, films, curios and camping supplies, as well as hire camp equipment, boats and fishing tackle. Other shops sell safari clothes and wildlife books. There is a shady camping and caravan site near the river.

The Cresta Mowana Lodge has been built on the old airfield site and there is a fairly basic Chobe Safari Lodge (PO Box 10, Kasane; tel 650336), only a kilometre from the 'centre' on the river. Some rooms have air-conditioning.

Game Lodges

The more attractive Kubu Lodge (PO Box 43; tel 650312) has thatched chalets by the river, seven km from Kasane towards Kazungulu. Some rooms have air conditioning and rates are reasonable. It consists of thatched rondavels or family cottages and there are attractive camping sites in the grounds. A far more luxurious, exclusive and – inevitably – expensive lodge only two km out of Kasane and overlooking the river is Chobe Chilwero (PO Box 22, Kasane; tel 650505, fax 650352). This is a small, thatched, bush lodge, quite luxurious in its way and where the game viewing is outstanding. It is run by the same people as the Linyanti Safari Camp, described below. However for many people the ultimate place is the Chobe Game Lodge.

By comparison with the rest of the Chobe Game Lodge (PO Box 32, Kasane; tel 650340) is a palace although discreetly designed to blend with the riverine woodlands. It is where Richard Burton married Elizabeth Taylor for the second time, has six suites with private swimming pools, very comfortable other rooms, and the shortest trip by boat or vehicle will take you close to elephant and other game. In fact signs warn 'Please do not leave your laundry outside your rooms for fear of baboons destroying your clothing. The lodge runs its own double-decker game viewing boat, complete with a bar. Transfers from Kasane are often made by launch and the lodge is linked with Chobe Air, which has twice weekly flights from Lanseria airport, Johannesburg (tel Kasane 250226). The lodge is expensive, though not wildly so. Because it is inside the park you have to pay daily park fees in addition.

Chobe National Park

The 11,700 sq km (4,570 sq mile) Chobe National Park, blessed with abundant grazing and well watered, offers a great variety of game. You can see lion, leopard, cheetah, zebra, buffalo, and 18 types of antelope including lechwe, roan and sable. But nowadays its greatest asset is that roughly 35,000 of Africa's remaining 600,000 elephant are here. At the time of writing a hunting ban since 1982 had made them less wary and you could watch hundreds in the north of the Park, where they go to bathe and drink in the river (see our cover photograph). Crocodiles and hippos lie in the shallows. Fish eagles swoop over the smooth water. Huge monitor lizards patrol the banks. The Chobe, rising under another name in the Angolan highlands, and running into the Zambezi, is one of the great rivers of the region. Given a boat and a passport you could drift down to the Victoria Falls in a matter of hours.

The river swarms with tiger fish, often called the freshwater barracuda, bream and barbel – a delight to any fisherman. You may fish anywhere from the boat, but fishing from the banks is restricted to certain areas as elephant and other big game may get in your way. Fishing licences can be obtained from the Department of National Parks and Wildlife. There is no closed season.

The park is a bird-watcher's paradise, too, with most types of Central African bird life, particularly aquatic birds along the river. Experts reckon you could identify as many as 200 different birds on a five-day trip.

Chobe's Differing Habitats
The park has three principal areas; the riverine forests, the Ngwezumba area of mopane woodland, and dead lake area in the south west around the Savuti Channel. At the southern tip the park adjoins the Moremi Wildlife Reserve and the southern entrance to the park is four hours drive from Maun. The well-known, though remote, Linyanti Swamps are outside the park to the north west. The only part of Chobe accessible by ordinary car is the riverine area where the northern lodges are. The best time to visit the park is from May to October. There are campsites run by the National Parks (PO Box 17, Kasane; tel 650235 and PO Box 11, Maun; tel 660230).

The Savuti Channel
Savuti is a dried up marsh that is now grassland, where great herds of buffalo, wildebeeste and zebra congregate and the lion are famous. Originally there was a flow of water along the Selinda spillway from the Okavango, which fed the Savuti marsh and was then lost in the Mababe Depression. But, as happens all over this part of Africa, lakes and streams come and go. For over a hundred years up to 1957 the Savuti was dry. Then it was flooded occasionally. Since 1982 it has been dry again. The area has magnificent game viewing and bird watching.

Botswana

There are three camps. Lloyds is on the channel and is personally run by Lloyd Wilmot (Private Bag 13, Maun; tel 660361. Gametrackers run two camps jointly, Savuti and Allen's, both with twin-bedded luxury tents in the classic safari style, electricity and so on. There are a resident naturalist and trained rangers. You can drive in via the main Maun-Kasane road or fly in. The Savuti is closed from January to March.

The Linyanti Swamp and the Selinda Game Reserve
Right up on the Caprivi Strip of Namibia is the Linyanti swamp, created by the Linyanti river running in a V shape. Basically it is a papyrus marsh with small islands and narrow waterways that you can explore by boat. The marsh is a habitat of the rare sitatunga – a water antelope – while there are elephant in the riverine forest; and the surrounding floodplains are home to a variety of other game and myriad birds.

The Selinda Game Reserve covers 1,350 sq km between the Linyanti swamps in the east and the Okavango in the west, which are linked by the Selinda spillway. Broadly the centre is dry, while the ends are wetlands. All the big game are here, notably lion, elephant and buffalo. The concession for the reserve is held by Brian Graham, an experienced Safari organiser, whose Linyanti Explorations run the camps. Clients can go on expeditions monitoring the fauna and flora. There are canoe trips and walking trails.

Selinda camp is at the eastern end of the spillway and Moporota Camp at the western, both with airstrips. The Zibalianja Camp is near Selinda, by a lagoon. They are all small tented camps. Clients are normally flown in. Selinda is closed December to February, the others longer. Bookings through Linyanti Explorations, PO Box 22, Kasane; tel 650505, fax 650352. They are represented in Britain by a man who knows the area expertly himself. This is Bill Adams of Safari Consultants (Orchard House, Little Cornard, Sudbury, Suffolk CO10 0N2; tel 01787 228494).

Lake Liambezi
This is another lake that has dried up, but very recently. Also in the Caprivi Strip, it projects marginally into Botswana, on the Linyanti river. It was both full of fish, providing a living for many Africans, and alive with waterbirds, hippo and crocodile. In the early 1980s low rainfall in Angola reduced the flow of the Kwando river into the system and in 1985 the lake totally dried out. Then the peat moss in its dried-out bed caught fire spontaneously and burned until rains came in 1987. The lake may well fill again and the game return.

Factfile

This should be read in conjunction with the General Information at the start of the book.

Getting There

Remember that the capital, Gaborone, is a very long way from Maun and the Okavango, which are more accessible from the Victoria Falls.

Air

European airlines serve Gaborone only indirectly through Johannesburg, using either Air Botswana or Comair. Air Botswana flies daily from Johannesburg to Maun. Air Namibia makes useful connections from Europe to Maun, via Windhoek. Air Botswana operates from Gaborone, Nairobi, Harare, Lusaka, the Victoria Falls and Windhoek, with flights to Maun from Gaborone and the Victoria Falls. Air Namibia connects Maun with Windhoek and Katima Kalima Mulilo. Minimum check-in time is 80 minutes for international flights. A departure tax is being introduced. Air Botswana's reservations number is 351 921. There are no airport buses at Gaborone but the bigger hotels send courtesy ones! At Maun Riley's hotel provides courtesy transport and safari firms always meet their clients, though it is easy to hitch a lift into the town, which is very close.

Air Charter is possible at Gaborone through Kalahari Air Services (PO Box 10102, Gaborone; tel 351804) or Okavango Air Services (PO Box 10088, Gaborone; tel 313308). Several firms operate at Maun, see the Maun section.

Rail

The train from Johannesburg departs at 1330 and runs up through Mafikeng to Lobatse, Gaborone and Francistown, going on to Bulawayo and the Victoria Falls. The service to Gaborone takes 12 hours approximately and operates daily in each direction. First and second class compartments are quite comfortable, and not expensive.

Long Distance Buses

Greyhound buses run from Johannesburg to Gaborone. For tickets contact Manica travel in Gaborone (tel 352021) or Greyhound in South Africa (tel 011 403 6463).

Backpacking

Hitchhiking to remote areas is not easy. One place to seek lifts is the noticeboard at the supermarket in the Mall in Gaborone. You will be expected to contribute to fuel costs in return for lifts. You need to have food and water with you when hitchhiking. Using National Parks campsites should ensure a reduction in the park fee. There are local buses and the train is a cheap way of getting north from Gaborone. Overall, the official attitude to backpackers is equivocal. Officially Botswana does not want low-cost visitors, but in practice people are very helpful.

Banks

Barclays Bank International Ltd and the Standard and Chartered Bank Ltd have branches. Gaborone banking hours are 0900 to 1430 Monday to Friday and 0830 to 1145 on Saturdays. On Wednesdays banks close at 1300. In small towns the hours are 0815 to 1245. Mobile banks visit villages.

Car Hire and Driving

Hire cars, including 4WD vehicles, are available at Gaborone airport and in towns. Avis (PO Box 790, Gaborone; tel 313093/4/5) is the main firm. Other companies include Holiday Car Rentals (Private Bag 0016, Gaborone; tel 353970), who are also represented in Kasane. Driving is on the left. Vehicle renters must be over 25 and your home driving licence is acceptable. Remember that driving on gravel or sand roads is quite different to tarmac – see hints in the General Information.

Currency

The basic unit is the Pula (which means 'rain'), divided into 100 thebe. There are bank notes for P100, P50, P20, P10, P5, P2 and P1. Coins are for P1 and 50t, 25t, 10t, 5t, 2t and 1t. The Pula is a hard currency and exchange controls are reasonable. You can take out up to P500 and it will be readily exchanged in other countries. In 1995 the rates were P4.25 to £1.00 and P2.70 to US$1.00. Botswana is not in the Rand monetary area.

Customs Regulations
You can bring in duty-free 2 litres of wine, 1 litre of spirits, 400 cigarettes, 50 cigars, 250 gms tobacco, 50 mls perfume and any amount of film.

Gratuities

Ten percent is a reasonable restaurant tip. After a game drive give the driver/guide P4 or P5. Give hotel porters P1 or P2.

Health

Do not drink water without first boiling it and do not bathe in either pools or dams; there is bilharzia in Botswana. In Chobe and the Okavango it is possible to contract malaria. Take a prophylactic drug such as Paludrin plus Deltaprim. If you enter a tsetse fly area and are bitten you should advise a doctor within ten days that you may be infected with sleeping sickness. If you arrive from a yellow fever area you must have a valid vaccination certificate. Finally, AIDS a notice at the border posts says it all 'One in 7 sexually active young adults has the AIDS Virus .... condomise'. The AIDS/STD unit phone is 306148.

Hotels, Lodges and Camps

Accommodation is not graded. The Tourism Development Unit publishes a list, with useful comments on facilities, and prices. Some campsites are included. Prices increase annually, or more often. Camping in the relatively few campsites costs little.

Immigration

No visas are required for visits of up to three months by citizens of the British Commonwealth or of Austria, Belgium, Denmark, Germany, Finland, France, Greece, Iceland, Ireland, Israel, Italy, Liechtenstein, Luxembourg, Netherlands, Norway, Switzerland, the United States of America and Uruguay. If you want to stay more than three months you must apply before arrival to the Chief Immigration Officer (PO Box 942, Gaborone; tel 352950).

Language

The language of the people is Setswana. However, English is widely spoken and is the country's official language.

Photography

Photographing the military, government buildings or the police can cause problems. Film itself is expensive - see also the General information.

Public Holidays

New Year's Day (January 1), January 2, Good Friday, Easter Monday, Ascension Day, (May), Sir Seretse Khama Day (July 1), President's Day (two days in-mid July), Botswana Day (September 30), October 1, Christmas Day (December 25), Boxing Day (December 26).

Representation Abroad

Botswana has diplomatic missions in Beijing, Brussels, Harare, Hong Kong, London, Lusaka, New York, Pretoria, Stockholm, Washington and Windhoek. Visas are obtainable from them.

Telephones

The trunk dialling system works well. All numbers have six figures, with the first three indicating the district. For example Maun numbers start with 660. The international prefix for Botswana is 267.

Time

Two hours ahead of GMT and seven hours ahead of New York (six during daylight saving).

Tourist Information

Enquiries can be made to the Tourism Division, Private Bag 0047, Gaborone; tel 353024; fax 371539. The Botswana diplomatic missions have some brochures, but cannot give detailed advice.

Mountain Village

Lesotho

The Country

Lesotho is a tiny mountain kingdom with a proud history, similar in size to Belgium, and entirely encircled by South Africa. Its 30,355 sq km (11,718 sq miles) lie between, or rather sit above, the borders of Natal, the Orange Free State and the Cape Province. No other country in the world has all its frontiers higher than 1,000m sea level and Lesotho is often called the 'Switzerland of Africa': although the breathtaking landscapes of its main mountain range, the Malutis, seem more Tibetan than Swiss and might not be in Africa at all.

In short, this is a country of total individuality, characterised by the handsome Basuto horsemen, splendidly dignified in their multi-coloured blanket cloaks and conical straw hats, magnificent scenery, isolated hill villages and fine handicrafts. Along with these come the added lures of pony trekking, excellent freshwater fishing, bird watching and climbing. What's more, expeditions can now be made from comfortable hotels and lodges: though it is safer not to go alone.

Topography
Topographically the western plain is an extension of the highveld of the Orange Free State, some 5,000 to 7,000 feet above sea level. But you are aware of the distant peaks of the Maluti mountains before you even reach Maseru bridge and driving only a short distant east from the capital takes you rapidly into them. The Malutis run roughly parallel with the Free State border, while the central range is like a spine down the middle of the country. The greatest altitudes are over in the Drakensberg, on the Natal border, where Thabana-Ntlenyana is the highest peak in southern Africa at 3,841 m (12,598 ft). Great rivers have their origin here: the Senqu (Orange), the Mohokare (Caledon) and the Tugela. But whereas lower down they are broad and sometimes muddy, here they and their tributaries are perfect highland streams, alive with fish. They also provide South Africa with water and the Orange is the focal point of a water development scheme that is currently the largest civil engineering project in Africa.

Climate

The climate is bracing and healthy, there are no tropical diseases and the rivers are free of bilharzia and so safe to swim in - if you don't mind very cold water. In the lowlands, which comprise a quarter of the country, temperatures vary from 32°C (90°F) in summer (October to February) to 13°C (20°F) in winter. The seasons are distinctive, unlike those of tropical Africa. Summer, from November to January, is ideal for fishing and swimming; autumn (February to April) is good for hiking and ends with the harvest; from May to July the mountains are snow-covered. Spring brings blossom and late spring - October - sees both thunderstorms and superb clear, warm weather.

The high mountains' climate, however, is another story. Snow may fall in the highlands at any time, especially from June to August, when roads are closed and areas cut off. So if you are driving keep an eye on your retreat and if camping make sure you have ample food and fuel as well as warm clothing and bedding. It can be very cold at night.

The rains are unpredictable, the average of 71cm (28 ins) falling mainly from October to April. But every month has showers and firework displays of thunderstorms can blow up suddenly, turning roads to streams. You definitely need a raincoat.

History

The Malutis – also called the Blue Mountains – still have the rock shelters in which prehistoric men lived 50,000 years ago: shelters subsequently decorated with rock art by the Bushmen, who drew animals now extinct here. But modern Lesotho first realised its own identity as a place of refuge for various clans of Sotho-speaking cattle owners who were spread across the South African highveld at the end of the 18th century. The stability of their existence was shattered by the warlike Zulu and Matabele living east of the Drakensberg mountains, until they were rallied by an astute and humane Chief called Moshoeshoe (1786-1870), who led them to safety in the mountains around 1818. Initially his stronghold was at Butha-Buthe, but by 1824 he had established a fortress capital at Thaba-Bosiu just east of present-day Maseru. By the 1840s his Kingdom extended well into what is now the Orange Free State.

Inevitably, Moshoeshoe came into conflict with European settlers moving up from the Cape on the Great Trek and, over two decades, lost more and more farmland to the founders of the Free State. In 1868 he sought protection from the British Government, who anglicised the tribal name into Basutoland and moved the capital to Maseru. But Moshoeshoe's troubles were not over. In 1871 Britain declared the country part of the Cape Colony. Nine years later the Basutos rebelled (specifically against having to surrender their firearms). They held out through the resultant 'Gun Wars' until in 1884 direct British rule was restored. In 1909, when the Union of South Africa was being created, the Basutos sent a delegation to London and insisted on preserving their colonial status, and thus their identity. This lasted until October 4, 1966 when Lesotho regained independent sovereignty as a monarchy under King Moshoeshoe II, the great-great-great-grandson of the nation's founder, with a Constitution and National Assembly on the British model.

During the 1970's the then Prime Minister, Chief Leabua Jonathan, annulled the 1970 elections and ruled illegally until he was removed in January 1986 by a Military Council. This Council restored authority to the King as Head of State. Eventually elections in 1993 brought the Basutoland Congress Party (BCP) back to power.

Meanwhile, in 1990 the King had fallen out with the Military Council, been exiled, and eventually been deposed in favour of his son, King Letsia III. In August 1994 a Palace coup removed the government from office. International protests followed and much foreign aid was suspended. South Africa, Botswana and Zimbabwe acted as mediators. The result was that the military returned to barracks and democratic government was restored. The old King was re-instated in January 1995. King Letsia III, who had been a reluctant monarch, was not debarred from succeeding his father.

Even so, Lesotho lost both in prestige and money. Many foreign aid missions, notably Scandinavian, German and Canadian, were transferred to South Africa at exactly the time when drought and unemployment made their help important.

The People

As in most of Africa there is one root word for the nation and its language –Sotho – to which prefixes are added. Thus the people of the Sotho nation are the Basotho, a man is a Mosotho and the country is Lesotho. The British used a phonetic variant of this to call the people 'Basuto' and the country 'Basutoland'.

Despite their scattered historical origins, the Basotho are very much one nation and are a colourful people, friendly to strangers. Of the present population of 1,884,000 (1991) one third live in the mountains and in many areas the Basotho pony is the sole means of transport. Owning one of these sturdy and amazingly sure-footed horses is a man's prerogative, but most womenfolk can ride and children learn to sit a saddle almost as soon as they can walk. Surprisingly, in view of poor internal communications, the standard of literacy is among the highest in Africa. There is a small expatriate community and no racial discrimination.

Dependence on South Africa and International Aid
Lesotho's population growth is relatively high at 2.6 percent a year, agriculture is declining and the economy is heavily dependent on South Africa. But whereas the old South Africa was generous, the new SA Government is likely to cut both Basotho employment in the Republic and Lesotho's share of revenue from the Customs Union.

In 1994 some 100,000 Basotho's worked in the gold mines and their remittances constituted 50 percent of the GNP, while 60 percent of government revenue derived from Customs duties. The country is heavily dependent on international aid, especially from Britain, and the economy was badly damaged by the 1992/93 drought.

However, there is one big bonus in sight, which could be a tourist one as well: the Highlands Water Project.

Lesotho Highlands Water Project
One commodity Lesotho has in abundance is water and substantial development and revenue will derive from the Lesotho Highlands Water Project on a tributary of the Senqu (Orange) river. This huge and complex dual project, in which South Africa, the World Bank, the EU, and donor countries including Britain are participants, will pipe water to South Africa's dry industrial heartland, starting in 1995 and not being complete until 2019. At the same time it will give Lesotho its own hydro-electric power, irrigation and a greatly improved infrastructure of roads, opening up hitherto inaccessible areas to visitors and creating lake-based mountain recreations like sailing and bird watching.

National Parks
Lesotho's only National Park, Sehlabathebe, is in the Qacha's Nek district on the country's remote eastern borders. It has accommodation and is described at the end of the chapter.

Accommodation
Hotels and Lodges
Lesotho's hotels are not classified, though they are regularly inspected. Outside the capital facilities are simple and some hotels exist more for their bars then for residents. A hotel list is obtainable from the Tourist Board on Kingsway in Maseru (PO Box 1378, Maseru 100, Kingdom of Lesotho. (Tel 312896). The country's top hotel is the 236-bed Lesotho Sun. Country hotels and lodges are small and modestly priced. There is a 10 per cent government tax on hotel bills.

There are a number of lodges in the mountains, designed as bases for expeditions and outdoor recreation. The most comfortable is the New Oxbow Lodge in the north, where there is skiing as well as riding and fishing. The Molimo Nthuse Lodge (PO Box 212 Maseru; tel 32 2002) is well situated in the Blue Mountains close to the Basotho

Lesotho

Pony Trekking Centre. The others are self-catering, including two run by the National Parks (PO Box 92, Maseru; tel 32 3600). The Sehlabathebe Lodge can only be reached with 4WD. The private Malealea Lodge, described later, is situated 85km south of and well placed for hiking and pony trekking. There are other mountain lodges at Qaba, Marakabei and Semonkong run by Fraser Lodge System (PO Box 7423, Maseru 100; tel 312601. Maseru office inside Fraser's store). Bedding, linen, crockery and so on is provided, also a servant to help with chores, but you do your own cooking and bring your own food. Charges are correspondingly low.

Youth Hostels and Camping

The Lesotho Youth Hostels Association (PO Box 970 Maseru; tel 322900) can help with information. Youth hostels include large ones at Phomolong, near Maseru and at Morija Ecumenical Youth Centre south of Maseru; plus smaller ones near the St Paul's Mission at Butha-Buthe and in the hills near Bela Bela, reachable from Maphutsoe by bus. These all have camp sites, you have to do your own cooking and may need your own blankets and towels. Fresh meat, milk, butter and eggs are usually available at village stores.

In general, although Lesotho has few organised camp sites, there are many suitable spots to camp in the mountains. No permits are necessary, but you should tell the local police station or village headman.

Outward Bound Centre

Lesotho has one of Africa's few Outward Bound centres, with a variety of courses for young people that are designed to provide character-building adventure. The centre is in the foothills of the Malutis, near Thaba Phatsoe, Leribe. (Address PO Box 367 Leribe, Lesotho).

Transport and Tours

Local bus services go to most places cheaply and crowded. Car hire is dealt with under in the Factfile at the end of the chapter. Pony Trekking is dealt with below. The only tour operator is the Lesotho Tourist Board (PO Box 1378, Maseru; tel 312 896, fax 310108), which offers a variety of conducted excursions (see below). There are also expeditions up the Sani Pass in the Drakensberg run by the Mokhotlong Transport Co, but these start from Natal, not Maseru and require a passport. The address is PO Box 12 Himeville, Natal.

Finally Air Maluti (tel 350314) runs services to about a dozen mountain destinations, including Mokhotlong, Qacha's Nek and the Sehlabathebe Park. It has no town office.

Recreations

Riding, walking and fishing are the main sports, although tennis and golf are available in Maseru.

Fishing

Although the rivers only have seven species of fish, they include rainbow trout, brown trout and carp, as well as indigenous yellow fish and barbel. The highland streams were stocked with trout in the early 1930s and some of have hardly been fished to this day. The best trout fishing is around Semonkong, Mokhotlong and in the Tsoelike river (a tributary of the Orange). But in truth streams everywhere offer opportunities and one of the largest trout ever caught in southern Africa was hooked at Sehlabathebe, weighing over 4 kg (9lb 5ozs). The trout season is September 1 to May 31.

There are barbel, carp, yellowfish and mudfish in the Caledon river and for some distance up the Orange river, as well as in their tributaries. Catches have included carp up to 11.34 kg (25lbs) and barbel to 13.61 kg (30lbs). The upper reaches of the Orange teem with yellowfish – a small fish with fighting qualities equal to the rainbow trout, but seldom exceeding 2.72 kg (6lb). A yellowfish will run 55m on trout tackle and take 25 minutes to subdue.

Fishing licences are obtainable at most border posts, from the Livestock Division of government, the Angling Society of Lesotho and from Fraser's Store in Maseru.

Pony Trekking

This is a real Basotho speciality: and hardly surprising given that the Basotho horse is exceptionally sturdy and agile, while – as we have already remarked – Basothos themselves are practically born in the saddle. The surefooted ponies are never shod and will take you safely across rivers and up precipitous mountain tracks. In a four-hour ride ours stumbled only once. Getting completely away from it all in Lesotho's vast landscapes is the joy of pony trekking. Virtually every country hotel and lodge can arrange riding and no great skill is needed. What you must take is waterproof clothing, sweaters, a hat and – if you are going to camp – your own sleeping bag, tinned food and cooking utensils. The pony trek organisers will provide capacious saddle bags. Treks last up to five days, normally staying in mountain villages, and are very reasonably priced. The season is September 1 to April 30, avoiding the winter snow, though there is no hard and fast rule. The best pony trekking firm is Basotho Pony Trekking (PO Box 1027, Maseru 100; tel 314165) out at Molimo Nthuse. Another is Maluti Pony Trekking and Riding (PO Box 593; tel 344382).

Maseru

Postal code 100. No area telephone code. Tourist info 312896.
The capital, Maseru, is Lesotho's principal town and communications centre. You really need to start a visit here, because only Maseru has all the necessities, from changing money to car hire and permits. Originally chosen by the British as a site in preference to King Moshoeshoe's Thaba Bosiu mountain fortress in 1869, it grew very slowly at first. The railway from Bloemfontein reached it in 1905, when the road bridge across the Mohokare (Caledon) river was also opened. The population was then 6,000. The Secretariat, designed by Sir Herbert Baker, was built in 1911. But the main street, Kingsway, was not tarmaced until 1947 and it has been the 1980s which have seen the greatest expansion. Today the city has a population of 106, 000, modern office blocks and hotels and the official urban area has burgeoned from 23 sq km (9 sq miles) to 145 sq km (57 sq miles), while cracked sidewalks and litter contrast with new developments like the Kingsway shopping mall.

Nonetheless Maseru remains a pleasant, town with many trees, interesting markets and an easy atmosphere: albeit that there is a rush hour of vehicles down Kingsway in the morning and evening. This street is the main axis, running straight through the town from Maseru bridge to the Cathedral Circle roundabout on the eastern side, where the main roads north and south branch off. Kingsway's centre of activity is the stretch between the Basotho Hat craft shop, with its thatched conical roof surmounted by a looped topknot and the Queen Elizabeth II hospital, a distance of about a kilometre.

The other principal highway, Moshoeshoe Road, loops around to the north from the Golf Course to end up at Cathedral Circle, enclosing the low hill on which the Royal Palace, the National Assembly and the Cathedral stand.

Information
The Lesotho Tourist Board's offices are at 209 Kingsway in the Victoria Hotel building (tel 322892), the board can provide maps of Lesotho and Maseru, a 'hotel guide' and tour brochures.

Secretarial Services
Maseru Secretarial Services provides typing, photocopying and fax facilities at the Maseru Sun Complex in Orpen Street.

Handicrafts
Lesotho's big thing is handicrafts, including tapestries and sweaters made from the angora goat mohair that is among the country's main exports, but more often exploiting the craftsmanship in clay, wood,

grass and other media that Basothos learn from childhood. Beadwork, woven grass baskets in rich reds, purples, greens and blues, colourful wall hangings of village scenes and abstract designs, and modern jewellery are among the products. The Basotho Hat is one place to see them, though its better to seek out the specialist shops, or go into the countryside to craft centres, where you can see things being made. Prices are somewhat higher than in South Africa.

Several of Maseru's handicraft centres are on Mohlomi road, off Moshoeshoe Road near the Industrial Area about one and a half km from the town centre. The Royal Crown Jewellers use silver, gold, copper, brass and semi-precious stones to make necklaces, rings and bangles. Basotho Tanners make sheepskin articles, handbags and shoes. Round the corner in Makoanyane Road is Thorkild Hand Weaving making tapestries, place mats and carpets. These are all open during normal shopping hours of 0800 to 1700 Monday to Friday and on Saturday mornings.

Right in town on Kingsway handicrafts are sold at an informal open air market, with another on Saturday mormings by St John's Church, as well as the Basotho Hat and Basotho Shield shops.

The best country towns for handicrafts are Teyateyaneng (known as TY), Tetebeng and Kolonyama in the Berea District north of Maseru; Maputsoe, Leribe and Butha-Buthe also in the north; and Mazenod and Morija to the south.

Hotels and Restaurants
The large Lesotho Sun splendidly set on a hill above Maseru brought completely new standards to Lesotho's hotel business. With 100 acres of its own gardens, all its rooms have private baths, the standard of cuisine is high and there are a casino, cinema, sauna, tennis courts, pools and shops, including a hairdresser. The hotel can organise pony trekking and other expeditions. At weekends it is usually full of South Africans taking advantage of the casino, so you need to book ahead (tel 313111 or Sun International central reservations in South Africa 011 780 7800). The same company owns the smaller Maseru Sun on Orpen Road.

Alas, the once-illustrious Lancers Inn (Private Bag A216, Maseru; tel 322114) on the corner of Pioneer Road and Kingsway needs renovating. The Hotel Victoria on Kingsway (PO Box 212; tel 322002) is better value and the rooms have baths. The Lakeside Hotel (PO Box 602; tel 313646) is four km out of town by Lake Mejametalana and considerably cheaper.

Eating Out

We like the Auberge Restaurant on Kingsway by Parliament Road (tel 312775). It has a menu ranging from seafood to wild boar. Boccaccio on Orpen Road is an Italian restaurant (tel 325853). The Chinese Palace on Orpen Road is what its name suggests (tel 323815). Cheap snacks are available in various places, including the Lancers Inn. The town's most luxurious establishment, with music for dancing, is the relatively expensive Lehana Grill at the Lesotho Sun Hotel.

Sightseeing Excursions

The capital itself does not offer much in this regard. The Royal Palace is not open to the public, though there is a statue of King Moshoeshoe on the hill near the Government offices. Sadly there is no National Museum. Virtually all the places worth going to involve hiring a car or joining a group to go out into the country. The nearest of these are Lancers Gap and Thaba Bosiu, while there are very fine rock paintings further out at Ha Baroana. Pony trekking at Molimo Nthuse, described later, is also within a day's excursion from the capital, as is the old Mission Station at Morija.

Lancers Gap and Thaba Bosiu.

The 'Lancers Gap' in the hills four km from Maseru leads to the Berea plateau, where British cavalry under General Sir George Cathcart were defeated in 1852. A tarmac road leads through the gap to fine views back to the capital.

Thaba Bosiu is where King Moshoeshoe established his capital, holding off both the Matabele under Mzilikazi in 1831 and later the Boers. Indeed it was never taken by an enemy: and if it had been Lesotho might not be independent today. The site is roughly 40km (25 miles) by road from Maseru, taking the main south road, turning left at Masianokeng and left again at Ha Makhalanyane. You have to climb a track up the hill to find the remains of the King's compound, the cairn that is his grave and his small house, now restored. There are splendid views.

Ha Baroana

Considered one of the finest series of rock paintings in southern Africa, the Ha Baraona site is within a small nature reserve 46 km (29 miles) from Maseru by the mountain road (see further on). The paintings can be seen for a fee between 0900 and 1700.

Routes from Maseru

For exploring Lesotho, there are basically three directions to take from Maseru: north to Butha-Buthe, the resort of Oxbow and ultimately Mokhotlong; east to the Pony Trekking Centre and the central range of mountains; or south to Quthing. These all ultimately involve some tough driving and a lot of time. From Quthing it is possible to drive along the country's southern perimeter to Qacha's Nek, as the road has been improved. With 4WD you could then reach the Sehlabethebe National Park in the Drakensberg in a long day, though it's a lot easier to fly.

Maseru to Butha-Buthe

From Maseru's Cathedral Circle you take the Main North road and will be on tarmac almost all the way to Oxbow, a three to four-hour journey of 198 km (124 miles) as the roads curve and climb along the edge of the Maluti mountains. There are some fine views on the way and also badly eroded soil, but little else. Occasionally you'll see Basotho horsemen, cantering across the landscape, wives or children on the saddles with them.

Teyateyaneng
The neighbourhood of 'TY' as everyone calls Teyateyaneng, has a number of craft centres. You can watch weavers at work at St Agnes Mission, 35 km (22 miles) from Maseru. TY itself, 12 km further on, has the small Blue Mountain Inn (PO Box 7; tel 500362), which is sadly rundown but tolerable if you're stuck. There is a campsite by the Inn. Local attractions are Bushman rock paintings near the mountain road from TY up to Mohatlanes and the Setsoto Designs shops selling handwoven rugs and tapestries both in TY and at Tebetebeng. Some ten km (six miles) along the Hlotse road you pass the Kolonyama pottery, which produces attractive and sophisticated stoneware. It is open everyday except Christmas and you can picnic in the garden.

Hlotse
Hlotse is the administrative centre of Leribe District and was founded in 1876 when the Rev'd John Widdicombe pitched a tent on a grant of land from King Moshoeshoe, who encouraged missionaries. The church dates from 1877 and the fort – which saw fighting in the Gun Wars – in 1879. Gordon of Khartoum, the famous British General later killed in the Sudan, lived here briefly in a small rondavel, which is preserved. Hlotse is 52 km (32 miles) from TY during which you pass two border posts, Peka bridge and Ficksburg bridge.

Accommodation and Sightseeing
The Leribe Hotel (PO Box 14, tel 400362) is clean and friendly and the rooms have baths. A scenically interesting side-trip is on tarmac up to Pitseng in the mountains, while 8 km (5 miles) north on the main Butha-Buthe road you can walk to fossilised dinosaur footprints in the bed of the Subeng stream, 400m downstream from the bridge. These are reckoned to be 200 million years old and are in what was once a

swamp. There are other dinosaur remains in the south; evidently these prehistoric monsters roamed all over the mountains.

Butha-Buthe

Reaching Butha-Buthe – which means 'place of safety' and was so named by Moshoeshoe because it was his first mountain stronghold – you are noticeable higher up. The town stands at 1,993 m (6,527 ft) as against Maseru's 1,713 (5,610 ft); the climate is colder because temperature decreases with height and from here on the climb to Oxbow is almost continuous. The town is a trading centre, with a small Indian population, shops, fuel and a bank. There are three small hotels, the Moteng Lodge (PO Box 526; tel 460350), the Crocodile Inn (PO Box 72; tel 460223) and the Butha-Buthe (tel 460233).

The Roof of Africa road
From Butha-Buthe the road to Oxbow and Mokhotlong is being reconstructed and tarmaced, which will reduce the distance by 20 km. Part of the 900 km (562 miles) Roof of Africa car and bike rally is run along this route past the barren upper slopes of the Drakensberg, made hazardous by everything from snow to rock boulders. There are bus services to Mokhotlong and you could reach the Sani Pass from Oxbow in an ordinary car in about five hours. (But if you descend the

Lesotho woman in traditional dress

pass the South African authorities will not let you return unless you have 4WD).

Oxbow to the Sani Pass

The New Oxbow Lodge above the Moteng Pass is definitely out of the ordinary. Its thatched chalets are set in rugged and wild country 3,000 m (10,000 ft) up, where you can hike, ride, swim, fish and even ski – if only from June to August and on short runs. The lodge has all the necessary sporting equipment for hire. The address is PO Box 43 Maputsoe, but the reservations address is in South Africa, (PO Box 60, Ficksburg 9730; tel 05192 2247, fax 6093). You should book in advance.

Expeditions

Worthwhile expeditions from Oxbow are trout fishing in the Tsoloane pool, a breeding haven for trout; and to the Mont aux Sources, on the brink of the Drakensberg amphitheatre, with wide views over Natal. Roughly half way to Mokhotlong there are disused mine diggings at Letseng-la-Terae, where a 527-carat diamond was once found. There are several disused mines in these mountains.

Mokhotlong

Mokhotlong itself has an airfield and the Senqu Hotel (PO Box 13; tel 920330). It is likely that the Highlands Water Project will bring more tourist development here eventually. Mokhotlong Mountain Transport, based in Himeville, Natal, runs daily transport between the two places.

The Sani Pass

This dramatic crossing into Natal has far-reaching views and is almost in the shadow of southern Africa's highest peak, Thabana Ntlenyana. But it is unwise to attempt either the road or the pass without good brakes and plenty of food, water and warm clothing, since if you break down you will be very much on your own up here.

Mountaineers' Chalet

An unexpected mountaineers' chalet is located 8 km (5 miles) from the pass on the Lesotho side, close to a hillside village. In appearance much like an Alpine refuge hut, it sleeps 22 people in bunk beds distributed between five simple bedrooms. The sitting room has a cast iron coal stove in the middle for warmth and there is a dining area. You bring your own food, though a local girl serves wine and beer: making this southern Africa's highest licensed premises! Hot showers are possible and bedding is provided, while a stack of ancient skis challenge the adventurous. Bookings through PO Box 12, Himeville

4585; tel 1302, ot the chalet's phone (033 702 1069). An Indian-run store 500 m away sells such essential as blankets, tinned fish and milk cartons long past their 'sell by' date.

The Mountain Roads to the Central Range

The route past Molimo Nthuse to the central range of mountains is as breathtaking as the names along it suggest: 'God Help Me Pass' is one. Beyond Thaba Tseka the road degenerates into a 4WD track, although a surprising amount of traffic goes in the direction of the villages and Mission Stations in the Senqu valley, crossing the river by the Koma Koma causeway. When it is not raining it is possible to reach Sehlabathebe National Park via this last section of the Trans-Lesotho Track, which will no doubt be improved one day. But most outsiders will be content with getting as far as the lodge at Makarabei, as near in the dead centre of Lesotho as it could be. Another mountain destination is Semonkong, with southern Africa's highest waterfall.

Molimo Nthuse
Leaving Maseru on the main south road you turn left after 20 km (12 miles) at a Caltex petrol station (the last chance for fuel) and then left again after another 10 km at St Michael's Mission, where the main tarmac road continues to Lesotho's University at Roma. After St Michael's you're in for a steep, winding climb up the Bushman's Pass at 2265 m (7,419 ft), though with rewarding views of the bare grass hills and basalt rock faces of the Blue Mountains. Close to the God Help Me Pass is the pleasant, rondavel-shaped Molimo Nthuse Lodge (PO Box 212, Maseru; tel 370211). Set among trees by a cascading stream, the lodge is a good stop for a meal or to stay when pony trekking at the Pony Project a little further on.

Pony Trekking
The tarmac ends by the entrance to Basotho Pony Trekking, 55 km (34 miles) from Maseru and roughly an hour's drive. In origin this was an Irish aid scheme to improve the indigenous Basotho horses by crossing them with Connemara stallions at a breeding station three hours drive further on. As a sideline the project developed pony trekking. You can roam all over the mountains on horseback, never seeing a vehicle and visiting waterfalls, such as the Qiloane Falls a couple of hours ride away, passing undisturbed villages to which your guide will give yodelling greetings across the valleys as you pass. Treks last from four hours to six nights and seven days, the longest being way across country to the Lebihan Falls near Semonkong (see below). You bring your own food and sleeping bags and pay a small fee to the villages where you stay. The season is September 1 to April 30. Bookings PO Box 1027, Maseru; tel 314165.

Marakabei
Beyond the Pony Project the gravel road levels off and takes you 45 km (28 miles) through a boulder-strewn and rugged landscape to the small village of Marakabei in the Senqunyane river valley. On the other side of an iron bridge is the self-catering Lodge PO Box 7423 Maseru; tel 312601). The lodge has a bar and is licensed. Recreations centre on riding, swimming in the unpolluted river, and fishing for trout and yellowfish.

Semonkong and the Lebihan Falls

The road through the pleasant university town of Roma – a cosmopolitan campus with students from all over Africa – takes you after 68 km (42 miles) to Semonkong, with horseback access to the Lebihan Falls in one of the most magnificent parts of Lesotho. Named after a French missionary who saw them in 1881, these falls are the highest in southern Africa with a sheer 192 m (629 ft) drop over a cliff. Rare spiral aloes grow near them and on the mountain to the west of Semonkong. The Falls are also called Malutsenyane, after the river, further up which the improved self-catering Semonkong Lodge is situated (bookings PO Box 243, Ficksburg 9730, South Africa; tel 051 92 2730, fax 3313. Or PO Box 5, Maseru). Horses are available and it's a splendid, though long, ride to the Falls. Alternatively you can fly from Maseru to an airstrip with Lesotho Airways and then ride a mere four km. Fishing in the river is excellent. The Ketane Falls, described later, are about a four-hour ride from Semonkong.

South to Quthing and Qacha's Nek

The tarred road down to Mohale's Hoek takes you past a variety of attractions and possible side trips. If you intend going on through Quthing District to Qacha's Nek you will need plenty of time, however. Fortunately this part of Lesotho has some of the best country hotels.

Morija
This is where Lesotho's first Mission Station was opened by the Paris Evangelical Society in 1833. As well as the Mission book depot and a handicraft centre there is a small Museum, which is the nearest thing the country has to a National Archive, thanks to grants from the Ford Foundation, the Dutch Government and Goldfields of South Africa. Incidentally the evangelical movement remains strong. Driving out of Maseru we had seen a poster which summed it up; 'Miracle Revival. Blind See. Sick are Healed. Venue Bible College.'

Malealea, Qaba and Ketane Falls
A turn off the main south road 10 km (6 miles) after Morija leads on

gravel to two mountain lodges. Malealea is an inexpensive self-catering one owned by a South African (PO Box 119, Wepener 9944, South Africa; tel 051 473 200, Lesotho number 785 727). It has an airstrip. Qaba (Fraser Lodge System) is the other side of the Gate of Paradise Pass, looking over a valley and next door to the Qaba Inn. From either lodge you can organise a five-day pony trek to the Ketane Falls and back. In wild country, these are so remote that few non-Basothos have seen them, although they are only four hours ride from Semonkong. At about 150 m (500 ft) the fall is less than Lebihan, but those who have been there say the setting is equally beautiful.

Mohale's Hoek
Passing through Mafeteng, with the turn-off to the Van Rooyen's Gate border post, you come to Mohale's Hoek and usefully situated accommodation at the Hotel Mount Maluti (PO Box 10; tel 785224). The hotel has a pool and tennis court. There are dinosaur footprints in the hills at Maphutseng (near the Mission), an old Griqua village south of the town, and 'cannibal' caves inhabited in the 1820s are located near Trollip's gate by the Makhaleng river. Both Mohale's Hoek and Moyeni are convenient bases for mountain trout fishing.

Moyeni
This town, also called Quthing, is in the extreme south of Lesotho. Its Orange River Hotel (PO Box 37, Quthing 700; tel 750252) has a high reputation. From it you could do a day's walking tour to the Kokobe rock paintings, yet more dinosaur footprints and a witch doctor's cave.

Fort Hartley
The road to Qacha's Nek – improved recently – runs part of the way along the Senqu river and past the historical sites of Fort Hartley, a camp used during the Gun Wars against Chief Moorosi and the chief's own hill fortress, sited above the river. They are both near Moyeni.

Qacha's Nek
This town is on a pass through the Drakensberg mountains, 2,033 m (6,658 ft) up at an altitude where mountain mist enables giant redwood trees, brought from California, to grow. Qacha's Nek has a small hotel, the Nthatuoa (PO Box 13; telephone 950260), and the associated Nthatuoa Lodge. Air services come in from Maseru and petrol is available, while improved tourist infrastructure should derive from the Highlands Water Scheme. It is possible to drive on to the National Park, provided you have 4WD.

Sehlabathebe National Park

Gazetted as a National Park in 1970, Sehlabathebe covers 6,500 ha

(23 sq miles) of grassy plateau and mountain high in the Drakensberg, through which the Tsoelikana river runs. Game protected in the park includes mountain reedbuck, oribi and wild cat, while there are rare wild flowers and a unique minnow-like fish, Oreodaimon, in the rivers. Bushman rock paintings and ancient rock shelters can be seen along the cliffs.

Development has been minimal in order to conserve the area. However hiking, rock climbing, riding and fishing are allowed. There are a lodge, a hostel and camping sites in the Park, but no food supplies or petrol. The nearest source of supplies within Lesotho is Qacha's Nek. The self-catering accommodation is cheap and can be booked through PO Box 92, Maseru; tel 323600.

Road access demands 4WD, whether it is from Thaba Tseka, Qacha's Nek or Mataliele in the Transkei. The lodge is a 10 km (6 mile) hike or pony ride from the Bushman's Nek border post in Natal. The easiest way in is to fly on Air Maluti from Maseru to the Ha Paulus airstrip, where transport can be arranged.

Factfile

Getting to Lesotho

Air

Lesotho Airways (PO Box 861 Maseru; tel 324513 or in South Africa 011 970 1046) operates between Maseru International Airport and Johannesburg and also to Manzini. Royal Swazi Airways connect Maseru with Manzini in Swaziland. The airport is 24 km (15 miles) south of Maseru, via the Main South road. There is an airport bus service leaving Maseru at 0630, 1000, 1200, 1400, and 1600 hours. The Lesotho Sun Hotel operates a courtesy bus. There is a small departure tax.

Road

There are 12 border posts on roads from South Africa. Access is easiest on the western side of the country, notably from Ficksburg, Ladybrand and Wepener. Access from Natal on the east via the Sani Pass requires 4WD. From the Cape Province entry is easiest via Aliwal North and the Telle Bridge border post to Moyeni (Quthing). Principal border posts like Caledonspoort linking Fouriesburg to Butha-Buthe, and Ficksburg are open 24 hours a day. Maseru Bridge is open 0600 to 2200, lessor ones from 0800 to 1600. A vehicle toll is charged when leaving.

Banks

Barclays the Lesotho Development Bank, and Standard provide foreign exchange service in Maseru, but procedures can be very slow

Car Hire and Driving

Avis (tel 314325) is at Kingsway and Hertz (tel 314460) at the Lesotho Sun Hotel.

Seat belts are compulsory and the speed limit is 90 kph (58 mph). It makes sense to drive carefully both because many roads are poor and out of respect for the many pedestrians, cyclists and horsemen. Drivers must have their driving licences with them, and possession of an International Driving licence is desirable.

Courier Service

DHL has an office in the Options Building, Pioneer Road (tel 311082).

Currency

The Loti (plural Maloti) is divided into 100 Lisente. There are notes for M2, M5, M10, M20 and M50. The Loti is at par with the SA Rand and Rands are generally accepted. Coins are distinctively different, but the brown R20 and M2 notes can be mistaken for each other. Foreign currency may only be exchanged in Maseru and you should change your Maloti before leaving. Foreign currency exchange desks are not operational on Saturdays.

Customs

Lesotho is in the South African Customs area and visitors arriving from Botswana, South Africa and Swaziland are not allowed to bring in liquor. Otherwise allowances are as in the General Information. Customs declarations are required.

Diplomatic Representation

Lesotho has Embassies/High Commissions in Bonn, Brussels, Gentofte (Denmark), Johannesburg (trade), London, Maputo, Nairobi New York (UN), Ottawa, Rome, Washington. Elsewhere the country is represented by British diplomatic missions.

Countries with Embassies/High Commissions in Lestho include Germany, Great Britain, Ireland, South Africa and the United States.

Electricity

220 volts AC.

Health

Lesotho is not malarial and is generally healthy. If you are coming from an area affected by yellow fever or cholera you must have the appropriate immunisation. There are hospitals in Maseru and in the countryside.

Language

Sesotho and English are the two official languages.

Passports and Visas

All visitors need a passport. Nationals of Britain and Commonwealth countries (except Ghana and Nigeria) do not need visas. Nor do nationals of Belgium, Denmark, Finland, Iceland, Italy, Liechtenstein, Luxembourg, Netherlands, Norway, San Marino, South Africa, Sweden, Switzerland, USA and Uruguay. Entry permits are for up to 30 days. For a longer stay you must apply in advance to the Director of Immigration and Passport Services, PO Box 363, Maseru 100. If you drive in from South Africa be sure you have a South African re-entry visa if you are on business.

Postal Service

Post Offices are open 0800 to 1300 and 1400 to 1630 Monday to Friday, and 0800 to 1100 on Saturdays.

Public Holidays

New Year's Day (January 1), Moshoeshoe's Day (March 12), National Tree Planting Day (March 21), Good Friday, Easter Monday, Ascension Day, Family Day (First Monday in July), Sports Day (First Monday in October), Independence Day (October 4), Christmas Day (December 25), Boxing Day (December 26). If the holiday falls on a Sunday, the next day is a holiday.

Telephones

Local calls can be dialled direct. Automatic international dialling is possible from some telephone numbers beginning 31, but not with numbers starting 32, otherwise dial 100 for the international operator. The code for Great Britain is 0044, for the USA 001 and for South Africa 0027.

Lesotho

The code for Lesotho from outside the country is 266.

Time

Two hours ahead of GMT, seven hours ahead of Eastern Standard Time (six during daylight saving).

Tourist Information

Some brochures are available from the High Commission of the Kingdom of Lesotho in London (10 Collingham Road, London SW5; tel 0171 373 8581) and the Embassy of the Kingdom of Lesotho in Washington (2511 Massachusetts Avenue, Washington DC 20008; tel 202 797 5533). Or contact the Lesotho Tourist Board direct (PO Box 1378, Maseru 100, Lesotho; tel 312 896, fax 310108).

Fort Namutoni in the Etosha National Park

Namibia

The Country

If you look at a map of Namibia you see some outlandish names –
'Solitaire', 'Kokerboom Forest', Fish River Canyon' and 'Skeleton
Coast' among them. This vast chunk of territory, bounded to the west
by the Atlantic and the Namib desert and to the east by the Kalahari, is
no ordinary place. It includes the most challenging and intriguing
wilderness areas anywhere. It's also the largest and least densely populated country in Southern Africa, with only 1,500,000 inhabitants of
all races in 824,268 sq km (321,979 sq miles), an area four times the
size of Britain.

It has the largest national park in Africa, fabulously rich diamond
mines, quixotically strong German traditions dating from its original
colonisation and a relatively tiny population, which is however multiplying by three percent a year. The landscapes range from woodland
around the Etosha Pan in the north through savannah and arid wilderness to the starkly dramatic 300-metre high dunes of the Namib. The
country became an independent nation in 1990 and joined the British
Commonwealth in 1991. Overall it is one of the most individual and
rewarding countries to visit in the whole continent.

Climate
The climate inland on the plateau is magnificent, with summer
daytime temperatures up to 35°C (95°F) and cool nights, but very little rain. In winter the maximum is around 25°C (76°F) and the
minimum 9°C (48°F). In the more low-lying areas of the north east
(including Etosha) and the south east it can be very hot in summer
(November-march), going above 40°C, particularly when the east
wind - the Bergwind - blows in off the Kalahari. On the coast the air is
kept fresh by the Atlantic, there is frequent fog and it can be chilly. The
short rains fall from October to December and the thundery long rains
in mid-January to April. Otherwise the days are cloudless and dry.

Communications
In sprite of the rugged terrain many millions of dollars have been spent
on road and rain improvements. However, flying remains the most
convenient way to travel. Details are given in the Factfile at the end of
the chapter.

History and People

Namibia's present diverse population is the outcome of extensive
African and European migrations within southern Africa from the
16th century onwards; migrations that led to continual wars. The first
Western explorer to land here was Diogo Cao, who erected a cross at

Cape Cross on the Skeleton coast in 1486. Two years later Batholomeu Dias did the same at Luderitz and named it Angra Pequena. But it was another 200 years before European traders, prospectors and missionaries began to discover the upland veld of the interior, which the 100 km wide barrier of the Namib protected from seaward intrusion. During those two centuries great conflicts among the African peoples took place.

Ancient Inhabitants

The most ancient inhabitants had been Bushmen and Namas (Hottentots), who together with the Damaras speak Khoisan languages and are often called Khoisan people. Some of the Bushmen paintings found on rock faces in the mountains are 28,000 years old, but the Bushmen's ambitions never progressed beyond the nomadic hunting that was their tradition all over southern Africa and they inexorably lost territory to stronger and more energetic tribes. Today they number a mere 37,000, living mainly in the north east and are both underprivileged and impoverished, making their living from craftwork.

Migrations

Namas traditionally lived in the south, on both sides of the Orange River, being joined in the 19th century by a migration from South Africa. It was a Nama Chief, Kaptein Josef Fredericks, who sold Adolf Luderitz coastal land in 1883, leading to Germany declaring the country a Protectorate in 1884.

Meanwhile Bantu-speaking Owambos and Kavangos had moved in through what is now Angola during the 16th to 18th centuries, eventually coming into bloody conflict with the Herero from east and central Africa. At first the Herero, who were nomadic cattle herders, settled in the barren north western area of Kaokoland. The primitive Himba still there are related to them. But the bulk of the Hereros were forced towards the Okahandja and Windhoek areas by the drought of 1829/30, Here they came against the Nama moving up from South Africa. Protracted wars ensued. Eventually, in 1872, Maherero, the Herero Chief, appealed to the Cape Colony for protection. However the upshot was only that the Cape annexed the harbour of Walvis Bay, a 1,124 sq km (434 sq miles) enclave which South Africa relinquished to Namibia in March 1994.

Before this happened, a community of Cape coloured people had moved up to the area south of Windhoek around Rehoboth, under the leadership of Kaptein Hermanus van Wyk. On September 15, 1885 the 'Basters', as they became known, signed a Treaty of Protection and Friendship with the Germans. They remained a 'state within a state' until Independence.

Namibia

Far from saving the Hereros, whose women still wear a stunningly colourful adaptation of 19th century missionary wives' dresses, Maherero's appeal led ultimately to their near-destruction. German colonisation followed and when the Hereros rose up against the white invaders a bitter war from 1903-1907 ended with three quarters of the tribe either dead or in exile. But for this the Owambo might not have become the dominant tribe today.

German Colonisation
In the early years of the 20th century settlers flowed in from the Fatherland, mines were established, towns, roads and railways built, game reserves proclaimed and a surprisingly durable heritage of German culture established. But the political hegemony was short-lived. On July 15, 1915 the colonial army – the *Kaiserliche Schutztruppe fur Deutsch Sud-West Afrika* – surrendered to South African forces in what had been one of the most remote theatres of the 1914-1918 war.

The South African Mandate
The League of Nations confirmed South Africa's mandate to govern South West Africa as a Protectorate on December 17, 1920. The Second World War saw the end of the League and the post-war era brought the disagreements that eventually led to independence.

Independence Achieved
Although the World Court supported South Africa's position in 1950, by 1971 it found the Republic's continued presence illegal. In the meantime SWAPO had started its armed struggle in 1966. Two-and-a-half decades of protracted fighting, conducted across the border in Angola between Cuban-supported SWAPO guerillas and the South African Defence Force, counter-pointed by endless international negotiations, finally led to peace accords under which South Africa agreed to withdraw from Namibia if Cuba withdrew from Angola. Elections for a Constituent Assembly were held under United Nations supervision in November 1989, a constitution was agreed and the country became independent as a Republic on March 21, 1990. The President is the SWAPO leader, Mr Sam Nujoma, whose party was re-elected in December 1994. His government is generally credited with having done a good job. The overall feel of Namibia is relaxed and friendly. Other parties are represented in the Assembly, notably the multi-racial Democratic Turnhalle Alliance.

The population's 11 ethnic groups include some 641,000 Owambos, 120,000 Kavangos, 97,000 Hereros, 62,000 Namas, 48,000 Caprivians, 37,000 Bushmen, 52,000 Coloureds and 82,000 Whites.

National Parks and Reserves

Since Independence Namibia's magnificent conservation areas have become internationally recognised. All the classic big game are present in the north, as well specialities such as the gemsbok, or giant oryx, the southern greater kudu and the mountain zebra. At 99,616 sq km (66,400 sq miles) the reserves total 15 percent of the country's land. Article 95 of the Constitution guarantees protection of the environment. This protection of the unusual range of flora and fauna dates back to 1907 when Governor von Lindequist proclaimed Game Reserves Nos 1, 2 and 3. He did so because the German settlers had realised that large scale hunting threatened the survival of the game. Reserve No 1 was the Namib and No 2 was Etosha.

Today 15 areas of scenic beauty or ecological interest are preserved by the Ministry of Environment and Tourism, which runs camp sites and excellent rest camps in many of the parks (see under Hotels below), where gravel roads are well maintained. Speed limits are 60 kph (37 mph) everywhere and 20 kph (12 mph) in camp. Admission charges are low. Generally speaking it is best to make game viewing drives in the early morning or late afternoon.

The Principal Parks
These – all described later – are the Etosha National Park, which is one of Africa's greatest reserves around the shimmering Etosha Pan in the country's north, six hours drive on tarmac from Windhoek; the Namib Naukluft Park, a coastal desert with an unique ecology and at 49,768 sq km (19,440 sq miles) the fourth largest conservation area in the world, now with adjacent accommodation as well as camp sites; and the Waterberg Plateau Park, a flat mountain top where such threatened species as sable antelope and white rhino are enabled to breed, only three hours drive from Windhoek. Permits to enter the Namib are available from the Environment Ministry's reservation office on the corner of John Meinert Street and Independence Avenue (Private bag 13267, Windhoek; tel 236975). Low entry fees are payable at the gates of others, which include the Daan Viljoen Park near the capital, the Cape Cross Seal Reserve the Skeleton Coast Park and the Sesriem entrance to the Namib Naukluft. The Fish River canyon is not a park, though it has a resort at Ai Ais run by the Ministry.

Hiking Trails
There are organised hiking trails in the Fish River Canyon, the Waterberg Plateau Park, the Naukluft mountains inland from the Namib Naukluft Park near Reheboth and on the Ugab river, adjoining the Skeleton Coast Park. Details from the Environment Ministry, as above.

Safaris

Camping and Photographic Safaris

One effect of Independence has been to open - if not to open up - northern areas adjacent to the Angola Border in Kaokoland, and the game areas in the Caprivi Strip. These and the Skeleton Coast are where the adventures beckon. Various firms offer expeditions. Desert Adventure Safaris (PO Box 339, Swakopmund 9000; tel 0641 4072) specialises in the Kaokoveld. Skeleton Coast Safaris (PO Box 2195, Windhoek; tel 061 224248) fly clients into their own camps in the Kaokoveld, while Olympia Reisen (PO Box 43, Windhoek; tel 62395) has the sole concession actually on the Skeleton Coast itself. Charly's Desert Tours (PO Box 1400, Swakopmund 9000; tel 0641 4341) take out safaris of up to 18 days in the same areas and into the Namib desert, as do Luderitz Safaris (PO Box 76, Luderitz; tel 06331 2719).

Tours

The big destination is always likely to be Etosha, followed by the Namib-Naukuft Park, Luderitz, and the Fish River Canyon; although all most tours do is stop for a picnic to gaze at the canyon itself. However, Swakopmund is coming to life and the remoter regions mentioned above will gradually pull in more groups.

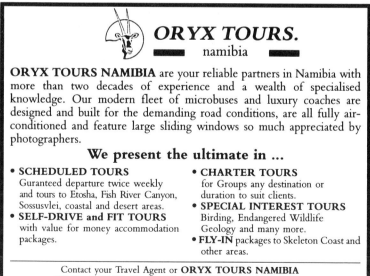

The number of firms offering tours, usually called 'safaris', has mushroomed. One of the best for scheduled departures at sensible prices is Oryx Tours (PO Box 2058, Windhoek; tel 061 217454, fax 263417), who also offer self-drive tours in conjunction with Avis. The Namib Travel Shop, run by Rosalind and Dennis Rundle (PO Box 6850, Windhoek; tel 061 225178, fax 061 239455) has built up a reputation for both road and fly-in safaris, especially to Caprivi, on which few firms are knowledgeable.

An increasing number of firms combine Namibia with Botswana and Zimbabwe. See page 27 for those we particularly recommed. The hefty list of British firms offering Namibia is obtainable from Namibia Tourism at 6 Chandos Street, London W1M 0LQ; tel 0171 636 2924.

Hunting Safaris
The two hunting seasons of around June/July and August/September are announced in May. Hunting is limited to these seasons and the restriction covers several antelope species and such birds as francolin, duck and sandgrouse. However, trophy hunters can hunt outside the seasons on registered guest farms, except in December/January, provided thay have a permit from the Ministry of Environment and Tourism. They must be hunting under the supervision of a professional hunter or guide, a list of whom can be had from the Namibia Professional Hunting Association (PO Box 11291, Windhoek; tel 061 234455, fax 222567). Hunting firms are graded and they will arrange clearance of clients' firearms through Customs, or guns can be hired locally.

Hotels, Rest Camps and Guest Farms

Hotels, game lodges, park rest camps and guest farms are graded by the government. One-star is standard, two-star means 50 percent of the rooms have private baths and floor service for refreshments 16 hours a day, three-star guarantees 24-hour reception service and some luxury. There is only one four-star hotel as yet. The Accommodation Guide for Tourists published by Namibia Tourism has detailed information and prices, which are in Namibian dollars, at par with the SA Rand. Usually prices are higher than in South Africa.

Rest Camps in National Parks
Rest camps in National Parks and at government-run resorts have been hugely improved in recent years. Accommodation varies from tents to air-conditioned bungalows. Rest camps have good restaurants, although shops sell food for people who prefer self-catering and bring their own gear. Value is excellent. Details are in the Accom-

modation Guide or can be had from the Environment and Tourism Ministry's reservation's office on John Meinert and Moltke Streets in Windhoek (Private Bag 13267, Windhoek 9000; tel 061 36975). Travel cheques and Visa and Mastercard credit cards are accepted.

Guest Farms
Some 80 ranches and farms accept visitors and should be seriously considered. A list is printed on the government's tourist road map. They are graded one to three star. Some have purpose built accommodation and very high standards. Nearly all have game on the estates and seven only welcome hunters. One company organising guest farms – as opposed to individual owners providing rooms – is Namib-Sun Game Ranches (PO Box 2862, Windhoek; tel 35111). Full board prices at guest farms are upwards of R150 per person per day in a double room and some will be twice that.

Windhoek

Postal code 9000. Telephone code 061.
This small, though growing, capital of 125,000 people is situated 1,650 m (5,400 ft) up in the country's central highlands. Both the climate and the place itself are enviably pleasant. New hotels, shops and office buildings have blended well with preserved examples of old German architecture. The city always had an informal feeling about it and still does, with German cooking and hospitality much in evidence. Despite the growth of industry and of residential areas like Pioniers Park and Eros Park, the centre of activity remains Independence Avenue. In total contrast you will see the tall and stately Herero women in colourful Victorian Style dresses which they copied from Rhenish missionaries' wives in the mid-19th century and which they still consider fashionable.

Windhoek was founded in 1890 by Major Kurt von Francois, who hoisted the German flag and built the Alte Fest (the old fort) on the hill off Leutwein Street, now part of the Museum. But the city owes its name to the Nama leader Jonker Afrikaner, who called it Winterhoek after the farm in the Cape where he worked as a boy. Eventually the name contracted to Windhoek. Formerly it had been known as *Ai-gams,* a native word for hot springs, while Sir James Alexander, the famous explorer, tried to name it Queen Adelaide's Baths. The springs, in the suburb of Klein Windhoek, used to supply the town with water.

Information

Three bureaux serve visitors. The commercially-sponsored Tourist

Rendezvous (PO Box 107; tel 221225, fax 224218) is in the Sanlam Centre on Peter Muller Str. You can book tours and accommodation there. The Windhoek Municipal Publicity Association is in the Post Street Mall (tel 290 2092), has various publications available, and can also find you a place to stay. The Namibia Tourism office of the Ministry is at 272 Independence Avenue (Private Bag 13346; tel 284 9111, fax 221930).

Shopping

Independence Avenue is the main thoroughfare and business and shopping centre. Business starts early at 0800 and ends at 1730. There are well-stocked chemists, clothing shops and other stores. For sporting guns try Rosenthal or Safari Guns, and for fishing tackle Metje and Ziegler of the Sports Centre. If you fancy a holiday home here, estate agents will sell you anthing from a bungalow to an ostrich farm, complete with jackal-proof fencing.

Namibia's most famous products are diamonds, semi-precious stones, and Karakul, or Persian lamb, pelts. Overseas visitors do not have to pay the local sales tax, on major purchases, subject to showing a passport.

Diamonds and Semi-Precious Stones

Diamonds are barely cheaper than elsewhere, but you will get purer quality for your money. Semi-precious stones like agate, jasper, rose quartz, chalcedony, amethyst and amazonite are gratifyingly cheap – after all, the territory is stiff with them. The tourmalines here are the world's finest, the most valuable being those with emerald or ruby lights in them. You can get semi-precious stones roughly polished by 'tumbling' quite cheaply. A well made gold ring, set with a properly cut stone, will cost substantially less than in Europe. Among curiosities one of the most interesting is the many faceted 'Desert Rose', actually a freak rock formation with crystals like petals.

Persian Lamb

Karakul sheep originated in Afghanistan and Bokhara, Southern Russia, being introduced to Namibia in 1907. Today, 2,900,000 sheep flourish in the dry and inhospitable south of the country. Often called 'black gold', they provided a record export of pelts in 1980; since then demand from West Germany and United States has slumped. They are sold under the trade name Swakara. Tailoring them is a local speciality. A full-length Persian lamb coat uses 20-28 pelts, while broadtail coats are more expensive. Pelzhaus Huber on the corner of Independence Avenue and Goring Street is one shop to find them.

Crafts and Curios
Local curios include Owambo baskets and Bushman quivers for
arrows, made from the bark of the curious kokerboom tree (see pic-
ture in the colour pages). Every first and third Saturday of the month
there is a street market in the Post Street Mall.

However, the place you must not miss is the Crafts Centre at 40
Mudume Street (formerly Tal Street). This displays and sells the
indigenous crafts of the nation's ethnic groups, from Baster karosses
and Nama woodcarving to European handbags and shoes. It is open
weekdays and Saturday mornings.

The Post Street Mall
The big shopping development is of the old Post Street on Independence Avenue. At one end is a startling display of modern sculptures;
that are actually a selection of the 77 meteorites that were found
around Gibeon. Quite apart from its shops and official street markets,
the mall is crowded with souvenir sellers all the time, and with picket-
pockets. In late afternoon the police clear them all away and then the
terrace of the Kaiser Krone hotel becomes a pleasant place for an
open-air drink.

Taxis and Car Hire

Taxis cannot usually be hailed on the street. There is a taxi rank (tel
237070) on Independence Avenue and Peter Muller Street, behind
the bus terminal. Radio Taxi numbers include 226119, 225222 and
223220. For car hire Avis is on Jeans Street (PO Box 2057,
Windhoek; tel 233166); Budget is on Mudume Street (PO Box
1754, Windhoek; tel 228720); and Imperial on Peter Muller Street
(PO Box 1387, Windhoek; tel 227103). Kessler 4 X 4 Hive (PO Box
20274; tel 233451) is on Mudume Street near the Tourist
Rendezvous.

Hotels

The only four-star hotel is the Kalahari Sands (PO Box 2254; tel
222300) on Independence Avenue, while the three-star Hotel Safari
(PO Box 3900; tel 240240) is slightly out of town. The Kalahari
Sands is genuinely luxurious, the Safari and Safari Court have a large
pool and many facilities, but both are somewhat characterless. All
three are being challenged by the new Windhoek Country Club Resort
(tel 205 4111, fax 205 4141), alongside the golf course. Built to five-
star standards, it has a casino, an entertainment centre, and shopping
arcades. The older two-star Thuringer Hof (PO Box 112; tel 226031)
on Independence Avenue is very pleasant, with an outdoor restaurant
in a shady courtyard. Windhoek has many pensions, normally clean,

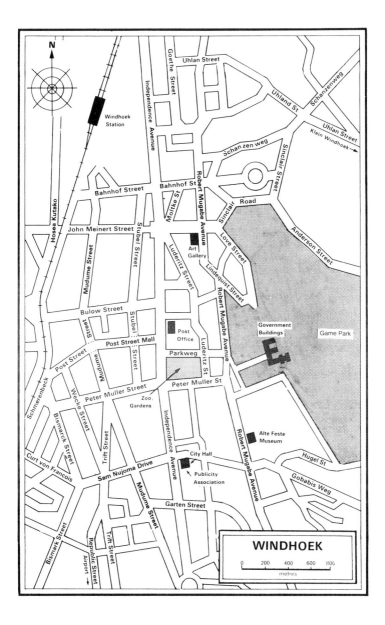

comfortable and with good cuisine. The Cela (PO Box 1947; tel 226295) on Van Rhijn Street, the Moni (Box 2805; tel 228350) and the Steiner (PO Box 20481; tel 222898) on Wecke Street are reliable, with good German food.

Places to See

Many of Windhoek's landmarks date from Colonial German days, like the Christuskirche. The Railway Station, unexpectedly, has great character. It was built in 1912. There is an art gallery close to the Windhoek theatre. Near the town are three small Rhineland style castles, each on a hill, called Schwerinsburg, Heinitzburg and Sanderburg. They are privately owned. Heinitzburg was the home of Mrs Olga Levison, the authoress who wrote 'The Ageless Land' about this country. In the 1890s she recorded that the first hotel was 'just a hut of thatch without any rooms .... guests had to sleep outside under a bush.' The Roman Catholic church's vineyard in the suburb of Klein Windhoek deserves a visit. The Zoo is behind the Administration Buildings of the Tintenpalast and harbours antelope, giraffe, zebra and ostrich in natural surroundings. The Daan Viljoen Game Park is a tiny reserve a few miles west of the city off the C28 road, with a restaurant.

The Alte Feste and the Transnamib Museum

This striking, white, battlemented fortress commands the city and now houses the Independence collection, depicting events and personalities that led to Namibia's freedom, and cultural history exhibits.

On the first floor in the railway station there is exhibition on railways and transport in Namibia - once you've seen the country you'll appreciate that building railways at all was quite a feat.

Festivals

The city has two traditional German festivals, each of which lasts for several days. These are the Carnival at the end of April, which is autumn, with processions and a masked ball, and the beer-drinking Oktoberfest, when the streets are hung with decorations.

North to Etosha; Ruacana Falls

Although the shimmering white landscape of the Etosha National Park is world famous, other fascinating parts of the sub-tropical north of Namibia have opened up to visitors. The Waterberg Plateau Park is off the route to Etosha, a number of game farms have good facilities, there are little known Game Reserves in both eastern Kavango and the Caprivi Strip, while Bushmanland on the Botswana border may become more accessible. Kaokoland, the home of the nomadic Himba tribe in the north east is described in the Coast chapter.

Driving to the North and the Caprivi Strip

The main B1 road to the north is tarred past the mining town of Tsumeb and the Etosha Park right up to the Angola border, while the B8 through Grootfontein is tarred to Rundu in the Kavango district. That colonial geographical oddity, the Caprivi Strip of Namibian land running between Angola and Zambia to the north and Botswana to the south, could become a travel route to the Victoria Falls, as two thirds of the road between Rundu and Katima Mulilo is now tarred. Meanwhile the communications are so good to the nearer part of the north that there is plenty worth exploring.

Okahandja

Postal code 9000. Telephone code 06228.

This small farming town, 72 km (45 miles) from Windhoek, is where the B2 road to Swakopmund and the coast branches off from the B1. There is a Rhenish Mission dating from 1870, while the graves of both Jonker Afrikaner and of the great Herero leader, Maherero, are in the public gardens. At the time of the full moon in August the Herero people gather here to pay tribute to their ancestral chief. The town has banks, shops, petrol and a one-star hotel, the renovated Okahandja (PO Box 770; tel 3024) while the Okahandja Bakery is a good place to stop for coffee and cake. The main attraction for locals is the resort based on the Von Bach dam in the hills nearby, which supplies Windhoek with water. The resort offers fishing for black bass, carp and bream, as well as sailing and windsurfing. There is a camp site with toilets.

Guest Farms

The area has seven guest farms, several of which rate three stars: Otjisazu (PO Box 149; tel 06221 2259) is near the Von Bach dam.

Gross-Barmen

Only 26 km (16 miles) west of Okahandja are the Gross-Barmen hot springs (formerly called Otjikango). Situated around the ruins of a Mission station, Gross-Barmen has air-conditioned bungalows, a shop and restaurant. The mineral water itself comes out of the ground at 65°C, but is cooled to 40°C for the thermal baths and cooler again for a swimming pool. The sulphide and fluoride in it are beneficial for rheumatism. To use the thermal baths you must be staying overnight. Bookings are through the Ministry of Environment and Tourism.

Okahandja to Otjiwarongo

From Okahandja the next town on the B1 is Otjiwarongo, 174 km (109 miles) further north. On the way you pass both one of the best game viewing ranches at Otijwa and the Waterberg Plateau Park.

Otijwa Game Ranch
This is 10,000 ha of splendid open bush and hills that shelter a herd of white rhino and large numbers of kudu, wildebeeste and other plains game among its 26 major species. Founded as a private reserve in 1958, Otjiwa has 13 dams and 14 game waterholes, hiking trails, hides and three safari camps. Though two-star, the main camp's units are somewhat depressing; better to stay at the Hilltop house, right out in the reserve. Game viewing vehicles are provided. Bookings (PO Box 1231, Otjiwarongo; tel 0658 11002). The ranch entrance is on the west side of the B1 road, 138 km (86 miles) from Okahandja.

Waterberg Plateau Park
The Waterberg is a dramatically distinctive flat topped mountain east of the B1 road, actually an escarpment of sandstone cliffs topped by hard dolerite. Well wooded and with plenty of water, it has been made a sanctuary for endangered species. The handsome sable antelope, roan antelope and white rhino are among them. The mountain is also known for its Bushman rock paintings, while historically it was the scene of a particularly bloody battle between the Herero and the German *Schutztruppe* in 1904. The Herero made the last stand of their rebellion against the cliffs below the plateau and were savagely defeated. In all some 75 percent of the Herero tribe either perished or fled, as did 50 percent of the Nama, permanently altering the population structure of the country. Today tribal Hereroland is east of here, while many Herero still live across the frontier in Botswana.

The park has excellent stone bungalow accommodation on the lower slopes of the mountain and an agreeable restaurant. Bookings through the Reservations office in Windhoek. Take the C22 tarmac road off the B1, then after about 40 km (25 miles) a gravel road leads to the park and the restcamp.

Otjiwarongo

Postal code 9000. Telephone code 0651.

This town, whose name means 'the pleasant place', is a good half-way stop on the drive north, as well as being where you have a choice of routes to Etosha, one via Outjo (described further on) to the Okaukuejo camp and the other via Tsumeb to Namutoni at the eastern end of the park. Otjiwarango is also where the tarmac road from Swakopmund via Karabib joins the B1 and it is on the railway. The two-star Hamburger Hof Hotel is clean and well run (PO Box 8; tel 2520) while you can get excellent coffee, cakes and apfelstrudel at the small Cafe Carstensen on Garden Street. There is a crocodile farm outside the town.

Otjiwarongo to Tsumeb

The fast, almost straight, B1 road continues north through a changing landscape. The acacia thorn savannah of the central plateau gives way to mopane bush and the temperature rises. Geophysically the low lying Bushmanland in the north east is an extension of the Kalahari, and even here the minimum economic size for a cattle farm is 5,000 ha, while game animals are everywhere.

Otavi Hills, Khorab and the Hoba Meteorite
However, the Otavi hills have a high rainfall and although Otavi itself has little more than flowering trees, banks, petrol stations and a caravan park to recommend it, there are a couple of local sights of interest. One is the memorial to the surrender of Governor Seitz and Lt Colonel Franke to General Louis Botha at Khorab on July 15, 1915. The other, on the Hoba farm on the road to Grootfontein, is the largest meteorite ever found. This 70-ton chunk of shooting star is 82 percent iron and 16 percent nickel.

Tsumeb

Postal code 9000. Telephone code 0671.
The largest town in the north, Tsumeb nonetheless has only 14,000 inhabitants and with its bougainvillea and jacarandas looks more like a garden town than a mining centre. There are shops, banks and filling stations. However it is Tsumeb's history of mining and the associated Museum that make it definitely merit a stop. The Eastern Park information office is in the town.

The Malachite Hill
The name Tsumeb means 'green mountain', deriving from a 10 m (33 foot) hill of malachite, which the local Bushmen first discovered. They guarded the hill and exchanged ore for goods. Yet they never smelted it themselves, leaving that to the Owambos who came from Owamboland for the purpose. In due course the Bushmen lost control and European traders moved in, giving a major boost to the early development of the German colony. The hill was in fact the visible sign of a staggeringly rich pipe of ore, containing over 184 different minerals. Today 11 are actively extracted, including gold, silver, copper, lead and tin. The mine has also yielded superb crystals and gemstones. One collection is in the Smithsonian Institute in Washington, another in the Tsumeb Museum.

Accommodation and Communications

The two-star Minen Hotel (PO Box 244; tel 21071) is owned by the mining company and well run by a German couple. The town has an airfield, sometimes used for fly-in safaris from Botswana and Windhoek. From Tsumeb it is an hour-and-a-half's drive up the B1 to the Etosha National Park turnoff and the Mokuti Lodge outside the park, while Namutoni is a distance of 119 km (74 miles).

Otjikoto Lake

On the way, just outside Tsumeb, you pass the curious Otjikoto lake. This small sunken pool is actually a cave, the roof of which collapsed, and is fed by an underground stream. About 36 m (118 ft) deep, the dark green lake was where the *Schutztruppe* dumped guns and ammunition during their 1915 retreat. Some of the cannon have been restored and are in the Tsumeb Museum.

Tsumeb to the Ruacana Falls

The B1 road continues past Etosha – described next – and via Ondangwa to the once spectacular Ruacana Falls on the Kunene river, which forms the Angolan border; in 1994 the river had dried up, due to lack of rain.The Owamboland country north of Etosha is heavily populated. You can go right up to the frontier and the falls (which generated electricity for Namibia, with power lines controversially crossing the Etosha National Park). However, it is wise to go with an organised group or tour if you are going to explore this part effectively, particularly if you are continuing along the Kunene through Kaokoland. See the chapter on the coast.

The B8 road runs north east to Rundu and the Caprivi, described after Etosha.

Etosha National Park

Even in a continent as amazing as Africa, Etosha is something special. Its heart is the Etosha Pan, a shimmering gray white expanse of salt and dusty clay that is roughly 130 km (80 miles) long and covers 6,133 sq km, or 1,690 sq miles. within the nearly 23,000 sq km (9,000 sq miles) National Park. Thousands of years ago the pan was a lake fed by the Kunene river. But the river changed course and the lake shrank and dried up, the wind and heat eroding its surface so that it became slightly lower than the surrounding bush. The name means 'the place of dry water': an apt enough description of the mirages which hover over its blinding surface. An abiding memory of Etosha was of a troop of wildebeest crossing the pan in glaring sun and seeming to float above the surface, their shapes coalescing in the haze.

Other pans adjoin the main one and they all fill partially after the rains, while there are many waterholes – assisted by nearly 80 windpumps – along its southern shore. The result is that the area attracts game like flies to a jampot. Springbok shelter in the shade of camelthorn trees; giraffe stretch their necks to nibble at acacia leaves; tiny Damara dik-diks, looking like models for Walt Disney's Bambi, watch one wide-eyed from the road verges.

Game around Etosha
At a recent count the numbers of game in the park were estimated at: elephant 2,500, rhino 350, lion 500, giraffe 2,400, springbok 30,000, wildebeest 2,200 (anthrax has killed thousands), Burchell's zebra 8,800, kudu 5,200, gemsbok 5,600, hartebeest 3,000. And there are lion, leopard, cheetah, rare black-faced impala and mountain zebra as well.

After the first rains around January a large percentage of the zebra, wildebeest, gemsbok and springbok leave the southern border of the Pan and trek west, right into Owamboland. The apparent reason is that the grass is literally greener on the other side, being of an annual and not a perennial kind. So the best time for game viewing is May to October, though there are many species all the year round at the eastern end, attracted by the waterholes near Namutoni. Here, after the rains (January-March), the veld is as green as such a stony wilderness can ever be and flamingoes and pelicans fly in to breed on the pans, adding to the 300 species of birds and making the spectrum of wildlife close to unique. Ask camp or park officials where it is best to go during your visit.

The story of conservation at Etosha
The preservation of game here has passed through many vicissitudes, the conservation efforts having historically been amongst the earliest in Africa. In the late 19th century hunting all but exterminated some species and Etosha's last herd of elephant was shot in 1881. The following year hunting regulations began a process of control. Then in 1907, after the Herero wars, a vast area of Kaokoland and the Etosha hinterland totalling 93,240 sq km and extending north to the Kunene river was declared Game Reserve No 2 (the Namib was No 1) and a German officer, Lt Adolf Fischer, became the first warden.

In 1947 Kaokoland was detached for the Hereros and another 3,406 sq km was given away for farming: farming pressures are a threat to wildlife throughout Africa. However the 1950s saw conservation become more organised and tourism begin. In 1956 the boundaries were again extended to the Skeleton Coast, making Etosha the largest game reserve in the world at 99,526 sq km. This, alas, was too good to last. In 1963 over three-quarters was taken away again, provoking international protests. As a result the park was brought to its present size of 22,270 sq km. Over time the main roads north were re-routed outside the park, gravel roads and tourist accommodation created inside and an Ecological Institute founded at Okaukuejo (pronounced Okkakuuyo). Today Etosha is exceptionally well-maintained.

The West of the Park
The western half of the park has fewer roads than the part near the Pan and no rest camps. It includes the Fairytale Wood or Haunted Forest, a dense stand of a curious tree unique to Namibia called *Moringa Ovalifolia,* which resembles a thinner baobab. But these trees are really only worth seeing in flower after the rains. The area also protects several thousand pelicans at breeding time. Incredibly they bring fish for their young from Lake Oponomo, 100 km (62 miles) away, each parent taking it in turn and riding thermals to make the journey.

Park Entrances
The two park entrances are in the east at Namutoni and in the centre/south leading to Okaukuejo. Entrance fees are payable at offices near the respective rest camps.

Rest Camps in the Park
There are three rest camps run by the Ministry at Namutoni, Okaukuejo and Halali. All have airstrips, first-aid posts, swimming pools and shops, and sell booklets about Etosha, but only Okaukuejo and Halali have spot-lit waterholes for night time game viewing – a real asset in the evenings. Bookings can be made through travel agents or to the Reservations office, Private Bag 13267, Windhoek 9000; tel 061 236975. Camps must be reached before sunset. If you want you can buy food from the shops and cook it yourself – there are barbecues provided.

Fort Namutoni
Namutoni is a spectacular whitewashed Beau Geste style fort, originally built in 1903. Three years later seven German cavalrymen briefly held out against 500 Owambo tribesmen, but the fort was razed after the seven escaped. In 1906 it was rebuilt with four towers and three gates, quickly acquiring the reputation of being the most striking fort in the German colonial empire. This hectic history – now illustrated in a museum in the main tower – ended after Etosha became a reserve and gradually Namutoni fell into decay. In the 1950s it was reconstructed as one of the most historic game lodges in Africa. In 1984 another renovation gave it air-conditioning. There is also a camp site. Happily the palm trees the German officers planted have been kept and their swimming pool has been improved. The only serious lack is of a waterhole for night game viewing.

Okaukuejo
Okaukuejo has traditional thatched bungalows and luxury air-conditioned rondavels, student dormitories and tents. There was a 1902 fort here, of which only the stone observation tower remains. This is an excellent place for game viewing from May to October.

Halali
Halali, situated among low hills midway along the pan's southern shore and between the other two camps, has luxury bungalows, dormitories and camp sites. The word *halali* means a single bugle call after the hunt is over. To us it was less appealing constructionally than Okaukuejo, though several waterholes and the only causeway running out into the pan are in the vicinity.

Lodges outside the Park
With the growth of tourism, lodges have multiplied around the park. The three-star Mokuti Lodge stands just outside the park's eastern gate. It is luxurious and offers game drives in a 4,300 ha (17 sq mile) private game reserve, but is centred on the swimming pool like a resort hotel, and lacks a waterhole to attract animals at night. Bookings Resorts International PO Box 2862, Windhoek; tel 061 233145.

The others are much simpler places. The Etosha Aoba (reservations PO Box 21783, Windhoel; tel 226979, fax 226999) near Mokuti has thatched cottages in woodland. Ongava Lodge (PO Box 186, Outjo; tel 248526, fax 248529) has twice won 'best guest farm' awards. It has thatched chalets and tents near a waterhole, on the park's south western boundary. Hobatere Lodge is near the western boundary in a 32,000 ha concession area adjoining the park (PO Box 10, Kamanjab; tel 0652 ask for 2022).

Planning an Etosha Visit
One good way to see Etosha is to divide your trip between two different lodges, for example starting at Namutoni for a couple of days, then driving on to stay at Halali or Okaukuejo. Doing this you will get a feel for the park's diversity.

From Okaukuejo you can drive out of the park down the C38 road to Outjo and then divert to Khorixas, the capital of Damaraland. From Khorixas there is a reasonable road to the West Coast Recreation Area and Swakopmund.

The Caprivi via Rundu
But first we deal with the Caprivi, reached on the B8 road through Rundu, where there are no hotels, but two rest camps. The Kaisosi

Namibia

Safari Lodge (tel 067372 265) rates one-star, the Kavango Guest Lodge none. They are self-catering, very cheap, and you should book in advance.

The Caprivi

This eccentric strip of territory, 500 km long but only 30 km wide and attached to the north east of Namibia, is totally different to the rest of the country; ethnically and topographically. Permanent rivers - the Chobe, the Kwando, the Okavango and the Zambezi - give it riverine forests and swamps, as well as open savannah. it is a fine game viewing area, with two national Parks, but few lodges. The whole area is very flat.

Katima Mulilo   *Telephone code 067352.*
The only town is on the Zambezi, 12,52 km (782 miles) from Windhoek; or two days drive, but an easy one from Victoria Falls, via Zambia. A ferry takes cars across the river to Zambian at Wenela. The airport is 18 km out of town and has three flights a week on Air Namibia from/to both Windhoek and Victoria Falls.

The town itself has many flamboyant trees and is quite pleasent. There is a Caprivi Art Centre, a few shops, a bank, petrol stations and a well-equipped hospital. The Zambezi Lodge (PO Box 98; tel 203) is on the river (see below) and the Hippo Lodge is 9 km out of town, also on the river.

History
From around 1700 to the end of the 19th century what is now Caprivi was ruled by the Lozi kings of Barotseland, whose empire centered on the flood plains north of the Zambezi in present-day Zambia. The Lozi considered themselves born free, but sold other tribes into slavery. All this changed with the arrival of the Germans in South West Africa.

In 1890 the Germans struck a deal with the British, which gave the Caprivi Strip to Germany in exchange for the Island of Zanzibar, off the coast of the German Tanganyika colony. The Germans hoped that by obtaining access to the Zambezi, they could link South West with Tanganyika navigationally. The strip was named after the German Chancellor, Count George Leo von Caprivi di Caprara di Montecuccoli; even though it sounds tropical. The link was never achieved, both because Rhodes created what is now Zimbabwe and because of the Victoria Falls.

For much of the 20th century the Caprivi was ruled by a Magistrate and it still has its own legislation. It was an early stronghold of the present ruling Namibian political party, SWAPO.

National Parks
Proclaimed since independence, the Mamili Park of 319 sq km 125 sq miles) is a wetland at the confluence of the Linyanti and Kwando rivers. You'll find sitatunga and red lechwe, buffalo and Cape hunting dogs among the animals. The nearby Mudumu Park of 1,009 sq km (394 sq miles) is mopane woodland on the Kwando, with similar game and 430 recorded species of birds.

The largest game area is the Caprivi Game Park, through which the B8 road runs, and which is a 180 km (112 miles) long stretch of densely wooded country, with elephant, buffalo and roan antelope. Since independence many Bushmen have moved into it; some Bushmen were emphatically on the wrong side then, having served as trackers in special units of the South African Defence Force fighting SWAPO.

Finally the small Mahango Game Reserve at the western end of Caprivi has plentiful game, including buffalo and lion. The Popa falls are nearby, best seen in the dry season.

Lodges
The Zambezi and Hippo lodges have already been mentioned. The Zambezi Lodge has air-conditioned double-bedroome chalets and a substantial hotel boat for cruising on the river, called the Zambezi Queen. Attractive as the boat cruises are, they only operate from January to May and are expensive.

The best lodge is the Lianshulu, on the banks of the Kwando river in the Mudumu Park, 'the only true wilderness lodge in the east Caprivi'. Activities include fishing, game viewing, nature walks and river cruises. It can be booked through the Namib Travel Shop in Windhoek, already referred to, whose associated company Wilderness Safaris are Caprivi experts.

The Popa Falls has a camp run by the Ministry of Environment and Wildlife.

Erongo (Damaraland)

Driving either down from Okaukuejo or up from Windhoek you come to the outpost ranching town of Outjo, which is the inland turn-off for Damaraland. Basically this part of the country has three attractions: game, rock paintings and geological formations, plus magnificent mountainous scenery. However you are in for some rugged driving.

Outjo to the Brandberg

Outjo *Postal code 9000. Telephone code 06542.*
Outjo has a couple of hotels and a museum devoted to the history of
the area, especially its gemstones and wildlife. There is quite a lot of
game in this area and several guest farms, including the three-star
Bambatsi Holiday Ranch (PO Box 120, Outjo; tel 1104). on the C39
road to Khorixas. Or you could base yourself at the two-star tourist
camp further on at Khorixas, (tel 065712 196), which has a restaurant and is a lot closer to the mountains. On the way you pass
relatively near the Vingerkip, a 35m high eroded rock pillar on a farm,
hardly worth deviating for.

The Petrified Forest and the Twyfelfontein Rock Paintings
The petrified forest of fossilised fallen tree trunks, said to be 200
million years old, is off the C39 gravel road that eventually leads down
the escarpment and to Torra Bay in the Skeleton Coast Park.
Specimens of the grotesque succulent *welwitschia mirabilis* grow
among the fossils. A turn-off further on leads, via the minor 3524
road, to the Twyfelfontein rock paintings – some 3,000 of them – and
to the Brandberg or Burnt Mountain, a barren ridge of purple and red
coloured hills. Of these sights Twyfelfontein is the most remarkable,
since the drawings of game are not only artistically satisfying, they
also constitute one of the largest known collections of rock art. They
are located in a mass of rocks south west of the Petrified Forest, both
of which are signed.

Palmwag Lodge
Roughly 160 km (100 miles) north west of Khorixas is the small two-
star Palmwag Lodge by the river Uniab. Its thatched bungalows set
among palm trees make a base for game viewing on the borders of the
Skeleton Coast Park, which is a part of the Namib desert and home to
the rare desert elephant as well as gemsbok (oryx) and other species.
You need 4WD to get there and more often expeditions start from
Swakopmund and drive up the coast, or fly in. The lodge has a pool
and is exotically situated in the midle of nowhere. Bookings
through Desert Adventure Safaris in Swakopmund (PO Box 339; tel
0641 4459).

The Brandberg and the White Lady
Finally from Khorixas – or from Swakopmund – you can reach the
Brandberg, the mountain with the highest peak in Namibia (2,579 m),
and one of the best known rock paintings in the world, the White
Lady. Actually the White Lady is one of a group of paintings, thought
to be 16,000 years old. The name was given one of the figures, which
might be a pale skinned girl or young man, by the Abbe Breuil in

1948: and has excited reasearch and controversy ever since. He suggested the figure might be of Cretan or Egyptian origin. Anyone who has seen young African men daubed in white for manhood ceremonies might think otherwise. The figures have, shockingly, been damaged by tourists putting Coca Cola on them to heighten the colours for photographs. The Brandberg mountain is visible for many miles and the paintings are in a signposted cave reached via the C35 road. Between the Uis mine and Khorixas you turn off to the foothills of the Brandberg. When you reach the sign it is a half-hour walk to the cave. There are countless other Bushman paintings around.

The Coast

The coast, as the map shows you, is enormously long and one of the strangest in the world, being separated from the inland plateau by the Namib desert. It has only three towns, the delightful and unexpected resort of Swakopmund, the port of Walvis Bay, and Luderitz. The West Coast Tourist Area and the Skeleton Coast Park are north of Swakopmund (see map) and the Namib-Naukluft Park to the south. Due to the diamond concession areas and the Namib Park the only place south of Sandwich Bay open to visitors is Luderitz.

The Namib-Naukluft Park

In 1978 the Namib Desert Park, founded by the Germans, was amalgamated with the Naukluft Mountain Zebra Park into a single 23,000 sq km reserve, ranging from granite mountains to the shifting dunes of the coastal desert. Mountain zebra can be found in the area where the hills descend to the desert around the Kuiseb River Canyon and near Ganab. The character of the Namib is described in the accompanying special article and here we deal with routes through it and the best places to visit. The famous Sossusvlei oasis is as accessible from Windhoek as it is from Swakopmund or Luderitz. A safari route to it is outlined after the Luderitz section.

Exploring the Park

The simplest way to explore the Namib is to fly or drive to the coastal town of Swakopmund and there hire a 4WD vehicle and a guide. Safari firms also operate into the central and southern parts of the park from Luderitz. However, Luderitz is pretty remote, while three main roads and one secondary road lead down through the park from the Windhoek to Swakopmund. A sketch map of the few other public roads in the park is available from the Tourism office in Windhoek or the Namib-I publicity office in Swakopmund.

Namibia

Sossusvlei

If you see glorious photos of the ochre-coloured Namib dunes, glow-ing in the light of early morning, their ridges curvingly sharp; then they were probably taken around Sossusvlei. This oasis deep in the desert, where a small lake sometimes forms and birds sing in the stunted thorn trees, is a traveller's Mecca. All round it the dunes rise 1,000 ft high, even tempting skiers. These days solitude has partly gone, even though there are only picnic sites at the vlei itself.

In practical terms, Sossusvlei is 66 km (41 miles) from the park entrance at Sesriem, where there is a small shop and a large Wildlife Ministry campsite, with rather brackish water supplies. The gravel road goes 45 km before you sight the first memorable dune, Dune 45. At 61 km there is a parking place, beyond which you can only go with 4 WD. Another five km through the dunes takes you to the vlei, or to be precise, a grouping of adjoining vleis. Campers within the park are allowed to start off at 0530 to catch the dawn light. They may also glimpse gemsbok or springbok.

Lodges

The Karos Sossusvlei Lodge (PO Box 6900, Windhoek; tel 06632 4322, reservations 061 248338) is just outside the Sesriem gate. Inspired by north African architecture, it solves the problems of high temperatures and occasionally tearing winds and is a pleasant place to stay, while gemsbok comes to its waterhole. 4 WD hire is available and Oryx Tours have a minibus service from Windhoek. Off the road from Solitaire is the delightfully situated Namib Naukluft Lodge (bookings tel 061 263086).

Balloon trips over the dessert are run from the Namib Rand Game Ranch south of Sesriem, but also depart from the Karos Lodge.

Getting There

Driving takes about six hours from Windhoek. The easiest route to follow is via the tarmac B1 to Rehoboth, then the gravel C24 to Solitaire. But it is worth deviating on the last part to the 1275 for superb views at the steep Spreethoogte Pass, then to Solitaire, which has 24 hour fuel. Sesriem is 69 km further. The road continues to Malthohe, past Duwisib castle (see chapter on the South).

Driving through the Namib to Swakopmund

The most interesting routes are two gravel roads, the C26 which joins the C14 from Maltahohe and the C28. Confusingly they are also known as roads 36 and 52 respectively. The C14 goes to Walvis Bay, joining the B2 to Swakopmund. Taking either route it is essential to start early, because of the heat. Even so, unless you have no curiosity, stopping will mean you take all day and if you want to see anything much of the Namib you should plan to camp at one of the sites in the park (permits and reservations from the Wildlife Ministry). There are no restaurants or petrol stations en route and the gravel surface demands a modicum of African driving experience. You must take food and water in case of breakdowns. The places we mention can be reached without 4WD. Park entry permits are not required if you do not intend leaving the main roads.

The C28 Road to Swakopmund
This relatively rough road goes direct to Swakopmund, starting through the hills of the Khomas Hochland via the ranchlands of the Khomas Highlands and descending the 1 in 5 gradient of the Bosua Pass (not negotiable by caravans). At the foot of the escarpment you come out on to the Tinkas Flats, where you can expect to see gemsbok, springbok, meerkat and other animals. There is a great variety of desert vegetation and a graded road leads to the Blutkoppie *inselberg* and its camp site. Unbelievably tadpoles breed in the pools of water in the Blutkoppe rocks after rain. 4WD tracks lead to watering holes on the flats, notably at Gemsbokwater. The C28 continues past the turnoff to the Welwitschia Flats 44 km (27 miles) from Swakopmund. described as an excursion from the town.

The 1982 Road via Ganab
This secondary road branches off the C26 at 32 km (20 miles) outside Windhoek and descends the easier 1 in 10 gradient Us Pass. Once inside the park the road passes near Ganab, where in March and April a lot of antelope come to graze, if it has rained. You may also see springbok, gemsbok, zebra, bat-eared foxes, hyaena, caracals and meerkat (a squirrel-like suricate which sits up on its haunches to watch passers-by). Eventually the road joins the C14.

The C26/C14 via Kuiseb Bridge
This well-graded road runs from Windhoek to Walvis Bay, descending through the scenically spectacular Gamsberg and Kuiseb passes (both 1 in 9 gradients) to the Kuiseb river canyon and finally into the desert. There is a campsite at the Kuiseb river bridge, Kudu, zebra, gemsbok and springbok come to the narrow Kuiseb canyon to waterholes in the evenings. The canyon itself, six km from the turn-off, has been eroded out of grey Damara schist.

28 km (19 miles) beyond the Kuiseb bridge a deviation south of 68 km (42 miles) will take you to the Homeb campsite further down the Kuiseb. There are many trees and, depending on the availability of ground water, numerous gemsbok as well as steenbok, baboons and some fifty species of birds. Furthermore, you are right on the edge of

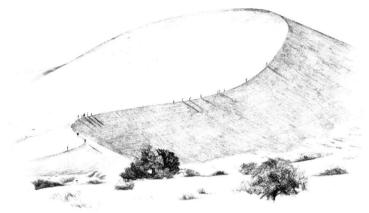

Namib Dunes

The Extraordinary Namib

The Namib is not only one of the oldest deserts in the world – its location has been arid for 80 million years – it also has a most unusual ecology, supporting plants, insects and animals where survival appears impossible among sand dunes up to 400 m (1,300 ft) high. In places as much as 200 km (125 miles) wide, though mostly less, the Namib runs eleven times that length from the Olifants river in the northern Cape Province of South Africa right up the Namibian coast and 500 km into Angola.

Two permanent rivers flow down from the highlands through the desert, the Orange and the Kunene, marking the southern and northern frontiers of the country to which it has given its name. Others like the Swakop are fed by underground water and run only infrequently, or are blocked by the dunes and disappear in oases, as the Tsauchab does at Sossuvlei. The river courses all support permanent vegetation and thus animal life. An easily reached example is the Goanikontes oasis near Swakopmund.

Between the Orange and the Kunene there are two main dune fields; the southern stretching from Luderitz to Swakopmund and extending inland almost to the first escarpment; the northern running from Torra Bay to the Kunene. The southern is within the Namib-Naukluft National Park and part of the northern is in the Skeleton Coast Park. The dunes themselves are composed of quartz grains and near the coast shift continuously north, driven by the prevailing southerly wind to form transverse slopes at right angles to it. Sand is blown up from the base to create a sharp crest at the top of the ridge, down the front of which – the slipface – it then tumbles, thus edging the whole dune forward. However this cross-country movement is limited by dry rivers, like the Kuiseb and the Swakop.

Further inland variable winds and the escarpment providing water for vegetation stabilise the massive dunes, which come in many shapes, some parabolic, some star-shaped. Sossusvlei, in the centre of the Namib, is the best place to observe them and the monster dunes surround an oasis that attracts a variety of game. On the plains you can see the most curious kind, called *barchans*, created where isolated quantities of sand are blown by the wind into crescent shapes, the horns of which advance across the desert.

Desert Habitats

The dunes are the most photographed characteristic of the Namib, but they are interspersed with mountains, strangely weathered rock formations known as inselbergs that you see rising out of the desert plains along the C14 and C28 roads through the park, unexpected oases and grassy interdune valleys. Between them they comprise three types of habitat; dunes, plains and vegetated riverbeds.

Life is sustainable in the dunes, despite the minimal rainfall, thanks to two factors. The first is a remarkable adaption by all sizes of creatures to the heat; beetles burrowing into the sand during the day, for instance. The second is the cold Benguela current sweeping up the coast from the Antarctic. This creates fogs up to 50 km inland. Fog droplets condense on rocks, on tiny plants, even on the backs of *tenebrionid* beetles, and enable an astonishing variety of flora and fauna to survive. If you fight your way up the steep slipface of one of the constantly movng coastal dunes – for instance between Walvis Bay and Swakopmund – you will find that tiny pieces of wind-blown detritus maintain spiders, dune ants and beetles; and lizards feed on them. Dune grasses and succulents take moisture from the fog. Plants vary from lichens to the grotesque 'living fossil', the *welwitschia mirabilis*, a plant related to the conifer, which has only two leaves. These sprout from the plant's base, absorb moisture from the fogs and grow up to three metres long in a grotesque tangle. There are complete separate male and female plants, the females having seed cones that are larger than the males'. The *welwitschia* is indigenous to the Namib, was only discovered in 1859 and is known to live up to 2,000 years.

The Plains and Riverbeds

Further inland, where the temperatures are harshest, larger species survive on the grass and the riverbed vegetation, as the Kuiseb river illustrates. There are still a few desert elephant in the northern Namib, while gemsbok, springbok and mountain zebra are fairly common in the Namib-Naukluft Park. There is even a herd of wild horses – descendants of abandoned German cavalry mounts – living in the stony plain near Aus.

Some routes are given in this guide's text. A useful locally published book is the 'Shell Guide to the Namib' by Mary Seely.

Namibia

the southern dunefield, with more vegetation, grasses and life than at the coast because Homeb enjoys both the fogs and slight rainfall. Further down the C14 you pass the Vogelfaderberg, a smooth-backed hump of granite worth stopping to investigate, both for the views from its top and to examine the aloes and other plants nourished by the rain it attracts.

From the Vogelfaderberg to Walvis Bay is 35 km (22 miles), though it seems longer across the hot gravel plain. It is a fast drive from Walvis Bay on to Swakopmund and on the way you pass some of the Namib's cresent-shaped barchan dunes.

The B2 to Swakopmund
The main tarmac road to Swakopmund, the B2, only skirts the park, though it passes through the desert. It goes near the Rossing uranium mine – the largest in the world – and then passes the turn-off to Goanikontes and the *Welwitschia* Flats, described later. The 326 km (226 miles) of tarmac takes six hours.

Swakopmund

Postal code 9000. Telephone code 0641.

Founded in 1892 as a port by the Germans because the British held Walvis Bay, this is an attractive, intriguing and friendly small German resort, incongruously beached on the African coast. During its October – March high season it is socially very much alive, while there's a German Carnival in August. Swakopmunders are at all times proud of their town, which architecturally is a complete turn-of-the-century period piece. Many of the houses have towers from which their merchant owners used to watch for arriving ships, just like their counterparts in Baltic seaports and 11 buildings are now protected as national monuments. Among notable ones are the former Administrator's summer residence, the jail – designed to look like a country house – and the imposing neo-Baroque extravagance of the railway station, now a hotel. They represent a heritage of German colonial architecture unparalled elsewhere.

Getting to Swakopmund
This is easy. The roads have been described. Intercape operates a luxury bus from Windhoek. Daily trains run overnight from Windhoek (though it has sleeping cars it no longer has a restaurant car) and there are flights four times a week by Air Namibia, but be sure you order a taxi to meet you at the airstrip. The taxi tel number is 2205.

Information
The Namib-I Publicity and Tourist office (tel 2224) is at 127 Kaiser Wilhelm Street.

Hotels and Restaurants

Every other hotel is dwarfed by the Swakopmund Hotel and Entertainment Centre created around the restored Railway Station (tel 63333, fax 63344). With its casino, shopping centre, tennis courts and use of the Rossing desert golf course, it has brought the big league to the resort. Even so, some may prefer the elegant if quiet three-star Hansa (Po Box 44; tel 311) though the traditional Bavarian-style Europa Hof (two-star; PO Box 1333; tel 5898) has better food and atmosphere. Another good two-star hotel is the Strand (PO Box 20; tel 315). There are many well-run pensions, among them the Hotel Adler Garni (PO Box 1497; tel 5045), and there is a Youth Hostel in the former German barracks. A couple of dozen restaurants include Anton's, noted for its cakes and pastries, and the Bistro.

Camping and Caravans

North of the town is a caravan and camp site, with some holiday houses; a reflection of Swakopmund being close to the National West Coast Tourist Recreation Area, a 200 km (125 miles) long strip of coast terminating at the Uchab river.

Shopping and Tours

The town has plenty of shops, hairdressers and garages. For Africana and pre-1914 militaria go to Peter's. Car hire firms include Avis (tel 2527), Budget (tel 4118) and Namib 4x4 Hire (tel 4100). Local tours are arranged by Charly's Desert Tours (PO Box 1400; tel 4341), who cover most of the places mentioned in this text and also offer full-scale camping safaris.

Local Attractions

Local attractions include the beach, which has the unusual habit of shifting all the time. 'It's a good beach this year,' people say. In the course of its wanderings it has silted up the harbour, originally constructed as the country's main facility for imports, via the railway. Before that an old steam engine, brought out in 1896, hauled goods inland. It now stands on a plinth outside the town at the spot where it finally broke down and is nicknamed 'Martin Luther', famous for saying (of his religious position) 'here I stand: I cannot do otherwise'. The Museum covers the coast's natural history and is well worth a visit. Close by it is the Namib Garden, where most plants known in the desert are grown.

Welwitschia Flats

Any botanist will want to see the indigenous and unique desert plant, the *Welwitschia mirabilis,* described in the special article on the Namib. One place to find it is on the Welwitschia Flats about 80 km (50 miles) drive from Swakopmund between the Khan and Swakop rivers, both dry most of the year. The flats are within the Namib park and so require a permit, obtainable from the Nature Conservation Office in the Ritterburg Building on Bismarck Street. There are two ways of getting there. The more interesting route is via the B2 road: turn right 40 km (25 miles) from the town, then drive 18 km (11 miles) through a desolate 'moonscape' to a palm oasis called Goanikontes on the Swakop river bed. There is a derelict hostelry, a camp site and a well-preserved 1903 road post at the point where you enter the Park. After that turn left and follow the track another 54 km (34 miles). A quicker, but less scenic, way is to take the C28 (road 52) from Swakopmund and turn left after 44 km (27 miles). A map is obtainable from Namib-I in the town.

The Coast North of Swakopmund

From Swakopmund north to Cape Cross is comparatively tame sandy seashore, unless you make the mistake of going there in a storm, though the fog will lie on the dunes in the morning. But from Cape Cross to the Angolan border is known as the Skeleton Coast with good reason. Gales, treacherous currents and rocks have caused many shipwrecks and the bones of both ships and men lie entombed in the stony shore, from sailing barques to passenger liners. It has been designated a National Park.

Henties Bay *Postal code 9000. Telephone code 06442.*
Driving up into the West Coast Tourist Recreation Area – which does not require a permit – you come first to Henties Bay, a small holiday resort with the one-star Hotel De Duine (PO Box 1; tel 1).

Welwitschia Mirabilis

Diversions Inland
From here you could venture inland to the Brandberg mountains via Uis, already described under Damaraland, a distance of 102 km (64 miles) on a fairly good road. A rougher road goes to Usakos, passing Namibia's 'Matterhorn', the instantly recognisable Spitzkoppe mountain, the lower slopes of which have a 'Bushman's Paradise' of rock art. If you have the time and inclination either of these trips would enable you to observe how the Namib changes as you approach the hills. Emerging from the dunes, with sparse vegetation dependent on the fog, you climb through grassland – if it has rained – and come out into a wide landscape of thorn tree savannah.

Cape Cross Seal Reserve
Continuing along the C34 coast road you reach the Cape Cross Seal Reserve at 131 km (82 miles) from Swakopmund. An estimated 80,000 seals live and breed on the rocks here, but you must ask about visiting times. The Reserve is open daily from 1000 to 1700. There is no accommodation. Swakopmund travel agents organise special tours to it. Beyond Cape Cross there is a caravan park at Mile 108 and then you reach the Ugab river and the Skeleton Coast Park. The rest of the road to Terrace Bay through the park can be travelled with a normal vehicle.

The Skeleton Coast National Park

Salt pans, dry water courses, occasional desert-dwelling elephant, lion and giraffe, curious dwarf shrubs and the wrecks of ships all characterise this desolate coast. The first ship you may see went aground near the Ugab river mouth. You are only allowed past the Ugab river if you have a permit, obtainable in Windhoek or at the Swakopmund Tourist office, or reservation advices: and you must enter the Park before 1500 hours. Day visitors may not go as far as Torra Bay.

Torra Bay and Terrace Bay
In the nearer, southern, part there are holiday camps at Torra Bay and Terrace Bay, run by the Wildlife Ministry. Terrace Bay is known for its surf fishing. Indeed the whole coast offers good angling for *kabeljou, steenbras* and *galjoen.* At Terrace Bay the all-inclusive charge covers meals and accommodation with hot showers. At Torra Bay there are camp sites with basic amenities, open only in December and January. There is an accompanied hike along the Ugab river trail twice a month, lasting Tuesday to Thursday. It's not very practicable for visitors, since you need to reserve well in advance and have a local medical certificate confirming your fitness.

The Northern Skeleton Coast
The northern part of the Skeleton Coast is closed to visitors, unless they are on a flying safari to a tented camp in the Khumib river valley north of Rocky Point (where the Sir Charles Elliot was wrecked in 1942). This is organised by Skeleton Coast Fly-In Safaris (PO Box 2195 Windhoek; tel 061 224248). Things to be seen on 4WD expeditions from the camp include the seal colony at Cape Frio (where the Dunedin Star went aground in 1942), the rock formations of the Hoarusib Canyon and the northern dune fields.

Kaokoland

Beyond the Skeleton Coast is Kaokoland, now opening up to limited tourism. The still-primitive semi-nomadic Himba people cattle herders live in a dramatically lovely wilderness of mountains and bush co-existing with the wildlife. Their bowl-shaped wood and mud huts, hairstyles and artefacts are noticeably reminiscent of the nomadic tribes of East Africa, from where they are thought to have come. The harsh climate is reflected in the women's piling their elaborately braided hair on their heads, as a protection against the heat as well as adornment. In the 1980s the wildlife suffered badly from poaching, especially of elephant and rhino, and a community game guard system has been introduced. Tourism helps the Himba get some benefit from preserving the animals, though game viewing is not the main attraction, more it is experiencing the strangeness and solitude of the area.

This is a rugged country, with few roads - and no signs - and DIY tourism is next to impossible. Professionals travel with a minimum of two vehicles. The soft option is the flying safari. For firms who specialise in the district see 'Safaris' earlier in the chapter. The Palmwag Lodge is often used as a base, otherwise there are no permanent facilities.

The Epupa falls on the Kunene river are the ultimate objective, set about with palm trees and baobabs. But at the time of writing the river had almost dried up.

The Coast South of Swakopmund

Expeditions south of Swakopmund are strictly limited by the diamond concessions and there are no public roads down the coast through the Namib Naukluft park. To reach Luderitz you must either fly or return by road to the highlands and drive via Mariental and Keetsmanshoop, which is at least a two-day journey. However you can enter the Namib Park from Walvis Bay along the C14 road and – with a permit – explore within the arc formed by the Kuiseb river, as already described, or go further via Solitaire to the Sossusvlei oasis.

Walvis Bay

Postal code 9190. Telephone code 0642.
The formerly South African controlled port of Walvis Bay is 33 km (21 miles) from Swakopmund via a fast road that gives some of the easiest access to the Namib's high dunes. On the way you pass Rand Rifles, a former 1914 war army camp, now a resort called Dolfinstrand. South Africa ceded the 1,200 sq km enclave to Namibia in 1994.

The Town
Walvis Bay – which means Whalefish Bay – lies below sea level. It is Namibia's only full-scale port, the terminal of the railway, and the home of a considerable fishing industry. So rich is the ocean here that trawling fleets come down from Europe, but their over-fishing causes much local resentment. The town has several hotels, notably the two-star Atlantic (PO Box 46; tel 2811), the Casa Mia (two-star; PO Box 1786; tel 5975) and the one-star Flamingo (PO Box 30; tel 3011). There are well-stocked shops, garages and other facilities, and local travel agents can arrange car hire, flights to the game reserves and safaris. One of Namibia's desert golf courses has the fairways marked by pegs. The surf fishing along the coast is excellent.

Bird Sanctuary
Flamingoes, pelicans and other waterbirds gather in their hundreds on the lagoons just beyond Walvis Bay town, which include a bird sanctuary. According to the indispensable 'Shell Guide to the Namib', this small area between the Atlantic and the desert constitutes 'the single most important wetland of Southern Africa for migratory birds.' It is estimated that 150,000 migrant birds come here every year from northern Europe, some in transit, some staying until they return for the European summer.

Sandwich Harbour
The old whaling harbour here is now a bird sanctuary, one species restricted to Namibia being the Damara tern. There are countless fish in the lagoon and seals that feed on them, but fishing by humans is prohibited. The harbour is 45 km (28 miles) south of Walvis Bay and being in the Namib-Naukluft park a permit is needed. This can be obtained from service stations in Walvis Bay. You need 4WD.

The Diamond Fields

This brings us to the subject of diamonds. All the way from Sandwich Bay to the Orange River – a distance of 600 km (375 miles) there are diamonds lying on the bedrock beneath the sand, as well as on a marine terrace under water formed during the Second Ice Age. They are thought to have been brought down the Orange River aeons ago and gradually washed up the coast by the Benguela current. Certainly the largest stones are nearest the river mouth, and diamonds are least easily found at the Sandwich Bay end of the concession areas. Originally they could be picked up on the sand and sometimes still can. This has led both to intricate security precautions by the concessionaires, the Consolidated Diamond Mines, and an unending series of smuggling attempts.

Diamond Smugglers
The facts are as hard as the stones themselves; firstly, when uncleaned these diamonds are extremely hard for an amateur to identify; secondly, the fine for going more than 5 m (16 ft) from the road without a permit in a concession area is theoretically heavy. If you find diamonds in Namibia you must hand them in to the police. One bold pilot was jailed after landing on a deserted beach to pick up a 'parcel' of diamonds hidden there by a C.D.M employee. Unhappily his aircraft's nosewheel stuck in the sand – and security men caught him. People joke that the only successful smugglers are the security men themselves. The whole vast and barren district is known as the *Sperregebiet* – the Forbidden Area – and more sections are still being opened up.

Luderitz

Postal code 9000. Telephone code 06331.
This town, perched on the rocks around a natural anchorage, often plagued by a howling wind, is unique: a German town in the middle of diamond fields on the least hospitable coast of all Africa.

First noted as a potential harbour by the Portuguese explorer Dias in 1498, it remained unexploited until 19th Century commercial interest culminated in Adolf Luderitz, a merchant from Bremen, establishing a trading post in 1883. Luderitz bought the whole coastal area from the Orange River up to 26° south and to a distance of 20 miles inland in 1883. He paid the local Nama Chief £500 and 60 rifles, acquiring one of the richest diamond areas in the world without realising it. Eventually diamond discoveries turned it into a boom town in the early 1900s, despite the lack of fresh water. When the local mines were exhausted and C.D.M's activity declined, so did the town. When the author first came here there were no tarred roads and water cost 75 cents a cubic metre. In 1968 water was piped from an underground river below the Koichab Pan, 70 km (44 miles) away in the desert. Today rock lobsters, pilchards and tourism have revived

Luderitz' prosperity, together with a new diamond field and offshore gas exploration.

Luderitz Town
Among notable examples of German colonial architecture are the Lutheran Church, windblown on the hill; the splendid former Magistrate's House, restored by C.D.M and open 1400-1500 on weekdays; and the Railway Station, completed in 1914 only a year before the territory was taken by South Africa in the Great War. Information can be obtained from the Tourist office in the Luderitz Foundation at the top end of Bismarck Street (tel 2532), or Luderitz Safaris in the same Street (tel 2719).

Hotels
The two-star Bay View Hotel (PO Box 387; tel 2288) and the 1904 Kapps Hotel (PO Box 100; tel 2701), often full of mining men on the way to camps down the coast, are the main hotels. The Sitz bar at Kapps used to be known for wild parties and miners shooting down the chandeliers. The Strand Motel is out of town on the beach (tel 2398). Don't expect haute cuisine or fresh milk.

Communications
Namib Air operates four flights a week from Windhoek via Swakopmund /Walvis Bay: a one night stay is possible. By train from Windhoek takes three days. The drive from Keetsmanshoop takes about four hours. There are no long distance bus services.

Museums and Crafts
The museum on Diaz Street has interesting displays on the area and diamonds. Kolmanskop (see below) is offically a museum too. And there is an Arts and Crafts Centre.

Local Sights and Sports
These include flamingoes on Second lagoon, jackass penguins on Halifax Island and the Agate beach. Sports are surprisingly plentiful: tennis, golf, swimming, yachting and excellent fishing.

Kolmanskop, Pomona and Bogenfels
The diamond mining village Kolmanskop, 9 km (6 miles) from Luderitz, was abandoned almost overnight in 1938. Founded 30 years before, it had a casino, skittle alley and school. Some buildings have been restored in this ghost town, others remain filled with drifting sand, memorials of how a boom can end. You can obtain a permit from the Tourist Information office. It is easily seen from the main road and guided tours start out at Kolmanskop itself at 0930 hours daily. All package tours take in Kolmanskop.

Another ghost town is Pomona. Local tours are authorised to visit it, the Maerchental Valley where the first prospectors allegedy worked by moonlight, the seal colony at Atlas Bay, and the natural rock arch of Bogenfels.

South of Luderitz

The entire coastline from Luderitz down to the Orange River is closed territory, except as just described. But you can drive east of the diamond area on the C13 to Rosh Pinah and with 4WD – and luck – reach the Fish River Canyon at Ai-Ais, described further on.

Elisabeth's Bay
Local mining fortunes are reviving with a new opencast mine 25 km (16 miles) south of Kolmanskop at Elisabeth's Bay. The original town is now a museum and there are tours to it and the plant from Luderitz.

Aus and the Schutschtruppe Camp

Postal code 9000. Telephone code 063332.
Out along the Keetmanshoop road, 122 km (76 miles) from Luderitz, is the tiny township of Aus, with its welcoming one-star Bahnhof Hotel (PO Box 20; tel 44). Close to Aus on the Rosh Pinah road, are the fallen mud bricks of the camp where the German colony's protection force, the *Kaiserliche Schutztruppe,* lived for four years after honourably capitulating to the South African forces on July 9, 1915. Apparently they wanted no part of the Great War, having come here to get away from Europe. There is a memorial. Near the road to Aus you can often see the wild horses, descendants of the Schutztruppe's mounts, that roam in a vast, sparsely grassed plain beyond which the pink Namib dunes are hazily visible. They go to drink at Garub, signed off the road.

Southern Namib Safaris
Although the Namib Naukluft Park borders the Luderitz to Keetmanshoop road, entry down here is not feasible. To enter the weird sand dune landscape you will have to go east up to the township of Helmeringhausen. From there drive on to Sinclair's Farm to Sossusvlei, already described. It is a very long way round.

Sinclair's Farm
This karakul ranch homestead, a mini-oasis near the former Sinclair mine, is one of the few really pleasant stopping-off spots in the whole huge area east of the Namib Park. It rates two stars. (PO Box 19, Helmeringhausen 9000; tel 06362 6503). It is roughly 60 km (37

miles) from Helmeringhausen. From here it is easy to reach the extraordinary Schloss Duwisib (see under Mariental, below).

The South

Southern Namibia is a vast, seemingly never-ending savannah, partly utilised for Karakul and cattle ranching, where towns are few and far between. The region's main centre is Keetmanshoop, beyond which the country gradually becomes hotter and more rugged. The Fish River Canyon is the most interesting feature of the 300 km (187 miles) between Keetmanshoop and the Orange River, which forms the frontier with South Africa.

Rehoboth
Driving south from Windhoek on the B1 road you pass what was once the Rehoboth Republic. The Rehoboth 'Basters' are a coloured people, a mixture of Europeans and Hottentots, who until independence largely ruled themselves in the wide karakul farming lands between Mariental and Windhoek. Today they number 32,000. The Reheboth Museum merits a visit and makes one understand the Basters pride in their heritage and their fears for its integrity.

Mariental and the Hardap Dam *Postal code 9000. Telephone code 0661.*
Mariental is a small town with two hotels on the Keetmanshoop-Windhoek road and railway, near which the Hardap Dam has created fishing and watersport facilities. There is some game in the reserve around the lake and a good restaurant overlooking it. Accommodation, bookable through the Tourism Ministry, is in bungalows. Hardap is open all year round.

Duwisib Castle
A more curious construction, over near the Naukluft mountains on the edge of the Namib Desert some 80 km (50 miles) south west of Maltahohe, is the German Rhineland style castle called the Schloss Duwisib. It was built by the Baron Hans-Heinrich von Wolf, who when serving with the German army allowed himself to be defeated near here by a force of Hottentots. He was sent home in disgrace, but returned in 1909 after marrying a wealthy American lady and began farming. He acquired 130,000 acres for about R1,400 and erected the Schloss, which he furnished with antiques. He was killed in the Great War, but the majestic, battlemented castle is still maintained by the Ministry of Tourism and can be visited. It is marked on maps.

Keetmanshoop

Postal code 9000. Telephone code 0631.
Keetmanshoop, the capital of the south, is a centre of communications and of a karakul farming district. It has banks, filling stations, a modern hospital and hotels, including the three-star Canyon Hotel, just outside the town, with comfortable rooms and a pool (PO Box 950; tel 3361).

The Kokerboom Forest
Some 15 km (nine miles) north east of Keetmanshoop there is a large stand of *kokerboom* trees. Although called the *Kokerboomwoud,* it is more a scattering of those curious high growing aloe *dichotoma* than a forest. Situated on an outcrop of volcanic rocks, it is worth seeing even though there are *kokerbooms* all over the south. Bushmen hunters use its bark to make quivers for their arrows; hence the colloquial name 'quiver tree'. The 'forest' is 16 km (10 miles) from Keetmanshoop. Take the B1 road, then the C16 for Aroab and it is well signed.

Fish River Canyon to the Orange River

The real attractions of the south are around the Fish River and the gigantic 85 km (53 miles) long Fish River Canyon, second in size only to the Grand Canyon in Colorado. It is 409 m (2,000 ft) deep, savage, and so sheer and unexpected in the landscape that you could walk into it by accident; not that anyone would walk through the heat of the surrounding semi-desert. The canyon is reached most directly from the main Keetmanshoop-Luderitz road, turning left at Seeheim and following the line of rail to Holoog, then turning right again. The main viewing point is on a U bend of the canyon. Part of the country around it is a National Park, protecting leopard, zebra, rockrabbits and antelope.

Ai-Ais Spa
Further on there are mineral hot springs in the floor of the Canyon at Ai-Ais. This is a natural oasis lower down the Fish River, with a spa which opens from mid-March to October 31; in summer it is unbearably hot. There are flats, a restaurant, bungalows, tents, camping facilities, a shop, a bottle store and a fine swimming pool using the hot spring water. The hotel/flat facilities are graded two-star. The mineral baths operate hourly sessions. An 86 km (54 miles) hiking trail has been created between Ai-Ais and the main vantage point on the canyon. It takes up to five days, but you need a medical certificate and a permit, and advance reservation from the Tourism Ministry.

The Orange River
Beyond the Canyon turn-offs, the tarred B1 leads down through a desolate volcanic landscape to the South African frontier at the wide, sandbanked Orange river. Just before the border post there is a restaurant and shop at Noordoewer. From Grunau the other B3 road runs 177 km (111 miles) east to the border and to Upington.

Factfile

Getting to Namibia and Internal Travel

By Air
Direct flights operate from Frankfurt, Johannesburg, Harare and London, and to Cape Town in conjunction with South African Airways to Windhoek's international airport on Air Namibia. Lufthansa and South African Airways serve Windhoek. From the United States there are daily connections via Johannesburg. Air Botswana operates once a week from Gaborone and Maun to the international airport, while Air Namibia operates to Maun from Eros, as well as to Victoria Falls.

Internally Namib Air serves Katima Mulilo, Luderitz, Swakopmund, Tsumeb and other towns from the smaller Eros airport. Charter flights are available to airstrips at all the main towns and in the Etosha National Park.

The international airport is 42 km (26 miles) east of Windhoek. A bus service operates before and after every flight going via the local Eros airport, which is very close to the city. The Air Namibia Central reservations number is 061 298 2552 and the international airport enquiries is 0626 40351.

By Rail
There are passenger trains twice a week to and from the South African network via Upington, with sleeping berths and restaurant cars. The journey takes 24 hours to Upington and two days to Johannesburg.

Internal rail services link Windhoek with Tsumeb and Grootfontein in the north, Gobabis in the east, Swakopmund and Walvis Bay. The southern line through Keetmanshoop to South Africa has a branch line to Luderitz. Trains are cheap but very slow.

By Road
Most main roads are well tarmaced and fast, though the road to Botswana via Buitepos is gravel and needs 4WD. The gravel road into the Kalahari Gemsbok Park at Mata Mata is closed at the frontier. To Windhoek from Cape Town is 1,493 km (933 miles) via Springbok,

and from Johannesburg 1,955 km (1,222 miles) on excellent roads. A trans-Kalahari highway from Windhoek via Gobabis and through Botswana to South Africa is planned.

Luxury Coaches from South Africa
The Intercape-Mainliner buses from Johannesburg and Cape Town to Windhoek take 19 and 15½ hours respectively at reasonable cost. They have reclining seats, complimentary meals are served, and films shown. Bookings tel 061 227847. Connex runs highly regarded seven day trips from Cape Town up to west coast.

Local Buses
The Intercape-Mainliner bus also operates four times a week between Windhoek and Walvis Bay/Swakopmund. Otherwise internal bus services are liable to be crowded.

Taxis
Taxis are available in Windhoek at the bus terminal (tel 37070), at Swakopmund (tel 2205), and at Walvis Bay (tel 2568). Hotels will phone for one. Taxis have meters, but the rates vary.

Hitch Hiking
You don't see many hitch hikers, but thumbing a ride is not a hazardous thing to do. Hitch hiking is, however, not allowed in the National Game Reserves.

Accommodation

Hotel, game lodges and guest farms are graded - see start of chapter.

Banks

Banking hours are weekdays 0830 to 1530 and Saturdays 0830 to 1100. Foreign currency can be exchanged at any commercial bank.

Business and Shopping Hours

Weekdays 0800 to 1300 and 1430 to 1730. Saturdays 0800 to 1300, although supermarkets stay open over lunch and on Saturday afternoon and on Sunday mornings.

Car Hire and Driving

Car rental is available through hotels and in the main towns, as well as in Windhoek and at the airports; see under Windhoek. It is more expensive than in South Africa. Major credit cards are accepted. The minimum age for rental drivers is 23 and there are severe restrictions on taking vehicles into neighbouring countries, for which a letter of authority must be obtained from the car hire firm. No vehicles may be taken into Angola, Zambia or Zimbabwe.

Driving
Driving is on the left. Seat belts are compulsory. Maximum speed is 120 km/hr and in built-up areas is 60 km/hr. Overseas visitors require international driving licences, and one with a photograph is desirable. If you've never driven on gravel remember it can be tricky, particularly at speed; it is easy to get out of control and overturn.

Automobile Association
The Automobile Association head office is in the Carl List Building, Windhoek. (PO Box 61, Windhoek, tel 224201).

Churches

The predominant churches are Lutheran, but other denominations are represented.

Currency

The unit of currency is the Namibian dollar, linked to the Rand. In early 1995 the rate was N$5.85 to £1 and N$3.60 to US$1.00.

Customs

Namibia is in the South African Customs area.

Diplomatic Representation

Namibia has diplomatic missions in Addis Ababa, Brussels, Lagos, London, Luanda, Lusaka, Moscow, New York (United Nations), Stockholm and Washington. See also under Tourist Information below.

Among 59 countries with diplomatic missions in Windhoek are: Angola, Botswana, Brazil, Britain, Canada, China, Cuba, Denmark, Egypt, Australia, Finland, France, Germany, Ghana, Kenya, India, Italy, Japan, Malawi, Nigeria, Norway, Portugal, South Africa, Spain, Sweden, Switzerland, USA, USSR, Yugoslavia, Zambia and Zimbabwe.

Electricity

220/230 volts AC. Electric plugs have round-shaped pins, as in South Africa.

Health

Yellow fever certificates are required if you arrive from an area where the disease is endemic. The 61 hospitals and 156 clinics in Namibia are well-run and equipped. There have been cases of meningitis. Malaria is endenic north of Windhoek. It is well worth taking out cover with Medical Rescue (PO Box 31220, tel 061 230505, fax 24 8114). See also General Information.

Language

English is the official language, though Afrikaans and German are more widely spoken.

Passports and Visas

Bona-fide tourists are allowed in for a maximum of 60 days, provided they have a passport valid for at least six months after the intended date of departure from Namibia, and have return or onward air tickets, or proof of other transport. You must have sufficient means of support (money, credit cards, cheques) and not be making financial gain from the visit. Nationals of the following countries do not require visas; Austria, Benelux countries, Britain, Canada, France, Germany, Ireland, Italy, Japan, Scandinavian countries, Switzerland, the USA and the USSR. Visits longer than 60 days can be authorised locally.

Public Holidays

New Year's Day (January 1), January 2, Independence Day (March 21), Good Friday, Easter Monday, Workers' Day (May 1), Cassinga Day (May 4), Ascension Day, African Day (May 25), Heroes Day (August 26), Human Rights Day (December 10), Christmas Day (December 25), Family Day (December 26).

General Sales Tax

A GST of eight percent is levied on goods and 11 percent on services. Tourists are exempt from tax on such luxury items as furs and jewels.

Telephones

International calls can be dialled from Namibian exchanges, which have a direct dialling system. The international code for Namibia is 264

Tourist Information - See page 25

Swazi market

Swaziland

The Country

This small, though surprisingly varied, country is one of the few kingdoms left in Africa. The landscape of the mountains that are its natural fortifications is magnificent. These rugged, mist-shrouded peaks protect the sacred burial grounds of the Swazi kings and are the source of powerful Swazi legends. Their strange and mystical beauty has seldom been better described than in Rider Haggard's classic adventure thriller 'King Solomon's Mines': and some of the interior has remained unexplored by visitors in the many decades since he wrote the book. Yet in spite of their heritage Swazi people bring an easy-going and friendly lifestyle to their land of contrasts.

Topography
Poised between the Transvaal, Natal and Mozambique, Swaziland is something of a topographical jumble. Within a roughly oval shape only 193 km (121 miles) long from north to south and much less east to west, God has contrived there to be everything from peaks and upland plateaux, through rolling grassland in the middleveld to the hot, arid bush of the lowveld on the Natal border. A century ago gold in the Pigg's Peak area of the north brought sudden wealth to adventurers: today citrus, cotton and sugar plantations in the south bring it. Wherever you venture in the country's 17,364 sq km (6,783 sq miles) you will find something different. The main routes into the mountain kingdom are listed at the end of the chapter.

Climate
In the mountainous area, commonly called the highveld, on the western side of the country, it is pleasantly warm (21°-30°C or 70°-85°F) from October to March. In the winter months, however, temperatures drop considerably, early-morning frost is not uncommon and hotel keepers light log fires in the evenings. This said, April to September is a beautiful time and it is much less hot in the lowveld. The middleveld, averaging 700 m (2300 ft) above sea level is warmer and drier, as is the Lubombo plateau in the east. The lowveld, running down to Natal, is sub-tropical, hot and dry and often suffers drought. Swaziland's rain falls mostly in the hot summer months of November to March. The lowveld is malarial, so take prophylactics if you go there.

History

Little is known of Swaziland's ancient history, although there are traces of human occupation from the late palaeolithic period onwards. However the Swazis themselves are relative newcomers – as are most of South Africa's peoples, black and white – having been part of a migration from the great lakes of central and east Africa around 1750 when the Nguni people moved down the east coast to Delagoa Bay and later settled between the Lubombo mountains (now Swaziland's eastern border) and the Indian ocean. Among their clan leaders was Nkosi Dlamini, forefather of today's royal clan. The Zulu and the Xhosa took the same route and the Zulu expansion under Shaka later led to the Dlaminis crossing the Lubombo. At their high point of power the Swazi nation controlled part of the Transvaal and their kingdom was twice its present size.

Conflicts
The confederation of clans which made up the nation was ruled by Mswati I between 1840 and 1868, from whom the word 'Swazi' derives. But at the same time other influences were intruding: those of Boer farmers and English missionaries. The Boers were also interested because Swaziland blocked their way to the Indian Ocean coast. Then in 1879 gold was discovered and a torrent of fortune hunters arrived seeking concessions from the King for anything and everything, from refreshment bars to clothing shops. The conflicts of interest led to the British and Transvaal governments defining the north, west and south boundaries: and the Swazis losing much agricultural land.

Independence
For a time dual control of the territory by the British and the Boers was tried, but without success and after much political manoeuvring the interests of the Swazis themselves were to some extent preserved by the establishment of a British Protectorate in 1903, when the Anglo-Boer war was over. Successive kings tried to achieve independence, finally succeeding in September 1968 under King Sobhuza II.

The People

Life can be tough for many of Swaziland's 850,000 people. Many work in the South African mines and this migrant employment – unaccompanied by the men's families – is a major factor in an economy beset by a high birthrate and population increase. Peasant agriculture has suffered from inadequate investment in the 'national land' which is held in trust by the king for the people. Grassland is heavily overgrazed by cattle that outnumber the population, but are not often slaughtered because they are regarded as wealth. However the big sugar and citrus estates belong mainly to local companies. Despite international aid schemes, Swazis are leaving the land and becoming more and more dependent on tourism and handicrafts for a living. Happily the European Union is helping small crafts people to find markets in Europe.

Swazi Kingship

The present monarch, King Mswati III, who was educated in Britain, acceded to the throne on April 25, 1986 at the age of 18. The principles of succession are both traditional and sensible. When an Ngwenyama or 'lion', as the king is known, dies the Royal council chooses one of his children to succeed him, normally the only child of a senior wife. As a Dlamini relative explained to us: 'The throne must go to a young man, not married. Then he thinks of nothing else in his life. This also prevents other families influencing him beforehand'. If the choice is a minor, then the Queen Mother or Ndlovukazi acts as Regent until the prince is crowned and becomes Head of State and the embodiment of the nation, albeit advised by his Council. However the Queen Mother remains the second pillar of the State throughout her life. There is a Parliament of two houses, a House of Assembly and a Senate, but legislation requires the King's consent. The King must always be a Dlamini: and he must always marry a noble girl from outside the Dlamini clan.

Traditional Ceremonies

Ancestral rituals matter considerably to the Swazis. There are two major traditional ceremonies, the *Ncwala* first fruits ceremony in December-January, and the Reed Dance in late August-early September. Visitors are allowed to attend the main day of the *Ncwala* and watch men of the Swazi Regiments, panoplied in skin tunics, dance at the Royal Residence at Lobamba in the Ezulwini valley, 16 km (10 miles) from the capital of Mbabane. The culmination of the Reed Dance, in which many hundreds of Swazi maidens take part to honour the Queen Mother and repair the reed windbreaks around her palace, may also be watched. Cine cameras are not permitted at either ceremony but you may take as many still pictures as you wish. The Tourist Office publishes an illustrated brochure about these and other rituals.

National Parks and Reserves

Although nothing in Swaziland can rival the Kruger, it does boast a surprising number of Reserves for a small country, described in detail later. With one exception they are administered by the National Trust Commission. Admission fees are charged. The 405 sq km Hlane National Park in the east is typical big game country with large herds of wildebeest, also rhino, giraffe and lion. There is limited self-catering accommodation in chalets. The other big game reserve protecting rhino, buffalo and a few elephant is the 15,500-acre Mkhoya, off the main Manzini to Big Bend road, which is privately managed with its own lodge. It has a privately run lodge. The somewhat tame 11,000-acre Mlilwane Wildlife Sanctuary close to Mbabane and the much larger Malolotja Nature Reserve in magnificent hills near Piggs Peak have antelope and other game, but no predators, buffalo, rhino or elephant. They have simple self-catering rest camp accommodation. The Mlawula Nature Reserve near the Hlane Park is a largely ironwood forest with walking trails and camping facilities. Game includes impala and bushbuck. Trips to the reserves and accommodation can be arranged through Umhlanga Tours Ltd, PO Box 2197 Mbabane; tel 44005, 44522, fax 42485. Their longer packages include the Kruger National Park.

Booking Accommodation

For Malolotja and Mlawula Reserves contact the National Trust Commission, whose offices are next to the National Museum at Lobamba, some 20km from Mbabane on the Manzini road (PO Box 100, Lobamba; tel 61178, fax 61875). Rates are low. For Hlane Mlilwane and Mkhaya contact Big Game Parks of Swaziland in Mbabane (PO Box 234; tel 44541, out of working hours 61591, fax 61594). Rates at Mkhaya are much higher than at the other two, but include game drives.

Hotels

The better hotels are mentioned in the text. Hotels are not graded, but a full illustrated list can be had from the Swazi Government Tourist Office (see below). By South African standards most are of two star quality, though the Mountain Inn at Mbabane would rate higher, as would the Protea Piggs Peak. Only the Royal Swazi Sun is of five-star standard.

Information

The Swaziland Government Tourist Office publishes an excellent range of brochures (PO Box 338 Mbabane; tel 44556, fax 42774). The town bureau is on the Swazi Plaza shopping complex in Mbabane. However the best map is produced by the AA of South Africa. It is called 'Motoring in Swaziland' and has a great deal of basic information on the back. Swaziland is represented in Johennesburg by SARTOC, PO Box 600, Parklands 2121; tel (011) 788 0742, fax 788 1200.

Craft Markets

Dolls, kaftans and skirts, baskets, mats, soapstone carvings, tapestries, decorative glassware and even solitaire boards are among the products of Swazi craftsmen and women, whose work retains a skill now rare in more commercialised African countries. Among quite a number of craft centres a few off the beaten track are Tisheshwe Cottage Crafts in the Malkerns valley, not far off the main Mbabane to Manzini road; Swaziland Tapestries at Phumalanga, reached off the

Swaziland

Mbabane to Oshoek road five km (three miles) before the border post; Ngwenya Glass in the same area and Mantegna Craft off the Mbabane to Manzini road close to the entrance of the Miliwane Game Sanctuary. The Handicraft Market is on Allister Miller Street in the capital and there are others in Manzini, Piggs Peak and Nhlangano.

Mbabane

No area telephone code. Tourist Info 44556

Swaziland's capital, sheltered by the Dlangeni hills at a climatically agreeable 1,200 m (3,930 ft) above sea level, was founded in 1902. The name means 'something sharp and bitter' and the town does lack any great attractiveness. Its real assets are the nature reserves you can so easily reach from it, the recreations and sports available, and the transformation in facilities brought about by Sun International's hotels a short distance away in the Ezulwini valley. It is also, happily, a place where none of its rapidly multiplying inhabitants appear to be in any other kind of hurry. 'Go straight', people say when giving you directions and there is a nice symbolism about the phrase, because there are not many city slickers around.

Town Centre

Mbabane's main street is named after Allister Miller, who founded 'The Times of Swaziland' newspaper back in 1896. At the southern end a bridge takes the road across the Mbabane river, past the Swazi Plaza shopping complex and on down the Ezulwini valley. The Plaza has parking, shops selling most things a visitor will need and restaurants, while alongside it is the rival centre of the Mall. Between them they have revolutionised the capital's shopping facilities. The bus station is by the Mall, while the open air market is back on the other side of the bridge.

Taxis

Taxis are available at the Swazi Plaza, or ask your hotel to call one. There are no taximeters, so agree a price in advance.

Hotels

The older and less expensive places are either in town or close by, easily the best being the Mountain Inn (PO Box 223; tel 42773, fax 45393) a kilometre out on the Ezulwini valley road, with fine views, en-suite bathrooms and a pool. The Tavern (PO Box 25; tel 42361) is at the western entrance to town and sports an oak beamed 'olde-English' atmosphere and a swimming pool. If you want to be centrally located in moderate comfort this or the City Inn (PO Box 15; tel 42406) is the best bet. Slightly further out are the picturesque thatched cottages of the Swazi Inn (PO Box 121; tel 42235).

Royal Swazi Sun Complex

In terms of luxury, however, these are all dwarfed by the Royal Swazi Sun down the Ezulwini valley (Sun International reservations. Local address Private Bag Ezulwini; tel 61001; fax 61859). A resort in itself this hotel has a casino, its own 18-hole championship golf course, squash, tennis, bowling greens and shops. However its partner hotels, the less expensive package tour-style Ezulwini Sun (tel 61201) and Lugogo Sun (tel 61101) were designed for South African trippers and the Royal Swazi becomes packed in the evenings when they swarm into the casino and disco. That said, the standards of the Royal Swazi Sun itself are very high and it is elegantly furnished. Part of the complex comprises a spa and health studio called 'The Cuddle Puddle'.

Eating Out and Entertainment

Three restaurants worth trying if you do not want to eat in a hotel are the Calabash (tel 61187); the very informal Mozambique (tel 52489), which serves Portuguese-style prawn dishes; and the more sophisticated First Horse (tel 61137), on the way out to the Ezulwini valley. Gigi's at the Royal Swazi Sun is the most up-market restaurant, usually with a cabaret singer. Friar Tuck's at the Mountain Inn is pleasant. There is a snack cafe at the Indigilizi Art Gallery in Johnson Street.

The town has a cinema, but the obvious entertainment and late-night centre is the Royal Swazi Sun complex with its casino and nightclub.

Sports

Visitors can play golf at the Royal Swazi Sun's 18-hole course and the Mbabane Club's 9-hole course, close to the capital. Squash, tennis and bowls are available. Horses are easily hired for riding. There are hiking trails in the reserves. The only thing to be careful of is swimming in mountain pools because you could become infected by bilharzia.

Museum

Out at Lobamba in the Ezulwini valley, the National Museum has archaeological cultural and historical exhibits. It is not far from the Royal Kraal where the most important ceremonies are held.

The Ezulwini Valley, Mlilwane and the Malkerns

Called the 'Valley of Heaven' by Swazis, the Ezulwini valley runs down towards Manzini with the Malkerns valley – actually rather more

Swaziland

attractive – coming into it from the west. Ezulwini's main attraction – aside from the Royal Kraal and drives through tea estates along the signposted Tea Road – is the Mlilwane Wildlife Sanctuary.

Mlilwane Wildlife Sanctuary
The 44 sq km (17 sq miles) Mlilwane reserve is the most easily visitable in Swaziland, being six km (four miles) only from Mbabane in what is called 'sourveld': grassland that does not develop much nutritional value due to the high rainfall. It is signed off the main Manzini road. You cross a bridge over the river, with glimpses of the mountain upstream and find yourself at the main gate (closes at sunset). A map is usually on sale showing the sanctuary's many tracks, most of which are negotiable in an ordinary car except after rain, while with 4WD you can climb to viewpoints in the foothills. Various species of antelope, buffalo, giraffe and zebra are among the animals, and also a few leopard and cerval cats. Locals boast that the game is among the tamest in Africa: probably true, but that does not make for a feeling of the wild. Beyond the hippo pool in the south – no hippos in evidence when we were there, alas – is a pleasant self-catering rest camp (reservations tel 44541). There is a shop. You may leave by the south gate after sunset, provided you obtained a permit on entry.

Mantegna Falls
The Mantegna Falls just outside the sanctuary are quite spectacular, but the access road is not secure. The hotel named after the falls has been refurbished.

The Malkerns Valley Route
This important pineapple and citrus growing valley provides the basis for an interesting and scenically beautiful circular drive of some 104 km (65 miles) from Mbabane and back again. A few kilometres from the turn off the main Manzini road is one of the best craft shops in the kingdom, Tisheshwe Cottage Crafts – Tisheshwe being the name of a kind of local cloth. Developed from a farm store by an English couple, it is effectively a sophisticated private aid scheme for the locals and sells everything from mounted semi-precious stones to carved soapstone heads. It is well worth a visit and is open every day.

University and Forests
Next you pass the campus of the University of Swaziland at Luyengo and follow the course of the Great Usutu river towards Bhunya, where there is a pulp mill. Before Bhunya turn right for Mhlambanyatsi and the huge, silent Usutu forest, one of the largest man-made forests in the world. Trees by the thousand, mainly pines, cover an area of more than 100,000 acres. After that you pass through the hilly Sipocosini area and, with the tarmac turning to gravel for the last part, cross

Meikles Mount, skirt a dam lake and a Bushman painting site before regaining the main road outside Mbabane.

Country Estates
Mhlambanyatsi has two places to stay on private country estates. The Forester's Arms Hotel (PO Box 14, Mhlambanyatsi, tel 74177) offers riding, fishing, golf and nature trails. Meikel's Mount (PO Box 13, tel 74110) has self-catering cottages, though with cooks and cleaning staff available. Both are good bases for hiking around the mountains and streams of a lovely area which lies geographically over the hills behind the Mwilwane sanctuary.

Manzini to Hlane and the Lubombo

Manzini
Described as the industrial hub of Swaziland, Manzini is 42 km (26 miles) south-east of Mbabane, in the middleveld. Although it is about the same size as the capital and with good shopping facilities it is built on flatter land and has fewer attractions for visitors. However the sports facilities at the Manzini Club include golf, squash and tennis, bowling greens and a swimming pool. Temporary membership is available.

The New George Hotel (PO Box 51, tel and fax 52061) is air-conditioned and has a terrace and a pool. There are several restaurants and night clubs, the best known being the Dallas.

Routes to Big Bend and Hlane
From Manzini the main road continues to the lowveld, Big Bend and – ultimately – Natal. Eight km (five miles) outside the town another tarmac road branches left to the Hlane National Park and the imposing Lubombo escarpment which forms the frontier with Mozambique. We deal with this direction first.

Hlane National Park

The park comprises 405 sq km (158 sq miles) of unspoilt acacia thorn bushveld and the road passes through it some 70 km (44 miles) from Manzini. Large herds of wildebeest and antelope are protected in the Park; there are white rhino and elephant, while lion were re-introduced in 1994. There is a small entrance fee to the park and simple self-catering accommodation in log cabins with bedding and towels provided. More luxurious chalets are at Bhubesi in the north of the park, also self-catering opened (reservations tel 44541 or through Umhlanga Tours in Mbabane, tel 44005). By prior arrangement the park authorities can arrange guided walks and tours and for campfire dinners. The roads are rough, so 4WD is advisable and you must take mosquito nets or insect repellent.

Mlaluwa Reserve and the Lubombo Escarpment
This area right on the Mozambique border is largely ironwood forest, noted for the rare Samanga (or green) monkey and for the shy oribi antelope. Otherwise there are some zebra, kudu, wildebest and duiker, over 300 species of birds have been recorded and there are many species of mountain flora. Energetic hikers can reach the top of the Lubombo and gaze right across Mozambique to the Indian Ocean on a clear day. A small, fully equipped, tented camp can be booked through the National trust (tel 61516).

Sugar – and Coca Cola
The sugar estates up here and south near Big Bend are, incidentally, a minor miracle of how irrigation can turn arid bush into acre upon acre of green sugar cane. Sugar is a major export earner, employing 12,000 people, despite the United States having reduced its import quota in 1988, because the European Union pays Swaziland well above world prices for a quota under the Lome Convention. Coca Cola has a syrup factory generating over E122 million a year in export revenue and bringing the government as much tax as is paid by the rest of private industry combined.

Siteki
A turn off to the right before you reach Hlane National Park takes you to Siteki, the largest settlement on the Lubombo escarpment. It is worth the deviation on a clear day for the magnificent views across the lowveld. The border post with Mozambique at Mhlumeni further on was closed at the time of writing, but Lomahasha to the north is open. Siteki has a small hotel, the Stegi (PO Box 33; tel 34126).

To Mkhaya Game Reserve and Big Bend

Driving down from Manzini to Big Bend, the road dropping constantly in altitude and the temperature rising, you could easily miss Swaziland's wildest reserve. The entrance is situated on the north of the road 50 km (31 miles) from Manzini. Where the road goes over the railway you must turn left on to a farm road and after three km, including crossing a riverbed, should find the Mkhaya homestead. But get detailed instructions: no visits can be made except by prior arrangement anyway.

Mkhaya
Mkhaya's 26 sq miles comprise savannah with some primaeval riverine forest. Elephant, black rhino, waterbuck, lynx and hyena are among a considerable range of animals and there are Bateleur, Mar-

tial, Walbergs and Crowned eagles among the 100 species of birds. It is pretty hot in summer and you must take anti-malarial prophylactics. In winter it's warm by day and cool at night. The Stone Camp has a central communal building and tents with their own piped water and lavatories. Walking, the owners say, 'is encouraged because it promotes an affinity with Nature'. Bookings through PO Box 33, Mbabane; tel 44541. Rates are very much higher than in other reserve camps, but they include all meals, hiking trails and tours. White-water rafting expeditions are possible on the Great Usutu river too.

Big Bend

Beyond Mkhaya you are fully into the lowveld. Huge sugar cane transporter trucks lumber along the main road, a hot wind blows, the outline of the Lubombo hills dominates the eastern skyline and where the serpentine Great Usutu river coils itself in a great loop is the town of Big Bend. Very much a Lonrho company town it is too. Actually located off the main road, its wide, tidy streets have banks, garages, company houses with well-watered lawns and a vast iron cogwheel mounted at the office entrance. Palm trees wave in that hot wind. The river winds greasy-brown with mud below the slight hill that the town is on, a wrecked concrete bridge a souvenir of rapacious floods. At the New Bend Inn (PO Box 37; tel 36111, fax 26384) there are air conditioned rooms and a pool. The restaurant's aspirations are modest, but it is a welcome stopping place.

On to Natal
Beyond Big Bend there is little save irrigation, water sprays and sugar cane until you reach a friendly border post at Lavumisa, though there is a 24hr petrol station at Matata, seven km south of Big Bend.

The Middleveld in the South

In the south of the territory, Hlatikulu, another of the several small settlements in Swaziland, lies on a beautiful mountain range above the Mkondo valley. Grand Valley, a worthwhile sight in both winter and summer, is accessible by way of a steep mountain road which leaves the Sitobela road five km (three miles) from Hlatikulu.

Nhlangano
Nhlangano, near the Transvaal border 27 km (17 miles) south of Hlathikhulu, is the administrative headquarters of the Shiselweni district. Mahamba Gorge, a few miles from the town and reached by a road through the Mahamba Methodist Mission, is a pleasent picnic spot.

Swaziland

Nhlangano Sun
The luxurious Nhlangano Sun (Private Bag Nhlangano, telephone 78211) is in the Makosini valley. Chalets have all their own facilities. Sports include tennis, badminton, swimming and golf at the nearby Country Club. There is a casino and a disco.

Mankayana and Mission Crafts
Sixty-nine km (43 miles) from Nhlangano, on the untarred road back to Mbabane via the Malkerns valley, is Mankayane (also on the main route from Piet Retief, in South Africa). At Enqabaneni Mission, a few kilometres from Mankayana, you can buy beautifully woven shawls and tablecloths and a host of other handicrafts made by the local people.

To the Highveld

Some splendid upland country, including the Malolotja Nature Reserve, lies north of Mbabane, with easy access up the King Mswati III Highway. It was travelling this road that I met two unforgettable people.

A Royal Relative
The first encounter was at the Highlands Inn in the one-time gold rush settlement of Piggs Peak. I had made the spectacular but barbarously winding drive into Swaziland from Barberton across the mountains, with the conveyor buckets taking asbestos from the Havelock mine swaying above the road on their 26 km aerial journey into the Free State. The Highlands Inn was a low colonial style building with lawns and jacaranda trees. Ordering a much needed beer I met Mr Peter Dlamini, a small man with a neat moustache and a quick wit. He gave me an introduction to Swaziland: and turned out to be one of the royal clan. He explained the succession always going to a boy: 'that size' he said, pointing to a youngster playing on the lawn. He also commented on the trees. 'These jacarandas must have been planted by you English. You brought them in everywhere.' Royally connected or not, he had done a two-and-a-half year stint in the mines at Barberton.

The Soapstone Carver
My second encounter was with a soapstone carver called Christian, selling his work from a small but tidy shack by the road. The carvings were coloured an unnatural black. 'I warm the stone and polish it with polish and paraffin wax three times. Then the colour does not change.' He earned what would be an hour's unskilled pay in Britain for a figurine that took three days to fashion. 'There is no work' he said simply, without complaint. One reason, of course is, the high birthrate.

Forbes Reef

I had encountered Christian near the former gold mine of Forbes Reef, half way between Mbabane and Piggs Peak. In theory there was a ghost town: in practice I was unable to locate it among the blue gum trees that have since been planted. (The mine shaft itself is inside the Malolotja Reserve.) So I retraced my route to see Malolotja instead, the entrance to which is roughly 35 km (22 miles) from both Mbabane and Piggs Peak.

Malolotja Nature Reserve

Although the wildlife is relatively limited – wildebeest, impala, reedbuck and zebra are the most commonly seen animals – this is Swaziland's most important park, with 230 species of birds and many varieties of flora, among them proteas and cycads. The habitats range from exotic mountain river valleys and waterfalls to open grassland. The less hilly eastern side has 20 km of roads (liable to be closed in the rains) which take one to a number of viewing points, while the mountains, cooled by the upland breeze, deserve exploring. In the west is Africa's oldest known mine, where haematite was extracted for ritual uses around 41,000 BC. There are five roughly mapped day walks, including ones to the Malolotja Falls which are Swaziland's highest at 100 m (328 ft) and the forested Majolomba Gorge. Backpacking trails, using overnight campsites with no facilities, require a permit. The main accommodation is in log cabins near the entrance gate, well sited looking across a valley. Cooking equipment is provided, but you must bring your own food and bedding. Nearby is a proper campsite with washing facilities and toilets. Make reservations through PO Box 234, Mbabane; tel 44541.

Piggs Peak

This small town is on a scenically fine mountain road and the Highlands Inn (PO Box 12; tel 71144) is an agreeable spot to stop for a meal or a night, though hardly for an entire holiday. In luxury terms the Inn is overshadowed by the hugely larger Protea Piggs Peak Hotel and Casino further up the road towards Jeppe's Reef. The Protea (Private Bag, Piggs Peak; tel 71104) is designed for tourists from South Africa, has numerous sports, a gym and car hire. The two establishments cater for very different kinds of people. A compromise for a few days could be the delightful Phophouyane Lodge (PO Box 199; tel 71319). Set in a small nature reserve near the waterfall of the same name, the lodge's charges are very reasonable for its self-contained thatched cottages. The lodge has a restaurant as well and you can find it signed seven km (four miles) north of Piggs Peak.

Swaziland

Mr Pigg and his 'Peak'

Alluvial gold was first found here in 1872. However the 'peak' where a prospector named Pigg subsequently located a gold reef was in the hills west of the present village. Mining began in 1883 and rapidly turned the tiny peak into a quarry, after which a proper shaft was sunk. The mine closed in 1954, although it had yielded 119,235 ounces of gold, the last year produced only two. Mr Pigg quit the area after his successful quarrying and settled in Natal. However other prospectors found other sources of the precious metal in the neighbourhood, workings now obscured by pine and blue gum plantations.

Local Attractions

Wherever you stay, the glories of this part of Swaziland are the natural ones of indigenous forests, waterfalls, birdlife and stunning views reached either on foot or horseback. Some renowned Bushman paintings of so-called 'birdmen' are along the Nkomati river at the Nsangwini Shelter south of Piggs Peak, while the town itself has a display of more modern African handiwork at Tintsaba Crafts.

Factfile

Getting There

Air

Royal Swazi Airways and Comair both operate between Johannesburg's Jan Smuts airport, and Matsapha airport eight km (five miles) west of Manzini. As well as these regular twice daily flights, there are services to Dar-es-Salaam, Durban, Gaborone, Harare, Lusaka, Maputo and Nairobi. Charter flights can be arranged with Royal Swazi Airways. A departure tax is payable. The airport telephone is 84451 for enquiries. For Royal Swazi reservations call 43433. There is an airport bus service to principal hotels.

Air-Hotel and Nature Trail Air packages are offered by Royal Swazi Airways, Comair and Airlink from Johannesburg and Durban. Tel Johannesburg (011) 331 9467 or locally 43433.

Bus

Local bus services run into Swaziland from South African towns nearby. A number of firms in South Africa are running luxury bus tours to the territory. They include Connex and Springbok Atlas. Within the country crowded local buses serve most areas. They leave Mbabane from a terminal near the Mall.

Roads

Internal travel is by road only. The main highways are all tarmac. The trans-territorial highway runs from Ngwenya on the western border to Lomahasha on the Mozambique frontier. The King Mswati III Highway runs from Matsamo on the northern border to the capital and the Grand Valley Road from Manzini to the Mahamba border post. The road via Big Bend to Natal via Lavumisa is good, as is the entry through Oshoek. Other roads are gravel.

Banks

Barclays, Meridien, Stanbic, the Standard Chartered and the Swaziland Development Bank have branches. Bank opening hours are 0830 to 1430 on weekdays and 0830 to 1100 on Saturdays.

Business Hours

Weekdays 0830 to 1700, Saturdays 0830 to 1300. Government offices are closed on Saturdays.

Car Hire

Car hire firms include Avis in Manzini (tel 86350) and at the airport (tel 86222), Hertz at the airport (tel 84396) and in Mbabane (tel 41384). You can use your home licence for up to six months, provided it is printed in English or has a certified translation attached. The minimum driver's age is 23. Cars have manual gear shift.

Churches

Most religious denominations are represented. There are Anglican and Roman Catholic churches in Mbabane and a Catholic Cathedral in Manzini. Some 60 percent of Swazis are Christians and vast crowds greeted the Pope on his 1989 visit.

Credit Cards

Amex, Diners Club, Master Card and Visa are usually accepted.

Currency

The unit of currency is the Lilangeni, plural Emalangeni, divided into 100 cents. One E is at par with one South African Rand and Rand notes (but not coins) are freely accepted. It is wise to change Swazi currency back into Rands before leaving.

Customs and Border Posts

Swaziland is in the South African Customs area, but Customs declarations are required. The border is manned on both sides and no border posts are open after 2200, many closing earlier. Ngwenya, Mabamba, Matsama (for Nelspruit), Lavumisa (for Durban), Lomahasha and Ngwenya (for Johannesburg) open at 0700.

Diplomatic Representation

Swaziland has diplomatic missions in Brussels, Copenhagen, Johannesburg, London, Maputo, Nairobi, New York and Washington. Visas are obtainable from them. There is an EEC Attache in Brussels.

Foreign countries represented in Swaziland include Belgium, China, Denmark, France, Germany, Great Britain, Israel, Italy, Mozambique, Portugal, South Africa, the United States, and the EU Commission.

Driving

Visitors can use their home country driving licences. The speed limit is 80 kph (50 mph). Drive on the left. Seat belts must be worn. Service stations are open on weekdays, Saturday mornings and Sunday afternoons.

Electricity Supply

220/240 volts AC in Mbabane and Manzini. Elsewhere variable. Round three pin 15 amp plugs are used.

Health Requirements

Yellow fever and cholera certificates are only required if you have come from an area where those diseases are endemic. Anti-malarial prophylactics are essential in the lowveld. Some slow-moving streams are infected with bilharzia. There are six main hospitals, including ones at Mbabane and Piggs Peak.

Language

English and Siswati are the official languages. English is spoken in hotels, offices, shops and markets.

Passports and Visas

All visitors need a passport. Nationals of the following countries may enter without visas: Britain and the Commonwealth, Belgium, Denmark, Finland, Greece, Iceland, Israel, Italy, Liechtenstein, Luxembourg, Netherlands, Norway, Portugal, San Marino, South Africa, Sweden, Switzerland, Uruguay, USA. EC nationals can obtain free vias at border posts. Otherwise they are obtainable from the Chief Immigration Officer or any British Consular office.

Public Holidays

New Year's Day (January 1), Good Friday, Easter Monday, National Flag Day (April 25), Ascension Day, King's Birthday (July 22), Umhlanga, National Day (late Aug/early Sept) National Day (September 6), Christmas Day (December 25), Boxing Day (December 26), Incwala Day (late Dec/early Jan).

Telephones

Local and external calls can be dialled direct. The code for South Africa is 07, for Australia 0061, for the UK 0044 and for the USA 001. The code for Swaziland from outside the country is 268. Despite improvements lines are frequently out of order.

Time

Two hours ahead of GMT.

Swaziland scener

Elephant crossing the Luangwa river

Zambia

Revised by Theo Bull, Gianna Molinar Min and Haslen Back

The Country

The unspoilt nature of Zambia and its magnificent National Parks are the country's greatest assets to the visitor, even though much of the nation's wealth is derived from mining and agriculture. The paradox is possible because Zambia is such a large country, at 752,614 sq km (293,989 sq miles) it covers an area as large as Austria, Hungary, France and Switzerland combined. From the tumultuous Victoria Falls on the Zambezi river to the great and varied wildlife of the Luangwa Valley, and from the lakes in the north to the vast floodplains in the west, the country offers an ever-changing spectacle.

This said, you are going to need to keep your cool and a sense of humour. There is plenty of unintentional inefficiency among officials, while it is nothing unusual to find one's hotel room has been given to a visiting delegation. Some necessities are in erratic supply, though the relaxation of exchange control has improved matters, if you can pay. Bear with problems because ordinary Zambians are usually good-humoured, patient, non-racist and friendly to strangers. Overall the atmosphere is curiously British, despite three decades of independence. This is due not just to the colonial legacy of language; it extends to socialising, dress and drinking habits. If you are staying with friends or acquaintances bring the latest paperbacks, garden seeds, nice handkerchiefs and the newspaper you were reading on the flight; all such items will be welcome.

Topography
Roughly kidney-shaped, Zambia is a landlocked tropical plateau of between 900 to 1,200 m (2,500 to 3,900 ft) above sea level, which makes the scenery undramatic. The beauty lies in trees, skies, grasslands and occasional lakes and rivers. The parts of greatest interest for visitors are the Zambezi river and the Victoria Falls, Kafue National Park and the Luangwa Valley. The country is bordered by Angola and Botswana to the west, Zaire and Tanzania to the north, Malawi to the east and by Mozambique, Zimbabwe and Namibia to the south.

Climate and Clothing
The climate is pleasant and there are two main seasons. Summer is between September and April with daytime temperatures ranging from 26°C to 32°C; there is a dry winter from May to August with temperatures from 15°C to 27°C, falling lower in the evening and early morning and even dropping below freezing on occasion. The rains come between November and mid-April and the best time to visit is April through to October, although October is the hottest month, and serious game viewing only starts around June. You need a light raincoat or umbrella and a lightweight pullover.

History

Human habitation in the area goes back as long as 200,000 years. At Mbala, in the far north, archaeologists have unearthed layers of occupation extending over much of that time. The earliest people would have been small hunter-gatherer bushmen, whose rock paintings can still be found in many parts of the country. But they were displaced by the arrival from the north of the first Bantu cattle herders and farmers, who established a number of kingdoms, notably of the Eastern Lunda in the northern region of Lake Bangweulu, and the Lozi in the south west around the Zambezi. However, a great part of the country was mercilessly exploited by Arab and Portuguese slave traders throughout the 18th and early 19th centuries and all the kingdoms save that of the Bemba and Lozi declined markedly.

Dr Livingstone
The area first became known to the western world through the travels of Dr David Livingstone, the great Scottish missionary who first travelled here in the 1850s. He died on the shores of Lake Bangweulu in 1873 and his heart was buried nearby in the village of Chief Chitambo. His memory remains highly respected.

British Rule
British rule began through the British South Africa Company at the end of the 19th century, when present-day Zambia consisted of North-Eastern and North-Western Rhodesia. In 1911 the two territories were amalgamated into the single entity of Northern Rhodesia and in 1924 the Colonial Office assumed direct rule of it as a Protectorate. In 1953 it was incorporated into the ill-fated Federation of Rhodesia and Nyasaland, which broke up a decade later after a campaign of civil disobedience.

Independence
On October 24, 1964 the independent Republic of Zambia was born.

The country is a democratic republic with an executive President. It was ruled as a one-party State by the United National Independence Party (UNIP) under Dr Kenneth Kaunda until late 1991, when the Movement for the Multi-Party Democracy (MMD) swept the polls and Mr Frederick Chiluba became President. Since the Zamibia has become a much more free and open society.

The People

Zambia's population totals around eight million, roughly half of whom live in or around towns. There are small minorities of Europeans and

Asians. Over 70 dialects are spoken, those most often heard being Nyanja, Bemba, Tonga and Lozi. In spite of this, English is the official language. African culture and traditional beliefs are prominent in Zambia although Christianity is widespread. Other Africans seem to think Zambians are rather conventional and boring. Zambians themselves find it hard to admit to being wrong and so, whilst appreciative of compliments, are slow to apologise for mistakes. But they are especially warm-hearted towards children and if you arrive with a family you will be very welcome.

Some Necessary Warnings

Zambians are also, in the words of a local, 'masterly thieves'; so watch your handbag or hip pocket and beware being duped by street money changers (illegal as well). Corruption is endemic and although you will not come across it when travelling by air, on other travels you need a supply of one dollar bills and cigarette packs to give away. However, the Government is strongly discouraging beggars. Finally, AIDS is widespread.

National Parks and Wildlife

The most compelling reason for coming to Zambia is to go on safari and the country has 19 national parks covering an area nearly 60,000 sq km (23,430 sq miles), totalling nine percent of the country and constituting one of the largest conservation areas in Africa. The best known – described in details later – are the Kafue National Park and the North and South Parks of the Luangwa Valley. There are a number of other national parks accessible to the public and well worth a visit, such as Lochinvar south of Lusaka on the Kafue Flats, Kasanka and Sumbu in the north, the Nyika plateau in the east and the Lower Zambezi National Park. The parks are generally inhabited by the large southern African mammals and the most comprehensive guide is 'Land Mammals of Southern Africa, A Field Guide' by Ray Smithers.

Birds

Zambia has a current bird list of around 750 species; broadly divided into five categories, birds of southern Africa, birds of eastern Africa, the wetlands birds, birds of the tropical rainforest (in the north-west), and the migrants whose passage to and from southern Africa regularly takes them through Zambia. Gems for the birdwatcher include the dodo-like shoebill found in the Bangweulu swamps, *Anchietas barbet* of the northern woodlands, and the increasingly rare taita falcon which breeds annually in the Zambezi gorge near the Victoria Falls. To identify them arm yourself with Robert's Birds of Southern Africa, or the Field Guide to the birds of East Africa by Williams and Arlott (Collins). Another useful publication is Newman's Common Birds of Zambia (Zambia Orthithological Society).

Conservation
The parks are managed and run by the Department of National Parks and Wildlife (Private Bag 1, Chilanga; tel 278636) with a large corps of game scouts and wildlife rangers. Their task is not only to maintain the parks and to guide tourists, but more importantly to patrol against the poachers who threaten the wildlife and therefore the economy of these areas. They are being assisted by western aid agencies, and the Wildlife Conservation Society of Zambia has worked hard to raise funds for game conservation with the help of such internationally renowned supporters as the late Gerald Durrell and the artist David Shepherd. The government also takes a hand through the small, but effective, Species Protection Department.

Safaris and Walks
Safaris are usually limited to six to eight persons per open-topped vehicle. But the most spectacular experience is the walking safari. Walks (accompanied by an armed National Parks scout and a knowledgeable trail leader) are organised during the dry season (June to end October) in the Luangwa Valley and Kafue National Parks. These walks were originated by Norman Carr, whose company now operates through Andrews Safaris (PO Box 31993, Lusaka; tel 223147). Effectively, they are a reversion to the traditional foot safari of the 1920s; the difference being that nowadays visitors are not normally allowed out of their vehicles in National Parks.

Fishing
Fishing is an untapped opportunity, apart from the one annual fishing competition, held at Kasaba Bay. The lakes and rivers are mainly unpolluted and sustain a tremendous fish population. The fighting tiger fish are found in Lake Tanganyika and the Zambezi river system. Nile perch, vundu (catfish weighing up to 100 kg) and tilapia are commonly found in the rivers. Safari firms can give advice, or contact the Tour Operator's Association (PO Box 30263, Lusaka; tel 224848, fax 224265) Several firms offer fishing tours.

Hunting
The official policy is that controlled hunting deters far worse destruction by poachers, who might otherwise be undisturbed. For further details see Safaris and Hunting, page 31.

Transport and Tours

Air and rail services, are detailed at the end of this chapter. The motto for Zambian travel is 'be patient, friendly and determined'. Anger will get you nowhere. There are several local travel agents and tour operators. The best are mentioned below.

European and American Tour Operators

An increasing number of European and American firms feature Zambia on their safaris. A few of the most knowledgeable are named on pages 26-27. Itineraries often combine Botswana, Malawi, or Zimbabwe with a Zambian safari.

Zambian Firms

Lusaka travel firms include Big Five Travel and Tours (PO Box 35317; tel 01 229237) at Pioneer House on Cairo Road and Eagle Travel (PO Box 34530; tel 01 228605). Both have branches in Livingstone. There are plenty of others.

Information

The head office of the Zambia National Tourist Board is just off Cairo Road (PO Box 30017, Lusaka; tel 229087): with offices in Livingstone. In Britain they are located at 2 Palace Gate, London W8 5NG (tel 0171 589 6343, fax 225 3221), and in the United States at 237 East 52nd Street, New York, NY 10022, USA (tel (212) 308 2155).

Hotels and Lodges

Hotels and motels are classified from five-star to one-star, plus ungraded. Lodges and camps are not graded. If you can afford it, do not stay in below two-star. Note that the National Parks neither run lodges, nor make lodge reservations. The best hotels are expensive; and on top of that bills are subject to a 10 percent service charge and 25 percent sales tax. Tipping in hotels and restaurants is illegal, but people often give a little extra. It is advisable to make hotel reservations before arrival in Zambia as the hotels are often full. Additionally it is important to have a written or faxed confirmation of this to produce on arrival.

Lusaka

Telephone code 01. Tourist Info 229087.

Zambia's capital is a spaciously laid out city, given a pleasant climate through being 1,315 m (4,270 ft) above sea level, yet with regrettably few amenities for the visitor, except in the hotels. It became the administrative centre (of what was then Northern Rhodesia) in 1935 because of its central position on the Cape to Cairo road and rail system and sits in rather flat, featureless country. The spine of Lusaka's downtown commercial area is Cairo Road, a mile-long avenue where you will find the Tourist Board, airline offices, banks, the General Post office, shops and the Lusaka Hotel. A number of suburbs have shopping centres, the largest and most varied being at Northmead. Street traders are in most areas and sell a surprising variety of things.

Hotels
The best hotels are all near each other up in the diplomatic quarter on the Ridgeway, a ten-minute taxi ride from Cairo Road. All have swimming pools and some have shops. The Pamodzi Hotel (PO Box 35450; tel 254455, fax250113), five-star, is the smartest and the Intercontinental (PO Box 32201; tel 250600, fax 251880), four-star, usually has the best food. As we warned before, these are not only expensive, you are liable to be evicted without notice in favour of visiting conference delegates and you must provide proof of booking on arrival. Personally we prefer the older, rambling Ridgeway Hotel (PO Box 30666; tel 251666, fax 253529), three-star. The Ridgeway has recently been taken over by The Holiday Inn Garden Court group from South Africa and should be given their acceptable standards and reasonable prices.

Overall, though, it will be cheaper and possibly less hassle to stay at a comfortable two-star place. Among these are the Ndeke Hotel (PO Box 30815; tel/fax 252779) also in the Ridgeway district; the Fairview (PO Box 33200; tel 212954, fax 218432) close to the city centre; or the Garden House (PO Box 30815; tel 287337, fax 289328) six km (four miles) west of town.

The Andrews Motel (PO Box 30475; tel 272301) six km south of town is a 'possible' and the small Hillview Hotel (tel 278554), 12 km south, does indeed have a hill view and a pleasant atmosphere. Both have swimming pools.

If you are on a tight budget, then get the ZNTB's Tourist Information booklet and check out some of the ungraded places. They are no rougher than the equivalents in Zimbabwe or Kenya.

Restaurants
Apart from the hotels, among the better places to eat are the Golden Bull (tel 274471) on Kafue Road; the Oasis (tel 251030) on the great East Road; the Polo Grill (tel 253848) opposite the polo ground; the Old Bakery at the north end of Cha Cha Cha road; and Zorba the Greek (tel 217119) six km south. For Indian food try Dil's on the Kabulonga Road extension or the Maharani Gardens on Suez Road, close to the Ridgeway. Zorba the Greek and the Oasis have discos in the late evening.

Shopping
Imported items are in sometimes short supply, so do not necessarily expect to find the brands of camera film, toiletries and so on that you

prefer. Local crafts can be a good buy, expecially silver jewellery – either plain or set with semi-precious stones – and copper ornaments. There are good jewellers in the Intercontinental and Ridgeway hotels. The best craft shops are Zintu at the Ridgeway and Bushcraft in the Farmers Co-operative Building on Cairo Road. Opposite Bushcraft are Thatcher's Silver Chain and Fredjoe, selling jewellery and malachite. The Wildlife Society has a tourist shop nearby. Copper Crafts in Dar-es-Salaam Place, the Gift Box on Cha Cha Cha Road and the Carousel Shopping Centre at the south end of Cairo Road are worth a visit. Numerous street vendors, often from Zaire, sell curios, malachite, illicit ivory and brass masquerading as gold. Check prices as the shops may be cheaper.

Excursions
There are a small zoo and botanical gardens at Munda Wanga, in Chilanga 12 km (seven miles) south of the city. Otherwise the best options – quite feasible for a day trip - are the Lechwe Lodge (tel 222073) one hour from the city, the Blue Lagoon and Lochinvar National Parks, both to the west. Lake Kariba, a favourite weekend watersports resort for locals, is 150 km (94 miles) to the south.

The Lower Zambezi National Park

This 4,092 sq km of superb game country lies on the north bank of the Zambezi, within easy driving distance of Lusaka. Most large mammals are here, except for giraffe. Most visitors coming by road go to the Chiawa pontoon on the Kafue river near the Chirundu bridge over the Zambezi. (the Kafue flows into the Zambezi) and then taken by river to the camps. These include the Chiawa Camp (tel 01 262683) inside the park, the Royal Zambezi Lodge (tel 01 223952) in lovely surroundings just outside, and St Nektarios Lodge (tel 01 252779) on the Zambezi, relatively close to Chirundu.

The Western Province

Although the Victoria Falls and the Kafue National Park are famous, much of western Zambia is a virtual secret, not least Barotseland and the upper reaches of the Zambezi.

Blue Lagoon National Park

This 420 sq km (162 sq miles) of flood plain north of the Kafue river is only two hours drive west from Lusaka. Like Lochinvar, it shelters large herds of lechwe, a wetland antelope of which there are three sub-species: red, black and Kafue. Roan and sable antelope, zebra and buffalo also live in the park, as well as many waterbirds. An elevated causeway facilitates viewing them. There is no lodge.

Lochinvar National Park

Lochinvar is three hours drive south west of Lusaka, via Monze off the road to Livingstone. Its 410 sq km (158 sq miles) are wetlands, the peak inundation being in May. Thousands of migratory birds stop here en route to and from South Africa and over 400 species have been recorded, so this is a birdwatchers' delight. Animals include around 700 zebra, 2,000 wildebeeste and 30,000 Kafue lechwe, which are unique to this area of Zambia. The Lochinvar Lodge is a converted colonial-style farmhouse by the park gate. Book through any travel agent.

Lake Kariba

The creation of Lake Kariba, one of the largest man-made lakes anywhere, is more fully described in the Zimbabwe chapter. Each country has its own hydro-electric plant at the 126 m (410 ft) high dam and its own resorts on the lake. Alas, you have only to visit the dam to see which side is the better maintained. Nonetheless the Zambia resort lodges at Siavonga are quite acceptable, spectacularly sited and less than 100 miles from Lusaka: Lake Kariba Inn, the Leisure Bay, the Manchinchi Lodge, and the Zambesi Lodge. Boating, fishing and watersports are available and the lake landscapes are worth seeing. Any travel agent can make bookings. The climate at the lake can be very hot and humid in summer.

Livingstone

Telephone code 03. Tourist Info 321404.
Named after the explorer, David Livingstone, and with many mementoes of him, this relaxed town was once the capital. It has a pleasant, old world charm, although it is becoming run down. Nevertheless, its closeness to the Victoria Falls is an unchangeable asset; it is on the line rail to Zimbabwe, and has frequent flights (see Factfile), the river landscape is beautiful and it is altogether a much more attractive place to visit than Lusaka. The ZNTB (PO Box 60342; tel 321404) is on Mosi-oa-Tunya Road, and both Big Five (tel 320775) and Eagle Travel (tel 320129) have branches. The flight enquiries telephone number is 321606.

Many visitors go to and from the Zimbabwe town of Victoria Falls. Border formalities are no longer troublesome and the train between the two towns runs morning and evening. You can also walk across the bridge : remember to take your passport and forign currency.

Hotels
The largest hotel, the four-star Mosi-oa-Tunya Intercontinental (PO

Box 60151; tel 321121) is at the Victoria Falls, not in the town. It has plenty of facilities and its standards are acceptable, though below what one would expect. The New Fairmount (PO Box 60096; tel 320726) has retained its three stars, but is not going to appeal to outsiders much. The Rainbow Lodge (tel 381806) on Mosi-oa-Tunya Road is delightfully situated and acceptable. But easily the most atmospheric spot is the Tongabezi camp 15 km outside the town in the National Park and on the Zambezi riverbank (Tongabezi Safaris, Private Bag 31; tel 323235). You can watch the rapids from the bar and its chalets are reasonably priced.

Local Attractions

The Livingstone National Museum has four galleries, which feature dioramas of wildlife with many well-mounted game specimens. The history section is an absolute 'must' for anyone interested in either Zambia's development or Dr Livingstone. The Railway Museum illustrates how the 'iron horse' opened up this part of Africa. Out at the Maramba Cultural Village you can see traditional crafts and tribal dances. There is also a rather rundown small game reserve, the Mosi-oa-Tunya, with around 1,300 animals, including rhinos. But the great draw is, of course, the falls.

The Victoria Falls

The world-renowned Victoria Falls are only five km (three miles) from Livingstone on a good road. The local name for them is Mosi-oa-Tunya, 'the smoke that thunders', and you soon see why. At high water the spray rising hundreds of feet above this great natural wonder can be seen from twenty miles away. The falls are at the point where the Zambezi river, flowing wide from its flood plains, suddenly reaches a mile-wide chasm. Plunging down 100 m (300 feet), it creates an unforgettable spectacle. At the height of the flood season 120 million gallons a minute cascade over the edge, though it is easier to see along the falls when the flow is less. By walking across the Knife Edge bridge you can get excellent close-up views, and also pass into the rain forest created by the spray, with frequent rainbows. But beware the wet; an umbrella will give partial protection, a bathing suit is best!

Experiencing the Zambezi/White-Water Rafting

The river trip above the falls on the launch Makumbi is well worthwhile, though American initiative in the late 1980s introduced a more adventurous way of experiencing the river – white-water rafting in rubber inflatables, below the falls. The rapids there are reckoned among the most challenging in the world and adventurers cross from the Zimbabwe side – where it is also done – for the Zambia start, just downstream of the 'Boiling Pot', the tumultous pool where the waters start their journey down the river gorge. You need to be fit for this rafting and canoeing (see under Victoria Falls in Zimbabwe chapter) and it is quite a climb to and from the Zambezi gorge. The people organising it are Sobek Expeditions (PO Box 60957; tel 321432), with rivals Makora Quest (tel 03 321 679).

For the bungee jump from the centre of the bridge see the Zimbabwe chapter.

Near the falls is the ancient baobab which Dr Livingstone used as look-out post. He actually stayed at the village of Chief Mukuni, still in existence, after finding the falls on November 16, 1855.

The Upper Zambezi

Although little visited, the flood plains and National Parks upstream of the Victoria Falls, which stretch up into Barotseland, are an area of special beauty. You ought, however, to consult a specialist safari organiser. They could be seen in conjunction with a trip to Kafue.

Sioma Ngwezi National Park and the Ngonye Falls

The Zambezi river flows down through western Zambia, gathering tributaries on the way, and forming the border between Zambia and the Caprivi Strip of Namibia. West of the river here is the Sioma Ngwezi Park, a flat and forested area between the Zambezi and the Kwando (or Cuando) river. There are buffalo, elephant, oribi and tsessebe; and a few visitors to the campsite on the Kwando. On the way in or out you should visit the Ngonye Falls close to Sioma, where a horseshoe-shaped cataract on the Zambezi cascades down a series of small falls and there is a white sandy beach, with a campsite. The park is roughly five hours drive from Livingstone. You need your own camping gear. The park staff are very helpful.

Traditional Royal Ceremonies

A traditional ceremony, the Kuomboka, takes place around the end of March, depending on the floodwaters. It celebrates the Paramount Chief of the Lozi tribe miving with his entourage in a fleet of canoes from his summer capital at Lealui on the Barotse flood plain up to his winter capital north of Mongu. The strongest young men contend for the privlege of rowing his 50 ft barge and 10,000 others come to watch. Some tour operators fix excursions to the festival. There is a one-star hotel at Mongu, the Ngulu (PO Box 910308; tel 07 221028).

Liuwa Plains National park

Situated at the head of the Barotse flood plain, this wildlife paradise has large herds of buffalo, tsessebe and wildebeeste; and only two tourist vehicles went there during 1994. It lies north of Mongu between the Zambezi and Luanginga rivers. Going from Mongu via the Kalabo ferry (May to January) you cross 25 km of totally unspoilt flood plain, still as Livingstone saw it. The other ferry at Lukulu runs all year. But you'll need a guide, as there are no tourist facilities. Abercrombie & Kent now operate a luxury tented safari here from Victoria Falls (see Zimbabwe chapter), and visit the Lozi festival.

Kafue National Park

Kafue, the largest and oldest of Zambia's national parks and the main lure of the western Province, was established by the veteran game warden, Norman Carr. Half the size of Switzerland, its 22,400 sq km (8,750 sq miles) are a vast undulating plateau cut through from north to south by the Kafue river, which forms part of its eastern boundary. Most African plains game are represented, with lion, leopard, cheetah and buffalo, the handsome sable antelope, roan, bushbuck and reedbuck. Sitatunga inhabit the swamps and on the Busanga Plains in the north there are large herds of red lechwe. The lechwe were once nearly exterminated by poachers, and indeed the numbers of most animals have declined, especially elephant and hippo. The game department continues to have difficulty patrolling the park due to its sheer size. Birds do not suffer and over 400 species have been recorded.

Administratively Kafue is divided into North and South, the demarcation being the Mongu to Lusaka road. The south is ideal for camping, if you have 4WD. Tongabezi of Livingstone take safaris there. Some areas have tsetse fly, so take insectisides.

Access
Much of the park is inaccessible during the rainy season (November to May) particularly in the north, but in the dry season it is a fascinating sanctuary to visit and is easily reached by the main road from Lusaka (330 km/206 miles). In the south there is an airfield at Ngoma, served by charters from Livingstone and Lusaka.

Just outside the park boundary is the Iteshi-teshi dam on the Kafue River, which has created a new lake and is a good birdwatching spot. But beware: the road connecting Iteshi-teshi to the main road is in poor condition.

Accommodation
The main lodge – out of eight lodges and camps – is the 52-bed Musungwa Safari Lodge. Musungwa is just outside the boundary,

overlooking Iteshi-teshi lake. It has a pool, twin-bedded rooms with en-suite bathrooms, is open all year round and can be booked through T G Travel on Cairo Road, Lusaka (PO Box 32591; tel 227807). Camps that are open June to November only include Lufupa Camp run by Busanga Trails (PO Box 31322, Lusaka; tel 224761) and the Hippo Camp run by Lubungu Wildlife Safaris (PO Box 31701, Lusaka; tel 253848). Both are on the Kafue river. You can take walks and drives in open vehicles from all the camps and lodges, whilst Hippo Camp has the added advantage of a flat bottomed boat; ideal for either game viewing or fishing for bream and pike. Chunga is a self-catering Camp (Wilderness Trails, Lusaka; tel 01 220112).

The Copperbelt

Zambia is the world's fifth largest producer of copper and the second largest of cobalt. The 'syncline' in which the rich mineral deposits lie runs through thousand million-year-old granite rocks in a twenty-mile-wide belt continuing into south-eastern Zaire. The mines themselves range from 1,850 m (6,000 ft) deep shafts to the enormous, three km (nearly two miles) long, Nchanga open pit at Chingola, the Commonwealth's largest. Although the mines are security areas, it is sometimes possible to visit them and their associated smelting plants. Apply well in advance to the Public Relations Officer, ZCCM (Zambia Consolidated Copper Mines) at its headquarters close to the railway station on Dedan Kimathi Road in Lusaka (telephone 229115). They are under no obligation to show people round, but will often help.

Kitwe and Ndola *Telephone code 02.*
Unless you are on business, there is little point in going to the Copperbelt, although two major towns have grown up there from the copper industry, Kitwe and Ndola. Some fifty miles apart, both are well laid out with local amenities like zoos and pleasure resorts. They are also better tended than other Zambian towns. They have flights from Lusaka and various hotels, of which the best are the three-star Mukuba (PO Box 72126, Ndola; tel 655545) in the showgrounds and the three-star New Savoy Hotel (PO Box 71800; tel 611097). The Edinburgh in Kitwe is disappointing. Ndola has a golf course. The memorial to the late UN Secretary General, Dag Hammarskjold, killed in an aircrash in 1961, lies off the Kitwe road a few miles out of Ndola.

The Luangwa Valley National Parks

The Luangwa River flows from Tanzania into Zambia, joining the Zambezi at a place also called Luangwa. It is a broad, slow flowing, silt laden river which has created many oxbow lakes and lagoons and greatly benefits both wildlife and farming. The abundance of wildlife long ago led to the creation of three national parks within the valley, South Luangwa, North Luangwa and Luambe National parks. The local airport is Mfuwe, where safari operators collect their clients and now officially 'international'. Equally it is perfectly possible to drive into the valley, provided you have 4WD and can take bad roads. The best time for visits is the dry season of May to November, but walking safaris only operate June to October. The valley as a whole used to be nicknamed 'The Kingdom of the Elephant'; there were once estimated to be 100,000. But poaching was rife in the 1980s and the herds suffered badly. although the poachers' activity has been reduced in the less remote parts.

Accommodation
Lodges are mostly on the outskirts of the parks and are open all year. They comprise twin-bedded chalets, constructed along the river, with their own bathrooms, a communal bar and often a swimming pool. Camps are generally inside the park, seasonal and often built of locally collected bamboo and grasses, with twin-bedded huts around a central dining room, from which there will undoubtedly be a view of the river and its hippo population. They can all be booked through travel agents in Lusaka. Tariffs usually include game drives.

South Luangwa National Park

This is the most famous of the parks in the valley, extending over 9,050 sq km (3,494 sq miles) between the Luangwa river to the east and the Mchinga Escarpment to the west. The vegetation is mainly *miombo* woodland with a few areas of open grassland in the north, but there are large tracts of mopane woodland (a favourite of the elephants) and beautiful groves of African ebony, known locally as *mchenja,* along the old river courses. The fauna includes lion, leopard, buffalo, elephant, hippo, crocodile, impala, puku, zebra, giraffe, waterbuck, bushbuck, and – near the river – greater kudu. There used to be a large population of black rhino, but they have been all but wiped out by gangs of armed poachers. The park is located 698 km (436 miles) from Lusaka in the east of the country.

Walking Safaris
The walking safari – now copied in many other countries – was pioneered in South Luangwa by Norman Carr, a former game warden and now a conservationist who is something of a legend in Zambia. Some walks last five to seven days, camping at night, and accompanied by armed scouts, guides and porters. The park also allows night drives, using searchlights to spot such nocturnal animals as leopard, civet cats, bushbabies and owls (notably the giant owl and

Zambia

Pels fishing owl). Otherwise gameviewing is based on the traditional early morning and late afternoon drives in open vehicles.

Kapani and Chinzombo Lodges
Kapani Lodge (PO Box 100, Mfuwe) is located just outside the park, 40 minutes drive from the airport. One of the best here, it is owned by Norman Carr, who gives occasional lectures on the park and its inhabitants. There are ten chalets, a large swimming pool and a shaded game viewing platform overloooking the lagoon. Chinzombo Lodge (PO Box 320169, Lusaka), also with a pool, is close to Kapani on the bank of the Luangwa in a shady grove of *Trichelia* evergreen trees. It is run by Zambia's Save the Rhino Trust. Phil Berry, who has been based at Chinzombo for many years, is an expert on the giraffe population and a fascinating person to go with on safari. Both these lodges are open all the year round.

Mfuwe and Chichele Lodges
Inside the park there are Mfuwe and Chichele run by Luangwa Safaris (PO Box 69, Mfuwe; tel 062 45018). Together with the President of Zambia's own private hideaway, these are virtually the only permanent structures allowed within the park. Mfuwe has a beautiful location on the edge of the Mfuwe Lagoon. Chichele is on a hill in the southern part of the park. A safari combining the two is an excellent idea, since their landscapes and settings are completely different. On the drive between them are a number of wooden banana trees; fairly inconspicuous except for their oddly shaped banana-like fruit. Both Mfuwe and Chichele have pools and conduct daily morning and evening game drives. Catering standards are acceptable.

Kakuli and Mchenja Camps
Kakuli Camp (Savannah Trails, PO Box 37783, Lusaka; tel/fax 01 224487) is a simple hutted safari camp about 23 km (14 miles) north of Mfuwe, on the bank of the Luangwa and overlooking the floodplain of one of the Luangwa's infrequently flowing tributaries. There are showers cut into the river bank and it is nothing odd to shower whilst watching elephants and kudu grazing opposite, or hippos and crocodiles a safe distance away in the river itself! Some 12 km (seven miles) north of Kakuli is Mchenja Camp (also run by Savannah Trails) a similar walking safari camp in a grove of African ebony trees. Both the camps offer walks, night drives and combined walk/drives or picnics.

Opposite: Gemsbok bulls at Etosha, Namibia (top)
             Basuto basket maker (below)
Overleaf: Swazi handicrafts stall (top)
             In the Moremi Wildlife Reserve, Botswana (below)

The Nsefu Sector

Whilst most of the South Luangwa National Park lies on the west bank of the river, it does extend east into a small area known as the Nsefu Sector. This covers only 175 sq km (68 sq miles) with similar game. There are opportunities to sight Cookson's wildebeest; a subspecies of the Blue wildebeest unique to the valley.

Tena-Tena Camp/Nsefu Camp

The park's only fully tented luxury camp is Tena-Tena (Robin Pope Safaris Ltd, PO Box 320154, Lusaka; fax 062 45076) in the Nsefu Sector. Robin Pope is one of Luangwa's most experienced and enthusiastic safari managers and you can easily combine Tena-Tena with trips to the Nyika Plateau (described below) and Lake Malawi. He also runs walking safaris to remote areas of the park, camping at night. Nsefu Camp (Wilderness Trails Ltd, PO Box 30970, Lusaka), is a 12-bedded camp located on a breathtaking bend in the river. From here, as at Tena-Tena, you can take walks or drives or just relax with binoculars and camera by the river watching the days events unfold.

Chibembe Camp

The larger Chibembe Camp (Wilderness Trails) is one hour's drive north of Nsefu Camp, just outside the park. The thatched chalets, are by a small swimming pool. The walking safaris often involve crossing the river in a small 'banana boat' in order to get into the park. This is an exciting way to begin the day, with sightings of the river's hippo and crocodile population. Chibembe has three small satellite camps for extended walking safaris and you can spend four days in the bush on foot completing a circuit of them.

North Luangwa National Park

The smaller North Luangwa National Park – separated from South Luangwa by the Munyamadzi Corridor – is a virtually unexploited wilderness in safari terms, with no permanent lodge. Its 6,000 sq km (2,400 sq miles) support a substantial wildlife and bird population. You will see cheetah here and hunting dog are common. Shiwa Safaris (Bookings Grand Travel, PO Box 35211, Lusaka; tel 01 223113) run a walking trip from Mpika (a town to the west of the Mchinga escarpment) into the park, which is the simplest way of seeing it. They pick up clients in Lusaka and get them to Mpika via a combination of road

Previous page: The main falls, Victoria Falls (top left)
                            Drowned woodland, Lake Kariba (top left)
                            Tree house lodge, Hwange (below)
Opposite: Hippos and Greater Kudu

and rail. They also have a base at Shiwa Ngandu, the family home of the owners, built in the 1920s as a great and romantic country house, where clients stay in chalets beside the local hot springs.

Ian Macdonald Safaris (PO Box 30684, Lusaka) has a base camp and two outlying camps in the park. He is well known for his bush skills and his safaris are exclusive trips for a maximum of five people, flying by chartered aircraft from Lusaka to Waka Waka airstrip near the base camp.

Luambe National Park

Between the North and South Luangwa National parks to the east of the river is the small Luambe National Park. Its 254 sq km (99 sq miles) consist almost entirely of woodland, which shelters most of the species seen in South Luangwa. There have been moves to renovate and re-open a small lodge there.

Nyika National Park

Nyika is one of Zambia's smallest parks, a short distance east of the Luangwa valley. Its 80 sq km (31 sq miles) are on the western edge of a high montane plateau area, which spans the Zambia/Malawi border and are most easily reached from the Malawi side, although a road runs from Chipata on the Zambian border through Lundazi to Nyika itself. Robin Pope Safaris run a resthouse 2150 m (7,000 ft) up on the plateau with (it is claimed) views of 100 miles across eastern Zambia. The park is primarily of botanical interest with montane grassland and relic forest, flowers and butterflies. The forest harbours the rare blue monkey, there are red, blue and forest duiker – alas not as highly coloured as their names suggest – and more standard animals like zebra, eland, roan antelope and reedbuck. You might see leopard and serval cats. Overall, Nyika makes an interesting contrast to Luangwa and the two areas can easily be incorporated into the same safari. But take note of Nyika's altitude. It can be cold.

Kasanka National Park

The nearest park to the Copperbelt, Kasanka is a small almost unknown one of nearly 400 sq km (156 sq miles), roughly six hours drive from Lusaka. After independence the animal stocks were almost totally depleted by poachers, but since David Lloyd (an ex-District Officer in colonial Northern Rhodesia) created the Kasanka Trust in 1987 the wildlife populations have begun to recover, though elephant, buffalo, hippo and lion are shy. The evening flight of the straw coloured fruit bats is a local spectacle. There are three simple camps with accommodation for up to 30 people and both walks and drives are available. Kasanka ia a very 'personal' park, which is well worth a visit. The creation of a private Trust to run a national park is a complete and refreshing break from Zambian tradition.

Lake Tanganyika and Sumbu

Way up on Zambia's northern border is one of Africa's greatest lakes, Lake Tanganyika, 700 km (437 miles) long and the second deepest in the world. It also offers – after Lake Kariba – the nearest thing Zambia has to seaside resorts. Three lodges – Kasaba Bay, Nkamba Bay and Ndole Bay – have been established on the lakeshore within the Sumbu National Park. They are served by scheduled flights from Lusaka. The park has a wildlife population including elephant, hippo, leopard, lion, buffalo and many antelope. Cruises on the lake depart from the port at Mpulungu.

Factfile

Getting to Zambia and Internal Travel

Air
Airlines serving Lusaka include Air France, Aeroflot, Air Namibia, Air Zimbabwe, British Airways, Kenya Airways, South African Airways. The Flight Enquiries telephone is at Lusaka airport is 271466. There is an international departure tax of $US20.00 or the equivalent. Taxis ply from Lusaka International airport to the city and the fare for the journey should be agreed in advance. The taxis tend not to be in very good condition, often with broken windscreens and rarely with seatbelts.

The collapse of Zambia Airways in late 1994 threw domestic services into confusion. Roanair flies from Lusaka to Kitwe, Ndola, Livingstone, Mfuwe for the Luangwa parks and Kasaba Bay (tel 01 228822, fax 221057). The internal airport tax is k 1,000. A number of charter companies also operate. Two are Eagle Air in Lusaka (Findeco House, PO Box 34530; tel 222792) and Star Avia (tel 01 271038).

Rail
The trains in Zambia are slow and the quality of the rolling stock and service is poor, but fares are low. From Lusaka you can travel up to Kitwe on the Copperbelt and south to Livingstone and Zimbabwe. Two trains a day run to Livingstone and vice versa, taking about 12 hours. The northbound Copperbelt train from Lusaka connects with a three-times-a-week service from Kapiri Mposhi to Dar es Salaam in Tanzania. This service is operated by the Tanzania Zambia Railway Authority (TAZARA). Tickets can be booked through the Lusaka office

Zambia

(PO Box 31784, tel 01 222274) located in Design House just off Cairo Road. The Livingstone trains continue to Zimbabwe, with connections to Bulawayo, Botswana and – eventually – South Africa.

Road
The roads are of a variable and mainly acceptable standard, though beware of potholes. There are a number of long distance buses, including those run by the postal services (PTC; tel 01 222299). Most buses are basic, crowded and often unreliable. It is not uncommon to see passengers waiting by the road in the middle of nowhere due to a broken-down bus. In addition Giraffe Buses (tel 01 221801) operate daily to Mufulira and on Mondays and Fridays to Harare in Zimbabwe. There are also buses to Johannesburg.

Banking
Banks are open from 0815 hours Monday to Friday and close at 1430 hours.Only Meridien Bank opens on Saturdays from 0815 to 1100. There is a bank agency at Luska International Airport, but it cannot convert local currencies back into foreign exchange; this can only be done at the branches in town.

In Lusaka

NDEKE HOTEL
Longacres
close to the city

GARDEN HOUSE HOTEL
6 km along Mumbwa Road

out of town

LEISURE BAY LODGE
Siavonga, Lake Kariba

ST NEKTARIOS LODGE
on the Lower Zambezi

CLEAN ROOMS, NICE FOOD AND FRIENDLY SERVICE
IN A VERY RELAXED ATMOSPHERE
Write to PO Box 30815 or phone/fax 252779

LUSAKA

Car Hire and Driving

Car hire is only possible with a driver. One reliable car hire company is Big Five Travel and Tours at Pioneer House, Cairo Road, Lusaka (PO Box 35317; tel 01 229237, fax 289362). They are also in Livingstone at Kent House, Mosi-oa-Tunya Road (tel 210811). The Hertz number is 01 229944, fax 227729.

The speed limits are 60 kph in built-up areas and 100 kph elsewhere. Some roads need 4WD, especially during the rains, so take advice. Beware hazardous driving by others and do not have cameras or binoculars visible in your vehicle.

Currency

The basic unit is the Kwacha, divided into 100 Ngwee. There are notes for 20, 50, 100, 200 and 500 Kwacha. Coins are of too little value to be useful. The rates of exchange decline steadily. In late 1994 it was around K 700 to US$1.00.

Customs

All valuables – such as cameras and jewellery – must be declared on entry and as personal effects are duty free, provided they are taken out again. Normal duty free allowances include one bottle of spirits and 200 cigarettes.

Diplomatic Representation

There are Zambian High Commissions or Embassies in Angola, Belgium, Botswana, Canada, China, Egypt, France, Germany, India, Italy, Kenya, Malawi, Namibia, Nigeria, Russia, Tanganyika, The United Kingdom, the USA and Zaire.

Electricity

The voltage is 220-240 volts AC. Most large hotels and game lodges provide electric razor points for 110 volt appliances.

Gratuities

Officially tips are disapproved of. In practice a 10 percent service charge is included in bills and hotel or restaurant staff appreciate a small gratuity for good service, even if it is only two percent.

Health

Cholera certificates are only required if you have come from an infected area. For further health advice see the General Information.

Language

English is the official language and is widely spoken.

Postage

Ordinary internal letters cost K100. Airmail letters abroad K350.

Passports and Visas

All visitors need a passport. British Commonwealth and Irish citizens do not need visas; US citizens do. Visas must be obtained in advance (see Diplomatic Representation above), though tourist visas are normally available at the point of entry.

Public Holidays

New Year's Day, Youth Day (March 12) Good Friday, Easter, Labour Day (May 1), Africa Freedom Day (May 25), Heroes' and Unity Day first Monday and Tuesday in July, Farmers Days (first Monday in August), Independence Day (October 24), Christmas Day.

Shopping and business hours

Most shops open from 0800 to 1700 Monday to Friday. Government offices also keep the same hours. On Saturdays shops and supermarkets open from 0800 to 1300.

Telephones

Coin boxes are few. Post offices have them and you can buy phone tokens. On subscriber lines direct dialing is available to major towns and internationally, though the functioning of the system can be erratic. The code for Zambia from outside the country is 260, followed by 1 for Lusaka, 2 for the Copperbelt towns, 3 for Livingstone.

Time

Two hours ahead of GMT, seven hours ahead of eastern USA.

Tourist Offices

See Information paragraph early in this chapter.

Conical tower at Great Zimbabwe Ruins

Zimbabwe

The Country

It is difficult not to become enthusiastic about Zimbabwe, for the country has practically everything. To start with, it's cinemascopic. A Canadian comments 'The greatest shock is that initially it looks and feels more like Florida than Africa'. Outside the towns your field of vision widens perceptibly – and it only takes a 15 minute drive in any direction to be in open veld. The air – even in the cities – is clean and fresh and generally the cities themselves are well maintained.

There are the exotic wonders of the Victoria Falls, the Zambezi and Lake Kariba in the north west almost alongside the big game bushveld of the Hwange National Park; the ruins of Great Zimbabwe are on the way south to imaginative projects in the lowveld; and the dramatic mountains of the eastern highlands, have inspired writers from Rider Haggard to Wilbur Smith. Virtually the whole of Zimbabwe is more than 300 m (975 feet) above sea level and much of it is on a higher plateau, ensuring an unusually fresh climate. Its 390,245 sq km (152,439 sq miles) make it three times the size of England.

Broadly, the area around Harare is the richest farmland; but across the country there is cattle ranching, tobacco farming, fruit farming and forestry; and sugar is grown in the lowveld. Many small mines yield copper, emeralds and chrome, titanium and other minerals, while Zimbabwe is the world's third largest exporter of gold.

However tourism is now second only to tobacco as a business and the 1990s have significantly broadened the activities available, from island lodges on Lake Kariba to adventurous white-water rafting on the Zambezi rapids. The varied landscapes and abundant wildlife make the Zambezi valley, Lake Kariba, the Victoria Falls and Hwange the most immediately rewarding areas to explore, though the mountains of the eastern districts, from Nyanga to Chimanimani, have a cool beauty that differs somewhat from usual perceptions of Africa.

Climate and Clothing

The climate is classified as 'temperate'. Actually, summer lasts eight months of the year, with daytime temperatures averaging 25°C to 30°C. In winter (May to August), warm clothing is generally necessary only at night or in the early morning, although frosts are not unknown on the highveld. Zimbabweans, however, tend to divide the year into two seasons; the rainy season and the dry season. The rains begin usually after the hottest month (October) and continue intermittently until the end of March. Because of the rains the best season for game-viewing and travelling is April to October. Rainfall in the low-lying areas varies from 152 to 254 mm (six to ten inches) a year, and in the highlands from 500 to 1,000 mm (20 to 40 inches). One point about clothing is that in Harare people do wear a jacket and tie, and often a suit, when they go out in the evening. If you have local introductions and expect hospitality in the cities, or are staying at top hotels, then you should be prepared. But Safaris are as relaxed as anywhere else.

Safaris Clothes
Safari clothing is on sale locally. Look for one excellent Zimbabwean product, the Courteney safari boot. These double-stitched gameskin boots are tough and comfortable.

History

The history of Zimbabwe was not chronicled in writing until the middle of the 19th century. The ruins and artefacts of Great Zimbabwe point to a well-organised state in the fifteenth century, and Portuguese explorers of the sixteenth century related contacts with a paramount ruler with the title of Monomatapa. Certainly leaders from here colonised further south, as both ancient ruins in the northern Transvaal similar architecturally to Great Zimbabwe and trees indigenous to Zimbabwe show. Overall, this was the seat of a powerful empire. In the early nineteenth century a branch of the Zulus, the Ndebele, were forced north by the Voortrekkers in South Africa and settled in what became known as Matabeleland, holding their northern neighbours, the indigenous Mashona, as vassals (a situation neatly reversed by the Independence elections). Even so it was left to the ivory hunters of the mid-nineteenth century, such as Hartley and Selous, to draw the attention of the outside world to the unknown interior north of the Limpopo; while subsequently the great ambitions of Cecil Rhodes prompted settlement and so development.

Cecil Rhodes
A hero to some, an expropriator to Africans, Cecil Rhodes was an extraordinary individual. He made his fortune from Kimberley diamonds, then sent himself to Oxford University (where he later founded the Rhodes Scholarships). He established the frontiers of Zimbabwe and his bones lie in the Matopo hills to this day. When he was only 36, in 1890, his British South Africa Company obtained a concession to exploit mineral resources from the Matabele King, Lobengula, and sent a pioneer column to move up from the Cape Province. This armed company effectively annexed Mashonaland and began to settle Europeans on the land. In 1896 the Matabele and Mashona tribes rose in rebellion but were crushed by the settlers. Thus began the European domination of what became known as Southern Rhodesia. The country was legally divided into white and

409

black areas to the great disadvantage of the Africans. White settlers came from South Africa and the United Kingdom, farming and small-scale mining became well established, and railways, roads and secondary industry followed. As time went by the settlers generally achieved a high standard of living.

The Independence Struggle
The British Government granted internal self-government to the settlers in 1923, and did not concern itself actively with the political development of the country until 1953, when the Federation of Rhodesia and Nyasaland was created, uniting present-day Zambia, Malawi and Zimbabwe. The decade of federation brought increased prosperity, but it foundered on the other two colonies' mistrust of the Rhodesians and was dissolved in 1963. Eventually the white government declared itself unilaterally independent in 1965.

A war resulted, as the guerilla armies of the two African nationalist parties, ZANU and ZAPU, headed by Robert Mugabe and Joshua Nkomo, struggled for universal suffrage. It was a tough and often bloody fight, known to Africans as the Chimurenga War. The United Nations imposed trade sanctions against Rhodesia. In 1979 the whites, although not defeated militarily in the field, were forced to negotiate with Britain and the General Election of 1980 returned Robert Mugabe's Zimbabwe African National Union – Patriotic Front (ZANU-PF) party to power. Zimbabwe became independent on April 17, 1980. The Parliament sits in Harare (formerly Salisbury) and Mr Mugabe is the executive president. Although theoretically a believer in Marxism, he has taken a pragmatic line. White settlers continue to farm and be involved in business; and the role of private enterprise is now expanding, especially in tourism.

The People

In 1994 the total population was 10,500,000, including around 100,000 Europeans and 11,000 Asians. Tribally the African people are divided into less than one quarter Matabele, who largely live in the south, and three quarters Mashona. Population growth is above three percent annually. Post-independence international aid has not reached expectations, and there is high unemployment. Nevertheless, Zimbabwe retains a fairly strong economy, has relaxed its exchange controls, maintains its roads and facilities well, and is competently governed.

Zimbabweans of all races are friendly and hospitable to visitors. Don't hesitate to ask strangers for help at any time. Ninety-nine times out of a hundred, they will be delighted. There is no racial discrimination and considering the long history of white supremacy, race relations are surprisingly relaxed; though politics is a good subject to stay off.

Communications

Internal travel is detailed in the 'Factfile'. Broadly, Harare is the centre for air and road routes, and Bulawayo for rail ones. Scheduled Air Zimbabwe services link the main towns. The railways serve all main towns, but are slow; the most useful service is the overnight one between Harare and Bulawayo. Coaches link Harare with the Midlands, Bulawayo and Mutare. Local bus services are worth using if you are on a tight budget and in no hurry.

National Parks and Game Reserves

'Wildlife Estate' is a favourite phrase for the 44,170 sq km (17,254 sq miles) of Zimbabwe set aside as national parks, botanical reserves, historic places, sanctuaries and recreation areas. They total 11 percent of the country's area and include some of the finest wildlife and scenic assets of the African continent.

There is only ever going to be one Victoria Falls, while the Hwange National Park of 14,650 sq km (5,722 sq miles) is one of Africa's greatest remaining elephant sanctuaries. Smaller parks like Mana pools on the Zambezi river below the Kariba dam and Matusadona, on Lake Kariba, also have exceptional wildlife. Overall, the National Parks do a noteworthy job of conserving Zimbabwe's wildlife heritage, not least by taking armed action against poachers – but they have a problem. Park entry fees only cover visitor services, not the high costs of animal management, for which they depend on the government. The solution may be managerial independence, so that they can attract World Bank aid. In 1995 most Parks charged non-residents Z$20.00, just about US$3.00.

The National Parks HQ is located some five km from the centre of Harare in Sandringham Drive, off Borrowdale Road. All bookings can be made there or by mail to Box 8151, Causeway, Harare (tel 706077). The Bulawayo address is Box 2283 (tel Bulawayo 63646).

Park Accomodation
Most parks have self-catering accomodation in lodges, cottages or chalets, where bed linen and cooking facilities are provided, at very reasonable rates. In 1995 a cottage sleeping four cost Z$100.00 per night. There are also caravan parks and campsites. These cost Z$10 per person, with ablutions and barbecues. It is advisable to book well

411

in advance. Pets are not allowed in the parks and you must be in camp by sunset. Increasingly parks also have privately-run lodges adjacent to them, like the Hwange Safari Lodge, or Fothergill Island, offshore from the Matusadona. Charges in these lodges are very substantially higher – see 'Factfile'.

Safaris

Safari Tours
In touring and photographic safari terms far and away the largest organisation is UTC which as United Touring International has British and American offices at Travel House, Springvilla Park, Springvilla Road, Edgeware, London HA8 7EB; tel 0181 905 6525; and UTI Inc, 400 Market Street, Suite 260, Philadelphia PA 19106-2551; tel 215 923 8700. UTC's head office in Zimbabwe is in the Travel Centre on the corner of Jason Moyo Avenue and Third Street, Harare (PO Box 2914; tel 792792, fax 735080). Typical safaris run from day game viewing trips from Victoria Falls to five-day canoeing on the Zambesi, and seven-day game viewing safaris. These will usually be in up-to-date minibuses.

Air Safaris
Air Safaris are run by Air Zimbabwe, under the title 'Flame Lily Holidays'. These use hotels and scheduled air services at Victoria Falls, Hwange, Kariba and elsewhere, and are good value. UTC also offer air tours. Air charters are run by Executive Air at Charles Prince airport (tel 302248). United Air (tel 731 7113, fax 52245) at the international airport, Zambezi Air Services (tel 302076, fax 304871) and others. Air charter can work out cheaper than flying by airline, if you can fill your plane's seats.

Rail Safaris
Train excursions, which utilise beautifully equipped vintage rolling stock, run from Bulawayo to the Victoria Falls, with game viewing en route. They have already been mentioned under the Great Trains on page 15. Their 'Enthusiast Expresses' last up to ten days.

Specialised Itineraries
A number of firms offer specialised, tailor-made, itineraries. UTC does this and so do Abercrombie & Kent, who combine Zimbabwe with Zambia and Botswana. Their Harare office is at 64 Union Avenue; (PO Box 2997; tel 759930, fax 759940). Their London office is at Sloane Square House, Holbein Place, London SW1; tel 0171 730 9600. Quite a number of local firms operate out of Victoria Falls. One seasoned manager commented caustically 'Anyone with a Land Rover and a pair of veldschoen calls himself a safari firm. 'There is some truth

in this. The good operators include Landela Safaris (PO Box 293, Kopje, Harare; tel 734043, fax 750785), who have their own lodges as does Touch the Wild (Private bag 6, PO Hill Side, Bulawayo; tel (19) 74589, fax 44696), in Hwange and the Matapos, and Run Wild at 55 Baker Avenue, Harare (PO Box 6485; tel 792333, fax 792343). Others are mentioned in the areas where they operate. A reliable travel agent for arranging individual safaris is Zambezi Trails at Suite 318 in Meikles Hotel, Harare (PO Box 825; tel 723719). They are associated with Safari Consultants in England.

Canoeing and Walking Safaris
Shearwater Adventures, the originators of white water canoeing and rafting on the Zambezi. Shearwater also represent Afro-Ventures of Johannesburg's overland trips. Their Harare office is in Edward House on the corner of First Street and Baker Avenue (tel 757831).

Golf Tours
Zimbabwe's excellent golf courses provide the basis of specialised itineraries, for instance by Run Wild above.

Professional Standards
The qualifications for becoming a professional guide are not easily obtained. They require a two-year course and a very detailed knowledge of wildlife. Quite a few young white Zimbabweans have become guides. Couriers, like tour bus drivers, are less highly qualified.

Staying on Farms
Many farms and ranches, often with plentiful wildlife, have facilities for visitors. Contact Farm Stays, tel 04 703978.

Hunting
Hunting has been dealt with in the general 'Safaris and Hunting' section at the beginning of the book.

Accommodation

Zimbabwe has a good network of both urban and country hotels and many have recently been refurbished. Zimbabwe Sun run hotels and lodges all over the country, including the famous Victoria Falls Hotel. The central booking address is 99 Jason Moyo Avenue, Harare (Box CY 1211, Causeway; tel 737944). The South African company, Cresta, is building up a chain of hotels.

Price are complicated by there being a two-tier system, giving a visitors' rate in US dollars, and a much lower residents' rate in local

Zimbabwe

currency. Visitors must normally pay in foreign exchange and major credit cards are accepted.

Youth Hostels, Backpacking and Campsites
There are two Youth Hostels Association offices. The Harare office is at 6, Chinamano Avenue; tel 796436. The Bulawayo office is at White Hollows, 52 Townsend Road; tel 76488. Young people get a real welcome in Zimbabwe and as well as youth hostels there is often cheap municipal camping available, as at Victoria Falls. A board at the domestic airport terminal advertises cheap accommodation. The Victoria Falls is the main backpacking centre - see that section.

Health

Don't take chances with malaris; supermarkets and pharmacies stock prophylactic tablets. AIDS is widespread. The tap water in towns is safe and bottled water is on sale. Remember that lakes and rivers are infected with bilharzia. This is a micropscopic organism in the water that gets into the body through cuts or scratches, causes blindness and can be fatal if untreaded. Emergency air and road ambulance services are operated by MARS (see Advertisement). Insurance for evacuation to a suitable medical facility costs US$18.00 for two weeks. Tours operators can arrange cover.

Harare

Telephone code 4. Tourist Info 705085.
The capital of Zimbabwe, set 1,478 m (4,850 ft) above sea level, is a clean, well laid out modern city, where blue skies and flowering trees soften the lines of the high rise blocks, which soar beside old colonial buildings. In Unity Square, site of the first pioneer encampment on September 12, 1890, and still the city's focal point, the jacaranda trees create a beautiful blaze of mauve in October. Other flowering trees, like scarlet flame trees, bauhinias and flamboyants, line the avenues north of the city, and the suburbs are remarkably attractive. Roughly speaking, Harare's north-south roads are numbered while the east-west roads are avenues. But their most astonishing aspect is the lack of crowds and traffic.

Information

The Harare Publicity Association (PO Box 1483; tel 705085) is on Unity Square and is remarkably helpful, not least with accommodation lists. The head office of the Zimbabwe Tourist Development Corporation (PO Box 8052, Causeway; tel 793666) is on the corner of Fourth Street and Jason Moyo Avenue. The Wildlife Society of Zimbabwe (tel 700451) is well worth consulting at its Wildlife Centre in the Monomatapa Hotel. The City Air Terminal is on Third Street and Speke Avenue, close to Unity Square.

For a stimulating and highly informative update on facilities and safaris seek out the monthly Travellers Times newpaper (tel 794106).

Hotels and Eating Out

Hotel rooms are at a premium in Harare and advance booking is essential. Unless you have good reason for staying in the capital it is better to avoid the expense and go straight to your destination. There are 16 graded hotels, plus many unregistered hotels and boarding houses. A listing of most is obtainable from the Publicity Association.

Unquestionably the best known is the five-star Meikles (PO Box 594; tel 795655), established on the corner of Third Street and Stanley Avenue since 1915, though totally rebuilt it still has a period feeling. The other five-star hotels are the towering 200 room Monomotapa, which has a shopping arcade, hairdresser and cafeterias (Zimbabwe Sun), and the Sheraton (PO Box 3033; tel 729771, fax 728450) on Jason Moyo Avenue. The four-star Cresta Jameson (PO Box 2833; tel 794641) is a well-known landmark. The Holiday Inn (PO Box 7; tel 795611) is also four-star and conveniently located. Three-star hotels are a third cheaper than four-star ones. Recommended are the Ambassador on Union Avenue (PO Box 8712; tel 708121) and the Cresta Oasis (PO Box 1541; tel 704217). Nor should you ignore suburban hotels, since they are not far out and tariffs are lower again. The Landela Lodge (tel 734043, fax 750785) is now on safaris circuits. The Red Fox (PO Box 11628; tel 45466) is an old-English style two-star hotel which serves pub lunches and is five km out on Greendale Avenue. For really cheap rooms and hostels get the Publicity Association's list of Lodges.

Restaurants

You are well served for restaurants in the city. Standards are high and prices reasonable, except in the five-star environment. Beefsteak is almost a national dish and is on most menus. Recommended restaurants are the Le Francais (tel 302706) at The Arts Centre, Avondale; the Carvery (tel 702484) on Fifth Street and Fife Avenue for beef; the Manchurian (tel 36166) on Second Street for stir-fry Chinese food; and the Cellar (tel 726598) in the Marimba Shopping Centre, reckoned the top place by many locals. For game meat as well as conventional food go to the Ramambo Lodge (tel 792029) in a gallery on the corner of Samora Machel and Leopold Takawira Avenue. The big hotels all have their restaurants, often with music. Local wines, for instance the Emerald Steen, are quite drinkable.

Nightlife

Restaurants which provide music for dancing include La Fontaine disco at Meikles and the Twelve Thousand Horsemen at the Monomatapa, which has a cabaret. Several nightclubs serve meals. The best are the Archipelago and Marilyn's.

Shopping

The main shopping streets are the First Street pedestrian mall, Baker Avenue, and Jason Moyo Avenue. Local buys include semi-precious

Zimbabwe

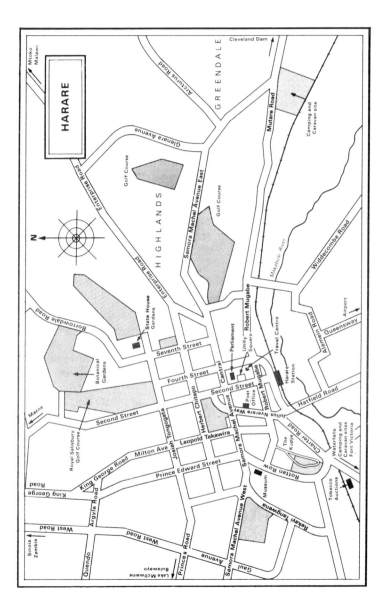

417

stones, stone and ebony carvings, skins, and decorative copper bowls, trays and souvenirs. Local Sandawana emeralds retain brilliant colour even in very small stones.

Get The Workshop's illustrated Harare map to find your way around. It marks and more interesting shops, like Rodo Arts and Jairos Jairi for crafts.

Museums

The Museum is at the Civic Centre and has an excellent wild life section, while archaeological and historical galleries illustrate the history of man in Zimbabwe from the earliest times. The National Gallery is a modern art centre, with a permanent collection and a workshop school of African art, which has received wide acclaim and offers some work for sale.

Transport

Car hire and driving is dealt with in the Factfile. Harare hire firms include Hertz (tel 793701) and Europcar (tel 706484). The long distance coach terminal is on Speke Avenue. Local buses are erratic and crowded. For advice or city tours go to the World Travel Bureau at 95 Stanley Avenue (tel 702831).

Sport

The city has 14 well-kept golf courses, including the championship-rated Royal Harare, close to town and the Chapman. Bowls, tennis and squash are available; Borrowdale has racing most Saturdays.

Places to See

This part of Zimbabwe is mostly fairly flat, though sprinkled with rock topped *kopjes*, or small hills, typical of the great Central African plateau. You should take a trip to Harare Kopje, from which you get a panoramic view of the city, where the perpetual Independence flame was lit on April 18, 1980. Skipper Hoste Drive leads out to it.

Chapungu Sculpture Park
Eight km out of the city, off the Mutare road, is an outdoor display of contemporary stone sculpture, where you can watch sculptors at work and there is a garden restaurant. It is open every day.

Snake Park
Fourteen km (nine miles) out of Harare on the Bulawayo road, the Snake Park adjoins the Harare Motel, with snakes from the non-

poisonous to the deadly.

Larvon Bird Garden
Also on the Bulawayo road, some 17 km (ten miles) out, is the Larvon
Bird Garden where there are 400 indigenous species of bird life
housed in well-tended aviaries and enclosures. The birds range from
the small Heughlin's Robin to majestic eagles, huge vultures and the
African ostrich, while waterfowl inhabit a natural lake.

Lake Chivero Park
Thirty-five km (22 miles) towards Bulawayo via the A5 road is
Harare's playground, Lake McIlwaine, where you will find yachting,
water skiing and fishing. The two-star Hunyani Hills Hotel (tel 172
236) is on the northern shore, as are tea rooms. Arrangements can be
made to go by motor launch to the notable Bushman rock paintings.
The lake is part of the 61 sq km (23 sq mile) Chivero Recreational
Park, including a lion and cheetah park and a small game park, part of
which can be traversed on foot. There are duiker, steenbuck, reedbuck, oribi, zebra, eland and the whole area is ideal for bird watching;
200 species have been recorded in a single weekend. For enquiries
on the self-catering park accommodation, camping and fishing in the
Park contact the Warden, Private Bag 962, Norton; tel 260 171.
Accommodation bookings are through the National Parks (see above).
Don't swim in the Mermaid's Pool; you could get bilharzia.

Ewanrigg Botanical Garden
Forty km (25 miles) north-east of Harare is Ewanrigg, a 283 ha botanical garden of aloes, cycads and cacti, no longer unique in Southern
Africa, but still a very good place for a picnic and a beautiful sight all
the year round. The best time to go is in June to August when the
aloes are in full flower. The cycad is a palm-like, prehistoric plant, described in our special article on page 74.

Mazowe Valley
Another 40 km (25 mile) journey, north of Harare by the A11 road,
brings you through attractive hills to the rich Mazowe Valley, fed by
streams and the Mazowe Dam. You will see rolling acres of citrus trees
on the local estates, founded more than 80 years ago.

Domboshawa and Chinhoyi Caves
If you are spending a few days in Harare, do not miss the opportunity
of visiting Domboshawa and the beautiful Chinhoyi caves. Domboshawa is about 32 km (20 miles) north-east of the city, with fine
views from the top of the large granite hill from which the area takes
its name. A cave on the eastern slopes contains many Bushman
paintings.

Zimbabwe

The Chinhoyi caves are about 128 km (80 miles) from Harare on the A1 road to Kariba. It is an easy hour and a half's drive. You pass through the town of Chinhoyi and six km (four miles) further on fork right to the Chinhoyi Caves Recreational Park. The caves are not very big, but they are breathtaking. The focal point is the Sleeping Pool, actually a limestone cavern, the roof of which has collapsed giving the appearance of a natural shaft. The water is at least 91 m (300 ft) deep and the light gives it a magnificent deep blue colour. The main entrance to the caves takes one down an inclined passage, or one can venture down steps that reach it through the Dark Cave. The caves were traditionally used as a retreat by the Mashona Chief Chinhoyi. Today there is a hotel and restaurant by them.

Iwaba Wildlife Estate

Down in the Midlands, though only three hours drive from Harare in the district where Frederick Selous first appreciated the wealth of Zimbabwe's wildlife, is a new 10,000 ha nature reserve. The Iwaba estate is in the Munyati valley and shelters species from elephant to buck and leopard. Night game drives, bird walks and hiking trails are among the facilities. Accommodation is in thatched rondavels. Iwaba is reached via the A5 road to Kewkwe and can be booked through Abercrombie & Kent (tel 4 759930).

The Zambezi and Victoria Falls

The western corner of the country not only contains one of those spectacles you have to see - the Victoria Falls - it is also has one of the continent's largest elephant populations in the huge Hwange National Park; while running up the border with Zambia is the often tumultuous Zambezi river and on it Africa's second largest artificial lake, Kariba. Not surprisingly the town of Victoria Falls has become a safari centre not only for Zimbabwe, but also for northern Botswana the Caprivi Strip, and Southern Zambia.

Getting to Victoria Falls

Victoria Falls has direct South African Airways flights from Johannesburg, Air Botswana flights from Maun, and Air Namibia flights to Tsumeb (for Etosha) Katima Mulilo and Windhoek. The town is well served by local transport, with daily scheduled air services calling at Kariba and Hwange en route; the rail line from Bulawayo; and good roads used by UTC and other tour firms. Or, if you have enough time, you could take the lake ferry from Kariba to Mblibizi, at the western end of the lake. This fascinating 22 hour voyage starts from Kariba at 0900 on Mondays, returning from Mlibizi at 0700 the next day. However, it does not always run to schedule.

Victoria Falls

Telephone code 13. Tourist Info 4202.

For such a tourist focal point the town of Victoria Falls is surprisingly small, although some of its facilities are out along the Zambezi. The main street, Livingstone Way, is actually part of the road through to Zambia, via the Victoria Falls bridge. The railway also loops through the town on its way to the bridge, which was crucial to Rhodes' 'Cape to Cairo' rail link dream and was completed in 1907. Appropriately the station is by the Victoria Falls hotel. Everything you need is within walking distance of the main shopping centre on Livingstone Way, where the Post Office, banks, the Air Zimbabwe air terminal (tel 4518), UTC, Hertz, and the Victoria Falls Publicity Association (PO Box 97; tel 4202) are located. This shopping centre is almost opposite the road to the station, while another small one is further up Livingstone Way, past the entrance to the municipal campsites and rest camps, and the craft market. In the opposite direction Livingstone Way runs down to the National Park entrance and the border post before the bridge. Overall it should take you all of twenty minutes to find your bearings in a town that is remarkably friendly to visitors. Even so, get The Workshop's nicely illustrated map.

Accommodation

Hotel accommodation has been increased significantly at the top end of the market. The Victoria Falls Safari Lodge overlooks the Zambezi National Park (PO Box 29; tel 4728, fax 4792) and Zambabwe Sun have rebuilt the Elephant Hills Casino and Country Club outside the town, overlooking the Zambezi and with its own golf course. However, the celebrated Victoria Falls Hotel (PO Box 10; tel 4751 or Zimbabwe Sun reservations) is not going to be eclipsed in a hurry. A graceful example of colonial architecture, within sight of the spray rising above the falls, its recent guests have included Prince Edward, the youngest son of Queen Elizabeth II; and Clint Eastwood, the film actor. So it is a hard act to beat, even if the hotel does struggle a little to maintain its standards.

Other hotels, all with air-conditioned rooms and swimming pools, include the four-star Makasa Sun (PO Box 90; tel 4275), with its casino is the closest to the falls; a three-star family hotel, the Rainbow (PO Box 150; tel 4585); and the worthwhile two-star Sprayview (PO Box 70; tel 4344), which is in the town with motel-type rooms around a large pool. Additionally the municipal campsite and the adjoining rest camp, just off Livingstone Way, are clean and very cheap.

Sports and the River Festival

The Elephant Hills golf course, designed by Gary Player, is being re-opened. Other serious sports are canoeing and white-water rafting, described in a moment, not to mention bungee jumping off the Victoria Falls Bridge. The Zambezi River Festival in October incorporates many events.

Shopping
The craft village is an overblown attraction. You can do better in the local shops, while vendors coming across from Zambia also sell artefacts like copper bracelets set with malachite, though hawkers can be a pest. It is worth bargaining.

Entertainment
The craft village is also the scene of traditional dancing most nights. There is a crocodile ranch, where you can buy crocodile skin articles. The casino offers roulette, blackjack, and slot machines; but you must play with foreign currency if you want to be able to take your winnings out of Zimbabwe.

Excursions
Two of the best local excursions are the well-known 'Flight of the Angels' air trip over the falls and river cruises. There are both standard launch cruises up the river to Kandahar Island and more exotic dawn champagne breakfasts, lunch cruises and sundowners, with the boat landing at an island. Any travel agent can fix these, notably UTC (tel 4267). Further afield UTC can take you to the Chobe National Park in Botswana for an overnight game viewing trip, while the Zambezi National Park is described below. Many visitors go across into Zambia for a day to see Livingstone (see Zambia chapter) and this is fairly hassle-free, though you need a passport and foreign currency. You can hire bicycles for such a trip in the town opposite the main shopping centre. Abercrombie & Kent, who brought Prince Edward here, have an office at 299 Rumsey Road (tel 4264) and a desk in the Victoria Falls hotel. Touch the Wild's phone is 4694. There are numerous other operators organising everything from birding to horse riding. Needless to say, the area's two big attractions are the falls themselves and the Hwange National Park, with various small private game-viewing lodges around it.

The Victoria Falls National Park

The falls are one of the greatest natural wonders of the world, second only to Niagara in size. They are created by the Zambezi river, the only major African river to flow eastwards into the Indian Ocean, plunging from its flood plain in Zambia into a 150 million years old fault, eroded by the water into its present shape. This rent in the earth is from 70 to 108 m (350 ft) deep and 1,700 m (one mile) wide.

Livingstone

David Livingstone was the first white man to see this mighty cataract, having been taken by local Africans to investigate the clouds of spray which are visible from 20 miles away. He wrote in his daily journal, in November 1855, 'scenes so lovely must have been gazed upon by angels in their flight'. Local Africans call the falls 'Mosi-oa-Tunya' or 'the smoke that thunders'. They do so with reason. When the river is in spate the clouds of spray rise 500 m (1,600 ft) into the sky and the falling water creates a continuous rumbling roar. In October, at the end of the dry season, nearly four million gallons a minute pour over. High water starts in mid-December and at the height of the flood, in April, 100,000,000 gallons descend and you can only glimpse the falls every few seconds as the spray parts. So the best time for seeing them is before or after low water in November.

Seeing the Falls

There are a series of vantage points along the cliff opposite the falls, which is the other side of the geological fault, from which the river escapes via a zigzag of ever-deepening gorges. These are likely to be irremediably changed if a planned dam further down in the Batoko Gorge is constructed, but the falls will not be, though they are threatened by a second bridge. Do not forget a plastic mac, because you'll get soaked, especially when the flow is high.

From the National Park entrance off the main road to the bridge and the border post you come to Livingstone's statue and the Devil's cataract. Near the statue is a famously huge baobab, 20 m (67 ft) in circumference, known as the Big Tree, and now fenced off. Another path leads to the viewing route. The falls are always slightly frightening – that torrent of raging water is an elemental force – but if you feel adventurous you can descend near the statue via the chain-assisted path to a point one third of the way down the gorge. Alternatively, having seen the cataract and probably a rainbow at its foot, you can follow a pebble-paved walkway along the top of the cliff. The falls' length is divided by rock outcrops and low islands.

Sequence of the Falls

Separated from Devil's Cataract by Cataract Island are the 731 m (half-mile) Main Falls. Beyond them are Livingstone Island and the crescent-shaped Horseshoe Falls. Then comes the highest of the cataracts, Rainbow Falls, which plunge from a height of 108 m (355 ft) and are the next widest to the Main Falls. A depression in the lip of the cliff, known as the Armchair, occurs below the last section, which is the 101 m (333 ft) Eastern Cataract.

Opposite the Main Falls the spray has created a thick tropical rain

423

forest, a tiny area of African jungle. A short distance beyond it you emerge on to grassland, where you can either follow straight on to Danger Point, or bear right for a sight of the Victoria Falls bridge. Danger Point is at the end of the cliff, below which the Zambezi churns through the whirlpool of the Boiling Pot and into the narrow gorge separating Zimbabwe from Zambia. Looking down you may well see groups of rafters edging their craft into the water.

White-water Rafting and Canoeing
The rapids in the gorges are numbered up to 19. Three companies organise rafting, through the gradings of one to six for the difficulty of rapids – with six being unrunnable – means that rafts must be portaged around rapid nine. On the Zambia side Sobek (tel 260 3 321432) starts at the Boiling Pot. On the Zimbabwe side Shearwater, who operate from Soper's Arcade in the town (PO Box 125; tel 4471) run some or all the 22 km (14 miles) of rapids four to 24 in their 16 ft rubber inflatables. This is 'very much a participating sport', though no experience is needed, so long as you follow the oarsman's orders. The season is July 1 to the end of March depending on the rains.

Canoeing upstream of the falls is also an exhiliarating, and less hazardous, experience. (see below).

The Upper Zambezi

If you are staying at Victoria Falls you should not miss touring in the Zambezi National Park, which is bounded by the river and covers 565 sq km (221 sq miles) of big game country. Beyond it, towards Kazungula and the Botswana border post, and occupying this whole corner of Zimbabwe upstream of Victoria Falls, is the Matetsi Safari Area, so there is a lot of game around. Although the main road goes through it, the Matetsi is private concession land, in which safari and fishing camps have been established.

Zambezi National Park
Within the park there are almost 128 km (80 miles) of scenic and game viewing roads, reached via the Park Way from Victoria Falls, and including the Zambezi Drive. The self-catering National Park accommodation is in a camp at the gate close to Victoria Falls town. There are designated stopping places for fishing along the river. Fishing permits are required and bream and the fighting tiger fish are likely catches. In the park you will have every chance of spotting elephant, lion, hippo and crocodile, as well as such rare birds as night herons, Pels fishing owls and African skimmers.

The Chamabonda Drive in the southern half of the park is reached from a turn-off on the Victoria Falls to Bulawayo road. In this beautiful bush country, you have outstanding opportunities to see elephant, buffalo, eland, kudu, waterbuck, impala, bushbuck, zebra and giraffe, as well as some of the finest and largest herds of sable antelope in Africa today. Lion, leopard and cheetah are occasionally seen. The drive is normally open May to November.

The Matetsi Safari Area
Several private camps in the Matetsi area offer canoe and river bank game watching, as well as fishing. The most exclusive is Vakatsha Lodge (PO Box 147, Victoria Falls; tel 433521), run by a very experienced guide called Piers Taylor. The camp has five thatched cottages, a pool and is 45 minutes drive from Victoria Falls. It is not, however, on the river. The other stone and thatched camps are by the water, namely the much larger Imbabala and Westwood. Imbabala is right up by the Botswana border with 11 km of private waterfront, where the Zambezi floodplain attracts large herds of buffalo and elephant. Westwood is on the borders of the National Park with its own 120,000 acres some 40 km west of Victoria Falls. Two lodges are being built (bookings Abercrombie & Kent). The most luxurious camp in the Matetsi is the very small Acacia Palm (tel 18 255512) by the river, run by Neil and Pattie Hewlett. Other activities in this direction include one to three day white water canoeing and walking trails, organised by Shearwater and Backpackers from Victoria Falls.

Hwange National Park

The great Hwange National Park, both rivals and complements Botswana's Chobe, because elephant move from one to the other, and is among the finest elephant sanctuaries left in Africa. Furthermore, its 14,650 sq km is hard for the Zambian poachers to reach, being some way from the Zambezi and being guarded effectively. The land is basically an extension of the Kalahari, the vegetation being scrub and sparse woodland, though it is less dry and there are more trees, including teak. It is located 121km (76 miles) south east of Victoria Falls, is reached via the A8 road to Bulawayo, and has its own modern airfield alongside the road leading from the A8 to the main camp. Two scheduled flights a day in each direction link it with Victoria Falls, Kariba and Harare. Airport transfers are arranged by UTC and are flexible, since flight timings are erratic. Trains from Bulawayo and Victoria Falls stop at Dett, but during the night, so you must arrange transport in advance. UTC runs a daily bus from Victoria Falls (three hours journey) and twice – daily game viewing tours from the Hwange Safari Lodge and from Main Camp in the park.

The most visited part of this 14,600 sq km park is the north and north east, where game congregates in the May to October dry season, and there is a network of gravel roads, connecting to a central road system. Even so Hwange can be frustrating. Vehicles are not allowed off the roads, one's views of game can be absurdly distant, even from the occasional viewing platforms, and many tour bus drivers are badly informed about wildlife. Equally no-one has informed the game about the boundaries, so there can be magnificent game-viewing from private camps on land adjoining the park, while there are a few privately run camps in the south of the park, which is completely undeveloped in a tourist sense. In the dry season the animals are largely dependent on boreholes. Due to lack of funds, 25 out of 30 were inoperative by 1994. Luckily British army volunteers repaired them.

The Wildlife
Hwange's wildlife includes 107 species of animals, from the elephant to the shrew, and 430 species of birds. The elephant population is often swelled by distinctively smaller cousins entering from Chobe. Each elephant is a member of a family group whose behaviour is particularly fascinating to watch at the waterholes. Newly arrived families wait until a previous herd has left before drinking and wallowing to cover their skins with mud as a protection against biting insects. Even crocodile will vacate the water when a large herd arrives. Among other game are buffalo, impala and numerous antelope, zebra, giraffe, wildebeest and lion, the latter being more frequently seen in the northern areas, near Robins Camp (see below). Game-viewing platforms have been erected at some of the principal waterholes and provide a safe vantage point for photography.

National Park Accommodation
The park authorities run three good camps, with serviced cottages, which are very cheaply priced. Main Camp, just inside the park on the main access road, has a restaurant called the Waterbuck's Head, a shop selling basic foods, and a curio shop. The other two are in the north west. Sinamatella is on a plateau overlooking the plains near the Lukosi river. Robin's Camp is close to the Botswana border but is only open from May to October. Both have shops and Simnatella has petrol and a restaurant. Petrol is also available at Main Camp, or at the Hwange Safari Lodge, described below. All three have camp sites. The Warden's Office is at Main Camp. Bookings should be made through the Parks Board in Harare.

Private Lodges and Camps *Dete telephone code 118*
Just outside the park boundary, very near Hwange airport and the small town of Dete, is the three-star Hwange Safari Lodge (Zimbabwe Sun; tel 118 331). Well-designed, very competently managed, the hotel is in its own 250 sq km game reserve and overlooks a swampy

vlei, where the great Frederick Selous used to hunt and which attracts many animals. Inevitably the lodge is a key stopping point in most package tours. However, it is linked with two small bush camps further along vlei that are ideal if you want to get away from the crowds. These are the delightful Sikumi Tree Lodge, with its thatched rooms up on stilts so that the game wanders around below; and the Sable Valley Lodge, which received a royal accolade when Queen Elizabeth II and Prince Philip stayed there in 1991. Both are run by Touch The Wild or can be booked through Zimbabwe Sun. Touch the Wild also operates a tented camp called Makalolo, deep in the south of the national park, where in the driest and hottest months of August to October great herds of elephant come to the waterholes. Clients are met at Hwange airport for the 85 km (53 miles) drive; or you can fly in.There is now a galaxy of small private lodges, but Malakolo remains special. You need to stay at least two nights.

Kazuma Pan National Park

This small 307 sq km (120 sq miles) park on the Botswana border north of the Hwange Park has recently been made much more accessible. Its natural pans flood seasonally, attracting gemsbok, oribi and other game, while a large variety of waterfowl fly in. There is a National Parks camp and safari operators from Victoria Falls take clients there. Game viewing on foot is allowed. though you need permission, which you can get from the Warden or through your safari firm.

Lake Kariba and the Zambezi Valley

Lake Kariba, the Matusadona National Park on its southern shore and the Mana Pools National Park downstream on the Zambesi, collectively offer safari opportunities unusual in Southern Africa; even if they do come second to the Victoria Falls as an attraction. Some of the island camps and houseboats are superb; yet other facilities second rate. The best places are not designed for mass-tourism and are mercifully less developed in that sense.

Lake Kariba
Everything here, whether unexpected or banal, derives from what was the largest man-made lake in Africa until the Aswan Dam in Egypt took Kariba out of the record books. What turned 1,390 sq miles of Zimbabwe's least coveted and most inaccessible land into a long expanse of blue, island studded, water was an ambitious colonial power scheme, shared by Zambia and Zimbabwe. The blocking of the narrow gorge where the Zambezi flowed out of this vast valley would

427

provide hydro-electric power for both countries' industries. Co-incidentally the project drowned huge numbers of animals, and created a new year-round sanctuary, with fishing, water sports, and wildlife resorts on its shores.

The Lake and the Batonka Tribe
Until 1960 this remote valley was the home of the Batonka people, whose primitive huts may still be seen in the Kariba area. The Baton-kas held that the river spirit, Nyaminyami, would never allow the completion of the dam, and many refused to leave their villages until they were forced to by the rising waters. They still believe he waits, in the depths of the lake, to free the river from its bondage. Appropriately a statue of the spirit god stands by the dam viewing point.

Wildlife Rescue
Humans were not the only ones displaced by the lake as it grew. Animals were marooned on hilltops that overnight became islands, and which often disappeared altogether. One of the most challenging wildlife rescue operations ever attempted was Operation Noah in 1959/60, when all kinds of creatures, from elephants to snakes, were saved. Nonetheless at least half the animals were drowned and, gruesomely, their corpses made the water nutritious for the tiger fish and kapenta (like a whitebait) which were introduced into the new lake. But that was a long time ago and the nutrients are now stabilised, although the resilient trunks of ironwood trees still poke up from the water along the shores.

Kariba Township

Telephone code 61. Tourist Info 2328.
The township built for the dam's construction workers has become a considerable holiday centre for Zimbabweans, helped by a good road from Harare and daily scheduled flights (going on to Hwange and Victoria Falls). The town is 369 km (231 miles) from the capital. The best time for a visit is between April and September, the dry winter months. The hottest months – and they really are steaming – are October and November. Take salt tablets if you visit Kariba during the rainy season, and malaria pills whenever you go. You will see game from the moment you arrive; it is nothing odd to find a herd of buffalo on the airport road, and elephant tearing the bark off roadside baobabs. An airport transfer bus run by UTC serves all the hotels, but it is a great deal quicker to take a taxi.

The township itself is on a steep hill 270 m (1,215 ft) above the lake. It has a bank, car hire firms, a hospital, a few shops and a notable modern church. The Publicity Association (PO Box 86; tel 2328) is among the shops, while hotels are mostly scattered along the bays and inlets of the lake shore. Getting from one to another involves detours 'inland'.

Hotels
These are not of a very high standard, although friendly and with adequate English cooking. Visitors from overseas are likely to use them only en-route to the top-class camps and lodges adjoining the Matusadona National Park on the lake and the Mana Pools National Park on the lower Zambezi. But these are expensive, so Kariba township hotels are an option as a base for seeing the lake. The following all have air-conditioned bedrooms.

The two-star Lake View Inn (PO Box 100; tel 2411) has a good pool and, fine views. Some boats to Bumi Hills and the island camps – all far more rewarding places to stay – leave from the Marina jetty by the two-star Cutty Sark (PO Box 80; tel 2321), which also has cheaper rooms, without air conditioning. The Caribbea Bay Resort and Casino (PO Box 120; tel 2453) is designed as a Sardinian style village, with self-contained casitas, and a restaurant, shop, marina, swimming pools, and camp site.

Sightseeing
A day tour should include the dam wall, the crocodile farm, and the unique church of St Barbara, which was built in the shape of a coffer dam to commemorate the 86 workers who lost their lives in the construction of the dam and power station. Many were Italian engineers. For the technical, the Kariba dam is a double-curvature concrete arch, with a maximum height of 128 m (420 ft) and a crest length of 617 m (2,025 ft). It carries a wide road, and contains about 1,275,000 cubic metres of concrete. There are six flood gates, each 9.14 m (30 ft) high by 9.45 m (31 ft) wide. The capacity of the lake when full is 40,837,500 million gallons, and the length from end to end is about 281 km (175 miles). The Information Centre at the dam viewing point also sells soft drinks.

Boating and Fishing
Only from the lake itself can the character of this inland sea be appreciated. Quite apart from taking the weekly ferry the length of the lake to Mlibizi, you can hire sailing dinghies and power boats from a number of operators, learn to waterski, or join regular cruises. Cruise Kariba (tel 2697) operates afternoon and sunset cruises from the Cutty Sark Hotel. These skirt the shoreline where, particularly in the late afternoons, animals come to drink or wallow in the shallows. The most luxurious vessel is the houseboat 'Lady May', which sleeps eight. Bookings tel 4 792333. Fishing here does not require a licence

Matusadona National Park

Along the southern shore of Lake Kariba, extending west from the dramatic Sanyati river gorge to the Ume river, with several areas of drowned forest, lies the wildlife heritage of the Matusadona National Park. The park covers 1,334 sq km (521 sq miles), which has only three bush roads. Many animals saved when the valley was flooded found refuge here and it provides a spectacular and genuinely wild habitat for them, from the heavily wooded and well-watered shoreline and plain up into the hills of the escarpment. At least 1,000 elephant are here, buffalo swim out to the islands, and there are two quite distinct and exciting ways of game viewing in the park. One is by shallow-draught boat or canoe along the shore, when you can get amazingly close to the game. The other is on wilderness hiking trails, sometimes near the shore, sometimes up over the escarpment, or in the Sanyati gorge. Apart from expeditions organised by the island lodges, you can go on foot from the National Park's camps and lodges at Tashinga on the Ume river and Elephant Point. These self-catering lodges are well built and comfortable. As already mentioned, the lake is well-stocked with fish and the Sanyati area is the venue for an annual Top Ten tigerfish contest, with participants based at Spurwing Island, following some months after the Tiger Fish Tournament at Kariba in October.

Island Camps

Many private lodges and camps are set around the Matusadona, several of them exceptional in their atmosphere and facilities. The smallest and most expensive is the Sanyati Lodge, (Po Box 4047, Harare; tel 703000) on the Sanyati gorge. Next around the shore is Spurwing Island (PO Box 101, Kariba; tel 2466, fax 2301), which has thatched cottages – and also cheaper thatch-sheltered tents – as well as a 'Tree House' on the main shore, where you can game view and stay overnight, accompanied by a guide.

Fothergill Island (Private Bag 2081, Kariba; tel 2253) is a little larger and more luxurious, with a delightful upstairs bar under a huge thatch roof and a swimming pool. Clint Eastwood was based here when shooting the film 'White Hunter, Black Heart'. The lodge is named after Rupert Fothergill, who masterminded the saving of the valley's wildlife and it maintains both floating and shoreline game viewing hides, as well as organising five-day hiking trails in the park. Both Fothergill and Spurwing have a daily boat service taking about 40 minutes, leaving Kariba's 'marina' at 1200.

On the Ume river is the Tiger Bay Lodge (PO Box 102, Kariba; tel 2569): the three-star Bumi Hills Safari Lodge (Zimbabwe Sun. PO Box 41; Kariba; tel 2353), plus Zim Sun's newer Katete Hills Lodge. Bumi Hills great attraction is the houseboats it maintains in the

Water Wilderness of drowned woodland on the nearby Chiuri river; a Zimbabwe version of Kashmir, with elephants instead of the Himalayas. You can fly in by light plane from Kariba.

Mana Pools National Park

This wildlife paradise is in the Zambezi valley east of Kariba, with a great variety both of habitats and animal species, extending for 70 km (44 miles) along the river and the river terraces, and back to the escarpment, which encloses the valley. It is in one of the most prolific game areas of the whole country. This middle-Zambezi valley as a whole is home to around 12,000 elephant and 16,000 buffalo. In the 2,296 sq km (897 sq miles) of the park you will encounter large herds of both, plus lion, leopard, warthog, wild dog, zebra, nyala – rare in Zimbabwe – and sable antelope. The pools are the remains of old river channels and in the dry season animals move down to them and the river for grazing, reaching a peak concentration by October. Both the pools and the river itself are renowned for fishing, though you need to keep an eye open for crocodiles. The park is only open during the dry season, from May 1 to October 1.

Although this part of the Zambezi flood plain was accorded World Heritage status in 1984, today the black rhino is extinct here. In 1984 there were 3,500 in the Zambezi valley, in 1991 still 1,500, now none; the last mother and child were evacuated to a 'special protection' zone in 1994. Whether the poachers do come from Zambia, which is the standard excuse, or the poaching is organised within Zimbabwe, the slaughter could not be stopped by National Park staff. The protection zones have, however, saved about 350 rhino overall.

Accommodation and Trails
As well as National Parks self-catering lodges and camp sites, the main one being at Nyamepi near the river, there are several private lodges just outside the park, which organise game viewing expeditions, canoeing safaris, and fishing. One of the best is Chikwenya (PO Box 292, Kariba; tel 2525) on the eastern boundary, where the Sapi river flows into the Zambezi. The Zambezi itself is one and half km wide at this point and Chikenya's thatched chalets look down on the flood plain, with riverine woodlands above, to which the game flock. The lodge has regular air transfers from Kariba, since driving is difficult. To the west of the park by a river is Ruckomechi, run by Shearwater, also with thatched cottages. They organise both self-help canoe trails and hiking trails, staying out for three to ten days and camping, and shorter 'luxury' canoe trails. Canoe trails are also organised by UTC. From Makuti a road leads to the National Parks lodge. The private camps are accessible by road, or by boat, or by light aircraft. It you are driving it is

advisable to obtain clear directions on the route from Makuti, past Marangora, a distance of 101 km (63 miles). You must take anti-malarial precautions; also take an insecticidal spray with you to guard against tsetse fly bites.

Matabeleland

Bulawayo

Telephone code 19. Tourist Info 60867.
Travelling south east from Victoria Falls by road or rail brings you to Zimbabwe's second city, Bulawayo. This is the former stronghold of the Matabele, who were led up from South Africa in the early 19th century by the legendary King Mzilikazi. Bulawayo was the Royal Kraal of both Mzilikazi and his son Lobengula, and its name means 'Place of Slaughter'. State House, a delightful white porticoed building nearly five km (three miles) out, occupies the site of kraal, of which there is a model in the rondavel in the garden, where Rhodes once lived. The building is not open to the public, but the model is.

In the 1890's Bulawayo became a speculators' boom town among European settlers, owing to the region's natural wealth, and in 1897 the advent of the railway confirmed its position as an industrial, mining and agricultural centre. Today it is a handsome city of 880,-000 people, the terminus of train services from South Africa and a focal point for this part of the country. The shopping district is around Main Street and Eighth Avenue and the Publicity Association is by the City Hall (PO Box 861; tel 60867).

Hotels and Restaurants
The city has nine registered hotels and many more, cheaper, unregis-tered establishments and boarding houses, of which the Publicity Association can provide a list. There are several three-star hotels, including the modern Bulawayo Sun on Tenth Avenue (PO Box 654; tel 60101), the Holiday Inn (Zimbabwe Sun) and the more countrified Cresta Churchill (PO Box 9140, Hillside; tel 41016). The old and reasonably priced Selborne (PO Box 219; tel 65741), is just across from the City Hall, but is ungraded. Easily the most spectacular place to stay is Nesbitt Castle, a medieval-style stone fortress built by a for-mer Mayor at 6 Percy Avenue, Hillside (tel 42726). It is very well res-tored but three times the price of three-star hotels. The choice of eating places is fairly wide.

Transport and Safais
For a taxi ring Bulawayo 60221 or 60704. Avis (tel 68571) and
Hertz (tel 74701) hire cars. The Railway Travel Bureau is at 87 Aber-
corn Street. Local buses to Masvingo start from the City Hall on Eighth
Street. There are several travel agents in the city. And, of course, the
vintage 'Enthusiast Express' of Rail Safaris start from here; see The
Great Trains, page 14.

One personally run safari operator is N'tabazinduna Trails (PO Box 7;
tel 26011, fax 78784), owned by Brian and Carol Davies, it has its
own tiny bus lodge north of Bulawayo. For tours contact UTC (tel
61402) on the corner of George and Silundika road and 14th Street.
There are many others.

Museums
Bulawayo's National Museum in Centenary Park illustrates the history
and mineral wealth of Zimbabwe, and its wildlife section of 75,000
specimens includes the second largest mounted elephant in the
world. The Railways Museum, on Prospect Avenue and First Street,
Raylton, displays steam locomotives, rolling stock, and railway
memorabilia dating to before 1900, which have given it world-wide
recognition. The Snake Park and the Aviary are in Hillside Road.

Crafts
Contemporary ceramic sculpture and pottery is made and sold at the
Mzilikazi Arts and Craft Centre (closed weekdays). A shop famous for
Africana is the Jairos Jiri Craft shop, on the corner of Grey Street and
Selbourne Avenue.

Sports
The city's bowls, golf and tennis clubs make visitors welcome, while
there is racing every fortnight at the Ascot course close to the city. The
Bulawayo Golf Club's course along the Matsheumhlope River features
in many Southern Africa golf safaris.

Chipangali Wild Life Orphanage
Situated 23 km (14 miles) south of Bulawayo, Chipangali provides a
home for orphaned, sick or abandoned wild animals. There are lion,
leopard cheetah; many species of antelope; bush pig and warthog,
and a large collection of reptiles and birds. The Orphanage is open
daily except Mondays.

Ancient Ruins around Bulawayo
Bulawayo is in flat, sparsely wooded cattle ranching country. To the
east, off the Gweru road, in the direction of Masvingo (formerly Fort
Victoria), are three interesting sets of ruins, at Dhlo Dhlo (96 km),

Regina and Naletale, the latter having the finest ancient decorative walling yet found in Zimbabwe. Twenty-two km (14 miles) south west of Bulawayo, at Khami, are even more extensive remains, with relics displayed in a site museum. Lobengula used the main hill here for rain making. The site consists of a series of terraces and passages supported by massive granite walls, some of them overlooking the Khami dam and gorge. Building in stone began in this area over 500 years ago, while some relics from it are 100,000 years old.

Matopos National Park

The main attraction near Bulawayo, however, is the Matopos National Park, where granite hills rise out of the flat landscape, creating a 2000 sq km region of unexpectedly stark and dramatic splendour. When Rhodes reached the hills' boulder-strewn crest he exclaimed 'I call this one of the views of the world'. The hill was in fact Malindidzimu, a place sacred to the Matabele as being the home of benevolent spirits. Rhodes decided to be buried there, and the firing party, in deference to Matabele beliefs, did not discharge their rifles. In addition to Rhodes' grave and the impressive granite monument commemorating the slaughter of Major Allan Wilson and his Shangani Patrol, the hilltop is also the burial place of Sir Leander Starr Jameson, Rhodes' friend and lieutenant.

The 70 sq km (44 sq miles) park combines Malindidzimu with some of the finest examples of Zimbabwe's prehistoric rock art, a game park covering 2,500 acres, wilderness areas, and many facilities for recreation. Ask for directions to the rock paintings, which are to be found in easily accessible caves, such as *Pomongwe* (small melon), *Bambata* (to caress), and *Nswatugi* (place of jumping). Among the wildlife are wildebeest, zebra, warthog, ostrich and both black and white rhino, the latter brought from Natal. The curious balancing rock formations are the haunt of the little dassie or rock rabbit, and the agile klipspringer. In the rock's more inaccessible heights are nests of the rare black eagle. Dams within the park provide excellent bass and bream fishing, as well as facilities for boating and picnicking.

Accommodation
Down by the Maleme dam within the park is a very pleasent fully equipped self-catering lodge. This and camping sites in the park can be booked through the Park Warden Private Bag K5142, Bulawayo). There are now quite a few private lodges. The Matobo Hills Lodge (bookings Zimbabwe Sun, in a private game reserve adjoining the park and with views down the Maleme valley, set the pace originally. The Malalangwe Lodge, the Amalinda and Big Cave Lodge are all well-regarded and are similarly on private land nearby.

Southern Zimbabwe

The renowned ruins of Great Zimbabwe have become a serious tourist attraction since Independence. They and the town of Masvingo lie on the edge of the highveld, south of which you come into both fine big game country and sugar plantations in the lowveld, with the Gona re Zhou National Park on the Mozambique border. Several smaller game reserves are located on the way south, among rolling miles of granite hills and deep ravines.

Masvingo

Telephone code 139. Tourist Info 62643.

Masvingo, formerly Fort Victoria, is the country's oldest town. It came into existence because the Pioneer column of 1890 kept well east to avoid the hostile Matabele tribes on the march to Mashonaland. So instead of taking the normal trail through Bulawayo the column reached the Mashonaland plateau through Providential Pass, which drops down to the present site of Masvingo. Even today the town has kept some pioneering atmosphere and there is a small pioneer museum in one tower of the Old Fort. During World War II many Italian prisoners of war were interned in the area, and the artists among them decorated the Roman Catholic Church just outside the town, giving it a richly coloured style not often found in Zimbabwe.

The town has the two-star Chevron Hotel (PO Box 245; tel 62054) and the Flamboyant Motel (PO Box 225; tel 62005), but has declined as a tourist centre, because Great Zimbabwe – the real attraction – has its own hotel. But there is a well-run municipal camp site in a park; bookings through the Town Clerk (tel 62431). The Publicity Association on Robert Mugabe Street (tel 62643) handles information on Great Zimbabwe and Lake Kyle.

Great Zimbabwe

The magnificent walled ruins of Great Zimbabwe are 29 km (18 miles) from Masvingo and well worth seeing, especially since post-Independence research has done much to elucidate the story of a civilisation which the settlers had merely regarded as 'mysterious'. This 'lost' Shona Karanga city was the power centre of a considerable empire in the 13th to 15th centuries. It had strong connections with east Africa, particularly through Arab gold traders, and its influence was felt down into what is now the Transvaal and eastern Botswana, along the Limpopo river. Western archaeologists first heard of it after a hunter, Adam Renders, stumbled on the ruins in 1868. It is now thought to have been totally abandoned by the 18th century; and

Zimbabwe

there is still some mystery as to why the sophisticated dry stone mason's techniques seen both here and in some 150 other sites were completely forgotten.

The Enclosures

The entire site of the National Monument covers 720 ha and contains various stone walled enclosures. The oldest part is the Hill Complex, crowning a precipitous hill and reached originally by a narrow stairway, wide enough for only a single man. The Great Enclosure, built later on below the fortified hill, has a vast outer wall 11 m (36 ft) high, inside which is a solid conical tower. Whether this swelling and slightly phallic tower was associated with fertility rites among the King's wives is not known. Certainly it is an example of stonework unrivalled anywhere in sub-Saharan Africa, while the zigzag pattern along the top of the main enclosure wall does represent the 'snake of fertility', which ensures a line of descendants. To learn more visit the Site Museum, open daily, to which the totemic carved soap stone birds found in the Hill Complex have been returned. One of these birds is now the symbol of the Republic of Zimbabwe.

Near the ruins is a reconstruction of a Karanga village, which illustrates the way of life of the local people at the time of the discovery of Zimbabwe. Huts and artefacts have been painstakingly re-created, and a potter may be seen at work making pots by the ancient African method – without the aid of a potter's wheel. A popular figure here in the village is the witchdoctor, who will 'throw the bones' and tell one's fortune.

The three-star Great Zimbabwe Hotel (Zimbabwe Sun. Private Bag 9082, Masvingo; tel 62274) has reasonable prices and is within walking distance of the ruins.

Lake Kyle National Park

This park is near Great Zimbabwe on the south-eastern edge of the highveld. Centred on Lake Kyle it offers beautiful scenery, boating and fishing. The park is best known, however, for its 69 sq miles of game reserve on the lake's northern shore, where pony trails and walks are organised. There are white rhino in this reserve, plus a variety of antelope including the rare oribi, Lichtenstein's hartebeeste and nyala, plus zebra and other plains game. The park is open the whole year round, although in extremely wet conditions some of the roads may be closed. Camping and caravanning facilities and lodge accommodation are available. Contact the Warden (Private Bag 9136, Masvingo; tel 62913) or the central booking in Harare.

Mushandike Sanctuary

Mushandike, 38 km (24 miles) from Masvingo, provides fishing and

boating in lovely surroundings. Sable, kudu, waterbuck and smaller
antelope are in the vicinity. There are two National Parks' camps.

The Lowveld

South of Masvingo you come into big game country, where the towns
of Buffalo Range, Chiredzi and Triangle – all on the tarmac A10 road –
are minor centres for hunting and safaris. By road they are four and a
half hours from Harare and Buffalo Range airfield has two scheduled
flights a week. On the way are two less-accessible parks around lakes,
Bangala and Manjirenji.

Chiredzi   *Telephone code 131*
This outback township has two hotels, the two-star Tambuti Lodge
(PO Box 22; tel 2575) being 10 km out of town and the one-star Plan-
ters Inn (PO Box 94; tel 2281, fax 2345) on the main street. There are
good golf courses and local crocodile, ostrich, and sugar farms that
can be visited. There is also climbing on splendid mountains, though
on private land.

New Game Conservancies
But the big news is the establishment of the two vast conservancy
areas, Save and Chiredzi, with a gradual opening up of the lowveld to
tourists as well as hunters. Sugar was going to be the economic
saviour here, now conservation and tourism may join it, though the
wildlife suffered greatly in the 1992 drought. The town serving both
conservancies is Chiredzi, While the Gonarezhou National Park is
quite close.

The Save Conservancy
This 'living experiment' in restoring the original environment of
bushveld and woodland is creating the largest private game reserve in
Africa. By tearing down fences former cattle farmers have joined up
320,000 ha (810,000 acres) west of the Save river, which eventually
flows into the Limpopo. With the cattle trucked out, wildlife is being
brought back, including elephant from Gonarezhou. The conservancy
is four to five hours drive from Harare and can be reached from Mutare
via Birchenough Bridge, as well as by flights to Buffalo Range. There
are a number of simple camps. For details ask travel agents or call
Harare 793701.

Chiredzi River Wildlife Conservancy
This 93,117 ha (230,000 acres) of 'prime big game country' is north
of Chiredzi town along the Chiredzi river towards the Manjirenji dam,
The 1991/92 drought put paid to cattle ranching and ten farms
joined together to recreate a wildlife wilderness, into which elephant,

buffalo and rhino have been re-introduced. During the drought a capture and feeding programme ensured that a nucleus of the species already there survived, so it is now well-stocked with game, and approved by the National Parks. Now the veld is recovering and 'eco-friendly camps and lodges will start to encourage limited tourism. The conservancy is close to Buffalo Range airport.

One ranch taking visitors is the 19,238 ha (47,500 acres) Mungwezi, whose owners run a fully equipped self-catering by a river. (Bookings PO Box 297 Chiredzi; tel 2865). There is unrestricted walking and driving, horses for hire, fishing on the dam, and a game scout. Flights to Buffalo Range can be met and guided visits arranged to local attractions and to Gono-re-Zhou.

Gona-re-Zhou National Park

The name means 'place of many elephants' and this park, which is 40 km or so from Chiredzi, certainly has them. However they are very wild, due to poaching. Normally the 2,500 sq km (976 sq miles) Mabalauta section of the park in the south is open from May 1 to October 31. It has a rest camp and camping sites, near the Warden's office and run by the National Parks. In the north east corner of the park there is a very large vlei, with marvellous birdlife. Nearby the first private lodge has been built, with an airstrip. This is the Mahenye Wilderness Lodge (Zimbabwe Sun) of thatched chalets on a small island near the Save and Runde rivers. Scheduled flights to Buffalo Range are met and United Air can provide charters.

The Eastern Highlands

The highlands define Zimbabwe's eastern border with Mozambique, extending for about 350 km (219 miles) from Nyanga in the north down to the Chimanimani mountains, with a fine, cool climate. Although they possess some of the country's finest scenery of peaks, forests and grassland slopes, with almost endless possibilities for fishing, hiking, and riding, as well as good golf courses and some excellent hotels, they are little known outside Zimbabwe. Partly this is because you need a car, as the highlands are not served by Air Zimbabwe, and the train and coach services only go as far a Mutare. The Publicity ofice for the region, known as Manicaland, is in Mutare.

Nyanga National Park

This district has some of the highlands' finest scenery and sports, not to mention ancient ruins. Mt Inyangani is the country's highest mountain at 2,790 m (9,154 ft), while the contiguous Mtazazi Falls National Park has the greatest waterfall, descending a breathtaking 762 m (2,476 ft) in two stages. Among flora characteristic of the east are aloes, with the rare *aloe inyangensis* growing on the Inyangani peaks, while the dwarf massa forests clothing the westward facing slopes are a botanical curiosity. Despite its elevation, the Nyanga area is open and accessible, with delightful walks past waterfalls and along paths through fragrant pine forests, though there is little visible wildlife except for birds.

There is a strong local association with Cecil Rhodes, who donated his estate here to form the nucleus of the park after his death. His house is now a hotel, while Nyanga village is inside the park. The trout fishing has no season in the park's dams, but is limited to October 1 to May 31 in streams. Licences are obtainable from the Park Warden.

Nyanga Hotels *Telephone code 129-8*
The village has a post office and store, but most hotels are outside the park in locations exploiting the scenery. Taking them in order as you approach on the A14 from Rusape, the three-star Brondesbury Park (Private Bag 8070, Rusape; tel 129 342) has a golf course; the four-star Montclair Casino (Zimbabwe Sun. PO Box 10, Juliasdale tel 129 441), is near Juliasdale in an area with many sporting facilities; the one-star Rhodes Nyanga (Private Bag 8024N, Rusape; tel 129-8 377) is Rhodes old lodge by a lake inside the Park; and the three-star Troutbeck Inn (Zimbabwe Sun. Private Bag 2,000, Nyanga; tel 129-8), is 14 km beyond the village by the Troutbeck Lake. The quality of these hotels underlines how popular the Nyanga district is among Zimbabweans; although your stay need not be expensive. There are several Park lodges, camp sites and a Tourist Office near the Park offices, some six km before the village.

Historical Sites
You should go a short way off the beaten track to see some of the extraordinarily preserved forts, pits, enclosures, and terraces covering some 129 sq km (50 miles), especially ones near the road to the Mare dam from the Rhodes Hotel. The Van Niekerk ruins, discovered in 1905, are a single complex of 80 sq km alone. Human habitation goes back to the Stone Age, as displayed in the Nyahokwe Field Museum. Later ruins date from the Iron Age and from the time of the empire based on Great Zimbabwe, although architecturally the ruined forts and pits are different. Nyanga Fort, for instance, signed inside the park, is about 60 m in diameter and has loopholes in its stone walls that, very curiously, do not command a field of fire. What the fort does have is a splendid view, which enabled its men to send signals along the chain of other forts. The archaeology is typical of the Tonga culture.

There is a small historical museum next to the Rhodes Hotel with displays covering ancient sites, Portuguese incursions in search of gold in the 16th century, and the part played by present day leaders in the Independence struggle.

Mutare

Telephone code 120. Tourist Info 64784.
The city is set halfway along the Eastern Highlands, where the roads from Harare and Chimanimani meet. Situated among steep, wooded hills, and attractively laid out with extensive parks and wide, jacaranda-lined streets, it lays a strong claim to being Zimbabwe's most beautiful town. The setting the founders chose 1,120 m above sea level in a mountain valley is magnificent too, though it was also logical, since the valley is the gateway to Mozambique, with both road and rail lines to the lowlands beyond. The town has two golf courses and a small local game reserve.

If you are driving here from Harare, which takes about four hours, a good place to break the journey is the Halfway House, between Marondera and Rusape.

Hotels and Information
Of several hotels the three-star Manica (Zimbabwe Sun. PO Box 27; tel 64431) is on Victory Avenue; while if you want to be in the country try the two-star Inn on the Vumba (PO Box 524; tel 63818) some nine km out in the Vumba foothills, with a swimming pool. Both have a la carte menus or go to the White Horse Inn (see below). The Manicaland Publicity Association (PO Box 69; tel 64784) on Main Street provides both local and general Eastern Highlands information. Camp sites exist in the Vumba (see below). Local tour firms collect clients from their hotels.

Museum
A history of this part of the Eastern Highlands is graphically shown in the local museum on Aerodrome Road, which also has a transport gallery showing examples of horse-drawn carriages and early locomotives.

La Rochelle
Thirteen km (eight miles) from Mutare is La Rochelle National Trust, the beautiful former home of the late Sir Stephen and Lady Courtauld. Here 14 ha (35 acres) of both formal and landscaped gardens feature rare orchids, unusual trees and ornamental shrubs. There are also numerous water gardens, waterfalls and fountains, all within the setting of the forested Penhalonga Valley.

The Vumba Mountains

A few km outside Mutare a side road to the Vumba mountains begins its scenic climb, winding through steep mountains and rolling farmland. At each turn new vistas over the surrounding countryside are revealed, and various viewpoints have been created. The name Vumba means 'mist', and the sight of the mountain peaks appearing through morning clouds gives the area a fairyland quality. There are many walks and rides (horses available through hotels). However the 70 km circuit of the Vumba, mostly on gravel through banana and wattle plantations, is not as rewarding as it is made out to be.

Botanical Garden
The Vumba Botanical Garden is twenty-nine km (18 miles) out beyond the dense Bunga Forest. Its 30 ha (74 acres) of landscaped flower gardens are set within a larger area of 'natural' woodland on the eastern slopes of the mountains. Indigenous and exotic flora provide year-round colour and the hydrangeas, azaleas and fuchsias are numbered in their thousands. There is a camp site, with a swimming pool. Bookings through the National Parks. The road leads on to Leopard Rock.

Accommodation
The two-star White Horse Inn (PO Box 3193, Paulington; tel Mutare 60325) is a small country hotel, with a very agreeable atmosphere, an a la carte menu and a pool. The hotel specifies 'no jeans, tee shirts, or shorts, ties appreciated'. It is 17 km (11 miles) from Mutare. Otherwise there is the Eden Lodge (tel 62000) but what is revitalising the district is the Leopard Rock.

The Leopard Rock Hotel, damaged during the Independence war, has been lavishly recconstructed with a casino and its own 18 hole golf course in what always was a marvellous position. It is a resort in itself. bookings PO Box 1297, Harare; tel 4 60467, fax 704457. The owners spent millions on it and the price's reflect that.

Just before you reach it there is a turnoff to the intriguing Castle (Bag V7401, Mutare; tel 210320). Built during World War II by Italian prisoners of war, it is a miniature Renaissance castle, but you have to book its few rooms as a group.

Chimanimani Mountains and National Park

Driving south from Mutare on the A9 one can divert by the scenic road through Cashel to the village of Chimanimani and the rugged splendours of the Chimanimani Mountains, the peaks of which, rising to over 2,500 m (8,200 ft), dominate the eastern horizon. This is a place for ardent hikers and climbers, since access to the mountains is by foot only. But the hills should always be treated with respect as the region is subject to sudden storms and mists. Three hours' hard walk from the foot of the mountains takes you to the mountain hut accommodation, provided by National Parks, where there are separate dormitories for men and women with bunk beds and sleeping bags with linen available.

Chimanimani *Telephone code 126*
The only hotel is the one-star Chimanimani (PO Box 5; tel 511) facing the mountains. A golf course is less than a km (half a mile) away and there is trout fishing high up in the mountains. Bridal Veil Falls, just behind the village, is a favourite picnic spot, where a delicate curtain of mountain water plunges into a large pool.

Chirinda Forest
An hour's drive south of the mountains brings you to the green tea estates of Gazaland, and the Chirinda Forest Botanical Reserve. Chirinda is one of the last remaining areas of the great tropical forest which, in primeval times, covered the whole of this part of Africa. Within its cool peace you will find rich bird life and magnificent age-old trees. In spring, the ironwoods bloom with white pea-like flowers.

The stopping place for this area is Chipinge, where the one-star Chipinge Hotel (PO Box 27, tel 127 2226) is a true 'local', frequented by farmers.

Factfile

Getting There and Internal Travel

Air
Air Zimbabwe and British Airways fly to Harare from London. Air Zimbabwe and Lufthansa fly from Frankfurt. Qantas flies twice weekly from Sydney. Other airlines operating from their own countries include Air Botswana, Air France, Air Malawi, Air Namibia, Ethiopian, Kenya Airways, KLM Qantas, Royal Swazi, South African Airways, and TAP. Harare Airport is 20 minutes drive from the city and buses leave hourly from the Air Terminal, opposite Meikles Hotel. The airport departure tax of US$20 can be paid in advance at banks and airline offices. Fares vary so hugely that it is vital to consult a travel agent. Air Botswana, Air Zimbabwe, Air Namibia and South African Airways also operate regional services out of Victoria Falls. The Harare flight

enquiries telephone is 575111 Ext. 2497 or 2360 and the Victoria Falls telephone is 4316.

Airport Formalities

Procedures after checking in require your passport and exit form, then your departure tax stamp (attach it to your ticket). The business is slow, but friendly. There is a bank at Harare and the departure lounge has a bar and an adequate duty-free shop, but no restaurant. The bank is open 0830 to 2230 for currency exchange - see also below.

Rail

The service from Bulawayo to Johannesburg runs daily overnight and the 'Limpopo Express' weekly. The Bulawayo to Victoria Falls train is also daily overnight, leaving at 1900.. Rail travel to Mozambique is possible. Internal rail services link Harare with Bulawayo, and so with Victoria Falls, with Mutare, and the Midlands.

Road

Border posts are open from 0600 to 1800 daily at the road frontier crossings at Beit Bridge, for South Africa, and on the roads to Botswana via Plumtree to Francistown, and via Kazungula to Kasane. The formalities are simpler than at airports.

Domestic express coach services link the main towns. The principal operators are Blue Arrow and Express Motorways (tel Harare 720392, bookings 2 Julius Nyerere Way; tel 737438). There are local bus services in most towns, but they are crowded and infrequent.

Hitchhiking

Zimbabwe is more friendly to backpackers than many African countries. It is not hard to get a lift and most towns have clean municipal campsites.

Banks

Barclays, Grindlays, Standard Bank, Stanbic and Zimbank are the principal banks. banking hours are from 0830 to 1500 on Monday, Tuesday, Thursday, and Friday (although some country branches close at 1300); from 0830 to 1200 on Wednesday; and from 0830 to 1130 on Saturday.

Car Hire

Self-drive, 4WD and chauffeur-driven cars are available in Harare, Bulawayo, Victoria Falls, and all resorts. Avis, Hertz, and Europcar also have offices at Harare and Victoria Falls airports. Hertz have offices in the main hotels. Give 14 days notice for taking a car across the borders, e.g. to Botswana.

Currency

The unit of currency is the Zimbabwe dollar, divided into 100 cents. Early 1995 exchange rates were Z$13.00 to £1 and Z$8.00 to US$1.00. The currency has been declining in value.

Currency Regulations

Visitors may bring up to Z$250 in Zimbabwe banknotes and any amount in foreign banknotes, but must declare these on the customs declaration form at entry, as otherwise they will be allowed to re-export only US$200 in banknotes. Officially these provisions do not apply to travellers' cheques, though it is advisable to declare them as well.

On leaving you can change back Zimbabwe notes into foreign currency, provided you have a bank receipt for the exchange Zimbabwe dollars.

Customs and Entry Requirements

You may bring in used clothing and personal effects, such as cameras tape recorders etc, without duty. Consumable stores are liable to duty, but there is a duty free allowance of Z$300 worth, which includes up to five litres of alcoholic drinks (only two litres can be spirits). Families can pool their allowances. The import of citrus fruits, bananas, and tomatoes – or their plants – is forbidden, without a licence.

Firearms and ammunition require your home country's permit. You then complete a Zimbabwe form, which allows them in for a limited time.

All visitors require passports. Visas are not needed by the citizens of many countries; including Australia, Great Britain, the USA, Canada, and most Commonwealth and European nations. You should have a return ticket and sufficient funds for your stay. If you have been in yellow fever infected areas you must have vaccination certificates. See also under Health below.

Diplomatic Representation

Countries with diplomatic missions in Harare include Australia, Belgium, Canada, Denmark, Egypt, France, Germany, Great Britain, Holland, the Holy See, India, Italy, Japan, Kenya, Malawi, Portugal, Sweden, Switzerland, Tanzania, the United States, Zaire, Zambia and other neighbouring countries, including South Africa.

Zimbabwe is represented in Addis, Ababa, Beijing, Bonn, Brussels, Cairo, Canberra, Geneva, London, Moscow, Nairobi, New Delhi, New York, Ottawa, Paris, Rome, Stockholm, Tokyo, Washington and the neighbouring African Countries.

Driving

You can use your home licence, provided it is printed in English. If not it must have a certificated translation and your photograph attached. Or get an International Driving Licence, issued by the AA.

Driving is on the left. You give way to traffic coming from the right, except where intersections are controlled. It is advisable to stop at both 'stop' and 'give way' signs. Police and emergency vehicles take precedence over all traffic. If the Presidential Cavalcade, with its out-riders, approachers you must pull into the left and stop. The general speed limit is 100 kph (62 mph) on open roads and 60 kph (37 mph) in towns which takes 20c coins. There are parking meters in main towns. Traffic lights are known as 'robots'. Both tarmac and gravel roads are well-maintained.

Automobile Association
The AA of Zimbabwe (PO Box 585, Harare; tel 707021) is affiliated to the Alliance Internationale de Tourisme and provides free maps and bulletins among its services.

Vehicle Insurance
Vehicles may be imported temporarily, but must be insured against third party risks in Zimbabwe. Short term policies are available at border posts. Remember there are restrictions on taking hired cars out of neighbouring countries.

Health

Malaria prophylactics are essential at Victoria Falls, Kariba and in the Zambezi valley and the lowveld. Bilharzia is present in lakes, so be cautious about swimming. See also advice on page 415.

Hotels

The Zimbabwe Tourist Development Corporation inspects and grades all tourist hotels. Gradings are from one to five stars and establishments that are not up to standard are recorded as such in official lists. Non-residents must pay hotel bills in foreign currency. There is a constant annual increase in prices, although this has been counterbalanced by exchange rate falls. Room rates are quoted in US dollars, but meals in local currency.

Cheap hotels charge as little as Z$65 single and Z$85 double per night, bed and breakfast, and backpackers lodges around Z$30. Campsites cost Z$25, including use of ablutions. These prices include the sales tax and may not have to be paid in foreign currency. Most towns have campsites and National Parks have good self-catering cottages for four people.

Languages

The main African languages are Shona and Ndebele. The official language is English, which is spoken everywhere.

Public Holidays

New Year's Day (January 1), Good Friday to Easter Monday inclusive, Independence Day (April 18), Africa Day (May 25), Heroes' Day (August 11), Defence Forces Day (August 12), Christmas Day (December 25), and Boxing Day (December 26).

Sales Tax

A sales tax of 10 percent is incorporated by law in the price of goods and services within Zimbabwe, including hotel accomodation and travel tickets. But it is wise to check beforehand that hotels and restaurants are doing so if you are on a tight budget.

Shopping Hours

Shops are generally open from 0800 to 1700.

Telephoning

There is a trunk dialling system. The international code for Zimbabwe is 263. It can be easier to get through internationally than locally.

Time

Local time is two hours ahead of GMT.

Tourist Information

The Zimbabwe Tourist Development Corporation (ZTDC) head office is on the corner of Fourth Street and Stanley Avenue in Harare (PO Box 8092, Causeway; tel 706511).

Southern Africa's Wildlife

Here are twenty-six of the animals you are most likely to see on safari or in National Parks and Game Reserves. The 'Big Five' are buffalo, elephant, leopard, lion and rhino.

The **African Elephant** is larger than the Indian Elephant, particularly its ears. A bull weights up to 6,000 kg (six tons) and stands 4 m (13 ft) high at the shoulder. Females are smaller. The tusks can weigh over 45 kg (100 lbs) each. Elephants are intelligent, live in family groups which often join up into herds and are vegetarians, consuming half a ton of food a day. Their life span is about 60 years.

The **African** or **Black Buffalo** basically grazes on grass, though often civilisation has driven it into the forests. Buffalo stay in herds and though shy are among the most dangerous big game animals. A grown bull averages 800 kg (1,760 lbs), females slightly less, and the span of its horns can be 1,270 mm (50 ins).

The **Hippopotamus,** whose name is Latin for 'water horse', is really of the pig family. Hippos congretate in 'schools' of around 15, led by a territorial male. They spend much of their day submerged in water up to their nostrils, emerging to graze at night. A grown hippo weighs 1,500 kg (3,300 lbs) or more and can outrun a man. Hippos can be aggressive and dangerous.

The **Black Rhinoceros** is smaller than the white rhino and distinguishable by its prehensile lip and small ears. It weighs around 850 kg (1,870 lbs). A solitary animal, fond of browsing in thorn scrub, it has poor sight but good smell and hearing. Although a vegetarian it is not pacific and will charge anything, even a car or a train. Poaching the rhino for its horn has led to its becoming an endangered species. A few survive in northern Namibia, the Zambesi valley and Hluhluwe in Natal. The horns of both species are composed of tightly packed hair, not real horn. Yemenis carve dagger handles from it while in the Far East powdered horn is considered an aphrodisiac.

The **White Rhinoceros** is larger, heavier and better tempered than its cousin. However it is not white. Its name derives from the Dutch *'weit'* meaning wide, which refers to its distinctive square jaw. Only occurring around Umfolozi in Natal, animals from there have been translocated to many other reserves.

The **Giraffe,** the tallest mammal, was first discovered in Namaqualand. It grows to 5.40 m (18 ft) and can weigh 1,200 kg (2,650 lbs). It eats leaves, likes open country and is unaggressive. It can move surprisingly fast. The **Reticulated Giraffe** is so called because its markings are square, within a network of whitish lines, instead of star shaped. In Southern Africa it is confined to Botswana and Namibia.

The **Crocodile** lives by rivers, lakes and swamps. It is not as slow moving as it looks and can swing its tail like a whip to hit an adversary. An average length is 3.66 m (12 ft) though it can be 4.57 m (15 ft) long. Its diet is mainly fish.

The **Zebra** is in fact the only remaining wild horse in Southern Africa. **Burchell's Zebra** feed on grass, leaves and shrubs, and usually move in herds, often with other species. A male zebra stands about 1.35 m (4.5 ft) high at the shoulder and weighs up to 320 kg (700 lbs). The smaller **Cape Mountain Zebra,** actually found as far north as Botswana and Zimbabwe, has a small dewlap, a brown nose, a woollier coat and stripes the whole way down its legs.

The **Lion,** the largest of African carnivores, used to roam the whole region. Today it is confined to the Kruger, reserves in Natal, the Kalahari and the countries further north. A full grown male weighs up to 240 kg (530 lbs). The lioness has no mane. 'Prides' of six to twelve, basically formed by lionesses, doze in the shade during the day and hunt at dusk. Males are itinerant and can charge at 80 kph (50 mph), killing by springing on the back of buffalo, zebra or other prey, but will feed on anything warm-blooded from mice upwards. They kill only when hungry, once in three or four days.

The **Leopard** hunts by night, is wary, cunning and dangerous when wounded or cornered. Unlike the cheetah its spots are arranged in a rosette pattern. A male weighs around 60 kg (133 lbs) and measures about 2.30 m (7.5 ft) from nose to tail. Leopards make their lairs among rocks in thick bush. Their favourite food is baboon, though they will descend to rodents and even insects if hungry. Their characteristic noise is a husky cough.

The **Cheetah** has relatively much longer legs and smaller head than a leopard, while its spots are isolated, not arranged in a pattern. It hunts by day, often in pairs, and is the fastest mammal – it has been timed at 96 kph (60 mph). Cheetahs stand 80 to 90 cm (32 to 35 ins) high at the shoulder and are about 2.13 m (7 ft) long. They are easily tamed and have been raced against greyhounds in Europe.

The **Spotted Hyena** is a night time scavenger, though it can be seen by day in Kruger Park, the Kalahari Gemsbok Park and throughout Botswana and Zimbabwe. Though its powerful jaws can crush bones it is cowardly and usually only attacks weak or aged live animals. Its colour is yellowish with dark brown spots, its weight about 60 kg (132 lbs) and it has a characteristic, unpleasant, howl. Hyenas 'laugh' when lions are around.

The **Warthog** is named after the warts on its grotesque head. It lives in families, or 'sounders', and breeds in holes. When running it holds its tail stiffly erect. During the day it crops grass, or digs for roots with its tusks, whilst kneeling on its forelegs. Males weigh around 100 kg (220 lbs) and can be aggressive. Warthogs are widely distributed in the north of the region.

The **Baboon** is a large dog-faced monkey, noted for its cunning and with a distinctive bark. It may live to 45 years old. Baboons usually move in large troops under the leadership of a big old male, and sleep under trees at night. Baboons will eat almost anything, animal or vegetable: and are themselves a leopard's favourite food. They are found all over Southern Africa. Males weigh up to 45 kg (100 lbs). The babies ride on their mothers' backs.

The **Vervet Monkey** is one of the only two true monkeys in South Africa, the other being the dark coated and rarer **Samango**. Its distinctive face is black, with an outline of white, and its body grey with white underparts. It is extremely cunning and omnivorous, eating chicks and insects as well as grain and fruit.

The **Blue Wildebeest,** or **Gnu,** is one of the commonest antelopes in Africa. It stands about 1.52 m (5 ft) high at the shoulder, weighs up to 250 kg (550 lbs), and its horns look slightly like a buffalo's. Its body is actually dark grey, with a shaggy mane, and it moves with a clumsy gait. Wildebeest live in herds. When alarmed they will gallop off, then suddenly turn in unison and face the danger. The **Black Wildebeest** was almost exterminated in South Africa in the 19th century, except in the Orange Free State. It has a high mane, black beard, black chest hair and white tail.

The **Reedbuck,** generally buff-greyish in colour, with a white underside, inhabits the east and north of Southern Africa. It stays by itself or in family parties, and rests in the heat of the day. It eats grass and when disturbed runs off with a 'rocking horse' motion, its white tail flashing. Males stand about 90 cm (35 ins) at the shoulder. Like most buck the female has no horns. The **Mountain Reedbuck** is smaller and more gregarious.

The **Waterbuck** is a large antelope that seldom strays far from water. Its coat is shaggy, greyish brown, with a white ring on the rump. The bull's curving horns are ringed with ridges and it stands about 1.3 m (4.25 ft) at the shoulder, weighing 250 kg (550 lbs). One bull may lead a herd of a dozen cows, who have no horns. Waterbuck are numerous in the Kruger Park, the Okavango and the Zambesi valley.

The **Duiker** is one of Southern Africa's smallest antelopes, though it is stronger than it looks. There are three species – **Blue, Red** and the larger **Grey,** or **Common Duiker.** The names rather overstate the variation in colouring, which runs from reddish yellow to grey. Common Duikers are found throughtout the region and stand 50 cm (19.6 ins) at the shoulder. The tiny blue duiker stands only 30 cm (12 ins). Duikers do not drink water, deriving moisture from browsing.

The **Eland,** the largest African antelope, is so placid that it was almost shot out in South Africa. It is now being reintroduced to the National Parks. Both sexes carry twisted horns. Eland are found in open country, like the Kalahari, the Kruger and Etosha. Their colour is greyish brown with light stripes and a grown bull can weigh 750 kg (1,650 lbs) and stand 1.7 m (5.5 ft) high at the shoulder.

The **Sable Antelope** is a splendid animal, standing 1.35 m (4.5 ft) high, weighing 230 kg (500 lbs) and bearing great scimitar-shaped horns. The body is almost black, with white on the underparts, rump and face. It stays in small herds and is relatively rare, being found in wooded areas of the north east Transvaal, northern Botswana and Zimbabwe.

The **Roan Antelope** is a close relative of the Sable, though more heavily built. Males stand about 1.4 m (4.6 ft) high at the shoulder and weigh up to 270 kg (595 lbs). Its colour is a light reddish brown, with the underparts white, and its tufted ears are often more noticeable than its horns. It prefers open woodland, but will take to living in forests, and tends to stay in herds of up to a dozen. Its range is similar to that of the Sable.

The **Gemsbok,** or **Cape Oryx,** a noble looking, savage and powerful animal, is generally fawn grey in colour. The male stands 1.2 m (4 ft) at the shoulder and weighs around 240 kg (530 lbs). Both sexes have straight horns up to 1,117 mm (44 ins) long. It is able to survive in very arid conditions, such as the Kalahari and Namib deserts, finding moisture from tsamma melons and wild cucumbers if there is no water.

453

The **Oribi,** a graceful small antelope, inhabits the grassveld in isolated areas of the Transvaal, northern Botswana and central Zimbabwe, usually between about 457 and 1,066 m (1,500-3,500 ft) above sea level. Oribi stand some 60 cm (23.5 ins) high at the shoulder and weigh 14 kg (31 lbs). They are rufous yellow in colour, with a white underside. They tend to stay in pairs, rather than herds.

The **Impala** is a timid, elegant, medium sized antelope, famous for leaping in the air when alarmed. It can jump 9 m (30 ft), rising as much as 3 m (10 ft) above the ground. Impala have smooth chestnut coloured coats. Males stand about 90 cm (35.5 ins) high and weigh 55 kg (121 lbs). The females do not carry horns and are fought for by the males in the rutting season. Both move in herds and are widely distributed in the north of the region, for instance in Namibia.

The **Springbok,** in English Springbuck, gets its name from its almost vertical leaps in the air. It is South Africa's national animal, where it is now mainly found in the northern Cape Province: there were once three million in the Karoo alone. Also common in Botswana, Namibia and many reserves. Its colouring is fawn, with a distinctive broad band of dark reddish brown on its flank, and a white underside. The male stands around 75 cm (29.5 ins) high at the shoulder. The females' horns are thinner and less curved. It is a species of antelope.

Elephants in the Kruger National Park

Wildlife Conservation

South Africa boasts the African continent's oldest reserves – dating back to 1889. But regional policies for the management of elephant herds in Botswana, South Africa and Zimbabwe have brought the National Parks authorities in those countries into dispute with CITES (the Swiss-based Convention on International Trade in Endangered Species of Wild Fauna and Flora). Many experts in southern Africa believe their conservation record deserves more recognition. **James Clarke** of 'The Star' newspaper in Johannesburg is a distinguished writer on wildlife. These are his comments.

When it comes to wildlife the news is good at the southern end of Africa. The success of local conservation policies is such that several once rare species of mammals are now common in South Africa and there are more of some kinds, notably elephant and rhino, than there were at the beginning of the 20th century. The biggest ivory-carrying elephants left in Africa are well protected. The endangered 1,000 kg black rhino is thriving. Its numbers have reached 600 (10 years ago there were 400) and it has been introduced to the Kruger Park, which could support 3,500 – as many as existed in the whole continent in 1990. The 2,500 kg white rhino have increased from 60 to more than 3,000, plus another 1,500 that have been translocated from the Republic to be reintroduced elsewhere in Africa, for instance in Kenya. Black wildebeest – the blond-maned gnu which was down to 40 animals before World War II – now number almost 10,000. In parts of the arid western Cape the springbok herds now flow through the valleys like brown rivers.

A New Deal with Wildlife

After years of being rather self-satisfied with their conservation efforts and their star attraction – the Kruger National Park – South Africa has a new deal going with wildlife and the public is much more involved.

Ten years ago there were only nine National Parks in South Africa. Now there are 17 and one of the old ones, the Addo Elephant Park in the Cape Province, has been almost doubled in size. There has been a huge expansion in the number of reserves. Not only have towns and municipalities established their own: so dide the independent states within South Africa (which were re-absorbed into the Republic). The 50,000 ha Pilanesberg National Park in the North West Province is an example of where local interests are intergrated with those of tourism. In one corner big game hunting looks after the culling, and also provides the locals with fresh meat at cost price. Other sections of the park, in a manner now widely copied, provide woodlots and thatching grass. And the visitors still view plenty of game. The Madikwe Reserve is the second largest in South Africa and the third largest south of the Limpopo (the Kalahari Gemsbok Park is the second). At the other extreme are tiny reserves like the Cycad Reserve in Lebowa.

Additionally some parks have created wilderness hiking trails. One of the most exciting is the Otter Trail in the Tsitsikama Coastal park, where hikers can watch buck, birds, seals, dolphins and whales, all on the same route.

There are also hundreds of new game farms – natural areas given over exclusively to wildlife – some of which allow big game hunting. So popular is wildlife utilisation becoming that cattle farmers are ranching antelope too and forming conservancies of up to 40 contiguous farms, to which the provincial nature conservation departments offer management advice and trained rangers.

Should Ivory be sold for Conservation?

South Africa, Botswana and Zimbabwe unsuccessfully opposed the 1989 CITES moratorium on international ivory trading, saying they would each lose millions of dollars and hundreds of jobs. In these countries and Namibia there are stockpiles of rhino horn from animals that have died and from confiscated poachers' hoards. The sale of these horns could earn millions to fund conservation – which South Africans argue would be "legitimate" as the "wise use of natural resources". However South Africa and Zimbabwe both toed the CITIES line again in 1994.

Equally some elephant HAVE to be culled. 80,000 elephant wander across the gap between Hwange National Park in Zimbabwe and the Okavango Delta in Botswana – a foraging range whose size has no rival in Africa today, but is still not enough to support such numbers. Hitherto the culling had been making money for conservation through the export of carved ivory and elephant leather.

The Kruger Park, both sells elephant to other reserves and has been forced to cull or else suffer the "Tsavo consequence". In the Tsavo National Park in Kenya, in the 1960s, public opinion stopped a culling programme. Two years later an over-population of elephant wrecked Tsavo's woodlands and demolished the habitats of other species. 5,000 elephant died of malnutrition. Although Tsavo's situation is different today, due to elephant poaching, the principle remains valid. From time to time protected elephant have to be culled.

Indeed South Africa's National Parks Board has ceased providing dams in areas that are chronically drought stricken. This is because animals are attracted to water and trample the grassveld around it, creating sheet erosion and damaging the veld for years to come – while the animals themselves either starve or become bogged in the mud, too weak to move. Drought is accepted as a natural way to deal with over-population.

Regional Co-operation

The South African National Parks Board has been helping Mozambique to restore its neglected game reserves and to train game rangers in the sometimes dangerous art of protecting big game. More imaginatively, there have been talks about the establishment of the biggest tourist attraction in Africa – a "mirror image Kruger" down the Mozambique side of the Kruger National Park. Meanwhile the private game reserves down the western edge of the Kruger – in the Sabi-Sand, Timbavati and Umbabat areas – are hoping to have had the fences between their 230,000 ha and the Kruger removed. So the unspoilt territory centred on the Kruger could one day be a 50,000 sq km wild region, dedicated to 200 species of animals and 500 species of birds.

Meanwhile KwaZulu-Natal's Greater St Lucia Wetland Park is being proposed by the new governemnt as a World Heritage Site and is expected to link with Mazambique's southerly Maputo Elephant Park, near the Natal border. This "international park" including lonely beaches, coral reefs and big game fishing waters in the Indian Ocean would add up to a revolution in African co-operation in the conservation of game.

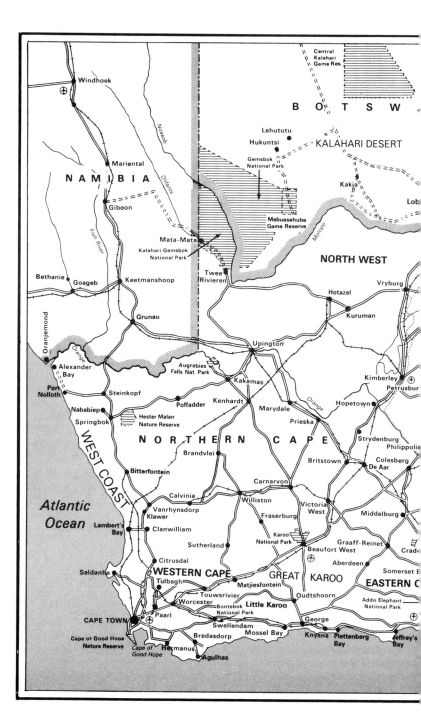

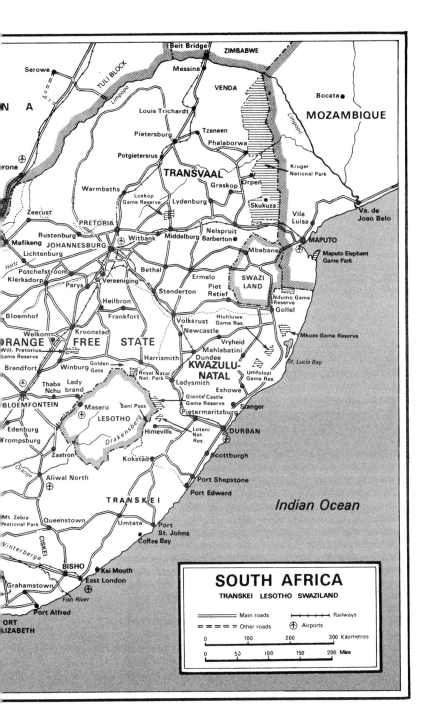

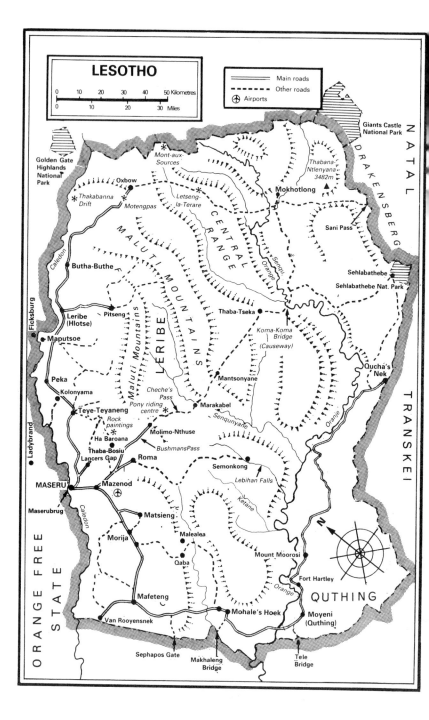

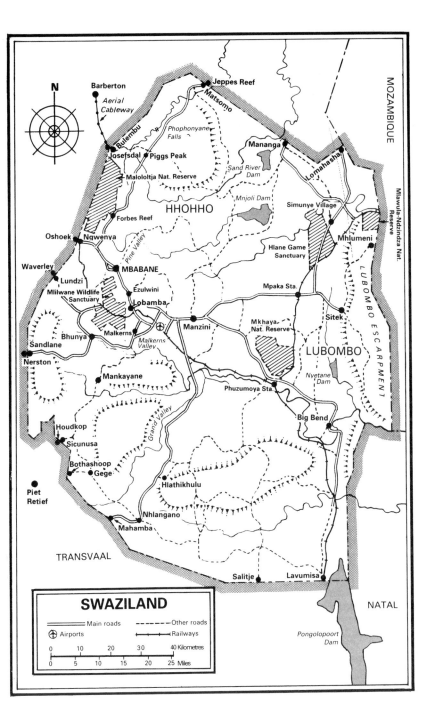

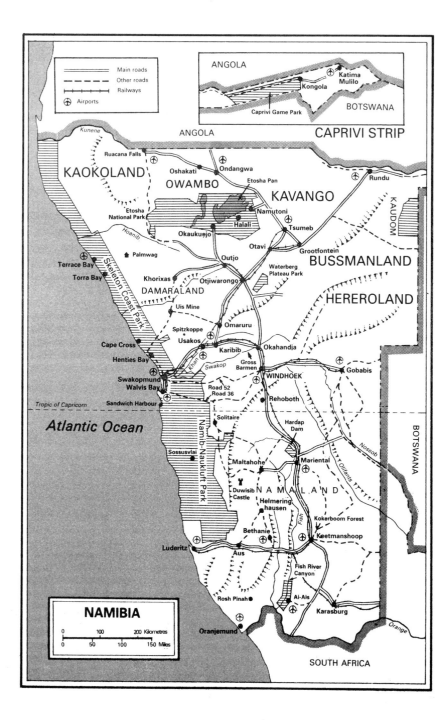

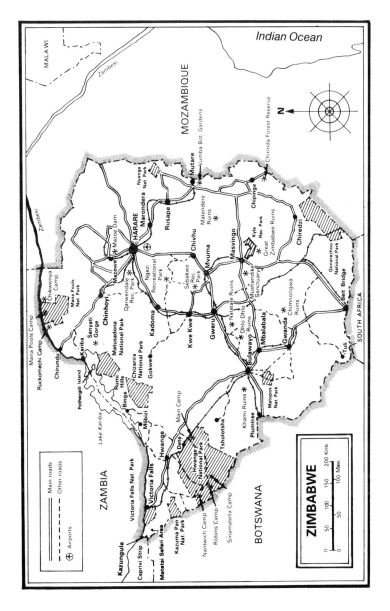

Index

Names of countries abbreviated as follows: Botswana (B); Lesotho (L); Namibia (N); Swaziland (S); Zambia (Z); Zimbabwe (Zm). Page references to photographs appear in **bold** type.

464

Ixopo Hills 141

Your Safaris Notes

Your Safaris Notes

Your Safaris Notes